Primate evolution

Selected Proceedings of the Tenth Congress of the
International Primatological Society, held in
Nairobi, Kenya, in July 1984

Volume 1

Primate evolution

Edited by

JAMES G. ELSE

Institute of Primate Research, National Museums of Kenya

PHYLLIS C. LEE

*Sub-Department of Animal Behaviour, Department of Zoology
University of Cambridge*

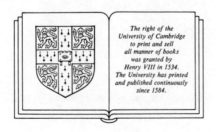

The right of the
University of Cambridge
to print and sell
all manner of books
was granted by
Henry VIII in 1534.
The University has printed
and published continuously
since 1584.

CAMBRIDGE UNIVERSITY PRESS

Cambridge

London   New York   New Rochelle

Melbourne   Sydney

Published by the Press Syndicate of the University of Cambridge
The Pitt Building, Trumpington Street, Cambridge CB2 1RP
32 East 57th Street, New York, NY 10022, USA
10 Stamford Road, Oakleigh, Melbourne 3166, Australia

First published 1986

Printed in Great Britain at the University Press, Cambridge

British Library cataloguing in publication data
Primate evolution. – (Selected proceedings
  of the Tenth Congress of the International
  Primatological Society . . . ; v. 1)
  1. Primate – Evolution
  I. Else, James G.   II. Lee, Phyllis C.
  III. Series
  599.8'0438   QL373.P9

Library of Congress cataloguing in publication data
Primate evolution.
(Selected proceedings of the Tenth Congress of the
International Primatological Society; v. 1)
  1. Primates – Evolution – Congresses.   2. Mammals –
Evolution – Congresses.   I. Else, James G.   II. Lee, Phyllis C.
III. Series: International Primatological Society.
Congress (10th : 1984 : Nairobi, Kenya).
Selected proceedings of the Tenth Congress of the International
Primatological Society; v. 1.
QL737.P9I53   1984   Vol. 1   599.8 s [599.8'0438] 86-8292

ISBN 0 521 32450 5 hard covers
ISBN 0 521 31011 3 paperback

CONTENTS

CONTRIBUTORS

H. F. Bär, *Institute of Functional Morphology, Ruhr University Bochum, 4630 Bochum 1, Federal Republic of Germany*

J. C. Barry, *Peabody Museum, Harvard University, Cambridge, Massachusetts 02138, USA*

M. A. Bassiouni, *Ains Shams University, Faculty of Science, Cairo, Egypt and University of Qatar, Scientific and Applied Research Centre, State of Qatar.*

G. Bouvrain, *Laboratoire de Paléontologie des Vertébrés et Paléontologie Humaine, University of Paris, 75230 Paris Cedex 05, France*

T. M. Bown, *United States Geological Survey, Denver, Colorado 80225, USA*

M. L. Cheng, *Genetics Department, Southwest Foundation for Biomedical Research, San Antonio, Texas 78284, USA*

G. C. Conroy, *Department of Anatomy and Neurobiology, Washington University Medical School, St Louis, Missouri 63110, USA*

R. T. Corlett, *Department of Botany, National University of Singapore, Kent Ridge, Singapore 0511*

N. Creel, *Department of Anatomical Sciences, State University of New York, Stony Brook, New York 11794, USA*

L. de Bonis, *Laboratoire de Paléontologie des Vertébrés et Paléontologie Humaine, University of Poitiers, 86022 Poitiers, France*

B. Demes, *Arbeitsgruppe für Functionelle Morphologie, Ruhr University, Bochum, 4630 Bochum 1, Federal Republic of Germany*

J. G. Fleagle, *Department of Anatomical Sciences, Health Sciences Center, State University of New York, Stony Brook, New York 11794, USA*

L. Ginsburg, *Institut de Paléontologie, Muséum National d'Histoire Naturelle, 75005 Paris, France*

S. Ishida, *Department of Geology and Mineralogy, Faculty of Science, Kyoto University, Kyoto 606, Japan*

N. G. Jablonski, *Department of Anatomy, University of Hong Kong, and Applied Oral Anatomy, Prince Philip Dental Hospital, Hong Kong*

B. Jacobshagen, *Anthropology Institute, Justus-Liebig University, D-6300 Giessen, Federal Republic of Germany*

G. Koufos, *Laboratory of Geology and Paleontology, Panepistemiou, Thessaloniki, Greece*

T. Koyaguchi, *Department of Geology, Faculty of Science, University of Tokyo, Tokyo 113, and Department of Earth Science, Ehime University, Matsuyama 790, Japan*

R. E. Leakey, *National Museums of Kenya, P.O. Box 40658, Nairobi, Kenya*

P. W. Lucas, *Department of Anatomy, National University of Singapore, Kent Ridge, Singapore 0511*

D. A. Luke, *Unit of Anatomy in Relation to Dentistry, Guy's Hospital Medical School, London SE1, UK*

J. E. Maiers, *Department of Anthropology, University of Wisconsin, Milwaukee, Wisconsin 53201, USA*

T. Makinouchi, *Department of Geology, Faculty of Science and Technology, Meijo University, Nagoya 468, Japan*

M. W. Marzke, *Department of Anthropology, Arizona State University, Tempe, Arizona 85287, USA*

T. Matsuda, *Department of Geology, Himeji Institute of Technology, Himeji 671-22, Japan*

S. Matsu'ura, *Department of Anthropology, National Science Museum, Tokyo 160, Japan*

P. Mein, *Département des Sciences de la Terre, University of Lyon, 69621 Villeurbanne, France*

J. Melentis, *Laboratory of Geology and Paleontology, Panepistemiou, Thessaloniki, Greece*

M. Meyer, *Institute of Functional Morphology, Ruhr University Bochum, 4630 Bochum 1, Federal Republic of Germany*

H. Mitsushio, *Department of Geology, Faculty of Science, Kochi University, Kochi 780, Japan*

C. S. Mott, *Department of Anthropology, University of Wisconsin, Milwaukee, Wisconsin 53201, USA*

J. D. Obradovich, *United States Geological Survey, Denver, Colorado 80225, USA*

M. Pickford, *National Museums of Kenya, P.O. Box 40658, Nairobi, Kenya, and Department of Paleontology, Johannes Gutenberg University Mainz, D-6500 Mainz, Federal Republic of Germany*

H. Preuschoft, *Arbeitsgruppe für Functionelle Morphologie, Ruhr University Bochum, 4630 Bochum 1, Federal Republic of Germany*

P. Schmid, *Anthropological Institute, University of Zurich, CH-8057 Zurich, Switzerland.*

G. H. Schneck, *Anatomy Department, University of Frankfurt-Main, D-6000 Frankfurt 70, Federal Republic of Germany*

B. Senut, *Laboratoire d'Anthropologie, Muséum Nationale d'Histoire Naturelle, 49 CNRS, and Institut de Paléontologie, 8 rue Buffon, 75005 Paris, France*

P. K. Seth, *Department of Anthropology, University of Delhi, Delhi 110 007, India*

S. Seth, *Department of Anthropology, University of Delhi, Delhi 110 007, India*

E. L. Simons, *Primate Center and Department of Anthropology and Anatomy, Duke University, Durham, North Carolina 27705, USA*

F. F. Steininger, *Institute of Paleontology, University of Vienna, A-1010 Vienna, Austria*

Z. Stratil, *Anthropological Institute, University of Zurich, CH-8057 Zurich, Switzerland*

C. Tardieu, *Laboratoire d'Anatomie Comparée, Muséum National d'Histoire Naturelle, 75005 Paris, France*

M. F. Teaford, *Department of Cell Biology and Anatomy, Johns Hopkins University, Baltimore, Maryland 21205, USA*

M. Torii, *Department of Geology and Mineralogy, Faculty of Science, Kyoto University, Kyoto 606, Japan*

T. R. Turner, *Department of Anthropology, University of Wisconsin, Milwaukee, Wisconsin 53201, USA*

J. L. VandeBerg, *Genetics Department, Southwest Foundation for Biomedical Research, San Antonio, Texas 78284, USA*

M. W. Vannier, *Mallinckrodt Institute of Radiology, Washington University Medical Center, St. Louis, Missouri 63110, USA*

A. Walker, *Department of Cell Biology and Anatomy, School of Medicine, Johns Hopkins University, Baltimore, Maryland 21205, USA*

P. J. Whybrow, *Department of Paleontology, British Museum (Natural History), London SW7 5BD, UK*

U. A. Zeller, *Department of Anatomy, University of Goethingen, 3400 Goethingen, Federal Republic of Germany.*

PREFACE

Our understanding of the primate fossil record has increased enormously over the past decade. We now have available fossils of primates that allow us to link together many of the trends leading towards the evolution of man. The papers in this volume represent some of the new ideas about primate and human evolution, and in the different sections, the fossil finds are integrated with current research on functional anatomy, on genetics and on the distribution and dispersion of primates in the past. Some papers also cover aspects of the behaviour of fossil primates and attempt to use these ideas to increase our understanding of the fossil primate record.

The volume is introduced by R. E. Leakey, whose work on primate and human evolution has been a major stimulus to the field. He reviews the problems and questions of current interest in the study of hominid evolution.

In Part I, one of the major problems of paleontology, that of providing reasonably accurate dates for different events in the fossil record, is discussed. These papers review the dating of fossil primates that have been found in many areas of the world, and the different techniques available for accurately estimating ages of various primate fossils are presented. The papers, however, deal primarily with an attempt to calibrate fossil finds, and not with the problems of methodology in their dating. Reconstructions of events in the past, radiations and dispersions among the fossil primates, are made using radiometric dating, stratigraphy and biostratigraphy, and paleomagnetic stratigraphy. The general patterns of primate evolution and dispersion are summarised with suggestions for new and fruitful areas of further research highlighted by the papers.

In Part II, the emphasis shifts from questions of relative and absolute dating to the issues currently under discussion in the evolution of the higher primates, the apes and hominids. This series of papers deals with how details of the anatomy of fossil primates can reveal patterns of distribution and differentiation among the higher primates. All the papers in this section present novel ideas and data that help us reassess the status and importance of the different hominoid fossils, again from several different parts of the world.

The evolution of primates is approached using techniques of functional anatomy in Part III. Biomechanical principles, allometry and comparative morphology are all used to reassess how we interpret the changes in primate fossils through time, and their inter-individual and inter-specific variability. The importance of studies of functional anatomy to an increased understanding of trends in primate evolution is demonstrated by the excellent papers on biomechanics, allometric relations and sexual dimorphism among modern primate and non-primate species.

The final section on evolutionary genetics represents a field that has been the subject of controversy among paleontologists. Estimating the dates and episodes of differentiation among primates using genetic markers is still highly controversial, but the papers in this section demonstrate the increasing sophistication of the use of genetic techniques to interpret and explain the fossil record of primate evolution.

All the papers in this volume were based on presentations at the Tenth Congress of the International Primatological Society, in Nairobi, Kenya, in July 1984. The contributions of Kenya in particular and East Africa in general towards our understanding of the evolution of primates, make it appropriate that this volume collects and integrates current research and concepts of primate and human evolution. The theme of the Congress was 'Primates at their Source: Past, Present and Future'. As the source of mankind, African contributions to our understanding of past primates should have a major role in suggesting future investigations.

The papers that follow have been revised and reviewed and we are particularly grateful to the symposium and session chairs who worked so hard and successfully to integrate the papers and to ensure the quality of the writing. We would like to thank the Republic of Kenya and the National Museums of Kenya for hosting the Congress. We thank Dr. Robin Pellew of the Cambridge University Press for his support and encouragement of this publication. PCL would like to thank Professors P. Bateson and R. A. Hinde for providing facilities during the editing of these volumes.

James G. Else
and
P. C. Lee
Nairobi and Cambridge,
September 1, 1985

FOREWORD: PRIMATE EVOLUTION

R. E. LEAKEY

The idea of writing a short introduction to a topic as broad as primate evolution is made easier by the obvious: it is a contradiction in terms and cannot be achieved. What I have done, therefore, is to offer my own view, biased as it must be by my rather local outlook from Nairobi, on some of the areas which I feel can be usefully addressed by future work. My own interests are African and tend towards the hominid rather than those of the more enigmatic hominoids of the Miocene. The cercopithecoids are undoubtedly important but I could not attempt to offer a cohesive review of the state of our knowledge on this or the various other groups that were discussed during the course of the Congress.

Another problem that I face in attempting a review is the extraordinary diversity of interest that the study of primate evolution has attracted. There are currently many specialist studies, involving a host of disciplines, which relate to the considerably improved state of our knowledge. In spite of these coordinated efforts to increase our knowledge, there are still certain areas and issues for which a basic understanding is still sought. It is perhaps here that my own preferred activities can play a useful part; new fossils must be found to fill in the gaps in our record, and this requires further and prolonged field work in some of the more remote areas certainly of Africa, but also in Asia, Europe, the Middle East or Gulf region, and the Far East. Some authors have suggested that fossils will soon be secondary to molecular studies and all that these encompass, but I do not share this view.

From the standpoint of the fossil record, there are gaps in that record and some issues that must be addressed. The early Miocene hominoids and the phyletic relationship between the few recognized species is a case in point. Although a good number of early apes are now to be found in museum collections, there are too few specimens that are well enough preserved to answer rather basic questions satisfactorily. The relationship between the Oligocene primates from North Africa and the early Miocene species in East Africa is but one example. Another important but illusive issue is the complex relationship between the *Dryopithecus* species, the *Proconsul* species, *Sivapithecus*, *Ramapithecus* and *Kenyapithecus*. How can these species be related to extant species in a broad evolutionary framework? A great diversity of opinion can be found in the literature but the degree of divergence of the con-clusions is directly related to the quality of the fossil collections, which generally are still poor.

The so-called 'fossil gap' between some 10 million and 3 million years ago is at the top of the list of unresolved issues. Even the most incomplete fossil fragments from this period are of interest and attract attention. It is thought, perhaps without particularly good reason, that bipedalism was one major event during this time period. Certainly, by a little more than 3 million years ago there is evidence of an hominid where bipedalism had been achieved. The lack of evidence for bipedalism earlier than 10 million years ago could reflect one of two possibilities: either that it was not yet present or that our fossil samples simply have not picked up the species in which this special-ization first occurred. I do not necessarily favour the latter view, but believe that some caution is called for when being guided by presump-tions based on an absence of evidence.

An important subject which is seldom considered is palaeo-zoogeography. We are all aware of the distribution of certain species in the modern system, but it is not always possible to offer explana-tions. Dispersal and separation in Africa during the Miocene through to the end of the Pleistocene is of signal interest. Sadly, fossils are only found where conditions for their formation are appropriate and a vast proportion of the available habitats for primates would not have lent itself to this process. There may well be gaps that can never be filled by fossils and it is conceivable that, lacking such vital clues, our final documentation of primate evolution will always be conjecture.

The record for the past 3 million years is quite good, although even here the strongest evidence is from the period between 2 million years ago and the present. The advent of large-brained cultural hominids is placed at just over 2 million years ago and the earliest *Homo sapiens* somewhere close to 200000 years ago. There remain many questions, however, concerning regional and other relationships between these lineages.

It is my opinion that many of these missing parts to the story of our own evolution will be found in the next decade. The increasingly scientific approach to the study of human evolution and the great interest in primate evolution in general is a most positive circumstance. A convergence of ideas between the palaeontologists and the molecular biologists is apparent and will result in closer collaboration. The excellent geological context for many of the fossil primate sites is similarly of great value.

This volume has brought together a wide range of important papers that encapsulate the rich diversity of scientific interest in the field of primate evolution, and that address some of the important issues raised above. Since the Congress and the presentation of these papers, further advances have been made. New fossil specimens have been reported from China and Africa, new techniques are being employed in analysis and a greater insight has perhaps been gained on some issues. This selection of papers nonetheless provides an up-to-date account of the state of a science that is continually being refined.

Part I

Dating the fossil primate record

Introduction. *M. Pickford*

Calibration of the fossil record is central to understanding the tempo of evolution and the sequence of events which occurred in the past. The symposium 'dating of the Fossil Primate Record' was organised to fulfil this need in palaeoprimatological circles. The scope of the symposium was confined to the higher primates of the Old World, and its thrust was towards the results of dating programmes rather than towards the methodology of dating.

The contributions span the period of late Eocene to Pleistocene and include data for much of Europe, Eastern Africa, Saudi Arabia, Pakistan and Java. The majority of the papers are reviews and represent geochronological schemes obtained by using a variety of techniques: stratigraphy, biostratigraphy, radio-isotopic dating (both K/Ar and Fission Track), and magnetostratigraphy as applicable and where appropriate.

Much of the European sequence is still based on biostratigraphy calibrated by a distressingly small quantity of radio-isotopic dates. The East African sequence is liberally calibrated by radio-isotopic age determinations, but a great deal of refinement of existing ideas can and should be done. The Pakistan sequence is calibrated mainly by magnetostratigraphic methods allied to biostratigraphy and a few radio-isotopic dates. Matsu'ura's work (Chapter 1.10) on the dating of the Javan hominids requires special mention since the determination of their ages is dependent on two major steps: (1) the determination of the precise provenance of specimens collected many years ago, sometimes with inadequate controls; and (2) the independent calibration of the strata in Java, by means of radio-isotopes, palaeomagnetic stratigraphy and biostratigraphy. Such kinds of studies may become a standard feature of the geochronology of old collections, among which there are many specimens with inadequate stratal and geo-chronological pedigrees.

It would be utopian if all the studies agreed with one another, but such is not the case. In particular, regardless of the methods used to arrive at dates of specific sites or sequences, there is always room for improvement or refinement. There is still debate about the age of the *Hiparion* datum, an important faunal event in the Old World. Current concepts indicate that it is highly time-transgressive with the earliest occurrences in Europe. My feeling is that the European dates are far too old and that the datum is more nearly synchronous over large parts of the Old World, at about 11 + 0.5 million years ago. In my view, critical sites such as Howenegg in the Federal Republic of Germany and Bou Hanifia in Tunisia, which form the basis for the 'early' datum, require further study.

Finally, this symposium did not receive contributions about North Africa, South Africa, Turkey and China, information gaps that should be filled if possible. However, the response to this symposium was most encouraging and indicated a need in palaeoprimatology. Hope-fully future Congresses will address this need.

I.1

How old are the Fayum primates?

J. G. FLEAGLE, T. M. BOWN, J. D. OBRADOVICH
AND E. L. SIMONS

Introduction

The earliest higher primates of Africa come from extensive early Tertiary deposits in the Fayum Depression of Egypt, approximately 100 km southwest of Cairo. The 11 primate species from this area have played a critical role in our understanding of anthropoid origins and the evolution of monkeys and apes ever since their initial discovery in the beginning of the century (e.g. Schlosser, 1911; Simons, 1965, 1967, 1972; Kay, Fleagle & Simons, 1981; Fleagle & Kay, 1983). Likewise, the Fayum provides the most complete record of Paleogene mammals from all of Africa and is critical for understanding the evolution of many mammalian groups on that continent, including marsupials, pangolins, elephant shrews, bats, insectivorans, creodonts, hyracoids, elephants, anthracotheres, arsinoitheres, and hystricomorph rodents. Unfortunately, the overwhelming preponderance of apparently endemic African elements in the Fayum mammalian fauna has largely precluded any possibility of faunal correlation between the Fayum and other paleontological localities that could place this fauna in a worldwide chronological framework.

The purpose of this paper is to review the geology and paleoenvironment of the primate-bearing sediments from the Fayum Depression, to discuss the evidence for estimating the antiquity of the Fayum primates on the basis of faunal correlations and regional geological events, and to report a new radiometric age for the Widan el Faras Basalt. Finally, we will discuss the significance of current evidence on both the age and the phylogenetic position of the Fayum primates for understanding the history of anthropoid evolution in Africa.

The primates

There are at present 11 fossil primate species known from the Jebel Qatrani Formation in the Fayum Depression (Table 1). Although the relationships of the individual species to one another are generally agreed upon by most current authorities, the precise phyletic relationships of these early anthropoids with respect to later primates have been debated for many years. In many cases they remain unresolved. The two hominoid genera (*Propliopithecus* and *Aegyptopithecus*), usually placed in the primitive catarrhine family Pliopithecidae, have at various times been regarded either as evidence for an early appearance of lineages leading to hominids, or to living pongids, or to gibbons or, more commonly, as broadly ancestral to the early Miocene apes from Kenya and Uganda (e.g. Simons, 1972; Simons, Andrews & Pilbeam, 1978; Szalay & Delson, 1979). Recently, however, there has been increasing evidence to indicate that they are likely to be ancestral to all later catarrhines, including apes, humans, and Old World monkeys (Fleagle & Kay, 1983).

The other common group of Fayum higher primates, the Parapithecidae (including *Qatrania*, *Apidium*, and *Parapithecus*) has been suggested as being uniquely related to living cercopithecoids by some authors (Simons, 1970, 1972), and platyrrhines by others (Hoffstetter, 1980). More recently, however, this group has been considered as a specialized group of early anthropoids (or catarrhines) with no clear ties to any later primates (e.g. Szalay & Delson, 1979; Kay & Simons, 1983).

Table 1. *Fossil primates from the Jebel Qatrani Formation*

Hominoids (*sensu* Fleagle & Kay, 1983)
Aegyptopithecus zeuxis
Propliopithecus haeckeli
Propliopithecus chirobates
Propliopithecus markgrafi

Parapithecids
Qatrania wingi
Apidium phiomense
Apidium moustafi
Parapithecus fraasi
Parapithecus grangeri (=*Simonsius grangeri*)

Tarsiid
Afrotarsius chatrathi

Incertae sedis
Oligopithecus savagei

Oligopithecus has been considered as ancestral to the hominoids *Aegyptopithecus* and *Propliopithecus* (Simons & Pilbeam, 1972), as a very primitive anthropoid (Szalay & Delson, 1979), or as an adapid prosimian (Szalay, 1970; Gingerich, 1973). Its affinities remain ambiguous. The most recently discovered Fayum primate is a new tarsier-like species.

Stratigraphy and occurrence of fossil remains

All of the Fayum fossil primates occur in the fluvial Jebel Qatrani Formation (Fig. 1), which conformably overlies the nearshore

Fig. 1. A simplified section of the Jebel Qatrani Formation, showing the stratigraphic levels of the quarries that have yielded fossil primates and the primate genera from each quarry.

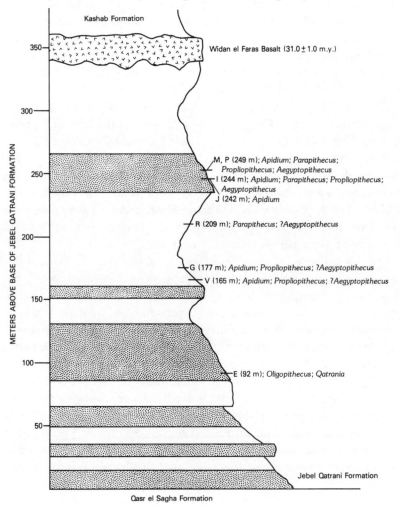

marine and fluvial Qasr el Sagha Formation (upper Eocene). In its type area, the upper part of the Qasr el Sagha Formation consists of 85 m of nearshore marine sandstones and alluvial channel deposits that record a late Eocene regression of the Tethys Sea and the northern and western advance of alluvial plain conditions. Paleocurrent data show that the principal marine strandline during most of the Qasr el Sagha and Jebel Qatrani deposition lay to the west and that source areas were east of the Fayum Depression, probably in the vicinity of the northern Galala Plateau approximately 130 km to the east (Bown & Kraus, in press). The Widan el Faras Basalt overlies the Jebel Qatrani Formation with erosional unconformity.

The Jebel Qatrani Formation (Fig. 1) is comprised of 340 m of variegated alluvial rocks; fine–coarse sandstones, conglomerates, sandy mudstones, carbonaceous mudstones, and limestones, all of which show evidence of profound mechanical and geochemical alterations due to ancient soil (paleosol) formation. Vertebrate fossils have been recovered from dozens of localities throughout the formation. However, most of the primate fossils have come from five quarries located at three distinct levels within the section (Fig. 1).

Fossil vertebrate Quarry E, the provenance of *Oligopithecus savagei* and *Qatrania wingi*, lies approximately 92 m above the base of the Jebel Qatrani Formation. Quarries V and G are 165 and 177 m above the base of the formation, respectively, and Quarries I and M occur 244 and 249 m above the base of the Jebel Qatrani section and about 90 m below the contact of the formation with the overlying Widan el Faras Basalt. The latter two quarries have yielded more fossil primates than any other area in the Fayum Depression. Seven species and over 80% of all primate specimens are from these two quarries.

Fossil vertebrate bones at Quarries I, J, M, and R occur in medium-coarse and gravelly sandstones representing coalesced point bar deposits of meandering streams. They are invariably associated with numerous coprolites, presumably of crocodiles. At quarries E and G, the fossils also occur in sandstones deposited by meandering streams, but in these instances they are found in mud pebble conglomerates forming relatively coarse scour fill deposits at the bases of channels. At each of these sites about 90% of the mammal bones show no abrasion, indicating that they were not hydraulically transported very far in the stream channels prior to burial. These unabraded specimens include tiny jaws and teeth of marsupials, bats, insectivores and primates in addition to larger bones. The remaining 10% of the fossils, together with a large proportion of the associated turtle shell fragments and crocodile scutes vary in showing minor to severe abrasion. However, the most complete specimens of all skeletal remains are invariably unabraded.

This and other evidence to be outlined elsewhere suggests that the majority of the bones accumulated gradually on point bars at Quarries I, J, M, and R. Although it is tempting to suggest that the fossils owe their concentration to crocodile predation and scavenging, there is little evidence to support this hypothesis. The surfaces of bones and teeth are not altered as commonly occurs when they pass through the digestive tracts of crocodiles (Fisher, 1981). Moreover, Gebo & Simons (1984) have shown that many of the tooth puncture marks commonly found on the Fayum fossils were probably made not by crocodiles, but by hyaenodontid creodonts.

Among the Fayum fossil primate sites, Quarry V appears to be a unique accumulation in that it is developed in the lower part of a sheetlike sandstone body that contains neither pebbles nor mud clasts and that it is probably not of point bar origin. Generally, the bones from this quarry are remarkably free of abrasion and tooth puncture marks and at least three skulls with attached mandibles have been found there. The remains occur in a coarse to granular sandstone and in part of the overlying medium-fine sand. At the six quarries described above, practically all of the bones occur widely separated in stratified sand with their long axes parallel to bedding. However, at Quarry V the bones are juxtaposed close together in a variety of unsystematic orientations ranging from parallel to perpendicular with bedding. These associations, coupled with absence of bedding in the deposit, development of dish and pillar structures in the coarse granular sand, and loading of the fine sand into underlying coarse sand suggest a shallow quicksand origin for the vertebrate fossil accumulation (Bown & Kraus, unpublished).

Paleoenvironment of the Jebel Qatrani Formation

The Jebel Qatrani Formation is a complex alluvial unit that is characterized by distinct large- and small-scale lateral and vertical facies changes (Bown & Kraus, in press). In general, deposition was by meandering streams. Local, small-scale changes in lithology reflect shifting from one local channel environment to another and transitions from channel to floodplain deposits. Larger scale changes from east to west and upward through the section record the approach and retreat of ancient marine strandlines and the change in dominance of the depositional setting from interior alluvial to coastal floodplain, mangrove swamp, and perhaps, lagoonal environments. Studies of Jebel Qatrani fluvial sedimentology, paleontology, paleopedology (fossil soils), and the regional relations of the formation provide detailed insights into the nature of the paleoenvironment of northern Egypt during the Eocene and Oligocene (see Bown, 1982; Bown *et al.*, 1982; Bown & Kraus, in press).

The Jebel Qatrani lithotope was low and had little relief. The occasional occurrence of sirenians and brackish water mollusks, sharks, and rays suggests that storms and/or tidal incursions increased the salinity of the streams for several kilometers inland. The floodbasins of the Jebel Qatrani streams were apparently heavily vegetated in many areas as evidenced by numerous fossil root casts and areas with abundant fossil trees (Bown *et al.*, 1982). There were really large, but shallow and probably ephemeral nonsaline ponds; soils were generally damp with probably seasonal rainfall.

The fossil megafloras show affinities with present-day tropical Indomalaysian floras. They suggest a 'tropical forest existing in a wet, perhaps monsoonal climate' (Wing & Tiffney, 1982). Like the paleof-. lora, the soils indicate seasonal wetness with good drainage in some areas and swampy conditions in others. There is no evidence for a dry, sahelien environment as suggested by Kortlandt (1980).

The mammalian fauna

There are over 40 genera and 75 species of fossil mammals known from the Jebel Qatrani Formation (see Bown *et al.*, 1982). The vast majority of families represented by the Fayum mammals, as well as many of the suborders and orders, are not known from any other continent before Miocene times. Thus they are of no help in pin-pointing the age of the Fayum deposits through faunal correlations. There are only seven groups of nonprimate mammals from the Fayum that are known from Eocene or Oligocene localities in Europe, Asia, or North America, and thereby offer any possibility for providing a relative age for the Fayum fauna. These are the didelphid marsupials, hyaenodontid creodonts, anthracotheriid artiodactyls, bats, lipotyphlan insectivores, pantolestid proteutherians, and a single sirenian specimen.

The didelphid marsupial *Peratherium africanus* from Quarry M in the Jebel Qatrani Formation is most similar to *P. cuvieri* and *P. elegans* from late Eocene and early Oligocene rocks, respectively, of Europe (Crochet, 1980; Bown & Simons, 1984). It does not permit a more precise correlation.

Nine species of hyaenodontid creodonts have been described from various levels in the Fayum sequence. Two of the Egyptian genera, *Pterodon* and *Apterodon*, are known from numerous localities in Europe and Asia. The former is a late Eocene genus and the latter is an early Oligocene genus (Lange-Badre, 1979; Savage & Russell, 1983). Lange-Badre (1979) has suggested that *Apterodon* could not have evolved from any known European Eocene species and must be an immigrant from some other continent. The presence of *Apterodon* in the Fayum would support either an early Oligocene age for the Fayum deposits *or* an African origin for the genus.

The anthracotheres (Artiodactyla) are another group of Fayum mammals that are well known from Europe and Asia as well as Africa. Unfortunately there has not been a recent review of this group that addresses the question of faunal correlations.

Numerous chiropteran specimens have been recovered from the upper levels (Quarries I and M) of the Jebel Qatrani Formation. Two specimens have been recently described as members of a new family with no close relatives among other presently known fossil bats (Sige, personal communication), and other specimens seem to be virtually identical to a living genus.

An undescribed genus of lipotyphlan insectivore is known from nine fragmentary jaws from Quarry E at the 92 m level of the Jebel Qatrani Formation and several new specimens of the pantolestan *Qarunavus* occur at Quarries V and I, at the 165 and 244 m levels, respectively (Simons & Gingerich, 1974). Preliminary studies indicate that both of these may be related to late Eocene forms known from Europe, but they are more derived in many aspects of their dental morphology and hence are of no use in precise biostratigraphic correlation.

One sirenian skull is known from the Jebel Qatrani Formation. Preliminary examinations suggest that it has morphological features intermediate between those of the late Eocene *Eotheriodes libycum* from Egypt and the middle Oligocene species *Halitherium schinzii* from Europe (D. Domning, personal communication). This is most compatible with an early Oligocene age for the fossil and the Jebel Qatrani Formation.

In summary, the few fossil mammals from the Jebel Qatrani Formation that resemble European (or Asian) forms are most comparable to late Eocene and early Oligocene genera. However, the differences between the Egyptian and European forms are such that they preclude a more precise correlation for most of the fossil mammals.

Geological and radiometric evidence

Since neither the rocks nor the mammalian fauna of the Jebel Qatrani Formation provide any precise evidence regarding the age of the formation and the fossil primates found there, the best evidence for the age of this formation comes from the respective ages of the immediately overlying and underlying rocks, i.e. the Widan el Faras Basalt above and the partly marine and partly fluvial Qasr el Sagha Formation below.

In the Fayum Depression, the upper Qatrani escarpment is capped by 2–25 m of the Widan el Faras Basalt (Bowen & Vondra, 1974), a dark, densely aphanitic, iron-rich extrusive basalt that is exposed for over 50 km. This capping of black basalt is responsible for the local name of the escarpment, the Jebel Qatrani or 'Tar Hills' (Figs. 2 and 3). Although highly variable in thickness due both to flow thickness and topographic irregularities, the basalt forms a continuous sheet from Elwaht Hialla in the east to the upper escarpment north of Tel Homar in the west (Fig. 2). Internally, the Widan el Faras Basalt appears to be composed of a single flow in those areas where it is thinnest; however, weathered and sometimes scorched contacts within the basalt, as well as thin coarse sandstone interbeds (some containing basaltic clasts), attest to the development of at least two or three separate flows over

Fig. 2. A simplified relief map of the Jebel Qatrani area showing the major escarpments, physical features, and location of major primate quarries.

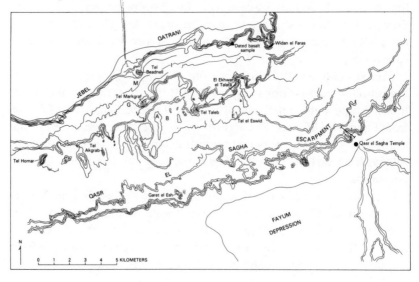

most of its exposure in the Fayum Depression (Bown & Kraus, in press).

Simons (1967; Simons & Wood, 1968) reported K–Ar ages of 24.7 ± 0.4 and 27.0 ± 3.0 million years for two samples of the Widan el Faras Basalt collected in the area between Widan el Faras and Tel Beadnell (where the flow is relatively thick). It is uncertain exactly where within the basalt these samples were obtained. A sample collected in 1981 from 70 cm above the base of the lowest flow west-northwest of Widan el Faras (Fig. 2) has been dated by one of us (JDO) and yielded a date of 31.0 ± 1.0 million years (Table 2). It seems likely that the two younger dates published by Simons either were on rocks obtained from different flows higher in the basalt or were determined on partially altered samples.

The age of 31 million years for the lowest part of the Widan el Faras Basalt provides a minimum age for the underlying Jebel Qatrani Formation that corresponds to late early Oligocene (Berggren *et al.*, 1978; Savage & Russell, 1983). Everywhere in the Fayum Depression, the contact of the Jebel Qatrani Formation with the overlying basalt is a pronounced erosional unconformity of unknown magnitude. At Widan el Faras there is a minimal erosional scour of 1–3 m; however, the contact descends markedly to the west such that about 4 km west

Fig. 3. A photograph of the Jebel Qatrani or 'Tar Hills', illustrating the basalt cap.

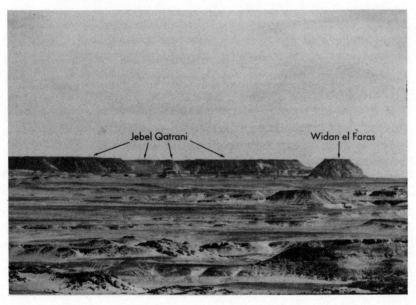

of Widan el Faras about 25 m of section is missing, which is present both further east and further west. West of the Fayum Depression, local deep erosional scars mark the unconformity between the basalt and the Jebel Qatrani Formation and record a pre-basalt topography of steep hills and narrow valleys with up to 40 m of regional relief. At present there is no way to estimate the time interval represented by the unconformity between the top of the Jebel Qatrani section and the base of the Widan el Faras Basalt.

The maximum possible age for the Jebel Qatrani Formation is provided by relatively inexact invertebrate faunal correlation of the conformably underlying Qasr el Sagha Formation. The uppermost part of this formation and its lateral facies equivalent, the Maadi Formation, contain an abundant echinoderm and oyster fauna, including *Anisaster gibberlus, Echinolampus crameri, Ostrea clotbeyi, O. reili, O. fraasi, Carolia placunoides,* and *Plicatula polymorpha.* In Egypt, these forms have traditionally marked the uppermost Eocene (Said, 1962).

Additional controls on the possible age of the lower contact of the Jebel Qatrani Formation with the underlying Qasr el Sagha Formation are provided from regional geologic evidence involving the change from marine to continental conditions at this contact. The Jebel Qatrani Formation records the first deposition of continental rocks in northern Egypt since the late Cretaceous. Because the uppermost part of the Qasr el Sagha Formation has been dated as the latest Eocene in Egypt

Table 2. *Analytical data for sample DKA 4550, whole rock basalt, Widan el Faras Basalt, Fayum Depression, Egypt*

Locality: 0.7 m above base of lowest flow in Widan el Faras Basalt; approximately 2.25 km N83 W of Widan el Faras (on Jebel el Qatrani), about 29 39′41″ North latitude and 30 36′22″ East longitude, Fayum Depression, Egypt

%K = 0.637
Moles $^{40}Ar^*/g$ = 3.45 × 10^{-11}
%Radiogenic ^{40}Ar = 12.8
Age (million years) = 31.0 ± 1.0 (+1σ)

Conventional isotope dilution techniques were employed for the determination of both argon and potassium (Dalrymple & Lanphere, 1969). Decay constants for, and isotopic abundance of, ^{40}K listed below are those recommended by Steiger & Jager (1977)

^{40}K = 1.167 × 10^{-4} mole/mole of K

$\lambda_{\epsilon \times \epsilon'}$ = 0.581 × 10^{-10} yr^{-1}
λ_β = 4.962 × 10^{-10} yr^{-1}

and because its upper 85 m record a substantial regression of the Tethys Sea in northeastern Africa, it is quite likely that the rocks near the Jebel Qatrani/Qasr el Sagha contact record the major early Oligocene/late Eocene regression found throughout western and southern Europe (Cavelier *et al.*, 1981; Plaziat, 1981). To the extent that this view is correct, the advent of continental deposition in northern Egypt might well be nearly synchronous with Stehlin's (1909) 'grande coupure'. In Europe this event records the turnover of Eocene to Oligocene land mammal faunas coincident with a worldwide decline of paleotemperatures (Wolfe, 1978; Wolfe & Poore, 1982; Morner, 1984).

In summary, the Jebel Qatrani Formation has a minimum age, based on the unconformably overlying basalt, of more than 31 million years. There is no radiometric age for the base of the formation which would provide a maximum age. However, most of the paleontological and geological data are concordant with the earlier observation by Simons (Simons & Wood, 1968) that the Jebel Qatrani Formation is probably mostly Oligocene and the underlying Qasr el Sagha Formation almost certainly Eocene. However, the new radiometric age of 31.0 ± 1.0 million years for the basalt unconformably overlying the Jebel Qatrani Formation and the presence of about 90 m of sediment between this unconformity and the highest fossil primate localities now indicate that the fossil primates from the Jebel Qatrani Formation come only from the early Oligocene rather than spanning the entire epoch.

The Fayum anthropoids and catarrhine evolution

Since they were first described in the beginning of this century, the Fayum anthropoids have been recognized as the earliest undoubted higher primates and have generally been regarded as broadly ancestral to the younger fossil apes from the Miocene of Europe, East Africa, and Asia. However, there has been considerable debate concerning the phyletic relationships of the various Fayum primates with regard to the evolutionary divergence of unique lineages leading to Old World monkeys, lesser apes, and hominids (e.g. Fleagle & Kay, 1983). When the Fayum 'apes' *Propliopithecus* and *Aegyptopithecus* were known almost totally from fragmentary dental remains, individual species of Oligocene 'apes' seemed to mark the evolutionary divergence of lineages leading to gibbons, great apes, and possibly even hominids (Simons, 1965, 1967; Pilbeam, 1967; Kurten, 1972). At the same time, the lineage leading to the living Old World monkeys seemed to be present in the sympatric and synchronic parapithecids (Simons, 1970, 1972).

With the recovery of more complete fossil material and the wide-spread acceptance of more rigorous phylogenetic analysis, it has become increasingly clear that the early 'apes' from the Fayum are extremely primitive with respect to living catarrhines (e.g. Simons & Fleagle, 1973; Szalay & Delson, 1979; Kay *et al.*, 1981; Fleagle & Simons, 1982; Fleagle & Kay, 1983). They lack most of the features that characterize living apes as a distinct group, as well as most of the features that unite the living Old World monkeys and apes as catarrhine primates. Even though they share with living catarrhines a reduced dental formula with two premolars, *Aegyptopithecus* and *Propliopithecus* seem to retain, in many aspects of their cranial and skeletal morphology, more primitive, platyrrhine-like features, suggesting they precede the Old World monkey–ape divergence. While they are primitive enough to be the ancestors of both groups of living catarrhines, they could only be placed on a lineage leading uniquely to the living apes by postulating that most of the features uniting living catarrhines evolved in parallel in separate lineages.

Likewise, any phylogeny deriving Old world monkeys from the parapithecids, to the exclusion of the Fayum 'apes', requires that all of the unique features uniting living catarrhines, including the presence of two rather than three premolars, were attained independently in monkeys and apes.

Compared with the Fayum anthropoids, the higher primates from the early Miocene of Kenya are much more advanced morphologically and more similar to living catarrhines. While there is reasonable debate regarding the precise relationship of the *Proconsul* group to living apes, they clearly have all the features that characterize living catarrhines and a few distinctly ape-like characters (Fleagle, 1983; Walker & Pickford, 1983). Similarly, the early Miocene monkeys from Napak (Pilbeam & Walker, 1968) and Buluk (Walker & Leakey, 1984) clearly document the presence of undoubted cercopithecoids in East Africa between 15 and 20 million years ago.

Thus, the new discoveries and analyses of the past 15 years have brought to light a considerable morphological gap between the early anthropoids of the Fayum and the monkeys and apes of the early Miocene of East Africa. The former show only a few features that distinguish them from a generalized higher primate condition, while the latter document the divergence of lineages leading to living cercopithecoids and (probably) hominoids.

With the new dating of the Widan el Faras Basalt, it now appears that this morphological gap corresponds to a rather substantial temporal gap of over 10 million years between the two groups of fossil anthropoids. At present, we have virtually no evidence of anthropoid evolution between 30 and 20 million years ago, the time that appears to have been characterized by a substantial adaptive radiation of catarrhines and the phyletic divergence of monkeys and apes.

Acknowledgments

We are grateful to the Geological Survey of Egypt for their generous assistance and cooperation in all aspects of this research, especially Dr Bahay Issawi, Dr Ragi Eissa, Dr Baher el-Khashab, Mr Ahmed el Awady Kandil, Mr Adb el Ghany Ibrihim Shellaby, and Mr Mohammed Askalany. Many of our colleagues contributed their expertise and insights to the contents of this paper including Mary Kraus, Prithijit Chatrath, Daryl Domning, Tab Rasmussen, Philip Gingerich, Richard Kay, Scott Wing, and David Krause. We thank Dr Martin Pickford for the invitation to participate in this symposium. This work was funded in part by Research Grants BNS 8016206, BNS 8114925, BNS 8209937 and BNS 8210949 from the National Science Foundation and 70869600 and 809479 from the Smithsonian Foreign Currency Program.

References

Berggren, W. A., McKenna, M. C., Hartenbol, J. & Obradovich, J. D. (1978) Revised Paleocene polarity time scale. *J. Geol.*, **86**, 67–81

Bowen, B. E. & Vondra, C. F. (1974) Paleoenvironmental interpretations of the Oligocene Gabel et Qatrani Formation, Fayum Depression, Egypt. *Ann. Geol. Surv. Egypt*, **4**, 115–38

Bown, T. M. (1982) Ichnofossils and rhizoliths of the nearshore fluvial Jebel Qatrani Formation (Oligocene), Fayum, Egypt. *Palaeogeogr. Palaeoclimatol. Palaeoecol.*, **40**, 255–309

Bown, T. M. & Kraus, M. J. (in press) Geologic and paleoenvironmental conspectus of the Oligocene Jebel Qatrani formation and adjacent rocks, Fayum Depression, Egypt. *Ann. Geol. Surv. Egypt*

Bown, T. M., Kraus, M. J., Wing, S. L., Fleagle, J. G., Tiffany, B., Simons, E. L. & Vondra, C. F. (1982) The Fayum Primate forest revisited. *J. Hum. Evol.*, **11**, 603–32

Bown, T. M. & Simons, E. L. (1984) First record of marsupials (Metatheria: Polyprotodonta) from the Oligocene in Africa. *Nature*, **308**, 447–9

Cavelier, C., Chateauneuf, J.-J., Pomerol, C.-J., Rabussier, D., Renard, M. & Vergnaud-Grazzini, C. (1981) The geological events at the Eocene/ Oligocene boundary. *Palaeogeogr. Palaeoclimatol. Palaeoecol.*, **36**, 223–48

Crochet, J.-Y. (1980) *Les Marsupiaux du Tertiare d'Europe*. 279 pp. Paris: Editions Fondation Singer-Polignac

Dalrymple, G. G. & Lanphere, M. A. (1969) *Potassium Argon Dating.* 258 pp. San Francisco: W. H. Freeman

Fisher, D. C. (1981) Crocodilian scatology, microvertebrate concentrations and enamelless teeth. *Paleobiol.*, **7**, 262–75

Fleagle, J. G. (1983) Locomotor adaptations of Oligocene and Miocene hominoids and their phyletic implications. In *New Interpretations of Ape and Human Ancestry*, ed. R. L. Ciochon & R. S. Corruccini, pp. 301–24. New York: Plenum Press

Fleagle, J. G. & Kay, R. F. (1983) New interpretations of the phyletic position of Oligocene hominoids. In *New Interpretations of Ape and Human Ancestry*, ed. R. L. Ciochon & R. S. Corruccini, pp. 181–210. New York: Plenum Press

Fleagle, J. G. & Simons, E. L. (1982) The humerus of *Aegyptopithecus zeuxis*, a primitive anthropoid. *Am. J. Phys. Anthropol.*, **59**, 175–93

Gebo, D. L. & Simons, E. L. (1984) Puncture marks on early African Anthropoids. *Am. J. Phys. Anthropol.*, **63**, 161

Gingerich, P. D. (1973) Anatomy of the temporal bone in the Oligocene anthropoid *Apidium* and the origin of the Anthropoidea. *Folia Primatol.*, **19**, 329–37

Hoffstetter, R. (1980) Origin and deployment of New World monkeys emphasizing the southern continents route. In *Evolutionary Biology of the New World Monkeys and Continental Drift*, ed. R. L. Ciochon & A. B. Chiarelli, pp. 103–38. New York: Plenum Press

Kay, R. F., Fleagle, J. G. & Simons, E. L. (1981) A revision of the Oligocene Apes of the Fayum Province, Egypt. *Am. J. Phys. Anthropol.*, **55**, 293–332

Kay, R. F. & Simons, E. L. (1983) Dental formulae and dental eruption patterns in Parapithecidae (Primates, Anthropoidea). *Am. J. Phys. Anthropol.*, **62**, 363–75

Kortlandt, A. (1980) The Fayum primate forest: did it exist? *J. Hum. Evol.*, **9**, 227–97

Kurten, B. (1972) *Not from the Apes*. New York: Vantage Books

Lange-Badre, B. (1979) Les créodontes (Mammalia) d'Europe occidentale de l'Eocene Superieur à l'Oligocene Superieur. *Mem. Mus. Natl. Hist. Nat., N.S.*, **XLII**, 1–249

Morner, N. A. (1984) Low sea levels, droughts and mammalian extinctions. In *Neogene Datum Planes*, ed. W. A. Berggren & J. A. VanCouvering, pp. 387–93. Princeton, N.J.: Princeton University Press

Pilbeam, D. R. (1967) Man's earliest ancestors. *Sci. J.*, **3**, 47–53

Pilbeam, D. R. & Walker, A. C. (1968) Fossil monkeys from the Miocene of Napak, Northeast Uganda. *Nature*, **220**, 657–60

Plaziat, J.-C. (1981) Late Cretaceous to Late Eocene paleogeographic evolution of southwest Europe. *Palaeogeogr. Palaeoclimatol. Palaeoecol.*, **36**, 262–320

Said, R. (1962) *The Geology of Egypt*. 337 pp. Amsterdam: Elsevier

Savage, D. E. & Russell, D. E. (1983) *Mammalian Paleofaunas of the World*. Boston: Addison-Wesley

Schlosser, M. (1911) Beitrage zur Kenntnis der Oligozänen Landsäugetiere aus dem Fayum (Aegypten). *Paleontol. Geol. Ost.-Ung. Orients*, **2**(24), 51–167

Simons, E. L. (1965) New fossil apes from Egypt and the initial differentiation of Hominoidea. *Nature*, **205**, 135–9

Simons, E. L. (1967) The earliest apes. *Sci. Am.*, **217**, 28–35

Simons, E. L. (1970) The deployment and history of Old World Monkeys (Cercopithecidae, Primates). In *Old World Monkeys*, ed. J. R. Napier & P. H. Napier, pp. 92–147. New York: Academic Press

Simons, E. L. (1972) *Primate Evolution*. 312 pp. New York: Macmillan

Simons, E. L., Andrews, P. & Pilbeam, D. R. (1978) Cenozoic Apes. In *Evolution of African Mammals*, ed. V. Maglio & H. B. Cooke, pp. 120–46. Cambridge, Mass.: Harvard University Press

Simons, E. L. & Fleagle, J. G. (1973) The history of extinct gibbon-like primates. *Gibbons and Siamang*, **2**, 121–48

Simons, E. L. & Gingerich, P. D. (1974) New carnivorous mammals from the Oligocene of Egypt. *Ann. Geol. Surv. Egypt*, **4**, 157–66

Simons, E. L. & Pilbeam, D. R. (1972) Hominoid paleoprimatology. In *The Functional and Evolutionary Biology of Primates*, ed. R. Tuttle, pp. 36–62. Chicago: Aldine–Atherton

Simons, E. L. & Wood, A. E. (1968) Early Cenozoic Faunas, Fayum Province, Egypt. *Bull. Peabody Mus. Nat. Hist.*, **28**, 1–105

Stehlin, H. G. (1909) Remarques sur les faunules de mammifères des couches Eocenes et Oligocenes du basin de Paris. *Bull. Soc. Geol. Fr.*, **9**, 448–520

Steiger, R. H. & Jager, E. (1977) Subcommission on geochronology: convention on the use of decay constants in geo- and cosmochronology. *Earth Planet. Sci. Lett.*, **36**, 359–61

Szalay, F. S. (1970) Late Eocene *Amphipithecus* and the origins of catarrhine primates. *Nature*, **227**, 355–7

Szalay, F. S. & Delson, E. (1979) *Evolutionary History of the Primates*. New York: Academic Press

Walker, A. C. & Leakey, R. E. (1984) New fossil primates from the lower Miocene site of Buluk, N. Kenya. *Am. J. Phys. Anthropol.*, **63**, 232

Walker, A. C., & Pickford, M. (1983). New postcranial fossils of *Proconsul africanus* and *Proconsul nyanzae*. In *New Interpretations of Ape and Human Ancestry*, ed. R. L. Ciochon & R. S. Corruccini, pp. 325–52. New York: Plenum Press

Wing, S. L. & Tiffney, B. H. (1982) A paleotropical flora from the Oligocene Jebel Qatrani Formation of northern Egypt: a preliminary report. *Bot. Soc. Am. Misc. Ser.*, **162**, 67

Wolfe, J. A. (1978) A paleobotanical interpretation of Tertiary climates in the northern hemisphere. *Am. Sci.*, **66**, 694–703

Wolfe, J. A. & Poore, R. Z. (1982) Tertiary marine and nonmarine climatic trends. In *Climate in Earth History*, pp. 154–8. Washington, D.C.: National Academy Press

I.2

The geochronology of Miocene higher primate faunas of East Africa

M. PICKFORD

Background to the context of East African primate faunas

The powerful combination of tectonic, volcanic and geomorphologic processes active in East Africa for the past 20 million years has led to the accumulation of a Tertiary vertebrate record which is unparalleled in Africa and which in many ways rivals the best in the rest of the world.

In particular the close association of more than 98% of East African vertebrate fossils with volcanic strata has led to extensive calibration of the fossil record by radioisotopic techniques. Although a great deal remains to be done, a stage has been reached where the East African sequence is often used as a yardstick against which fossil sequences in other parts of the Old World are compared. The development is particularly interesting since, until the advent of radioisotopic dating on a large scale, all East African fossil sites were correlated on a basis of European sequences, often with equivocal results.

The application of radioisotopic dating has not been without hiccups, there being several examples where the deduced ages for fossil sites were incompatible with other data. In most of these cases the record of the mammal fauna has indicated that the radioisotopic ages were suspect, but on other occasions stratigraphic mapping has led to resampling and hence revision of the radioisotopic data.

It is therefore necessary to recognise that dating of the fossil record should be based on as many techniques as possible. This review of the dating of East Africa's Tertiary higher primates takes into account all available data, including stratigraphy, radioisotopic dating and biostratigraphy. There are gaps in our knowledge, there are incompatibilities in our data, and there are voids in the stratigraphic record, but a general picture is emerging of the sequence of events which occurred in East Africa from 23 million years ago to the present.

Since the East African sequence is increasingly being used as a standard against which other sequences are compared, especially with regard to fossil primates, it is essential that every dated site be submitted to rigorous testing.

Too much reliance has frequently been placed on unrelated, isolated radioisotopic dates performed in the early days of the K–Ar dating method, when problems of technique had still to be solved, when context was usually not as rigorously studied as it is now, and when

Fig. 1. Distribution of Miocene fossil areas in Kenya and Uganda.

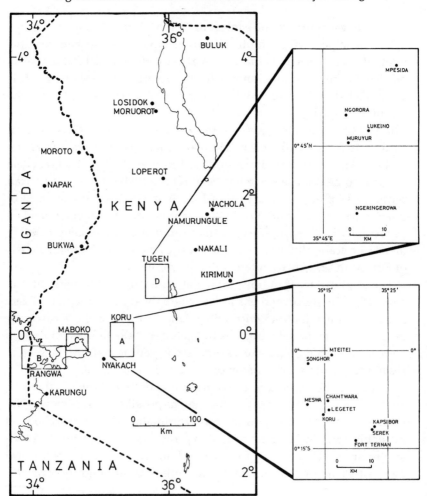

mapped sequences had not been established. Nowhere is this more so than in Western Kenya where the very first dates published for that region are still widely quoted regardless of inconsistencies with faunas and stratigraphy (see Fig. 1).

An example is the often quoted date of 23 million years ago (m.y.) for the site of Karungu. Faunally, Karungu is the same as Rusinga-Hiwegi (Pickford, 1981), dated at 17.9 m.y. Redating of Karungu has resulted in K–Ar dates of 17.7 m.y., essentially equal to 17.9 ± 0.16 for Rusinga Island (Drake *et al.*, unpublished). Other sites that need attention are Fort Ternan and Songhor, which have formed convenient pegs on which many authors have hung their correlation hats. In addition Rusinga has recently been redated (Drake *et al.*, unpublished) and plans are under way to refine the geochronology of other Miocene sites in West Kenya.

Other dated Miocene sequences in Kenya are also being refined or confirmed. The Baringo K–Ar sequence is being re-examined although previous geochronology was reasonably internally consistent with its faunas and stratigraphy (Hill *et al.*, unpublished). The Miocene sites in Northern Kenya, however, need further study because their dates and faunas are inconsistent in some cases with the West Kenya sequence as now understood. For example, the Buluk Fauna is widely divergent from that of Hiwegi, and is much closer to that of Maboko, yet the currently available K–Ar dates (Harris & Watkins, 1974) suggest that the Hiwegi and Buluk faunas were nearly contemporary. If the faunas were indeed contemporary, then the degree of ecological diversity in the lower Miocene of Kenya must have been very great. However, several of the Buluk mammals, especially the Suidae, seem to be

Fig. 2. Miocene fossil sites in Western Kenya, Winam Gulf area.

derived relative to Hiwegi species and are possibly descended from them; an implication which suggests that Buluk is younger than Hiwegi. Maboko is in turn expected to be slightly younger than Buluk.

Nearly 2000 craniodental remains of higher primates have now been collected from Miocene deposits of East Africa, the bulk of these (nearly 95%) having come from sites in the Nyanza Rift Valley (Table 1). Only 105 specimens have come from other parts of East Africa. In addition to the craniodental remains, several hundred higher primate postcranial fossils have been recovered, again predominantly from Western Kenya.

It is therefore essential to ensure that the Nyanza Rift stratigraphy and geochronology is as soundly based as possible. The potential of regional mapping was apparently not thoroughly appreciated by early workers in the area, who seemed to be more interested in what a specimen was, rather than where it came from. This is not to say that geological mapping was not done; several fine examples stand out from the literature (Kent, 1944; Shackleton, 1951; Whitworth, 1953, 1961), but the scope of these studies was generally either rather limited or at too great a scale.

Regional geological mapping by the Geological Survey of Kenya was a step in the right direction since it resulted in better understanding of the relationships between the sediments and volcanics of West Kenya; but for the purpose of palaeontology and biostratigraphy the maps were of too large a scale to be of much use.

In addition, early studies of the sediments in West Kenya were carried out within the framework of the Miocene Lake Hypothesis

Fig. 3. Miocene fossil site in the Maboko-Ombo area.

Table 1. *Miocene Hominoidea and Cercopithecoidea of East Africa; distribution and specimen counts*

LOCALITY / TAXON	Indeterminate hominoids	Micropithecus clarki	M. songhorensis	M. sp.nov.	Dendropithecus macinnesi	Limnopithecus legetet	L. evansi	Rangwapithecus gordoni	R. vancouveringi	Mabokopithecus clarki	Oreopithecoidea sp. A	Oreopithecoidea sp. B	Xenopithecus koruensis	X. hamiltoni	Proconsul africanus	P. nyanzae	P. major	P. sp.?	Kenyapithecus africanus	K. wickeri	K. sp.?	Nov. gen. A	Nov. gen. B	Australopithecinae ?	Victoriapithecus	Colobinae nov. gen.	Small colobine	Small cercopithecine	Medium cercopithecine	TOTALS	FAUNAL SETS
Lukeino																												1	3	4	VII
Mpesida																													1	1	
Namurungule																								1						1	VI
Nakali																											1			1	
Ngeringerowa																										1				1	
Ngorora	8															1			1		1									11	V
Nachola	4																		18											22	
Muruyur	1																													1	
Fort Ternan	2	9			?1			3											2	17										34	IV
Serek	1																													1	
Kapsibor										1																				1	
Nyakach																			1						2					3	
Maboko	1	26	13							2	102								61						497					702	IIIB
Majiwa	1															5									1					7	
Kaloma																1														1	
Kirimun	?1																													1	
Moruorot																				1										1	
Loperot			1																						1					2	IIIA
Moroto														1																1	
Buluk	1															?2		4												7	
Losidok	1												2																	3	
Angulo			1																											1	
Chianda	2																													2	
Kulu			3														1													4	
Bukwa			2																											2	
Hiwegi	1				114	7	4	3							90	80														299	II
Karungu			1													1														2	
Walangani			1												1	1														3	
Kiahera			3		1										17	11														32	
Gumba			1	1											1															3	
Makira	1		2												5	1														9	
Napak	14	13	2	4													11								?2					46	
Songhor		36	4		92	71	2								15	?4	35													259	I
Chamtwara		49	42	20		96									6	?4	17													234	
Legetet	14	8	30	1										1	8	9														71	
Koru	1		5												2	?1	2													11	
Mteitei	1	1		5											1	1														9	
Meswa															12															12	PreI
TOTALS	40	77	87	35	152	159	97	78	5	2	102	4	1	2	146	104	75	16	88	17	1	5	1	1	503	1	1	1	4	1805	

(Kent, 1944) with all the chronological, lithological and stratigraphic connotations that go with sediment accumulation in lake basins. With the full realisation that sedimentation in Western Kenya resulted from, and was controlled by, volcanic and tectonic activity and largely subaerial geomorphologic processes in the Nyanza area, the Miocene Lake Hypothesis has now been abandoned. Almost all the strata in West Kenya accumulated on the flanks, apron or arena of carbonatite–nephelinite volcanoes, or in a precursor of the Nyanza Rift Valley. Volcanic episodes occurred intermittently throughout the lower and middle Miocene period providing potentially datable horizons at many levels. Currently available radioisotopic dates calibrate only a small fraction of these horizons. The scope for further studies is obvious.

The impetus for such studies exists as a result of geological mapping by Van Couvering (1972) and Pickford (various unpublished reports in the Kenya National Museum) who have integrated the regional stratigraphy at all the major fossil bearing areas in this region, including Koru-Songhor, Rangwa (Rusinga, Mfwangano, Uyoma, Karungu), Maboko-Nyakach, and Fort Ternan which together have yielded all the important fossil primates from that region.

The primate fauna

The most common fossil higher primate in Western Kenya is *Victoriapithecus*, now known from nearly 500 dental and gnathic remains (Pickford, unpublished 1984 field report on Maboko Island). Also well represented are *Limnopithecus legetet* (160 specimens), *Dendropithecus macinnesi* and the two species of *Proconsul, P. nyanzae* and *P. africanus* (Table 2).

Recent work by the author in the Koru and Maboko areas has resulted in the collection of over 900 craniodental remains of higher primates allowing a reassessment of many of the taxa. As a result of recent studies several new species have been recognised and await formal publication (Table 2), and a general sorting out of established taxa has been possible. This reshuffling of fossils has inevitably resulted in changes in the distribution patterns of taxa (compare Andrews (1978), with Table 1) and several interesting distribution patterns have emerged which appear to result from a combination of chronological and ecological factors (Pickford, 1983).

There remain, however, several very poorly represented taxa such as *Xenopithecus* (Table 2), the status of which may be improved by future collecting.

Table 2. *Specimen frequency of Miocene higher primates in East Africa*

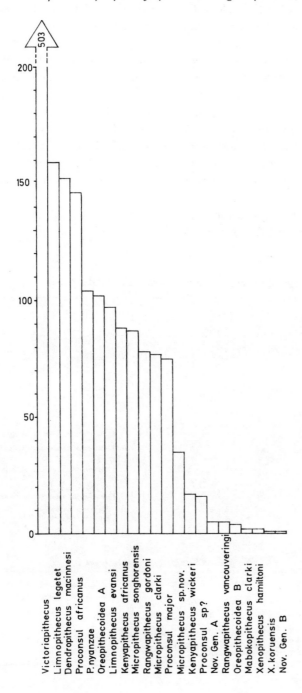

The current chronological framework of the sites from which these taxa came is provided in Table 3. This framework will hopefully soon be improved by additional K–Ar dating now in progress.

The geological context of the 105 fossil primates from Miocene deposits outside the Nyanza Valley is variable and should be studied more closely. In particular fossils from West and South Turkana (seven specimens) need much better contextual data. Material from Baringo (15 specimens) has better geological information (Pickford, 1975; Hill, *et al.*, unpublished) and specimens from east of the Gregory Rift (75 specimens) have good geological context (Ishida, Ishida & Pickford, 1984), but all this fossil material could have more refined geo-chronologic control which hopefully will be forthcoming in the near future.

The current available information on the dating of these fossil primates is given in Table 3.

Table 3. *Chronological ranges of higher primates in East Africa*

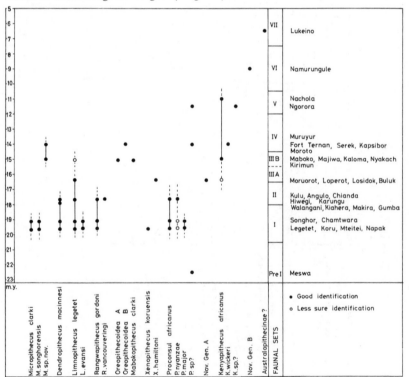

Acknowledgements

I am anxious to thank the L. S. B. Leakey Foundation, the Boise Fund and the Foundation for Research into the Origins of Man for supporting the research in Western Kenya. Research permission was granted by the Office of the President. I would also like to thank Mr. R. Leakey, Director/Chief Executive of the National Museums of Kenya, for encouragement and support during the duration of my studies in Baringo and West Kenya.

References

Andrews, P. J. (1978) A revision of the Miocene Hominoidea of East Africa. *Bull. Br. Mus. Nat. Hist. (Geol.)*, **30**, 85–224

Andrews, P. J., Harrison, T. & Pickford, M. (1980) Hominoid primates from a new Miocene locality named Meswa Bridge in Kenya. *J. Human Evol.*, **10**, 123–8

Andrews, P. J., Meyer, G., Pilbeam, D., Van Couvering, J. A. & Van Couvering, J. A. H. (1981) The Miocene fossil beds of Maboko Island, Kenya: geology, age, taphonomy and palaeontology. *J. Hum. Evol.*, **10**, 33–48

Bishop, W. W. (1967) The later Tertiary in East Africa – volcanics, sediments and faunal inventory. In *Background to Evolution in Africa*, ed. W. W. Bishop & J. D. Clark, pp. 31–54. Chicago: University of Chicago Press

Bishop, W. W., Miller, J. A. & Fitch, F. J. (1969) New potassium–argon age determinations relevant to the Miocene fossil Mammal sequence in East Africa. *Am. J. Sci.*, **267**, 669–99

Harris, J. & Watkins, R. (1974) New early Miocene vertebrate locality near Lake Rudolf, Kenya. *Nature*, **252**, 576–7

Ishida, H. & Ishida, S. (1982) Report of Field Survey in Kirimun, Kenya, 1980. In *Study of the Tertiary Hominoids and their palaeoenvironments in East Africa*, pp. 1–181. Osaka: Osaka University Press

Ishida, H., Ishida, S. & Pickford, M. (1984) *African Studies Monograph, Supplement 2*. Kyoto: Kyoto University Press

Kent, P. E. (1944) The Miocene beds of Kavirondo, Kenya. *Q. J. Geol. Soc. Lond.*, **100**, 85–118

Pickford, M. (1975) Stratigraphy and palaeoecology of five late Cainozoic formations in the Kenya Rift Valley. Ph.D. thesis, University of London

Pickford, M. (1981) Preliminary Miocene mammalian biostratigraphy for Western Kenya. *J. Hum. Evol.*, **10**, 73–97

Pickford, M. (1982) The tectonics, volcanics and sediments of the Nyanza Rift Valley, Kenya. *Z. Geomorphol. N.F.*, **42**, 1–33

Pickford, M. (1983) Sequence and environments of the lower and middle Miocene hominoids of Western Kenya. In *New Interpretations of Ape and Human Evolution*, eds. R. L. Ciochon & R. S. Corruccini, pp. 421–39. New York: Plenum

Pickford, M. & Andrews, P. J. (1981) The Tinderet Miocene Sequence in Kenya. *J. Hum. Evol.*, **10**, 11–33

Shackleton, R. M. (1951) A contribution to the geology of the Kavirondo Rift Valley. *Q. J. Geol. Soc. Lond.*, **106**, 345–92

Shipman, P., Walker, A., Van Couvering, J. A., Hooker, P. J. & Miller, J. A. (1981) The Fort Ternan Hominoid Site, Kenya: geology, age, taphonomy and palaeoecology. *J. Hum. Evol.*, **10**, 49–72

Van Couvering, J. A. (1972) Geology of Rusinga Island and correlation of the Kenya mid-Tertiary Fauna. Ph.D. thesis, Cambridge University

Van Couvering, J. A. & Miller, J. (1969) Miocene stratigraphy and age determinations, Rusinga Island, Kenya. *Nature*, **221**, 628–32

Walker, A. (1969) Lower Miocene fossils from Mount Elgon, Uganda. *Nature, London*, **223**, 591–3

Whitworth, T. (1953) A contribution to the geology of Rusinga Island, Kenya. *Q. J. Geol. Soc. Lond.*, **109**, 75–96

Whitworth, T. (1961) The geology of Mfwangano Island, Western Kenya. *Overseas Geol. Min. Res.*, **8**(2), 150–90

Appendix: Site locations and stratigraphy of Miocene fossil primates in Kenya

MESWA BRIDGE
(loc. 36. Discovered by M. Pickford in 1976)

A channel deposit in the Muhoroni Agglomerates dated radioisotopically at 22.5 m.y. (Bishop *et al.*, 1969); it has yielded 11 fossil fragments of a large hominoid species provisionally identified as *Proconsul major* by Andrews *et al.* (1981). Stratigraphically it is the earliest locality in the Koru-Songhor area.

MTEITEI VALLEY
(locs 32, 33. Discovered by R. Shackleton in 1947)

Two sites in the Koru Formation stratigraphically above the Muhoroni Agglomerates. Not yet radioisotopically dated, but faunally correlated to Set I. The sites have yielded 9 fossil higher primate specimens assigned to the following taxa: *Proconsul major, Proconsul africanus, Micropithecus songhorensis, Limnopithecus evansi.*

KORU
(locs 16, 25. loc. 16 discovered by Dr Gordon in 1927–28; loc. 25 discovered by M. Pickford in 1976)

Two sites in the Koru Formation which lies unconformably on the Muhoroni Agglomerates. Provisionally dated at loc. 16 to be 19.5 m.y. (Bishop *et al.*, 1969), the sites have yielded 11 fossils of higher primates assigned to the following taxa: *Proconsul major, P. africanus, Micropithecus clarki, Limnopithecus legetet, ?Proconsul nyanzae.*

LEGETET
(locs 10, 11, 14, 21, 29. loc. 14 discovered by Dr Gordon in 1927–28; other sites by M. Pickford in 1975–76)

Many sites in the Legetet Carbonatite Formation which unconformably overlies the Koru Formation, but which contains a similar fauna. Not radioisotopically dated. The sites have yielded 71 fossil specimens belonging to 7 taxa of higher primates, thereby yielding one of the most diverse fossil primate faunas yet known. *Micropithecus clarki, M. songhorensis, Rangwapithecus gordoni, Limnopithecus legetet*, Xenopithecus koruensis*, Proconsul africanus*, Proconsul major* (* = type site).

CHAMTWARA
(loc. 34. Discovered by M. Pickford in 1976)

A richly fossiliferous locality stratigraphically higher than the Legetet Formation, currently not dated by radioisotopic methods, but faunally similar to Legetet. This site has yielded a very diverse primate fauna comprising 7 taxa based on 234 dental and over 200 postcranial remains. *Micropithecus clarki, M. songhorensis, Dendropithecus macinnesi, Limnopithecus legetet, Proconsul africanus, P. nyanzae?, P. major*

SONGHOR
(Discovered by L. S. B. Leakey and D. G. MacInnes in 1932)

Songhor is thought to be stratigraphically equivalent to Chamtwara despite some differences in faunal content between the sites. Dated by Bishop *et al.* (1969) to be 19.6 m.y. Songhor has yielded abundant higher primate fossils ever since it was discovered.

Up to now, 259 fossil primate specimens assigned to 8 taxa have been collected. *Micropithecus songhorensis*, Dendropithecus macinnesi, Limnopithecus evansi*, Rangwapithecus gordoni*, R. vancouveringi, Proconsul africanus, P. major*, P. nyanzae?* (* = type site).

NAPAK (Uganda)
(Discovered by J. G. Wilson in 1958)
Napak fossil sites are believed, on a basis of K–Ar geochronology, to be about 19 m.y. old. The fauna from Napak is most like those from Koru, Legetet and Chamtwara, also dated by K–Ar methods to about 19.5 m.y. (Bishop *et al.*, 1969). Napak has yielded a rich assemblage of fossil primates comprising 46 specimens assigned to 5 taxa. *Micropithecus clarki*, Dendropithecus macinnesi, Limnopithecus legetet, Proconsul major, Victoriapithecus?* sp. (* = type site).

MAKIRA
(locs A, B, C, D, E. Discovered by L. S. B. Leakey in 1931)
The Makira deposits equated with the Wayondo Formation in Rusinga Island are the oldest exposed sediments in the Rangwa complex, overlying granites in the vicinity of Makira. They have yielded 9 fossil higher primate specimens assigned to 3 taxa. The sites have not been radioisotopically dated but faunally are evidently younger than Songhor and similar to Hiwegi, i.e. about 17.9 m.y. *Dendropithecus macinnesi, Proconsul africanus, P. nyanzae.*

GUMBA
(Discovered by East African Archaeological Expedition in 1931)
The Gumba redbeds are part of the Wayondo Formation on Rusinga Island which has recently been redated to be about 17.9 ± 0.16 m.y. (Drake *et al.*, unpublished). 3 fossil primate specimens have been found in these beds: *Dendropithecus macinnesi, Limnopithecus legetet, Proconsul africanus.*

KIAHERA
(R70, 71, 73, R113, Wayondo, Katuroe. Individual sites discovered at various times between 1931 and 1955)
Several sites in the Kiahera Formation on Rusinga Island have yielded fossil primates. The Kiahera Formation has recently been redated to be 17.9 ± 0.16 m.y. (Drake *et al.*, unpublished). Up to 32 primate fossils assigned to 4 taxa have been recovered from these levels. *Dendropithecus macinnesi, Rangwapithecus gordoni, Proconsul africanus, P. nyanzae.*

WALANGANI BEDS
(Discovered by L. S. B. Leakey in 1931)
The Walangani Beds, defined by Whitworth (1961) are now known to represent sedimentary intercalations in the Rusinga Agglomerate Formation. Originally dated at 19.6 m.y. by Van Couvering & Miller (1969) it has recently been redated to 17.9 ± 0.16 m.y. (Drake *et al*, unpublished). The strata are generally poor in mammals but have yielded 3 primate specimens belonging to 3 taxa: *Dendropithecus macinnesi, Proconsul africanus, P. nyanzae.*

KARUNGU
(Nira, Kachuku. Discovered by G. R. Chesnaye in 1909)
The Karungu Beds were originally thought to be 23 m.y. old (Bishop *et al.*, 1969) but were redated on the basis of its faunal similarity to Hiwegi to be 17.7 m.y. by Pickford (1981). New K–Ar dates confirm the younger date (Drake *et al.*, unpublished). Karungu has yielded a limited primate fauna comprising 2 taxa based on 2 specimens. *Dendropithecus macinnesi, Proconsul nyanzae.*

HIWEGI
(R1, R3, R5, R106 etc. Discovered by E. J. Wayland in 1929 and Leakey *et al.*, at various dates)

The various Hiwegi Formation sites have yielded the bulk of higher primate fossils from Rusinga Island. The strata were originally dated at about 18.5 m.y. by Van Couvering & Miller (1969) but have been redated recently to be 17.9 ± 0.16 m.y. (Drake et al., unpublished). Up to now 266 fossil primate dental specimens have been found, belonging to 6 taxa. Rangwapithecus gordoni, R. vancouveringi*, Proconsul africanus, P. nyanzae*, Dendropithecus macinnesi, Limnopithecus legetet. (* = type site).

BUKWA (Uganda)
(Discovered by MacDonald and Old in 1967)
Bukwa was originally thought to be younger than 17.5 m.y. on a basis of the first dating programme, but this estimate was revised downwards to 22.5 m.y. (Walker, 1969). The fauna is most like that from Hiwegi, which suggests that the original estimate was probably closer to the age of deposition of the strata. 2 hominoid teeth assigned to Limnopithecus legetet were recorded from Bukwa.

KULU
(R2–4 and Wakondu. R2–4 discovered by East African Archaeological Expedition in 1934; Wakondu discovered by L. S. B. Leakey in 1947)
Very few fossil primates have been collected from the Kulu Formation. Despite its unconformable contact with the Hiwegi Formation below, its faunal content is virtually identical, and its age is considered therefore, to be only slightly younger than 17.9 m.y. So far 4 primate specimens have been assigned to Proconsul nyanzae and Dendropithecus macinnesi* (* = type site).

CHIANDA
(Discovered by W. E. Owen in 1936)
Fluviatile deposits underlying Kiangata Agglomerates on the Uyoma Peninsula at Chianda, have yielded 2 primate fossils, so far not assignable with confidence to any of the better known taxa from Rusinga. The fauna at Chianda is most like that from Hiwegi. This fact and its stratigraphic position suggest an age of about 17.9 m.y.

ANGULO
(Discovered by M. Pickford in 1981)
The Rangoye Beds at Angulo are possibly stratigraphically equivalent to the Kulu Formation on Rusinga and are likely to be about 17.9 m.y. old. The only primate known from these beds is Dendropithecus macinnesi.

LOSIDOK
(Discovered by L. S. B. Leakey in 1951)
A poorly understood site which has yielded 3 primate teeth, notably of the large species Xenopithecus hamiltoni*. The fauna is limited but seems to be more advanced than that of Rusinga. (* = type site.)

BULUK
(Discovered by R. Watkins in 1974)
An interesting series of sites yielding a fauna distinctly more advanced in aspect than that of Hiwegi. Buluk was originally dated to be older than 17.1 m.y. by Harris & Watkins (1974), but new dates are expected soon. The sites have yielded 7 primate fossils assignable to 3 taxa, including the earliest known cercopithecoids in the world.

MOROTO (Uganda)
(Discovered by J. Wilson in 1960)
The fauna from Moroto is of limited use for biostratigraphy. The strata are overlain by a lava dated to be 14 m.y. (Bishop et al., 1969) an age which Bishop (1967) thought was close to the age of deposition of the sediments. Moroto yielded a virtually complete palate of a large hominoid, hitherto identified as Proconsul major, but possibly rather different from the Songhor species.

LOPEROT
(Discovered by F. Dixey in 1945)
Loperot is a poorly understood area yielding a fauna which is more advanced than that of Hiwegi but more primitive than that of Fort Ternan. It has yielded 2 fossil primate specimens including *Limnopithecus legetet* from the Williams Flat locality, and *Victoriapithecus*.

MORUOROT
(Discovered by C. Arambourg in 1933)
Moruorot strata have yielded faunal remains generally more advanced than those of Hiwegi. One fossil primate of uncertain affinities which has been collected from these beds, has usually been compared to *Proconsul*, but such identifications are by no means certain, especially in view of recent discoveries at Buluk and Maboko.

KIRIMUN
(Discovered by R. Shackleton in 1945)
The fluviatile strata at Kirimun have recently been dated to be older than 15 m.y. by fission track methods (Ishida & Ishida, 1982). The fauna has some similarities to that of Hiwegi, but in some respects is more evolved. It requires further study. A single tooth, doubtfully primate has been recorded from Kirimun.

KALOMA
(Discovered by M. Pickford in 1978)
The Kaloma strata are evidently part of the Maboko Formation. Among the few vertebrates from this locality is the most complete, but badly crushed, mandible of *Kenyapithecus* yet known from African deposits.

MAJIWA
(Discovered by W. E. Owen in 1933)
Majiwa has yielded relatively few mammal species all of which occur on Maboko Island. The primates from Majiwa comprise 8 specimens assigned to 3 taxa, *Kenyapithecus africanus*, *Victoriapithecus*, and *Micropithecus*. A phonolite overlying the Majiwa sediments has yielded an age of 11.8 m.y. (Andrews *et al.*, 1981).

MABOKO
(Discovered by J. O. Harper in 1933)
Maboko is one of the richest fossil primate sites known in Kenya, having yielded over 700 specimens. The fauna is distinctly more advanced in aspect than that of Hiwegi, but is only slightly different from that of Buluk. Its fauna is more primitive than that of Fort Ternan. Primates so far recognised at Maboko include *Micropithecus* sp., *Limnopithecus legetet?*, *Mabokopithecus clarki**, *Oreopithecoidea* A, *Kenyapithecus africanus**, *Victoriapithecus** (* = type site).

NYAKACH
(4 sites discovered by F. DaSilva in 1968; 20 sites discovered by M. Pickford in 1981)
The Nyakach Formation is evidently stratigraphically equivalent to the Maboko Formation and contains a fauna which is essentially identical to that of Maboko. A single Fission-Track age of 13.4 ± 1.3 m.y. has been obtained from a sample of tuff in the middle of the sequence. Site Koimoroon S has yielded one *Kenyapithecus* fossil and 2 other sites have yielded one *Victoriapithecus* specimen each.

KAPSIBOR
(Discovered by M. Pickford in 1980)
Kapsibor is at the same stratigraphic level as Fort Ternan. It has a slightly different fauna from Fort Ternan but the differences may be due to facies rather than time. Kapsibor has yielded a single hominoid specimen assigned to Oreopithecoidea B.

SEREK
(Discovered by M. Pickford in 1980)

Serek, like Kapsibor, is at the same stratigraphic level as Fort Ternan. Its fauna is comparable in most respects to that of Fort Ternan. It has yielded a single hominoid tooth of unknown affinities.

FORT TERNAN
(Discovered by F. Wicker 1957)

The Fort Ternan beds were dated in 1969 to be 14 m.y. old (Bishop et al., 1969). This date has been quoted so often that it has become a standard against which many correlations are made. A recent dating project to obtain a date from underlying lavas was not entirely convincing in its support for the 14 m.y. age (Shipman et al., 1981). A date of 12.6 m.y. has been obtained from an overlying lava (Bishop et al., 1969). Fort Ternan yielded a mammal fauna which is more evolved than that of Nyakach, dated by Fission-Track methods to be about 13.4 m.y. In view of this inconsistency, the radiometric dates for both Fort Ternan and Nyakach require further investigation. Fort Ternan has yielded 34 fossil primate specimens belonging to 5 taxa. Micropithecus sp., Rangwapithecus gordoni, Oreopithecoidea B, ?Proconsul sp., Kenyapithecus wickeri* (* = type site).

MURUYUR
(One site discovered by G. Chapman in 1969; several sites by M. Pickford in 1972)

The Muruyur Beds are considered to be about 13.5 m.y. old on a basis of K–Ar dates obtained from underlying and overlying lavas. The fauna is poorly known, but Diamantomys occurs. A single hominoid talus of medium size has been found in the deposits.

NACHOLA
(Discovered by M. Pickford, Japan/Kenya Expedition, 1982)

The Nachola Beds are interstratified between lavas dated at 10.8 and 11.1 m.y. (Ishida et al., 1984). The mammal fauna which is limited suggests an age nearer 14–15 m.y. Remains of primates are common, some 70 fossil primates have been found, assigned to four taxa. Kenyapithecus cf. africanus, ?Cercopithecoidea, Micropithecus sp., and ?Xenopithecus sp.

NGORORA
(Discovered by G. Chapman in 1969)

Ngorora Formation was originally radioisotopically dated between 12 and 8.5 m.y. on the basis of K–Ar dates obtained from underlying and overlying lavas. More recent K–Ar and magnetostratigraphic results now place the Ngorora Formation between 12.7 and about 9 m.y. (Hill et al., unpublished). 11 fossil primates have been found at different sites in the Ngorora Formation. A refined age estimate may soon be forthcoming as a result of recent work in the area. ?Proconsul sp., Cercopithecoid, small ape species, Kenyapithecus?

NGERINGEROWA
(Discovered by M. Pickford in 1972)

Originally mapped as Ngorora Formation, the Ngeringerowa area was subsequently found to yield a fauna with marked differences from that of Ngorora. In particular Hipparion and Nyanzachoerus suggest an age younger than 10.5 m.y. for the beds. A single higher primate fossil, the jaw of a new genus of small colobine, was found at Ngeringerowa (Benefit & Pickford, unpublished).

NAKALI
(Discovered by M. Golden in 1969)

The Nakali sediments are not well understood, but are thought to be between 8 and 10.5 m.y. Hipparion is common at several localities in the area. A single colobine tooth was recovered from Nakali.

NAMURUNGULE

(Strata discovered by Baker in 1953; fossils first found by W. W. Bishop and M. Pickford in 1974)

The Namurungule Formation in the Samburu Hills is interstratified between lavas dated at 12.3 m.y. below and 6.7 m.y. above (Ishida *et al.*, 1984). A fission track date obtained from a tuff in the sedimentary succession yielded a date of 6.7 m.y. at variance with the fauna which seems to be older, perhaps 9–10 m.y. A single hominoid specimen has been recovered from this formation.

MPESIDA

(Discovered by G. Chapman in 1968)

The Mpesida beds are intercalated between flows of Kabarnet Trachyte dated between 6.7 and 7.1 m.y. The sediments have yielded a sparse fauna which includes a medium sized cercopithecoid canine which is too poorly preserved to be positively identified.

LUKEINO

(Discovered by G. Chapman in 1968)

The Lukeino Formation overlies Kabarnet Trachyte dated at 6.2 m.y. It is overlain by the Kaparaina lavas, the oldest of which are dated at 5.7 m.y. (Hill *et al.*, unpublished). Its age is estimated to be about 5.7–6.1 m.y. The formation has yielded a single hominoid molar and 3 indeterminate medium-sized cercopithecoid fossils.

I.3

Geochronology of Miocene hominoids east of the Kenya Rift Valley

T. MATSUDA, M. TORII, T. KOYAGUCHI,

T. MAKINOUCHI, H. MITSUSHIO AND S. ISHIDA

Introduction

East Africa has been recognized as one of the most excellent fields for the study of the evolution of hominoids. However, Neogene hominoid fossils are scarce from the period prior to the Pliocene *Australopithecus afarensis* and later than the early Middle Miocene *Kenyapithecus africanus* or *K. wickeri*. Ages of *Australopithecus afarensis* determined by K–Ar and ^{40}Ar/^{39}Ar methods are 3.0 ± 0.2 million years (Ma) from Hadar, Ethiopia (Johansen and Taieb, 1976), and between 3.59 and 3.77 Ma from Laetolil, Tanzania (Leakey *et al.*, 1976). The K–Ar age of *Kenyapithecus wickeri* from Fort Ternan is about 14 Ma (Baker *et al.*, 1971). In 1982, two species of Miocene and Pliocene hominoid, *Kenyapithecus* and a large ape called the Samburu hominoid, were obtained from the west of Baragoi, east of the Kenya Rift Valley (Fig. 1) by the Japan/Kenya expedition team. Preliminary age estimates have been made on the basis of mammalian fossils which came from the same horizon as the hominoid fossils; *Kenyapithecus* is considered to be Middle Miocene, while the Samburu hominoid is thought to be Late Miocene in age (Pickford *et al.*, 1984). However, their radiometric ages have previously not been measured. In order to clarify their ages in greater detail, six K–Ar and two fission-track age determinations were made (Matsuda *et al.*, 1984). In 1980, the Japan/Kenya expedition team also studied the stratigraphy and paleontology of Miocene rocks of the Kirimun area east of the Kenya Rift, where Dr Louis Leakey obtained a canine of a hominoid and identified it as *Proconsul major* (Ishida *et al.*, 1982). Although no primate fossil was obtained from the area by the Japan/Kenya team, many vertebrate fossils were collected and two radiometric ages of volcanic rocks were measured by K–Ar and fission-track methods to determine the age of the fossil beds.

In this paper, we summarize the results of the age determination of the Miocene rocks west of Baragoi and in the Kirimun area.

Baragoi area
Geology

Baragoi is situated at about 80 km north of Maralal, northern Kenya. The area west of Baragoi is underlain by thick Miocene and Pliocene volcanic rocks with intercalations of sedimentary beds, and is bounded to the east by the El Barta plains which are underlain by Precambrian basement complex. To the west it is bounded by the Suguta valley which is a part of the Kenya Rift Valley in which recent volcanic and sedimentary rocks are accumulating (Fig. 2) (Baker, 1963). *Kenyapithecus* was obtained from site BG-X in the eastern part of this area called the Nachola area, and the Samburu hominoid was from site SH22 in the western part called the Samburu Hills (Makinouchi *et al.*, 1984).

Fig. 1. Locations of Baragoi and Kirimun, east of the Kenya Rift Valley. Rectangles outline areas of Fig. 2 and Fig. 4. Stippled area is underlain by Miocene and Pliocene volcanic rocks (Baker *et al.*, 1971).

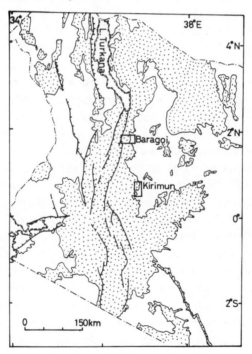

The Miocene rocks in the Nachola area are named the Nachola Formation (Fig. 3B). They are composed of sandstone, mudstone, and trachyte welded tuff. *Kenyapithecus* was obtained from the middle part of the Nachola Formation. Pickford *et al.* (1984) concluded that the fauna from this formation is in the pre-Hipparion stage, earlier than 10.5 Ma ago in the middle Miocene.

The Miocene rocks in the Samburu hills (Fig. 3A) are divided into three formations: the Aka Aiteputh, Namurungule and Kongia Formations. They are overlain by the Pliocene Nagubarat and Tirr Tirr Formations. K–Ar ages of the Tirr Tirr Formation were reported at about 4 Ma (Baker *et al.*, 1971). The Aka Aiteputh Formation is composed of basalt, trachyte welded tuff and lava, conglomerate and alternations of limestone and weathered basalt sediments. The Namurungule Formation consists of two horizons of alternations of sandstone and mudstone, mudflow deposits and sandstone. The Kongia Formation is composed of basalt lava flows. Many vertebrate fossils including the Samburu hominoid have been reported from the Namurungule Formation (Nakaya *et al.*, 1984; Pickford *et al.*, 1984). The age of the Namurungule Formation was estimated to be later than 10.5 Ma during the post-Hipparion stage, based on the fauna (Pickford *et al.*, 1984).

Fig. 2. Simplified geologic map of the area west of Baragoi and sample localities for K–Ar and fission-track dating.

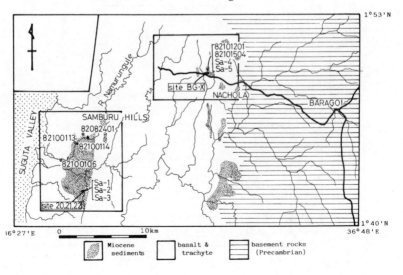

Fig. 3. Sequence of Miocene rocks in the Samburu Hills (A) and the Nachola area (B), and horizons of samples for dating. (See also Matsuda *et al.* (1984) for details of paleomagnetic measurements.)

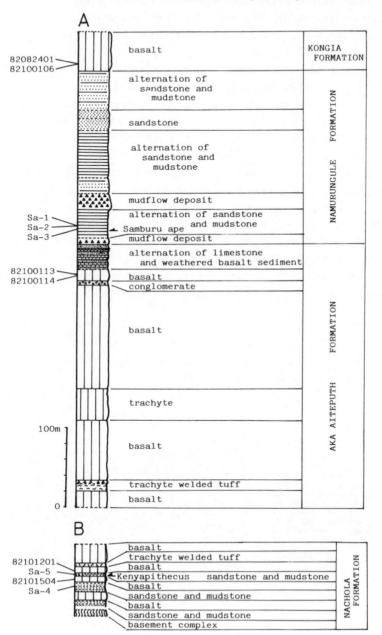

Radiometric ages

Four samples were collected from the Nachola area and seven from the Samburu Hills to determine the radiometric ages of the levels from which the hominoid fossils were obtained (Figs. 2 and 3). Six of the samples, 82082401, 82100106, 82100113, 82100114, 82101201 and 82101504, were for K–Ar dating, and the other five, Sa-1, 2, 3, 4, and 5, were for fission-track dating. All samples for K–Ar dating were basalt and for fission-track dating were pumiceous sediments.

Whole-rock K–Ar age determination on the six samples were carried out by Teledyne Isotope. The results of the K–Ar dating are shown in Table 1. The ages of the lower two samples, 82101201 and 82101504, from the Nachola Formation are 11.8 ± 1.4 and 10.1 ± 1.4 Ma, respectively. These ages coincide in their error limit. The middle two samples, 82100114 and 82100113, are of the Aka Aiteputh Formation. Their ages are 14.6 ± 1.2 and 12.0 ± 1.0 Ma, respectively. The ages of the upper two samples, 82100106 and 82082401, from the Kongia Formation, are 6.3 ± 1.0 and 6.4 ± 0.5 Ma, respectively. These samples were fresh, and the ages obtained within each horizon are quite similar, so these ages can be considered to be estimates of the age of extrusion of their constituent flows.

Results of fission-track dating are listed in Table 2. The only materials suitable for fission-track dating were apatite from Sa-2 and Sa-3. Apatite grains were also obtained from Sa-5, but their quantity was

Table 1. *Results of K–Ar dating of Miocene volcanic rocks from the Samburu Hills and Nachola area west of Baragoi (Matsuda et al., 1984)*

Sample number	Isotopic age (Ma)	scc $Ar^{40Rad}/g \times 10^{-5}$	% Ar^{40Rad}	% K
82082401	6.4 ± 0.5	0.036	37.8	1.49
		0.038	28.1	1.50
82100106	6.3 ± 1.0	0.028	16.0	1.12
		0.028	17.7	1.15
82100113	12.0 ± 1.0	0.032	27.7	0.69
		0.033	14.8	0.70
82100114	14.6 ± 1.2	0.061	36.5	1.11
		0.063	27.8	1.12
		0.066	29.3	
82101201	11.8 ± 1.4	0.033	20.8	0.73
		0.034	21.9	0.73
82101504	10.1 ± 1.4	0.036	17.7	0.91
		0.036	20.4	0.92

too small to permit a reliable determination of fission-track age. No material suitable for fission-track dating was obtained from samples Sa-1 and Sa-4. Therefore, the preliminary fission-track ages were determined on only two samples, Sa-2 and Sa-3, from the Namurungule Formation. Their ages are 6.7 ± 1.8 and 16 ± 4 Ma. However, the small number of grains and spontaneous fission tracks measured makes the age error large. Therefore, we need to get many more apatite or zircon grains in future expeditions in order to refine the age of the Samburu hominoid.

Summary

The K–Ar ages of the horizon of *Kenyapithecus* in the Nachola Formation are around 11 Ma (Middle Miocene). The ages are 2–3 Ma younger than the K–Ar ages, about 14 Ma for *Kenyapithecus* from Fort Ternan.

The K–Ar ages of the formations below and above the site of the Samburu hominoid are about 13 and 6.4 Ma, respectively. The age of the Samburu hominoid is, therefore, between them. The fission-track ages of the Samburu hominoid horizon are 6.7 ± 2 and 15 ± 4 Ma. An age of 6.7 Ma is consistent with K–Ar ages, but 15 Ma shows a very old age and is not consistent with the results of the stratigraphical and K–Ar studies. The reason that sample Sa-3 indicated an age older than expected is not clear. One acceptable interpretation is that the apatite crystals in Sa-3 are detrital grains from older rocks. As mentioned above, the fission-track ages have large errors. Therefore, at present, we can only state that the Samburu hominoid is Late Miocene in age. We need to measure the ages in more detail to restrict the age of the Samburu hominoid.

Table 2. *Results of fission-track age determination on apatite of pumices obtained from the Namurungule Formation which has yielded the Samburu hominoid (Matsuda et al., 1984)*

| Sample number | Number of grains | Spontaneous fission tracks | | Induced fission tracks | | Thermal neutron flux (/cm^2) | Age (Ma) |
		Number	Density (/cm^2)	Number	Density (/cm^2)		
Sa-2	8	30	3.42×10^3	728	1.66×10^5	5.45×10^{15}	6.7 ± 1.8
Sa-3	7	26	3.37×10^3	271	7.04×10^4	5.45×10^{15}	16 ± 4

Kirimun area

Geology

Kirimun is located at the eastern margin of Miocene plateau phonolite to the east of Rift Valley (Fig. 1). The phonolite overlies the Precambrian basement rocks which outcrop to the east. Between the phonolite and the basement rocks, sedimentary rocks are sporadically distributed (Fig. 4).

The Miocene rocks in the Kirimun area are divided into two formations, the Kirimun Formation and the Rumuruti Phonolite (Fig. 5) (Shackleton, 1946; Ishida *et al.*, 1982). The Kirimun Formation is composed mainly of mudstone, sandstone and conglomerate. Many vertebrate fossils have been recovered from the formation. Pickford (1981) pointed out that the fauna is of Early Miocene aspect. Paleontological results by Ishida *et al.* (1982) are consistent with Pickford's conclusion. A canine of *Proconsul major* from Kirimun was described by Andrews (1978).

The Rumuruti phonolites in this area are composed of three lava flows and underlying welded tuff. The three lava flows are called the Infra-Rumuruti Phonolite, Lower Rumuruti Phonolite and Upper Rumuruti Phonolite. Two K–Ar ages of the Upper and Lower Rumuruti phonolites were reported as 11.3 ± 0.3 and 12.3 ± 0.6 Ma, respectively (Baker *et al.*, 1971). (These ages are recalculated by adopting the decay constant and isotope abundance newly established by Steiger & Jäger, 1977).

Two samples, KE-8091101 from the phonolite welded tuff and KE-8090902 from the Infra-Rumuruti Phonolite, were collected from the horizon; these samples are stratigraphically closer to the fossil-bearing beds than Baker's sampling horizon. The age of the Infra-Rumuruti Phonolite was measured by whole-rock K–Ar dating. The age of the welded tuff was determined by fission-track methods using zircon.

The results of K–Ar age determinations on KE-8090902 are shown in Table 3. The age obtained is 11.4 ± 0.6 Ma. This age is almost the same

Table 3. *Results of K–Ar dating of the Infra-Rumuruti Phonolite (Ishida et al., 1982)*

Sample number	Isotopic age (Ma)	scc $Ar^{40Rad}/g \times 10^{-5}$	% Ar^{40Rad}	% K
KE-8090902	11.4 ± 0.6	0.194	66.2	4.37
		0.194	71.3	4.38

Fig. 4. Geologic map of the northern part of the Kirimun area (Ishida *et al.*, 1982) and sample localities for K–Ar and fission-track dating.

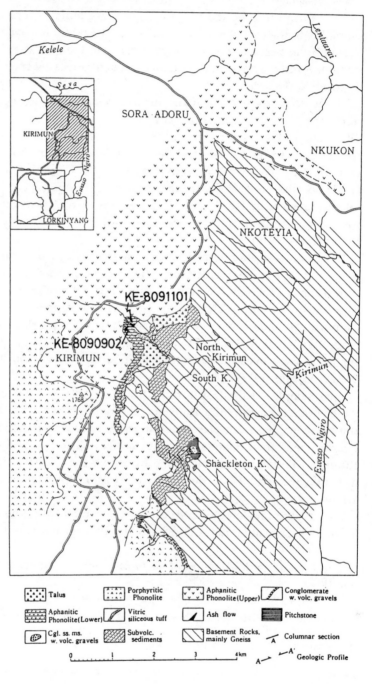

as those of the Upper and Lower Rumuruti Phonolites. The fission-track age of KE-8091101 is 15 ± 2 Ma (Table 4).

The summary of the stratigraphy, radiometric dating and paleomagnetic measurement of the Kirimun area is presented in Fig. 5. The lowest volcanic rock is the welded ash flow deposit dated at 15 million years. The Kirimun Formation is overlain by the welded tuff, so it is earlier than 15 Ma. This age is concordant with the paleontological results which imply that the formation is of Early Miocene age.

Table 4. *Results of fission-track dating of phonolite welded tuff of the lowest member of the Rumuruti Phonolite (Ishida et al., 1982)*

| Sample number | Number of grains | Spontaneous fission tracks | | Induced fission tracks | | Thermal neutron flux (/cm²) | Age (Ma) |
		Number	Density (/cm²)	Number	Density (/cm²)		
KE-8091101	16	709	6.35×10^5	2769	2.48×10^6	1.00×10^{15}	15 ± 2

Fig. 5. Generalized stratigraphy and results of radiometric age determinations and paleomagnetic measurements of Miocene rocks in the Kirimun area (Ishida *et al.*, 1982).

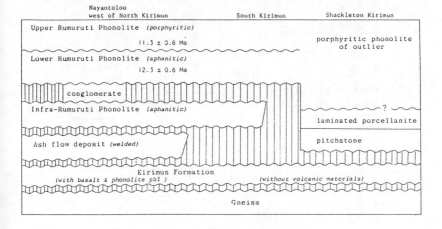

Concluding remarks

The sequence of Miocene rocks to the east of the Kenya Rift Valley, which has yielded many vertebrate fossils including hominoids, is summarized in Fig. 6. Preliminary estimates of their ages have been based on the vertebrate fossils. The Namurungule Formation in the Samburu Hills is Late Miocene, the Nachola Formation is Middle Miocene, and the Kirimun Formation is Early Miocene in age. Most of the radiometric ages reported here are concordant with the paleontological and stratigraphical results.

Three kinds of hominoid fossils have been obtained from this area. *Proconsul major* is from the Kirimun Formation, *Kenyapithecus* is from the Nachola Formation and the Samburu hominoid is from the Namurungule Formation. The ages of the hominoid fossils in this area are concluded to be as follows: *Proconsul major* is of the Early Miocene (earlier than 15 Ma); *Kenyapithecus* is of the Middle Miocene, in the pre-Hipparion stage (10–12 Ma); and the Samburu hominoid is Late Miocene, in the post-Hipparion stage (around 7 Ma).

Fig. 6. Schematic diagram of Miocene rocks east of the Kenya Rift Valley. Figures show K–Ar and fission-track ages.

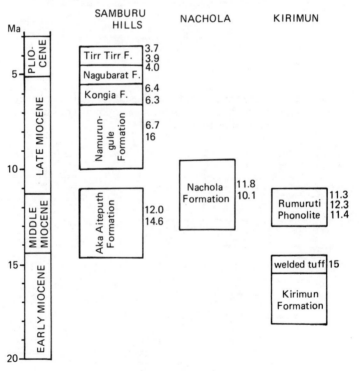

Acknowledgements
This study is supported largely by the Japan Ministry of Education, Science, and Culture with its Grant-in-Aid for Overseas Scientific Survey. We would like to express our gratitude to the Ministry. We would like to thank the National Council of Science and Technology and the Office of the President of Kenya for having granted us a research permit. We are also grateful to Mr. Richard E. F. Leakey and Dr. Martin Pickford of the National Museums of Kenya for their helpful advice. We would like to thank Associate Professor Hidemi Ishida of Osaka University who organized our survey and gave us much advice. We wish to thank Mr. Hideo Nakaya of Hokkaido University, Mr. Yoshihiko Nakano of Osaka University and Mr. Kiptalam Chepboi of the National Museums of Kenya for their strenuous support to our field survey.

References

Andrews, P. J. (1978) A revision of the Miocene Hominidea of East Africa. *Bull. Br. Mus. Nat. Hist. (Geol.)*, **30**, 85–224

Baker, B. H. (1963) *Geology of Baragoi area. Geological Survey Degree Sheet 27, N.E. Quarter*. Nairobi: Geological Survey of Kenya

Baker, B. H., Williams, L. A. J., Miller, J. A. & Fitch, F. J. (1971) Sequence and geochronology of Kenya Rift volcanics. *Tectonophys.*, **11**, 191–215

Harland, W. B., Cox, A. V., Llewellyn, P. G., Pickton, C. G. A., Smith, A. G. & Walters, R. (1982) *A Geologic Time Scale*. Cambridge University Press

Ishida, H., Ishida, S., Torii, M., Matsuda, T., Kawamura, Y., Koizumi, K., Nakaya, H. & Pickford, M. (1982) Report of field survey in Kirimun, Kenya, 1980. In *Study of the Tertiary Hominoids and their Palaeoenvironments in East Africa*, vol. 1. Osaka: Osaka University

Johansen, D. C. & Taieb, M. (1976) Plio–Pleistocene hominid discoveries in Hadar, Ethiopia. *Nature*, **260**, 293–7

Leakey, M. D., Hay, R. L., Curtis, G. H., Drake, R. E. & Jakes, M. K. (1976) Fossil hominids from the Laetolil beds. *Nature*, **262**, 460–6

Makinouchi, T., Koyaguchi, T., Matsuda, T., Mitsushio, H. & Ishida, S. (1984) Geology of the Nachola area and the Samburu Hills, west of Baragoi, Northern Kenya. *Afr. Study Monogr.*, supplementary issue no. 2, 15–44

Matsuda, T., Torii, M., Koyaguchi, T., Makinouchi, T., Mitsushio, H. & Ishida, S. (1984) Fission-track, K–Ar age determinations and paleomagnetic measurements of Miocene volcanic rocks in the western area of Baragoi, Northern Kenya: ages of hominoid. *Afr. Study Monogr.*, supplementary issue no. 2, 57–66

Nakaya, H., Pickford, M., Nakano, Y. & Ishida, H. (1984) The Late Miocene large mammal fauna from the Namurungule Formation, Samburu Hills, northern Kenya. *Afr. Study Monogr.*, supplementary issue no. 2, 87–132

Pickford, M. (1981) Preliminary Miocene mammalian biostratigraphy for Western Kenya. *J. Hum. Evol.*, **10**, 73–97

Pickford, M., Nakaya, H., Ishida, H. & Nakaya, Y. (1984) The biostratigraphic analyses of the faunas of the Nachola area and Samburu Hills, northern Kenya. *Afr. Study Monogr.*, supplementary issue no. 2, 67–72

Shackleton, R. M. (1946) Geology of the country between Nanyuki and Maralal. *Geol. Surv. Kenya, Rep.* no. 11

Steiger, R. H. & Jäger, E. (1977) Subcommission on geochronology convention on the use of decay constant in geo- and cosmochronology. *Earth Planet. Sci. Lett.*, **36**, 359–62

I.4

Chronology of the European Pliopithecids

L. GINSBURG

Introduction

Pliopithecus antiquus (Blainville), the type species of *Pliopithecus* (Gervais 1849), is the earliest recorded fossil primate in the history of palaeontology. It was discovered in 1834 by Edouard Lartet in the famous Miocene locality of Sansan (Gers district), in south-western France. Since that time, many other pliopithecid remains have been found in the Miocene of Europe. Until recently, pliopithecids were referred to, or closely related to, the Hylobatidae, but a reconsideration of their affinities, based on a phylogenetic character analysis, led to the conclusion that they are more primitive than the Hylobatidae and even the Cercopithecoidea, and are regarded as the sister group of all the other Catarrhini (Ginsburg & Mein, 1980) (Fig. 1).

The known history of the Pliopithecidae spans the Middle Miocene and the beginning of the Upper Miocene. Traditionally, the European continental Miocene was named according to the marine stratigraphical nomenclature (Burdigalian, Helvetian, Vindobonian, Tortonian,

Fig. 1. The genus *Pliopithecus*.

etc.). But, as our knowledge of the Miocene mammal faunas increased, it appeared that the major changes of the latter did not always coincide with the boundaries in the marine sequence, and that there was an urgent need for a more precise stratigraphical nomenclature for the continental Miocene. The first Miocene continental biostratigraphical scale was proposed by Mein (1975). Later, Fahlbusch (1976) organized an international symposium in Munich in order to discuss particular points of Tertiary mammal biostratigraphy and to work out the basis of a stratigraphical scale based on mammal faunas. There, the bio-stratigraphical zones of Mein were grouped into a number of stages and superstages. The results of this Munich Symposium were largely accepted and followed by most palaeontologists working on Neogene mammals.

Mein's biozones are defined by faunal associations and their lower limit is often characterized by either the first appearance of a new evolutionary stage in particular mammal groups, or by the first occurrence of an immigrant species. These mammalian stages and biozones are the stratigraphical framework in which I shall set the European Pliopithecids.

The age of the Pliopithecidae

The phylogenetic and systematic position of the primates referred to as the Pliopithecidae has been dealt with elsewhere (Ginsburg & Mein, 1980) and will not be reconsidered here except for minor points. The present discussion will be limited to the question of the precise biostratigraphical distribution of each pliopithecid species (Fig. 2).

Our classification is the following one:

Fam. Pliopithecidae
    Sub. fam. Pliopithecinae
            Pliopithecus (Pliopithecus) piveteaui Hürzeler 1954
            (?including *Pl. platyodon* Biedermann 1863)
            Pliopithecus (Pliopithecus) antiquus chantrei n. ssp.
            (Depéret 1887)
            Pliopithecus (Pliopithecus) antiquus antiquus
            (Blainville 1839)
            Pliopithecus (Epipliopithecus) vindobonensis Zapfe
            & Hürzeler 1957

Sub. fam. Crouzelinae
    Crouzelia auscitanensis (Bergounioux & Crouzel 1965)
    Crouzelia rhodanica Ginsburg & Mein 1980
    Plesiopithecus lockeri (Zapfe 1961)
    Anapithecus herniaki (Kretzoi 1974)

Pliopithecus piveteaui Hürzeler
This species is the oldest known pliopithecid in Europe. The type specimen comes from the Falun of Manthelan (Indre-et-Loire), near Loches, south of the Loire river. Many isolated teeth referred to this species have also been found in the Faluns of the Noyant-sous-le Lude basin (at Pontigné, Lasse, Noyant-sous-le Lude, Dénezé and Meigné-le-Vicomte in Maine-et-Loire district) and the Savigné-sur-Lathan basin (localities of Rillé, Channay, Hommes, Savigné-sur-Lathan and Pont-Boutard in Indre-et-Loire district), north of the Loire.

Fig. 2. Distribution map of the European pliopithecids.
1. Noyant-sous-le Lude basin; 2. Savigné-sur-Lathan basin;
3. Doué-la-Fontaine; 4. Manthelan; 5. Thenay-Pontlevoy;
6. Liet; 7. Sansan; 8. Castell de Barbera, San Feliu (Sabadell);
9. La Grive-Saint-Alban; 10. Rümikon; 11. Elgg; 12. Stein am Rhein;
13. Kreuzlingen; 14. Stätzling; 15. Diessen am Ammersee;
16. Trimmelkam; 17. Göriach; 18. Neudorf (Spalte + Sandberg);
19. Przeworno; 20. Oppole; 21. Rudabanya.

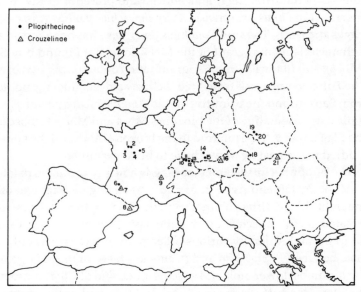

Two specimens have been found in the Pontlevoy-Thenay area: one belonged to the collection of the Abbé Bourgeois (Pontlevoy), and was mentioned by Stehlin (1925), the other was discovered recently in the marine layers of Thenay (Ginsburg & Sen, 1977). The former specimen has been destroyed, as was most of the Bourgeois collection, during the burning of the College of Pontlevoy at the end of World War II, and it is unknown whether it came from the marine or the continental deposits of Pontlevoy. All known specimens of *Pliopithecus piveteaui* are referred to the upper part of the MN 5 zone, and possibly occur also in the lower part.

One place deserves special attention. It is the lignites of Elgg, near Winterthur in the Zürich district of Switzerland, where Biedermann (1863) describe a palate that he referred to as a new species: *Pliopithecus platyodon*. Later, Hürzeler (1954) synonymized this species with the species from Göriach, *P. antiquus*. I have previously followed this view, but have now changed my opinion for the following reasons. von Meyer (1867) gave for this locality a list in which coexisted '*Mastodon*' *turicensis, Anchitherium aurelianense, Amphicyon intermedius* and *Titanomys visenoviensis*. *Zygolophodon* ('*Mastodon*') *turicensis* is typical for the middle and upper part of the Orleanian and the Astaracian, whereas *Titanomys visenoviensis* is characteristic of the MN 1 and MN 2a of the Agenian (Tobien, 1974). I did not see these fossils, but I had the opportunity to examine in the Museum of Basel some material from Elgg, and noticed the presence of the following species: *Conohyus simorrensis, Amphimoschus pontileviensis* and *Eotragus artenensis*. The suid *Conohyus simorrensis* has been considered as a characteristic immigrant of the MN 7 zone, but I found it in Sansan (MN 6), and in the Faluns of Touraine and Anjou (upper part of MN 5). The *Eotragus artenensis* from Elgg is clearly smaller than the population from Sansan, and the primitive cervid *Amphimoschus pontileviensis* is a typical representative of the biozones MN 4 and MN 5. Consequently, the Elgg fauna is to be referred to the biozone MN 5 and the specimens studied in the past by Meyer have to be re-examined.

The pliopithecid specimen of Elgg is a nearly complete palate with I^1–M^1 of the left and right sides and a small lingual fragment of M^2 of the right side. It differs neither from the Göriach material nor from the isolated teeth collected during the last 20 years in the Faluns of Touraine and Anjou by various collectors and myself. The only difference between *P. piveteaui* and *P. antiquus* rests on the enlargement of the hindmost lower molar (M_3) in the latter, and one may suppose that the same trend affects the upper M^3, but this tooth is not preserved in the Elgg specimen. Consequently, the Elgg palate cannot be determined at the specific level. Thus, the specific name *Platyodon* erected by Biedermann must be retained only for this specimen. One can thus neither confirm nor refute the synonymy of *P. piveteaui* with this 'species', yet its stratigraphical position in the MN 5 would rather suggest conspecificity.

Pliopithecus antiquus (Blainville)

Remains of this species have been discovered in many localities, from western France to Poland. The type specimen comes from Sansan (Gers, France), the reference locality for mammal biozone MN 6. Other localities for this species are: Liet (Gers) in France (Collier, 1978; Ginsburg & Mein, 1980); Kreuzlingen, Rümikon and Stein am Rhein in Switzerland; Göriach in Austria; Stätzling and Diessen am Ammersee in the Federal Republic of Germany (Hürzeler, 1954); Oppole (Wegner, 1913) and Przeworno II (Kowalski & Zapfe, 1974) in Poland; and finally Neudorf-Sandberg in Czechoslovakia (Thenius, 1952). All these localities are referred to the Astaracian. Liet belongs to MN 6, but somewhat older than Sansan. Rümikon is referred to the same old level of MN 6 by Engesser, Matter & Weidmann (1981). In contrast, Göriach is slightly more recent than Sansan, yet also in MN 6. Przeworno and Oppole, where *Euprox furcatus* occurs, are referred to MN 7. Neudorf-Sandberg, with the occurrence of a Tragocerine, is referred to MN 8. In the other localities, the associated fauna is generally too poor to be assigned a particular stratigraphical position, or deserves a re-examination because some associations are doubtful.

However, Depéret (1887) referred to as *Pliopithecus antiquus* var. *chantrei* a lower jaw from La Grive-Saint-Alban (Isère, France). This form is characterized, according to Depéret, by a slight reduction of its last molar. The comparative proportions of M3/M2 in this specimen and those from Sansan, Manthelan and Göriach are as follows:

	Manthelan	La Grive	Sansan I	Sansan II	Göriach
M3/M2	0.949	1.069	1.187	1.103	1.103–1.12

The measurements are those recorded by Hürzeler (1954). However, this author did not mention whether maximal and minimal lengths of the teeth of Göriach are taken from the same individual. Nevertheless, this may not have bearings on the result. Similarly, we note that the

M3 of the *Pliopithecus* from La Grive-Saint-Alban occupies an inter-mediate position between that from the Faluns of Manthelan (*P. piveteaui*) and those from Sansan and Göriach.

Some years ago, this remark would have sounded inconsistent, but Mein has revised the whole fauna of La Grive-Saint-Alban and came to the conclusion that, considering the date of the discovery of the *Pliopithecus* specimen, it must come from the Peyre and Beau quarry, which contains fissure fillings of various ages, some of them being slightly older than Sansan (Guérin & Mein, 1971). The *Pliopithecus* described by Depéret may come from one of these older fissures.

Pliopithecus sp. from Doué-la-Fontaine

Recently, a second lower molar of *Pliopithecus* sp. was found in the Faluns of Doué-la-Fontaine (Maine et Loire) near Saumur in western France. This marine deposit, containing *Hipparion primigenium*, *Korynochoerus palaeochoerus* and *Protragocerus chantrei*, is to be referred to the lower part of the first biozone of the Upper Miocene: MN 9 (Ginsburg *et al.*, 1979).

Pliopithecus (Epipliopithecus) vindoboniensis Zapfe

The type of this species comes from the fissure of Neudorf an der Marsch in Czechoslovakia. A long list of the associated mammal fauna was given by Zapfe (1960), and Cicha *et al.* (1972) gave good evidence that this locality is older than Sansan. Morever, Ginsburg & Mein (1980) noticed that the size of the giraffid *Palaeomeryx* from Neudorf fissure is that of the largest specimens from Pontlevoy-Thenay, and that the presence of the suid *Bunolistriodon lockharti* in Neudorf-Sandberg further supports this interpretation. It is note-worthy that this suid is obviously reworked from sediments of nearly the same age as the filling of Neudorf Spalte. Therefore, this locality is to be referred to the top part of MN 5, which Zapfe (1969) places in the uppermost Karpatian.

Crouzelinae

Historically, *Plesiopithecus lockeri* (Zapfe) is the oldest known Crouzelinae. This species is known from the Lignites of Trimmelkam (Austria) and is difficult to date because it has only a poor associated fauna. The latter consists of mustelids indet., rhinoceroids indet., *Palaeomeryx eminens* and *Deinotherium* cf. *bavaricum* (Zapfe, 1961), but Zapfe noticed that these lacustrine beds are discordant on marine sediments with a *Rzehakia* fauna referred to the upper Karpatian

(='Oberhelvetische'). Therefore, Zapfe's opinion is that Trimmelkam is at the base of the Badenian. He places the classical Göriach fauna just above Trimmelkam, the latter being thus referred to MN 6.

Plesiopithecus lockeri is referred to the subfamily Crouzelinae to which also belongs *Crouzelia auscitanensis* from Sansan (MN 6), *Crouzelia rhodanica* from La Grive-Saint-Alban (fissure L 7) (MN 7) and *Anapithecus herniaki* from Rudabanya (Northeastern Hungary) (lower part of MN 9) (Kretzoi, 1975, 1982).

Last of all, Crusafont-Pairo & Golpe-Posse (1981) described a new Pliopithecid from the upper Astaracian (or the base of Vallesian) of Castell de Barbera and Can San Feliu near Sabadell (Northeastern Spain). The lengthening of the last lower premolar (P_4) and the elongation of the tubercles of the lower molars into crests are the reasons why the authors referred their fossils close to *Plesiopithecus lockeri*. But they are not exactly alike and they named it *Pliopithecus* sp. It seems better in my opinion to call these Spanish fossils 'Crouzelinae indet. nov.'.

Radiometric dating

Only two radiometric dates are available within the time span of the Pliopithecidae in Europe. The first is for Howenegg, in southwestern Germany, which is a very rich mammal-bearing locality. Lithologically, it consists of marls and travertines interbedded within the Hegau volcanic series. The basalt of Hegau is dated to 12.4 ± 1.0 million years (M.Y.) (van Couvering, 1972). The mammal fauna consists chiefly of *Hipparion primigenium*, *Miotragocerus pannoniae*, *Chalicotherium goldfussi* and *Deinotherium giganteum* (Tobien, 1957), that is, a typical assemblage of the MN 9 biozone.

Secondly, in southern Germany, the Steinheim and Nördlingen Ries basins are rounded meteorite craters, both of the same age. The age of the Ries Crater has been determined by radiometric (K/Ar) and fission track methods on Suevit rocks, as 14.7 ± 0.7 M.Y. (Reiff & Groschopf, 1979). After the impact of the meteorite, the craters were filled with water and were the seat of lacustrine sedimentation including invertebrate- and vertebrate-bearing layers. In the Ries Crater, the small fauna of Steinberg is dated to the lower Astaracian (MN 6) (Heizmann & Fahlbusch, 1983). The populations of *Cricetodon sansaniensis* and *Miodyromys aegensi* are somewhat more primitive than those from Sansan. Consequently, the Steinberg fauna has to be referred to the beginning of MN 6, and has probably been deposited shortly after the impact of the meteorite. The Steinheim Crater, in turn, worked as a fossil trap somewhat later, in the time of MN 7.

Fig. 3. Stratigraphical distribution of the European pliopithecids.

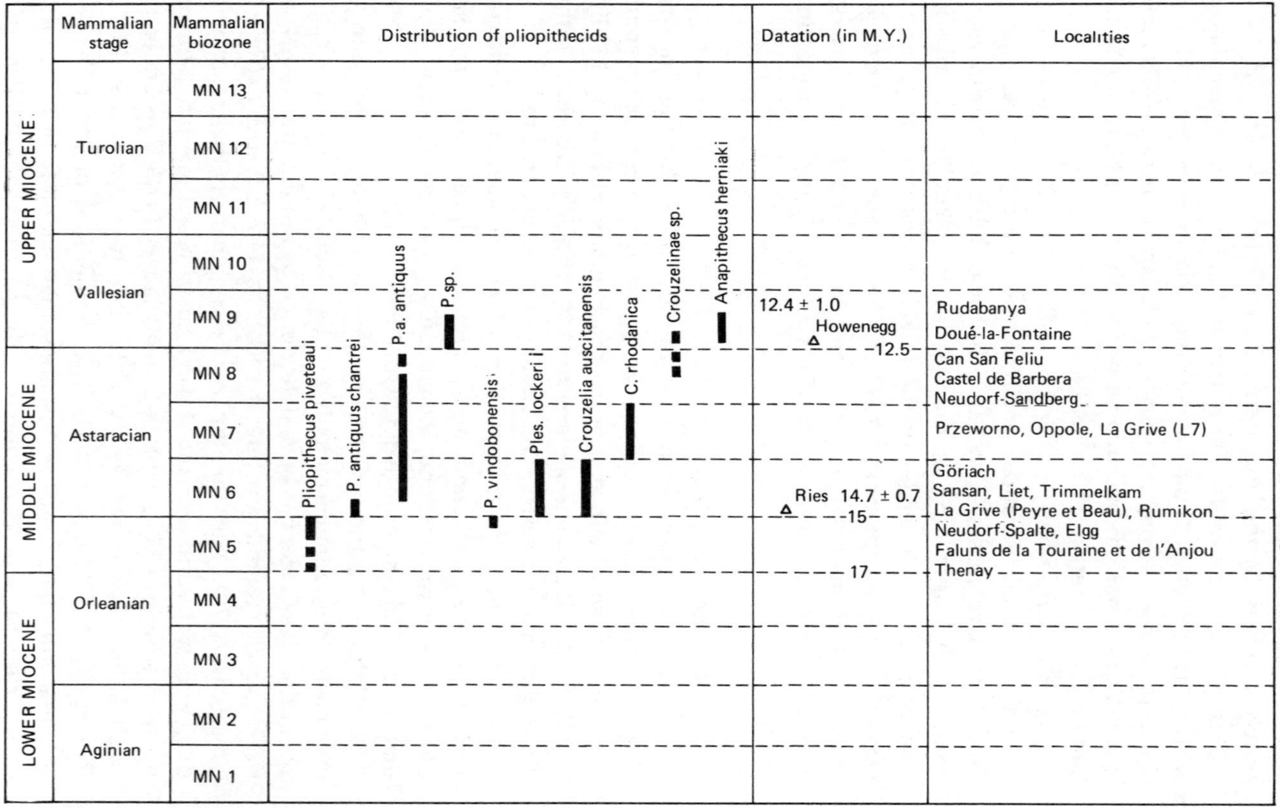

Correlations with marine sequences

In the Lissabon Basin (Portugal), marine layers are interbedded in continental deposits containing land mammals. The horizon V b (or regressive period R 4) has yielded *Gomphotherium angustidens, Deinotherium bavaricum, Bunolistriodon lockharti, Dorcatherium naui, Procervulus dichotomus* and *Phillotillon naricum*, an assemblage which clearly corresponds to the biozone MN 5, possibly its lower part. This horizon V b of the Lissabon Basin is interbedded between two marine transgressive phases, the lower one referred to zone N 8 of the Blow scale (with *Globigerinoides sicanus*), and the upper one referred to N 9 or N 10. Consequently, the horizon V b could coincide with N 9 (or the uppermost part of N 8) to N 10 or N 11 in the Blow scale, that is the Langhian, which is dated as 16.8–15.8 M.Y. (Rögl & Steininger, 1983).

Conclusions

The European pliopithecids are known during the Middle Miocene and the lower part of the Upper Miocene, from Spain to Poland (Fig. 3). Their record thus spans 4 million years. As I already pointed out, they are late representatives of the most primitive Catarrhini, the Eocatarrhini (Ginsburg & Mein, 1980). They probably arose from a stock of propliopithecids which lived in Africa during Oligocene times and disappeared when the first Eucatarrhini (e.g. the Cercopithecoidea) arose. An offshoot of Eocatarrhini thus migrated into Europe before the Eucatarrhini (Dryopithecidae) and survived there during the Middle and the Lower Upper Miocene. They became extinct, possibly because of the dryer climate, and also the concurrence of the more advanced and numerous hominoid primates which developed in the Upper Miocene.

References

Antunes, M. Telles (1960) Notes sur la géologie et la paléontologie du Miocène de Lisbonne. I. Stratigraphie et faunes de mammifères terrestres. *Bol. Soc. Geol. Portugal, Porto*, 13, 257–67

Antunes, M. Telles, Ginsburg, L., Torquato, J. R. & Ubaldo, M. L. (1973) Age des couches à Mammifères de la basse vallée du Tage (Portugal) et de la Loire moyenne (France). *C.R. Acad. Sci. Paris, Ser. D.*, 277, 2313–16

Biedermann, W. G. A. (1863) *Petrefakten aus der Umgegend von Winterthur. II. Die Braunkohlen von Elgg*. Winterthur: Bleuter-Hansheer

Cicha, I., Fahlbusch, V. & Fejfar, O. (1972) Die Biostratigraphie Korrelation einiger jungtertiärer Wirbeltierfaunen Mittleuropas. *Neues Jb. Geol. Paläont. Abt. Stuttgart*, 142(2), 129–45

Collier, A. (1978) Découverte de restes de Pliopithèques (Mammalia, Primates) dans les sable faunes de l'Armagnac. *C.R. Acad. Sci. Paris, Ser. D*, 286, 327–30

Couvering, J. A. van (1972) Radiometric calibration of the European Neogene. In *Calibration of Hominoid Evolution*, pp. 247–71. New York: Academic Press

Crusafont-Pairo, M. & Golpe-Posse, J. M. (1981) Estudio de la denticion inferior del primer Pliopithécido hallado en España (Vindoboniense terminal de Castell de Barbera, Cataluna, España). *Boll. Inf. Inst. Paleontol. Sabadell*, **13**(1–2), 25–38

Depéret, C. (1887) Recherches sur la succession des faunes de Vertébrés miocènes de la Vallée du Rhône. *Arch. Mus. Hist. Nat. Lyon*, **4**, 45–313

Engesser, B., Matter, A. & Weidmann, M. (1981) Stratigraphie und Säugetierfaunen des mittleren Miozäns von Vermes (Kt. Jura). *Ecl. Geol. Helv.*, *Basel*, **74**(3), 893–952

Fahlbusch, V. (1976) Report on the International Symposium on mammalian stratigraphy of the European Tertiary. *Newslett. Stratigr.*, *Berlin*, **5**(2–3), 160–7

Ginsburg L., Janvier, P., Mornand, J. & Pouit, D. (1979) Découverte d'une faune de Mammifères terrestres d'âge Vallésien dans le falun miocène de Doué-la-Fontaine (Maine-et-Loire). *C.R. Somm. Soc. Géol. France*, *Paris*, **5–6**, 223–7

Ginsburg, L. & Mein, P. (1980) Crouzelia Rhodonica, nouvelle espèce de Primate catarhinien, et essai sur la position systématique des Pliopithecidae. *Bull. Mus. Natl. Hist. Nat.*, *Paris*, **2**, 57–85

Ginsburg, L. & Sen, S. (1977) Une faune à micromammifères dans le falun de Thenay (Loir-et-Cher). *Bull. Soc. Géol. France*, *Paris*, **19**(5), 1159–66

Guérin, C. & Mein, P. (1971) Les principaux gisements de Mammifères miocènes et pliocènes du domaine rhodanien. *doc. Lab. Géol. Univ. Lyon*, 131–70

Heizmann, E. J. & Fahlbusch, V. (1983) Die mittelmiozäne Wirbeltierefauna von Steinberg (Nördlinger Ries). Eine Übersicht. *Mitt. Bayer. Staatsslg. Paläont. Hist. Geol. München*, **23**, 89–93

Hürzeler, J. (1954) Contribution à l'odontologie et à la phylogénèse du genre *Pliopithecus* Gervais. *Ann. Paléontol.*, *Paris*, **40**, 5–63

Kowalski, K. & Zapfe, H. (1974) *Pliopithecus antiquus* (Blainville, 1839) (Primates, Mammalia), from the Miocene of Przeworno in Silesia (Poland). *Acta Zool. Cracow.*, **19**(2), 19–30

Kretzoi, M. (1975) New ramapithecines and *Pliopithecus* from the Lower Pliocene of Rudabanya in north-eastern Hungary. *Nature*, **257**, 578–81

Kretzoi, M. (1982) Fontosabb Szórvanyleletek a máfi gerincesgyüjeményében: Funde der Hipparion-Faunen im Pannon des Karpatenbeckens. *Foldt. In. Evi Jel.*, *Budapest*, 385–94

Mein, P. (1975) Biozonation du Neogène méditerranéen à partir des Mammifères. *Rep. Activ. R.C.M.N.S. Working Groups, Ve Congr. Int. Neogène Méditerranéen*, 78–81

Meyer, H. von (1867) Studien über das genus Mastodon. *Paleontographica*, **17**, 1–72

Reiff, W. & Groschopf, P. (1979) Geology of the Steinheim Basin Impact Crater. *42nd Annual Meeting of the Meteoritical Society*, 9–18

Rögl, F. & Steininger, F. F. (1983) Vom Zerfall der Tethys zu Mediterran und Paratethys. Die Neogene Paläeogeographie und Palinspastik des zirkummediterranen Raumes. *Ann. Naturhist. Mus. Wien*, **85/A**, 135–63

Stehlin, H. G. (1925) Catalogue des ossements de Mammifères tertiaires de la collection Bourgeois. *Bull. Soc. Hist. Nat. Loir-et-Cher, Blois*, **18**, 77–277

Thenius, E. (1952) Die Säugetierfauna aus dem Torton von Neudorf an der March (CSR). *Neues Jb. Geol. Paläontol.*, **96**(1), 27–136

Tobien, H. (1957) Die Bedeutung der unterpliozänen Fossilfundstätte Höwenegg für die Geologie des Hegaus. *Jh. Geol. Landesamt Baden-Wurtemberg*, 2, 193–208

Tobien, H. (1974) Zur Gebisstruktur, Systematik und Evolution der genera *Amphilagus* und *Titanomys* (Lagomorpha, Mammalia) aus einiger Vorkommen im Jüngeren Tertiär Mittel- und Westeuropas. *Mainz. Geowiss. Mitt.*, 3, 94–214

Wegner, R. N. (1913) Tertiaer und ungelagerte Kreide bei Oppeln (Oberschlesien). *Paleontographica*, 16, 175–274

Zapfe, H. (1960) Die Primatenfunde aus der miozänen Spaltenfüllung von Neudorf an der March (Devinska Nova Ves), Tschechoslowakei. *Schweiz. Palaeont. Abh., Basel*, 78, 1–293

Zapfe, H. (1961) Ein Primatenfund aus der miozän Molasse von Oberösterreich. *Z. Morphol. Anthropol.*, 51(3), 247–67

Zapfe, H. (1969) Primates. In *Catalogus Fossilium Austriae*, 1–16. Wien

I.5

Chronological succession of hominoids in the European Neogene

P. MEIN

Introduction

Hominoids are rare in the European Neogene, and are generally represented by isolated teeth. The discoveries were mostly made many years ago and the localities are poorly dated. An attempt is made here to arrange the hominoid localities of Europe in the biostratigraphic scale of Neogene Mediterranean Mammals (Mein, 1975*). The proposed succession exhibits differences from earlier chronologies (Thenius, 1959; Szalay & Delson, 1979; Bernor, 1983). The nomenclature of the European hominoid remains follows to a great extent that of Szalay & Delson (1979); it is necessary to take into account the synonymy of *Ramapithecus* with *Sivapithecus* and the new determinations by Morbeck (1983) and Kay & Simons (1983). Contrary to the opinion defended by Bernor (1983), I consider that central and western Europe comprise a single biogeographic province. Greece and Georgia, in contrast, show oriental affinities characterised by specific taxa and by earlier appearances of faunal elements.

Spanish localities

Hostalets de Pierola

The lower beds at Hostalets de Pierola have furnished hominoids at two localities: one fragment of left mandible with M_{2-3} and one fragment of right M^1 at Can Vila and a lower deciduous canine at Can Mata. These remains, after various determinations (Villalta & Crusafont, 1941, 1944*), are currently ascribed to *Dryopithecus brancoi* by Szalay & Delson (1979).

* For details of reference see Szalay & Delson (1979).

Fig. 1. The chronological succession of hominoids in the European Neogene. Localities mentioned in the text, their ages and associated mammalian events are presented.

M.Y.	Stage	Mammals ages	Mammalian Neogene units	Selected localities for correlations with marine scale ⁰ or radiometric age *	European localities with Hominoids: Spain	Germany, France	Austria, ČSSR, Hungary	Greece, Georgia	Distribution of Hominoids	Mammals events (migrations)
7	TORTONIAN	TUROLIAN		Librilla *					*D. fontani*, *D. brancoi*, *S. darwini*, *S. metai*	
8	TORTONIAN	TUROLIAN	MN12	Samos *				Pyrgos		
9	TORTONIAN	TUROLIAN	MN11			Salmendingen				← Dipoides
10	TORTONIAN	VALLESIAN	MN10	Kastellios K2 ⁰	La Tarumba Polinya			Rain ravine Udabno, Eldar		← Progonomys ← Pliohyrax
11, 12	TORTONIAN / SERRAVALLIAN	VALLESIAN	MN9	Howe-negg *	Can Llobateres Castel de Barbera Can Ponsic El Firal	Melchingen Eppelsheim/Wissberg	Mariathal Rudabanya			Microtocricetus ← Hipparion
13	SERRAVALLIAN	ASTARACIAN	MN8	Neudorf-Sandberg ⁰	Hostalets inf. San Quirze	La Grive L 3 St. Gaudens	St Stephan Klein Hadersdorf Neudorf-Sandberg			← Tetralophodon ← Protragocerus Muscardinus
14	SERRAVALLIAN	ASTARACIAN	MN7							← Eurolagus
	SERRAVALLIAN	ASTARACIAN	MN6	Steinberg/Ries *						

San Quirze

The locality of San Quirze (Trinchera del Ferrocaril) has yielded a fragment of M_3 also attributed to *D. brancoi*. The fauna (Crusafont & Golpe, 1973*; Agusti, 1982), devoid of *Hipparion*, contains an association of *Megacricetodon ibericus* (Schaub) and *Fahlbuschia crusafonti*, Agusti. This fauna comprises part of the biostratigraphic unit MN 8.

Teutelaria del Firal

The locality of Teutelaria del Firal (=El Firal) in the Seu d'Urgell, Province of Lerida, yielded a mandible of *Dryopithecus fontani* (see Woodward, 1914). The fauna (Alberdi, 1974) is characterised by the presence of *Hipparion primigenium primigenium*, the oldest *Hipparion* of Spain. This locality is placed at the base of MN 9.

Can Ponsic

This locality has furnished numerous fragmentary remains of primates (Crusafont Pairo & Hürzeler, 1969), most of which are assigned to *D. brancoi* (=*Hispanopithecus laietanus*). One right M^3 (IPS 53) could appertain to *D. fontani* according to Szalay & Delson (1979). One right P^4 (IPS 51) has been attributed to *Sivapithecus* but its thin enamel indicates that it also is a *Dryopithecus*. The fauna (Crusafont & Golpe, 1973*; Santafe, 1978; Agusti, 1982) is clearly more recent than the basal Vallesian. *Fahlbuschia* and *Megacricetodon ibericus* have disappeared, and one finds the first *Cricetulodon*. It belongs to the lower Vallesian (MN 9) because of the presence of *Anchitherium* and *Tapirus*.

Castel de Barbera

The locality of Castel de Barbera, which has yielded an upper canine of a hominoid (Crusafont & Golpe, 1973*) determined as *D. brancoi* by Szalay & Delson (1979), is considered by Spanish authors (Crusafont & Golpe, 1973*; Santafe, 1978; Agusti, 1982) to belong to the upper Astaracian MN 8 because of the absence of *Hipparion*. To my knowledge the analysis of the rodent faunas (Agusti, 1982) shows clearly that the locality is in the Vallesian (MN 9 upper) near Can Ponsic, and that ecological reasons may explain the absence of *Hipparion*. Pickford (personal communication) records that *Hipparion* does in fact occur at Castel de Barbera, on the basis of dental and post-cranial remains seen in Sabadell Museum and in the field.

* For details of reference see Szalay & Delson (1979).

Can Llobateres

About 25 hominoid dental/gnathic fragments have been found at Can Llobateres. A large right M_3 could belong to *D. fontani*. A right canine (IPS 41) has been attributed to *Sivapithecus darwini* by Andrews (1983). All the best of the material represents *D. brancoi* (it contains the very small mandible with M_{1-3}, CLL8, on which is based the taxon *Rahonapithecus sabadellensis*). The fauna (Crusafont & Golpe, 1973*; Santafe, 1978; Agusti, 1982) is very reminiscent of that of Can Ponsic with a more modern aspect. Among the thousands of rodent teeth collected has been found one tooth of *Progonomys*. Can Llobateres marks the top of the lower Vallesian MN 9.

Polinya II

The site of Polinya II (Gabarro) has yielded a canine (IPS 50) (Crusafont & Golpe, 1973*) attributed to *D. brancoi*. The limited fauna (the six taxa of large mammals cited, occur at Can Llobateres) is of Vallesian type (Santafe, 1978), but the topography allows a more precise placement of the locality as younger than Can Llobateres and it is therefore in MN 10.

La Tarumba

At La Tarumba (Villadecaballs) an upper series of teeth, the type of *Hispanopithecus laietanus* has been published (Villalta & Crusafont, 1944*). It is now considered by Szalay & Delson (1979) to belong to *D. brancoi*. The fauna (Santafe, 1978) indicates an upper Vallesian age like the group of localities at Villadecaballs.

The hominoids of Spain come from MN 8 to MN 10. The majority of the fossils and taxa are found in the lower Vallesian. The opinion of J. Hürzeler is that the variability observed in all the primates of Europe is compatible with the existence of a single form. All the hominoid localities of Spain are situated in the provinces of Lerida and Barcelona which were particularly humid during the epochs under consideration.

French localities

St Gaudens

The site of St. Gaudens (Valentine) (Haute-Garonne) has furnished three lower jaws and two teeth belonging to four individuals of *Dryopithecus fontani* (Lartet, 1856*; Gaudry, 1890; Harlé, 1898, 1899).

---

* For details of reference see Szalay & Delson (1979).

The fauna comprising a dozen taxa is of upper Astaracian type (Harlé, 1898; Richard, 1946; Crouzel, 1957; Ginsburg, 1974*). It does not allow us to choose between MN 7 and MN 8. The topography (100 m above the large locality of Simorre) as well as the discovery of *Deinotherium giganteum* just above (Crouzel, 1957) and lateral to *Protragocerus chantrei* at Rieucasse (Ginsburg, 1974*) allows us to place this locality in MN 8.

La Grive-St-Alban

The rich karst locality of La Grive-St-Alban, comprised of many fossiliferous fissures of middle Miocene age, has yielded a hominoid M^3 (Depéret, 1911). More recently C. Artémiou has discovered in a drawer in the Museum of Basel an upper incisor determined as *Dryopithecus fontani* (Andrews, personal communication). The two teeth possess the grey patina characteristic of fissure L3 and belong to the fauna of upper La Grive (MN 8).

Montrejeau?

Montrejeau (Haute-Garonne)? The legend of the geological map of St Gaudens (1:80000) published in 1911 mentioned the presence of Dryopithecine teeth in the fossiliferous lignites at the base of the Vallesian. The citation is repeated by the following authors – Richard (1946), Crouzel (1957), and Ginsburg (1974*); but no one knows of what the material consists, if it exists, nor where it is preserved.

The hominoids of France are reduced to a single species which occurs in a short segment of time: MN 8.

German localities

Two types of sites have yielded hominoids in the Federal Republic of Germany: the *Deinotherium* sands (Dinotheriensande) of Rhenanie and the siderolithic deposits of the Schwäbian Alps (the Bohnerz of the Schwäbisch Alps). The first type of deposit occurs in a stratified formation of which the age is approximately homogeneous. Two localities have yielded hominoids.

* For details of reference see Szalay & Delson (1979).

Eppelsheim and Wissberg

The Eppelsheim locality has furnished a right femur: *Paidopithex rhenanus* Pohlig 1895. After various determinations (Dubois, 1895*; Von Koenigswald, 1956*), this femur is now attributed to a *Pliopithecus* (McHenry & Corruccini, 1976*). (For a review of this specimen see Morbeck, 1983). The locality has also furnished an upper canine, the type of *Semnopithecus eppelsheimensis* Haupt, 1935, later studied by Hürzeler (1954*) and Von Koenigswald (1956*); this canine is now attributed to *Dryopithecus brancoi* by Szalay & Delson (1979).

The locality of Wissberg has yielded a fragmentary M_1 (Von Koenigswald, 1956*) attributed to *D. brancoi* and an M_2 determined as *D. fontani*. The mammalian faunal list of the Dinotheriensande was recently revised by Tobien (1980). With the presence of *Hipparion primigenium primigenium* are numerous Astaracian taxa: *Anchitherium*, *Conohyus*, *Heteroprox*, and *Dicrocerus*. These localities belong to the lower Vallesian (MN 9). It is not possible paleontologically to differentiate between the ages of Wissberg and Eppelsheim. These sites range in the lower part of MN 9 and are therefore older than those of Can Ponsic and Can Llobateres, contrary to the table in Szalay & Delson (1979).

The siderolithic deposits of the Schwäbian Alps have yielded several isolated hominoid teeth from numerous localities. These discoveries were all made in the nineteenth century and there has not been a faunal revision since Schlosser (1902). The problem with karstic localities is that every fissure can have a different age. The sites of Trochtelfingen and Ebingen, which have each yielded a lower molar of *D. fontani* (see Branco, 1898*; Schlosser, 1901*), are of indeterminate Vallesian age.

Melchingen

The site of Melchingen has yielded six higher-primate teeth (Branco, 1898*; Schlosser, 1901*; Simons & Pilbeam, 1965*; Kay & Simons, 1983). Three of these, of a larger size than is normally the case in *D. fontani*, have been said to be close to *Sivapithecus*. However, according to an observation of Andrews (cited in Kay & Simons, 1983), the thinness of the enamel suggests the attribution of the six teeth to *D. fontani*. The rich faunal list indicates placement in MN 9.

* For details of reference see Szalay & Delson (1979).

Salmendingen

Salmendingen fissure has yielded a small M_3, the type of *Anthopodus brancoi* Schlosser (1901) now assigned to the genus *Dryopithecus*, as well as two larger M_1 attributed to *D. fontani* (in spite of their size which is smaller than the specimen from Melchingen). The fauna enumerated by Schlosser in 1902, shows a certain number of differences compared to that of Melchingen. There is no *Anchitherium*; in contrast, one finds Leporidae and it is the type locality of the Castoridae: *Dipoides problematicus* Schlosser. This *Dipoides* is an immigrant, now known in many localities of lower Turolian age: Dorn-Durkheim (Federal Republic of Germany), Dionay (France), Tortajada, Los Aguanaces (Spain). This site should be placed in the lower Turolian MN 11 between 10 and 9.5 m.y. It is the youngest discovery site of higher primates in Western or Central Europe.

Austrian and Czechoslovakian localities

Neudorf-Sandberg

The locality of Neudorf-Sandberg (Devinska Nova Ves) has yielded four teeth (right M_3, right dp^4, right M^2 and right M_3) of a hominoid: *Dryopithecus darwini*, Abel, 1902, later studied by Glaessner (1931[*]), Steininger & Thenius (1963), Simons (1983), Pilbeam (1965[*]), Zapfe (1969[*]), and Kay & Simons (1983); they are now attributed to the genus *Sivapithecus*. The fauna was studied by Thenius in 1952. It contains two artiodactyls which generally never occur together: *Bunolistriodon lockharti* and a tragocerine. In 1975 I proposed that this locality was in MN 6, that is to say an age younger than *Bunolistriodon*, and older than the tragocerine. A second analysis (Ginsburg & Mein, 1980) has led us to admit that in this marine locality the *Bunolistriodon* could have been reworked from an older level. Under this hypothesis the presence of *Protragocerus* makes the fauna younger, and it can be situated at the base of MN 8. This site contains planktonic Foraminifera N9/N13 and nannofossils NN6/NN7 (Rabeder & Steininger, 1975). The age deduced from this marine equivalence was 15 million years but, according to the latest Neogene time scale (Berggren *et al.*, in press), the limit is placed at about 13.5 million years. Neudorf-Sandberg remains the earliest hominoid site in Europe, but it is surely younger than Pasalar in Turkey.

[*] For details of reference see Szalay & Delson (1979).

Klein Hadersdorf

Klein Hadersdorf near Polysdorf has yielded a cuboid and a humeral diaphysis: *Austriacopithecus weinfurteri* Ehrenberg, 1937. These bones have been studied successively by Thenius (1948*, 1954) and by Zapfe (1960*, 1969*); they were finally attributed to *Sivapithecus darwini* by Szalay & Delson (1979). The age of the fauna is comparable to that of Neudorf-Sandberg; the presence of *Gazella stehlini* suggests an age of MN 8 rather than MN 7.

St Stephan

A mandible of *Dryopithecus fontani* from St. Stephan was studied by Mottl (1957*, 1958). The fauna contains a *Listriodon splendens*, and *Anchitherium* with large molars, and seems therefore to be slightly younger than that of Neudorf-Sandberg; it corresponds to MN 8; the locality is correlated indirectly with marine formations (Zapfe, 1969*; Steininger & Papp, 1979).

Mariathal

The locality of Mariathal near Hollabrun, contains a lower molar attributed to *D. brancoi* by Zapfe (1969*), Szalay & Delson (1979) and Thenius (1982). The fauna shows an association of *Anchitherium* and *Hipparion primigenium*. It is thus of lower Vallesian age (MN 9).

Hungarian localities

Rudabanya

The site of Rudabanya (Kretzoi, 1969*, 1974*, 1975*) has yielded dental and postcranial remains of two hominoids. *Rudapithecus hungaricus* Kretzoi, originally thought to be a Ramapithecine, possesses thin enamel (Kay & Simons, 1983) which allows us to place it in *Dryopithecus fontani*. *Bodvapithecus altipalatus* Kretzoi is a *Sivapithecus* (*S. darwini* for Szalay & Delson (1979); *S. indicus* for Kay & Simons (1983)). The teeth are larger than that of Neudorf-Sandberg. Simons (1981) considered the locality to be upper Vallesian or lower Turolian. The faunal list (Kretzoi et al., 1974*) indicates a lower Vallesian age with the presence of *Microtocricetus* and the persistence of *Sansanosmilus* and *Platybelodon*.

* For details of reference see Szalay & Delson (1979).

Greek localities

Rain Ravine

The Rain Ravine in Macedonia (de Bonis *et al.*, 1974*; de Bonis & Melentis, 1975*, 1977*, 1978*, 1979*) has yielded beautiful dental remains (palates and mandibles) of hominoids – *Dryopithecus macedoniensis*, for which a new genus *Ouranopithecus* was later erected. This form is put into synonymy with *Sivapithecus metai* (Ozansoy) by Andrews (1976*). Kay & Simons (1983) were astonished by the degree of sexual dimorphism which exceeds that observed in living Pongidae. The fauna (de Bonis *et al.* 1974*, 1979; Koufos, 1979, 1984) indicates affinities with a faunal province different from that of western Central Europe. The presence of the murid *Progonomys* indicates an upper Vallesian age. The presence of Giraffidae, *Bohlinia*, and the occurrence of several hipparions are unknown in Europe before the Turolian.

Pyrgos

Pyrgos (Tour La Reine) has yielded a mandible, badly damaged during World War II, described by Von Koenigswald (1972*): *Graecopithecus freybergi*. It possibly belongs to the same species as that of Rain Ravine, but because of the state of preservation of the piece a specific determination was difficult. Recently the holotype was redescribed following its removal from the matrix. Martin & Andrews (1984) demonstrated the conspecificity between *Graecopithecus*, *Ouranopithecus* and *Sivapithecus metai*. The fauna cited comprises nine taxa which are found in the Pikermi fauna, in particular the giraffid *Helladotherium*; it is a Turolian fauna, dating probably to MN 12.

Georgian localities (USSR)

Udabno

Two localities have yielded hominoids. Udabno contains a P^4 and an M^1 of a hominoid described as *Udabnopithecus garedziensis* (Burtschak-Abramovich & Gabachvili, 1950*; Delson, 1979*). There is no associated mammal fauna. Thenius (1959) associates the site of Udabno with that of Eldar. Szalay & Delson (1979) mention that *D. fontani* occurs in both localities, but I have not found the reference mentioning the discovery of the primate at Eldar. The mammalian fauna of Eldar, revised by Gabunia (1979), relates to the Chersonian stage and correlates to the Upper Vallesian, MN 10.

* For details of reference see Szalay & Delson (1979).

Chronologic and geographic distribution of European hominoids

If one defines *Sivapithecus* by large molar size and by thick tooth enamel, it seems that it never entered western Europe. *Sivapithecus darwini* of Neudorf and its descendant at Rudabanya lived in a forested environment. *Sivapithecus metai* from Greece lived in more open countryside (Andrews, 1983). *Dryopithecus* seems to have occurred throughout Europe. Its time range is shorter than that for the occurrence of *Sivapithecus*. *Dryopithecus* seems to have lived preferentially in swampy forest and its disappearance follows the climatic change in the Turolian. Nowadays, one has the impression of two parallel lines: *D. fontani* of larger size, of which the type comes from old strata; and *D. brancoi* of small size, of which the type comes from younger strata. Due to sexual dimorphism and insufficiency of material, it could be that these two apparent lines are really only one.

References

Agusti, J. (1982) Biozonacion del neogeno continental de Cataluna mediante roedores (Mammalia). *Acta Geol. Hispanica*, **17**, 21–6

Alberdi, M. T. (1974) El genero Hipparion en España. Nuevas formas de Castillas y Andalucia, revision e historia evolutiva. *Trab. Neog.-Cuatern.*, **1**, 146 pp.

Andrews, P. J. (1983) The natural history of *Sivapithecus*. In *New Interpretations of Ape and Human Ancestry*, ed. R. L. Ciochon & R. S. Corruccini, pp. 441–63. New York: Plenum Press

Berggren, W. A. & Couvering, J. A. van (1974) The late Neogene. *Palaeogeogr., Palaeoclimatol., Palaeoécol.*, **16**, 1–216

Berggren, W. A., Kent, D. V., Flynn, J. J. & Couvering, J. A. van (in press) Cenozoic Geological Chronology. *Bull. Geol. Soc. Am.*

Bernor, R. L. (1983) Geochronology and zoogeographic relationships of Miocene Hominoides. In *New Interpretations of Ape and Human Ancestry*, ed. R. L. Ciochon & R. S. Corruccini, pp. 21–64. New York: Plenum Press

Crouzel, F. (1957) Le Miocène continental du Bassin d'Aquitaine. *Bull. Serv. Carte Géol. France*, **248**, 1–264

Crusafont Pairo, M. & Hürzeler, J. (1969) Catalogo comentado de los Pongidos fosiles de España. *Acta Geol. Hispanica*, **IV**(2), 44–8

de Bonis, L., Bouvrain, G. & Geraads, D. (1979) Artiodactyls from the upper miocene of Macedonia. *VIIth Int. Congr. Medit. Neogene, Athens*, I, 167–75

de Bonis, L. & Melentis, J. (1980) Nouvelles remarques sur l'anatomie d'une Primate hominoïde du Miocène: *Ouranopithecus macedoniensis*. Implications sur la phylogénie des Hominidés. *C.R. Acad. Sci. Paris, Sér. D*, **290**, 755–8

Depéret, C. (1911) Sur la découverte d'un grand singe anthropoïde du genre *Dryopithecus* dans le Miocène moyen de la Grive-Saint-Alban (Isère). *C.R. Acad. Sci. Paris*, **153**, 32–6

Dubois, E. (1901) Zur systematischen Stellung der ausgestorbenen Menschenaffen. *Zool. Anzeiger*, **24**, 556–60

Gabunia, L. K. (1979) Biostratigraphic correlations between the neogene land mammal faunas of the East and central paratethys. *VIIth Int. Congr. Medit. Neogene, Athens,* I, 413–23

Gaudry, A. (1890) Le Dryopithèque. *Mem. Soc. Géol. France (Pal.),* **1,** 1-11

Ginsburg, L. & Mein, P. (1980) *Crouzelia rhodanica,* nouvelle espèce de Primate catarhinien, et essai sur la phylogénie des Pliopithecidae. *Bull. Mus. Natl Hist. Nat. Paris,* **2,** 57–85

Harlé, E. (1898) La machoire de Dryopithèque. *Bull. Soc. Géol. France,* 3, 377–83

Harlé, E. (1899) Nouvelles pièces de Dryopithèque et quelques coquilles de Saint-Gaudens (Haute-Garonne). *Bull. Soc. Géol. France,* 3, 304–10

Jäger, G. (1850) Ubersicht der fossilen Säugetiere welche in Würtemberg in verschiedenen Formationen aufgefunden worden sind und Nähere Beschreibung und Abbildung einzelner derselben. *Nova Acta Acad. Leop.-Carol.,* **22,** 767–934

Kay, R. F. & Simons, E. L. (1983) A reassessment of the relationships between Later Miocene and subsequent Hominoidea. In *New Interpretation of Ape and Human Ancestry,* ed. R. L. Ciochon & R. S. Corruccini, pp. 577–624. New York: Plenum Press

Koufos, G. D. (1979) Preliminary report on the study of mammalian fauna (carnivora, proboscidea, perissodactyla) of Axios valley (Macedonia-Greece). *VIIth Int. Congr. Medit. Neogene, Athens,* II, 631–5

Koufos, G. D. (1984) A new hipparion (*Mammalia, Perissodactyla*) from the Vallesian (Late Miocene) of Greece. *Paläontol. Z., Stuttgart,* **58**(3/4), 307–17

Kretzoi, M. (1976) Emberré vàlàs és az australopithecinàk. *Anthropol. Közl.,* **20,** 3–11

Martin, L. & Andrews, P. (1984) The phyletic position of *Graecopithecus freybergi* Koenigswald. *Cour Forsch. Inst. Senckenberg,* **69,** 25–40

Mein, P. (1976) Biozonation du Néogène méditerranéen à partir des mammifères. *Proc. VIth Congress, R.C.M.N.S., Bratislava 1975,* **2**

Mein, P. (1979) Rapport d'activité du groupe de travail vertébrés: mise à jour de la biostratigraphie du Néogène basée sur les mammifères. *Ann. Géol. Pays Hellen., Athens,* III, 1367–72

Morbeck, M. E. (1983) Miocene hominoid discoveries from Rudabanya. Implications from the postcranial skeleton. In *New Interpretation of Ape and Human Ancestry,* ed. R. L. Ciochon & R. S. Corruccini, pp. 369–404. New York: Plenum Press

Mottl, M. (1958) Weitere Säugetierreste aus dem Sarmat von St-Stefan im Lavanttal, Kärnten. *Carinthia II, Mitt. Naturwiss. Ver. Kärnten,* **68,** 46–48

Rabeder, G. & Steininger, F. (1975) Die Direkten biostratigraphischen Korrelationsmöglichkeiten von Säugetierfaunen aus dem Oligo-Miozän der zentralen Paratethys. *Proc. VIth Congr. R.C.M.N.S. Bratislava 1975,* **1,** 177–83

Richard, M. (1946) Contribution à l'étude du bassin d'Aquitaine. Les gisements de Mammifères tertiaires. *Mém. Soc. Géol. France,* **94**(52), 1–380

Santafe, J. V. (1978) Rinocerotidos fossiles de España. *Thesis Fac. ci. Geol. Fac. Barcelona,* **1,** 501 pp. + 1 vol. tabl.

Savage, D. E. & Russell, D. E. (1983) *Mammalian Paleofaunas of the World.* London: Addison-Wesley

Schlosser, M. (1902) Beiträge zur Kenntnis der Säugetierreste aus den süddeutschen Bohnerzen. *Geol. U. Pal. Abh.,* **9,** 117–258

Simons, E. L. (1981) Man's immediate forerunners. *Phil. Trans. R. Soc. Lond.,* B., **292,** 21–41

Steininger, F. F. & Papp, A. (1979) Current biostratigraphic and radiometric correlations of late Miocene central Paratethys stages (Sarmatian s. str., Pannonian s. str., and Pontian) and Mediterranean stages (Tortonian and Messinian) and Messinian Event in the Paratethys. *Newslett. Stratigr.*, **8**, 100–10

Steininger, F. & Thenius, E. (1963) Ein neuer Pongidenfund aus dem Miozän des Wiener Beckens. *Anthropol. Anz.*, 211–15

Szalay, F. S. & Delson, E. (1979) *Evolutionary History of the Primates*. New York: Academic Press

Thenius, E. (1952) Die Säugertierfauna aus dem Torton von Neudorf an der March. *Neues Jb. Geol. Palaeontol. Abh.*, **96**(1), 27–136

Thenius, E. (1954) Die Bedeutung von Austriacopithecus Ehrenberg für die Stammesgeschichte der Hominoidea. *Osterr. Akad. Wiss., Wien, Sitzung Math-Naturwiss. Klasse*, **13**, 191–6

Thenius, E. (1956) Funde Fossiler Menschenaffen aus Niederösterreich und ihre Bedeutung für die Herkunft des Menschen. *Unsere Heimat.*, **27**, 81–4

Thenius, E. (1959) Tertiär. Zweiter Teil: Wirbeltierfaunen. *Handb. Stratigraph. Geol.*, **3**, 328 pp.

Thenius, E. (1960) Die Jungtertiären Wirbeltierfaunen und Landfloren des Wiener Beckens und ihre Bedeutung für die Neogenstratigraphie. *Mitteil. Geol. Ges. Wien*, **52**, 203–9

Thenius, E. (1982) Ein kleiner Menschenaffe (Pongidae, Primates) aus dem Jung-Miozän (Pannon) von Niederösterreich und die paläoökologische und paläoklimatologische Problematik des Vorkommens. *Anz. Osterr. Akad. Wiss. Math.-Naturwiss. Klasse*, **4**, 37–44

Tobien, H. (1980) Taxonomic status of some Cenozoic mammalian local faunas from the Mainz Basin. *Mainzer Geowiss. Mitt.*, **9**, 203–35

Villalta, J. F. & Crusafont, M. (1941) Dryopithecus Fontani, Lartet, en el Vindoboniense de la cuenca Vallés-Penedés. *Boll. Inst. Geol. Min. España*, **55**, 131–43

Woodward, A. A. (1914) On the lower jaw of an anthropoid ape (Dryopithecus) from the Upper Miocene of Lérida (Spain). *Q. J. Geol. Soc. Lond.*, **70**, 316–20

I.6

Dating the Paratethys Miocene hominoid record

F. F. STEININGER

Introduction

For more than 100 years remains of various hominoids have been known from Miocene deposits of southern Germany, Austria, Hungary, Poland and Czechoslovakia. This area is part of a very characteristic Neogene marine-to-endemic bioprovince defined by Laskarev (1924) as the Paratethys realm.

The aim of this paper is not the discussion of the taxonomic status of the hominoid remains known from the Paratethys. Rather, the aims will be: (1) an accurate correlation of the Central and Eastern Paratethys Stages with the Mediterranean Stages and the 'European Mammal Ages'; and (2) a calibration of the Paratethys Miocene hominoid record. Another very important topic, the relation of geokinematic events and the Paratethys with respect to the Eurasian hominoid record, will be touched upon only briefly.

The Neogene Paratethys

In the late Oligocene the epicontinental seas north and south of the Alpine–Caucasian orogenic belt, with ever-changing seaways, were characterized by a distinct evolution of their biotas. This motivated Laskarev (1924) to separate this northern bioprovince – the Paratethys – from the Neogene Mediterranean Tethys bioprovince.

In the Early Miocene (Eggenburgian to Early Ottnangian) the sea extended from the western Mediterranean across the Rhône and Molasse Basins to the Ponto-Caspian region. During the later Early Miocene to the lower Middle Miocene (Ottnangian to Middle Badenian) a seaway across northern Yugoslavia provided marine connections from the Central Paratethys to the Miocene sedimentation areas in northern Italy. In the Late Oligocene and the Early and Middle

Miocene, the connection with the Indo-Pacific realm was faunistically very important although it was subject to rapid changes due to the active tectonic zones east of the Paratethys. The closure of the marine connection to northern Italy and the Indo-Pacific in the later Middle Miocene brought about the isolation of the Paratethys and triggered the evolution of the well-known endemic aquatic biotas. During the late Miocene and Pliocene, brief marine ingressions extended into the Eastern Paratethys from the Aegean Sea across the Dardanelles.

The Paratethys and Mediterranean paleogeographic and geokinematic development, the importance of these events in relation to aquatic and terrestrial faunal evolution and migrations, as well as the evolution of the Paratethys aquatic biotas have been recently discussed (de Bruijn & van der Meulen, 1981; Bernor, 1983; Rögl & Steininger, 1983; Adams, 1984; Steininger, Rabeder & Rögl, 1985).

Correlation of Paratethys and Mediterranean Neogene stages with European Mammal Ages (Fig. 1)

In calibrating marine plankton biochronologies and the Mediterranean stages we followed, with some modification, the biostratigraphy of DSDP-Leg 42 A, Bizon & Müller (1979) and Berggren *et al.* (1985, in press). The most important datum levels that can be used for a better correlation of the Central and Eastern Paratethys Stages and European Mammal Ages are briefly outlined below.

Late Oligocene/Early Miocene
Egerian; Caucasian; Chattian-Aquitanian

A horizon of larger Foraminifera, including *Miogypsina septentrionalis, Miogypsinoides formosensis, Lepidocyclina (Neophrolepidina) morgani, Cycloclypeus, Operculina* and *Heterostegina* occurs in the upper part of Nannoplankton zone NP25 (Steininger, Rögl & Martini, 1976; Drooger, 1979; McGowran, 1979; Adams, 1984).

Within this marine horizon, a vertebrate fauna known from Upper Austria can be assigned to mammal zone MN 0 (Rabeder & Steininger, 1975).

Nannoplankton zone NN1 is present in the uppermost Egerian of the Austrian Molasse zone (Rögl, Hochuli & Müller, 1979).

Early Miocene
Eggenburgian; Sakaraulian; Burdigalian

The Early Miocene horizon of 'giant' mollusc taxa within Nannoplankton zone NN2 correlates the Early Eggenburgian and

Fig. 1. Stratigraphic correlations of circum-Mediterranean marine chronostratigraphic regional stages, biostratigraphic zonations and European Mammal Ages, and a calibration of Paratethys hominoid sites.

GEOCHRONOMETRIC SCALE IN MILL. YEARS	EPOCHS	CHRONOSTRATIGRAPHIC-STAGE SYSTEMS			BIOSTRATIGRAPHIC ZONATIONS				EUROPEAN LAND MAMMAL ZONES (MEIN 1975, FAHLBUSCH 76, ALBERDI & AGUIRRE 1977, MEIN 1979)	EUROPEAN LAND-MAMMAL AGES	STRATIGRAPHIC POSITION OF PARATETHYS HOMINOID LOCALITIES
		MEDITERRANEAN	CENTRAL PARATETHYS	EASTERN PARATETHYS	PLANKTON - ZONES FORAMINIFERA BLOW 1969	DSDP LEG. 42A 1978	NANNO MARTINI 1971				
2 (1.8)	PLEISTOCENE	PLEISTOCENE			N22	G. truncatulinoides	NN19	NN19	MN 17	VILLAFRANCAN — VILLANY	
3	PLIOCENE LATE	PIACENZIAN	ROMANIAN	AKTSCHAGYL-IAN	N21	G. inflata / Globigennoides obliquus extremus	NN18 / NN17 / NN16	MN 16			
(3.4)							NN15			RUSCINIAN	
4	PLIOCENE EARLY	ZANCLIAN	DACIAN	KIMMERIAN	N20	Sp. subdehiscens	NN14	MN 15			
5					N19	G. margaritae evoluta / G. margaritae margaritae	NN13	MN 14			
(5.4)					N18	Sphaeroidinellopsis acme	NN12				
6	MIOCENE LATE	MESSINIAN			N17	G. mediterranea	NN11	MN 13			
7 (6.8)			PONTIAN	PONTIAN		Globorotalia humerosa		MN 12	TUROLIAN		
8								MN 11	CATALONIAN		
9		TORTONIAN		E — MAEOTIAN	N16	Globorotalia acostaensis	NN10		VALLESIAN	UDABNO, ELDAR, UdSSR; TRUCHTELFINGEN, SALMENDINGEN, DRESSEN, MELCHINGEN, EBINGEN, GERMANY
10			PANNONIAN	D				MN 10		
				C — CHERSON.						MARIATHAL, AUSTRIA
11	MIOCENE LATE			B/A — BESS-ARABIAN (EARLY SARMATIAN)	N15	Globorotalia menardii	NN9	MN 9		RUDABÁNYA, HUNGARY
12 (11.8)			SARMATIAN		N14		NN8	MN 8		
13	MIOCENE MIDDLE	SERRAVALLIAN		VOLHYNIAN	N13	Globorotalia mayeri	NN7	MN 7	ASTERACIAN — ARAGONIAN	ST. STEFAN i. L., AUSTRIA; OPOLE, POLAND
14			BADENIAN (MIDDLE LATE / EARLY)	KONKIAN	N12		NN6			PRZEWORNO 2, POLAND; KLEIN HADERSDORF, AUSTRIA; GORIACH, AUSTRIA; DEVINSKÁ NOVÁ VES, CSSR ("SANDBERG + SANDHILL")
15				KARAGANIAN	N11			MN 6		
				TSCHOKRAKIAN	N10		NN5			
16 (15.8)		LANGHIAN		TARKHANIAN	N9	G. peripheroronda / O. suturalis		MN 5		TRIMMELKAM, AUSTRIA; DEVINSKÁ NOVÁ VES, CSSR ("SPALTEN-FISSURES")
17 (16.8)	MIOCENE EARLY		KARPATIAN		N8	Po. glomerosa				
18			OTTNANGIAN	KOZACHURIAN	N7	G. trilobus	NN4	MN 4	ORLEANIAN	
19		BURDIGALIAN			N6		NN3	b		
20			EGGENBURGIAN	SAKARAULIAN	N5	G. altiaperturus / G. dissimilis	NN2	MN 3	a	
21										
22 (22.2)										
23 (23.2)	OLIGOCENE LATE	AQUITANIAN	EGERIAN	CAUCASIAN	N4	G. primordius / G. kugleri	NN1	MN 2	b / a	AGENIAN
24		CHATTIAN					NP25	MN 1		
25					P22	G. cip. ciperoensis		MN 0	ARVERN.	

Sakaraulian with the Early Burdigalian (Steininger *et al.*, 1976; Horvath & Nagymarosy, 1979; Rögl *et al.*, 1979; Martini, 1981).

An Early Orleanian (MN 3) micromammal association appeared in Early Eggenburgian marine sediments with NN2 nannoplankton flora (P. Mein, personal communication).

The first appearance of Proboscidea (MN 3b) in the Paratethys is dated as Late Eggenburgian by Nannoplankton zone NN3 (Rögl & Steininger, 1983).

Miogypsina intermedia appears in Late Eggenburgian time within sediments dated by nannoplankton as NN2/NN3 (Rögl *et al.*, 1979).

Ottnangian; Kozachurian; Burdigalian

Ottnangian nannoplankton ages from the central Paratethys range from zone NN3 to zone NN4 (Martini & Müller, 1975*a*; Baldi-Beke & Nagymarosy, 1979; Rögl *et al.*, 1979; Martini, 1981).

During the late Ottnangian regressive phase and the Early Karpatian, typical reduced-salinity to freshwater mollusc assemblages, the '*Oncophora*'-beds, are widely spread from the Western to the Eastern Paratethys (Ctyroky *et al.*, 1973). Nannoplankton floras from these beds still show assemblages characteristic for the NN4 zone (Baldi-Beke & Nagymarosy, 1979).

The '*Oncophora*'-beds overlie the important mammal fauna of Orechov, Czechoslovakia (Cicha, Fahlbusch & Fejfar, 1972), indicative for mammal zone MN 4a (Mein, 1979).

Radiometric dates for the 'Lower Rhyolitic Tuff' – a widely spread horizon of lower Ottnangian age in northern Hungary – average 19.6 ± 1.4 million years (Ma) (Hamor *et al.*, 1979) and range from 22.0 to 18.0 Ma (Hamor *et al.*, 1978). These dates are in accordance with its biostratigraphic age (Rögl & Steininger, 1983).

Karpatian; Late Burdigalian

The most important datum levels are the NN4 to NN5 nannoplankton floras and the First Appearance Datum (FAD) of *Globigerinoides bispherica* (sometimes incorrectly referred to as *sicanus*) in the upper part of the Karpatian Schlier formations (Martini & Müller, 1975*b*; Steininger *et al.*, 1976; Baldi-Beke & Nagymarosy, 1979). According to Rehakova (1977), diatom assemblages from the upper Karpatian 'Schlier' formations allow a correlation with Schrader's North Pacific Diatom Zonation – NPDZ-25/24. Since the Late Kozachurian of the Eastern Paratethys is characterized by endemic mollusc evolutions, its direct correlation with the marine sequences of the Karpatian in the Central Paratethys is not possible (Rögl & Steininger, 1983).

Middle Miocene
Badenian; Tarkhanian to Konkian; Langian to Middle Serravallian

The worldwide planktonic datum plane with the FAD of *Praeorbulina* is known from the base of the Badenian and Tarkhanian (Cicha, 1970; Steininger *et al.*, 1976).

The entire Badenian and the eastern Paratethys stages range from Nannoplankton zone NN5 into zone NN7 (Fuchs & Stradner, 1977; Lehotayova & Molcikova, 1978; Stradner & Fuchs, 1978). According to Rehakova (1977), the diatom floras of the Badenian can be correlated to NPDZ-24 – NPDZ-22.

Biostratigraphically well-controlled radiometric ages from various volcanic rocks are known throughout the Badenian. They range from 17.1 to 13.3 Ma (Hamor *et al.*, 1978, 1979; Vass & Bagdasarjan, 1978; Vass, Bagdasarjan & Steininger, 1978).

Important mammal faunas that can be directly controlled with the marine sequences belong to mammal zones MN 5 and MN 6 (Rabeder & Steininger, 1975; Mein, 1979).

The paleobiogeographic and geodynamic evolution of the Badenian was extensively treated by Rögl *et al.* (1979) and Rögl & Steininger (1983).

The more or less continuous marine sedimentation of the Paratethys is terminated at the end of the Late Badenian. The later part of the Middle Miocene – the Sarmatian – is characterized by a reduced-salinity facies, which prevails in the Eastern Paratethys into the Late Miocene. The late Miocene of the Central Paratethys is dominated by '*Congeria*–Melanopsid' assemblages and finally by fluviatil-limnic and continental deposits.

Therefore the correlation of the late Middle Miocene, Late Miocene and Pliocene stages is rather well established by the evolution of endemic invertebrate faunas between the central and eastern Paratethys (Kojumdgieva, 1979; Paramonova *et al.*, 1979; Semenenko, 1979; Andreescu, 1981).

Correlations of this time span with the marine Mediterranean stages could be established: (1) by mammal faunas interspersed into sediments with endemic invertebrate faunas; (2) through short marine transgressive events into the Ponto-Caspian realm; and (3) by radiometric and palaeomagnetic dating (Steininger & Papp, 1979).

Sarmatian-Volhynian to Early Bessarabian-Late Serravallian
Marine diatom floras of the Early Sarmatian correlate with diatom zone NPDZ-19 (Schrader, personal communication).

Late Asteracian mammal faunas of zone MN 8 are interspersed into Sarmatian sediments with endemic molluscs (Feru, Radulescu & Samson, 1980). A key feature is the lack of *Hipparion* in all Sarmatian mammal faunas found so far (Rabeder & Steininger, 1975; Steininger et al., 1976).

Biostratigraphically controlled radiometric ages of Sarmatian volcanic rocks range between 13.6 and 10.7 Ma (Vass & Bagdasarjan, 1978) and yield 13.7 ± 0.8 Ma for the 'Upper Rhyolite Tuff' of Hungary (Hamor et al., 1979).

Late Miocene
Pannonian; Bessarabian to Maeotian; Early to Middle Tortonian

Vallesian mammal faunas of zone MN 9 with the FAD of *Hipparion* are known from Early Pannonian and Late Bessarabian sediments. The FAD of *Hipparion* has been dated as Early Tortonian in the Mediterranean (Benda & Meulenkamp, 1979; de Bruijn & Zachariasse, 1979; Steininger & Papp, 1979).

Because of a marine ingression into the Euxinian Basin in lower Maeotian time, nannofloras of zone NN10 occur in Maeotian sediments. Simultaneously, endemic Maeotian Paratethys mollusc faunas migrated into the Aegean Sea as far south as Athens (Semenenko & Ljulieva, 1978; Papp & Steininger, 1979; Semenenko, 1979).

Pontian; Late Tortonian to Messinian

Early Pontian sediments yielded rich lower Turolian mammal faunas of zone MN 11. Mammal faunas of this zone are intercalated into marine late Tortonian sediments in the Mediterranean (de Bruijn et al., 1975; Steininger & Papp, 1979).

The typical rich Messinian mammal faunas of zone MN 13 are interspersed within Late Pontian sediments in the Central and Eastern Paratethys (Mein et al., 1973; de Bruijn et al., 1975; van Couvering et al., 1976; Steininger & Papp, 1979; Kojumdgieva, personal communication).

Biostratigraphically accurately controlled radiometric dates from this time span are scarce in the Paratethys; they range from 9.4 to 7.0 Ma (Berczi et al., 1982; Vass & Bagdasarjan, 1978).

Pliocene
Dacian; Kimmerian; Zanclian

The Early Pliocene marine transgression extended as far as the Ponto-Caspian realm in Early Kimmerian time; nannoplankton floras of zone NN12 are known from this area (Semenenko & Ljulieva, 1978).

Romanian; Aktschagylian; Piacenzian

A last marine transgression through the Dardanelles into the Black Sea provides typical late Pliocene Mediterranean ostracods and nanno-plankton in Aktschagylian sediments (Semenenko & Ljulieva, 1978; Taner, 1982).

Paratethyan sections in the Dacian Basin (Romania) and Black Sea area with endemic mollusc faunas and mammals allow an excellent correlation with the paleomagnetic time scale (Andreescu, 1981; Andreescu & Radulescu, 1981; Semenenko, 1979; Semenenko & Pevsner, 1979).

The correlation of the upper part of the Romanian and Aktschagylian stages was recently supported by paleomagnetic dating of mollusc- and mammal-bearing sections in Romania that even straddle the Neogene/Quaternary boundary (Andreescu & Radulescu, 1981).

Dating the Paratethys Miocene hominoid record (Fig. 1)

Hominoid remains are known from the later Early Miocene, the Midde Miocene and the lower late Miocene of various localities in the Paratethys. Since no taxonomic opinion can be given in this paper, we followed the taxonomy published by Kretzoi (1974), Thenius (1959, 1982) and Zapfe (1969) and have given the opinion of Szalay & Delson (1979) in parentheses after each taxon cited.

Early Miocene

Děvinská Nová Ves 'fissures', Slovakia, Czechoslovakia

Fissure fillings with *Pliopithecus* (*Epipliopithecus*) *vindobonensis* (=*Pliopithecus vindobonensis*). Stratigraphic position: due to the paleogeographic configuration the fissures were accessible only during the Early Miocene between the Eggenburgian/Ottnangian marine peak and the late Karpatian/Badenian transgressive phase (Rabeder & Steininger, 1975; Gasparik, 1979; Rögl & Steininger, 1983). The rich mammal fauna recovered from the fissures was recently assigned to the base of the mammal zone MN 5 (Mein, 1981) and is evidently younger than the mammal fauna of Ořechov near Brno (Czechoslovakia) assigned to mammal zone MN 4a which is overlain by typical 'Oncophora'-beds characteristic for latest Ottnangian and lowermost Karpatian. The fissure fillings themselves are overlain by late Badenian marine sediments. These arguments point to a stratigraphic position of middle-to-late Karpatian age for this important *Pliopithecus* locality. Marine correlations allow an estimated geochronometric age of approximately 17 Ma.

Trimmelkam, Upper Austria

The hominoid remains were recovered from a lignite mine (Zapfe, 1956, 1961; Weber & Weiss, 1983): *Pliopithecus (Plesiopliopithecus) lockeri* (=*Pliopithecus lockeri*). Stratigraphic position: the lignite sequence follows with a discordance above the late Ottnangian/lowermost Karpatian 'Oncophora'-beds. No relation to marine sediments exists, although terrestrial and limnic gastropods point to a Karpatian or lowermost Badenian age (Papp, personal communication).

Middle Miocene

Dvinská Nová Ves, 'Sand-Hill', Slovakia, Czechoslovakia

Marine nearshore sands with *Pliopithecus (Pliopithecus) antiquus* ssp.ind. (=*Pliopithecus antiquus*) and *Dryopithecus fontani darwini* (=*Sivapithecus darwini*). Stratigraphic position: Middle Badenian. The marine correlation allows an estimated geochronometric age of approxiomately 15 Ma. The mammal fauna itself is placed in mammal zone MN 6 (uppermost MN 5 – Mein, 1981).

Klein Hadersdorf, Lower Austria

Marine nearshore sands with *Austriacopithecus weinfurteri* (=*Sivapithecus darwini*). Stratigraphic position: Middle to late Badenian according to the poor microfauna. The locality is only about 60 km northwest of the 'Sand-Hill' locality (see Zapfe, 1969).

Göriach, Styria, Austria

Numerous remains of *Pliopithecus (Pliopithecus) antiquus* ssp. ind. (=*Pliopithecus antiquus*) were recovered from a lignite mine (Zapfe, 1956; Weber & Weiss, 1983). Stratigraphic position: the sediments of this small inner alpine brown coal basin have no connection to marine sediments. According to the rich mammal fauna, the fauna was placed into mammal zone MN 6 and seems to be very close to the Dĕvinská Nová Ves 'Sand-Hill' fauna which is of Middle Badenian age (Mottl, 1970; Rabeder & Steininger, 1975; Rabeder, 1978).

Przeworno 2, Poland

Fissure fillings with *Pliopithecus antiquus*. Stratigraphic position: no relation to marine sediments. A lower Badenian age is assigned for faunistic reasons by Rabeder (1978).

Opole, Poland

Lake deposits with *Pliopithecus antiquus*. Stratigraphic position: no relation to marine sediments. The mammal fauna is placed in mammal zone MN 7. Freshwater molluscs point to a Sarmatian age of the deposits.

St Stefan i. Lavanttal, Carinthia, Austria

The hominoid remains were recovered from a lignite mine (Zapfe, 1956, 1969; Mottl, 1957; Weber & Weiss, 1983): *Dryopithecus (Dryopithecus) fontani carinthiacus* (=*Dryopithecus (Dryopithecus) fontani*). Stratigraphic position: the brown coal seams interfinger with Early Sarmatian reduced-salinity sediments containing a typical microfauna. Marine correlation allows an estimated geochronologic age of approximately 13 Ma.

Late Miocene

Rudabanya, Hungary

The hominoid remains were recovered from a lignite mine: *Rudapithecus hungaricus* (=*Ramapithecus punjabicus*); *Pliopithecus hernyáki* (=*Pliopithecus hernyáki*), *Bodvapithecus altipalatus* (=*Sivapithecus darwini*). Stratigraphic position: according to the mammal fauna assigned to the lower part of the mammal zone MN 9; according to the molluscs, assigned to the Early Pannonian (Kretzoi *et al.*, 1974; Kordos, 1982).

Mariathal, Lower Austria

Fluviatile gravel beds with *Dryopithecus brancoi* (=*Dryopithecus brancoi*) (Thenius, 1983). Stratigraphic position: according to Thenius (1983), Pannonian approximately zones C to D.

Federal Republic of Germany

Mostly isolated teeth from *Dryopithecus fontani* and *D. brancoi* are known, generally from fissure fillings such as Salmendingen, Melchingen, and Ebingen. According to the accompanying mammal fauna these localities are of Vallesian age.

Udabno, Eldar, USSR

From sediments with endemic Eastern Paratethys molluscs, remains of *Udabnopithecus garadziensis* (=*Dryopithecus (Dryopithecus) fontani*) are known. Stratigraphic position: molluscs associated with the hominoid remains point to a Chersonian age. The mammal fauna of Eldar was assigned to mammal zone MN 11 by Mein (1979) and was recently transferred to mammal zone MN 10 by Gabounia (personal communication).

Pliocene

There is to date no hominoid record from sediments with a definite Pliocene age.

The Miocene hominoid dispersal events

Several attempts of the reconstruction of circum-Mediterranean paleogeography, seaways and migrational routes of mammals between Eurasia and Afro-Arabia have been published recently (Thenius, 1972; Coryndon & Savage, 1973; Biju-Duval et al., 1977; Baldi, 1980; de Bruijn & van der Meulen, 1981; Boccaletti et al., 1982; Bernor, 1983; Rögl & Steininger, 1983; Adams, 1984; Steininger et al., 1985; Thomas, in press).

It became evident that after a long period of isolation of Eurasian and Afro-Arabian mammal faunas during the Oligocene and lower Early Miocene, the plate collision between Arabia and Eurasia responsible for the disconnection of the Mediterranean Sea from the Indo-Pacific resulted in a first phase of extensive mammal exchange between Eurasia and Afro-Arabia in the middle to later Early Miocene. In the course of this event we find the first appearance of hominoids (*Pliopithecus*) in Eurasia and the Paratethys area. This event was lately described by Thomas (in press) as NDP-1 (Neogene Dispersal Phase).

In contrast to Adams (1984), Rögl & Steininger (1983) have pointed out that the Middle Miocene (Langhian) marine peak, which can be followed worldwide, again interrupted this mammal migrational route. This is also evidenced in the mammal record. Only in Serravallian time was this mammal exchange, called NDP-2 by Thomas (in press), reactivated. During this second phase, *Sivapithecus* and *Ramapithecus* migrated to Europe, followed later by *Dryopithecus* (Bernor, 1983).

In the late Miocene (Vallesian) a favorable climatic change might have caused the far-spread appearance of various hominoids throughout the Paratethys (Bernor et al., 1979; Thenius, 1982).

References

Adams, C. G. (1984) Neogene larger foraminifera, evolutionary and geological events in the context of datum planes. In *Pacific Neogene Datum Planes*, ed. N. Ikebe, & R. Tsuchi, pp. 47–67. Tokyo: Tokyo Press

Alberdi, M. T. & Aguirre, E. (1977) Round-table on mastostratigraphy of the W. Mediterranean Neogene. *Trabaj. Neogeno-Cuatern. Secc. Paleontol. Vertebrados Hum.*, **7**, 7–47

Andreescu, I. (1981) Middle–Upper Neogene and Early Quaternary chronostratigraphy from the Dacic Basin and correlations with neighbouring areas. *Ann. Géol. Pays Hellén.*, hors sér., **4**, 129–38

Andreescu, I. & Radulescu, C. (1981) Chronologie (Mollusques, Mammifères, Paléomagnetisme) des formations plio-pléistocènes de la zone de Slatina (Bassin dacique), Roumanie. *Trav. Inst. Speol. 'Emile Racovitza'*, **20**, 127–37

Baldi, T. (1980) The early history of the Paratethys. *Földtani Közlöny, Bull. Hung. Geol. Soc.*, **110**, 456–72

Baldi-Beke, M. & Nagymarosy, A. (1979) On the position of the Ottnangian and Karpatian regional stages in the Tertiary nannoplankton zonation. *Ann. Géol. Pays Hellén., hors sér.*, **1**, 51–9

Benda, L. & Meulenkamp, J. E. (1979) Biostratigraphic correlations in the Eastern Mediterranean Neogene. 5. Calibration of sporomorph associations, marine microfossil and mammal zones, marine and continental stages and the radiometric scale. *Ann. Géol. Pays Hellén., hors sér.*, **1**, 61–70

Berczi, I., Hamor, G., Jambor, A. & Szentgyörgyi, K. (1982) Characteristics of Neogene sedimentation in the Pannonian Basin. In *Evolution of Extensional Basins within Regions of Compression, with Emphasis on the Intracarpathians*, ed. F. Horvath, pp. 36–8. Budapest: Geol. Survey of Hungary

Berggren, W. A., Kent, D. V. & Couvering, J. A. van (1985) Neogene geochronology and chronostratigraphy. In *Geochronology and the Geologic Time Scale*, (ed. N. J. Snelling). London: Geol. Soc. Lond.

Berggren, W. A., Kent, D. V., Flynn, J. J. & Couvering, J. A. van (in press) Cenozoic Geochronology. *Geology*

Bernor, R. L. (1983) Geochronology and zoogeographic relationships of Miocene Hominoidea. In *New Interpretations of Ape and Human Ancestry*, ed. R. L. Ciochon & R. S. Corruccini, pp. 21–64. New York: Plenum Press

Bernor, R. L., Andrews, P. J., Solounias, N. & Couvering, J. A. H. van (1979) The evolution of 'Pontian' mammal faunas: some zoogeographic, paleoecologic and chronostratigraphic considerations. *Ann. Géol. Pays Hellén., hors sér.*, **1**, 81–9

Biju-Duval, B., Dercourt, J. & Le Pichon, X. (1977) From the Tethys Ocean to the Mediterranean Sea: a plate tectonic model of the evolution of the Western alpine system. In *Structural History of the Mediterranean Basins*, ed. B. Biju-Duval & L. Montadert, pp. 143–64. Paris: Editions Technip

Bizon, G. & Müller, C. (1979) Report of the Working Group on Micropaleontology. *Ann. Géol. Pays Hellén., hors sér.*, **1**, 1335–64

Blow, W. H. (1969) Late Middle Eocene to Recent planktonic foraminiferal biostratigraphy. In *Proceedings of the First International Conference on Planktonic Microfossils 1*, ed. R. Bronnimann & H. H. Renz, pp. 199–241. Leiden: E. J. Brill

Boccaletti, M., Conedera, C., Dainelli, P. & Gocez, P. (1982) The Recent (Miocene–Quaternary) regmatic system of the western Mediterranean region. A new model of ensialic geodynamic evolution, in a context of plastic/rigid deformation. *J. Petrol. Geol.*, **5**(1), 31–49

Bruijn, H. de, Mein, P., Montenat, C. & Weerd, A. van de (1975) Correlations entre les gisements de rongeurs et les formations marines du Miocène terminal d'Espagne méridionale, I: Provinces d'Alicante et de Murcia. *K. Ned. Akad. Wet., Proc., Ser. B*, **78**, 1–32

Bruijn, H. de & Meulen, A. J. van der (1981) The distribution of land mammals in the Mediterranean through the Neogene – is there a fit with the paleogeographic and paleoclimatologic reconstructions based on data from marine basins? *Ann. Géol. Pays Hellén., hors sér.*, **4**, 323–35

Bruijn, H. de & Zachariasse, W. J. (1979) The correlation of marine and continental biozones of Kastellios hill reconsidered. *Ann. Géol. Pays. Hellén., hors sér.*, **1**, 219–26

Cicha, I. (1970) Stratigraphical problems of Miocene in Europe. *Rozpr. U.U.G., Svaz.*, **35**, 134 pp.

Cicha, I., Fahlbusch, V. & Fejfar, O. (1972) Biostratigraphic correlation of some Late Tertiary vertebrate faunas in Central Europe. *N. Jb. Paläontol. Abh.*, **140**, 129–45

Coryndon, S. C. & Savage, R. J. G. (1973) The origin and affinities of African mammal faunas. *Spec. Pap. Paleontol.*, **12**, 121–35

Couvering, J. A. van, Berggren, W. A., Drake, R. E., Aguirre, E. & Curtis, G. H. (1976) The terminal Miocene event. *Mar. Micropaleontol.*, **1**, 263–86

Ctyroky, P., Senes, J., Strauch, F., Papp, A., Kantarova, V., Ondrejickova, A., Vass, D. & Bohn-Havas, M. (1973) D. Die Entwicklung der Rzehakia (Oncophora) Formation – M 2 c–d – in der Zentralen Paratethys. In *M²*, *Ottnangien. Chronostratigraphie und Neostratotypen 3*, ed. A. Papp, F. Rögl & J. Senes, pp. 89–113. Bratislava: Slovak Academy of Sciences

Drooger, C. W. (1979) Marine connections of the Neogene Mediterranean, deduced from the evolution and distribution of larger Foraminifera. *Ann. Géol. Pays Hellén.*, *hors sér.*, **1**, 361–9

Falbusch, V. (1976) Report on the International Symposium on mammalian stratigraphy of the European Tertiary. *Newslett. Stratigr.*, **5**, 160–7

Feru, M., Radulescu, C. & Samson, P. (1980) La faune de micromammifères du Miocène de Comanesti (Dép. d'Arad). *Trav. Inst. Spéol. 'Emile Racovitza'*, **19**, 181–90

Fuchs, R. & Stradner, H. (1977) Uber Nannofossilien im Badenien (Mittelmiozän) der Zentralen Paratethys. *Beitr. Paläontol. Österr.*, **2**, 1–58

Gasparik, J. (1979) Paleogeographical map of Slovakia. *Neogén. Geol. Ustav. D. Stura*, 1–34

Hamor, G., Ravaszne-Baranyai, L., Balogh, K. & Arvane-Soos, E. (1978) Radiometric age of the Miocene Rhyolite Tuffs in Hungary. *Inst. Geol. Publ. Hung.*, 65–73

Hamor, G., Ravasz-Baranyai, L., Balogh, K. & Arva-Soos, E. (1979) K/Ar dating of Miocene pyroclastic rocks in Hungary. *Ann. Géol. Pays Hellén.*, *hors sér.*, **2**, 491–500

Horvath, M. & Nagymarosy, A. (1979) On the boundary of Oligocene/Miocene and Egerian/Eggenburgian in Hungary. *Ann. Géol. Pays Hellén.*, *hors sér.*, **2**, 543–52

Kojumdgieva, E. (1979) Le IXième symposium de groupe de travail 'Paratéthys' (11–18.IX.1978 – Sofia). *Geol. Balcanica*, **9**, 112–13

Kordos, L. (1982) The prehominid locality of Rudabánya (NE Hungary) and its neighbourhood: a palaeogeographic reconstruction. *Mag. All. Földt. Int. Evi Jel*, **1980**, 394–404

Kretzoi, M. (1974) Az emberrevalas utjan. *Anthropol. Közlemenyek.*, **18**, 121–8

Kretzoi, M., Krolopp, E., Lörinzc, H. & I. Pálfalvy, I. (1976) Flora, fauna und stratigraphische Lage der unterpannonischen Prähominiden-Fundstelle von Rudabanya (NO-Ungarn). *Földt. Int. Evi Jel, 1974–rol*, 365–94

Laskarev, V. (1924) Sur les équivalents du Sarmatien supérieur en Serbie. In *Recueil de travaux offert à M. Jovan Cvijić par ses Amis etr Collaborateurs*, (ed. P. Vujevic) pp. 73–85. Beograd: Drzhavna Shtamparija

Lehotayova, R. & Molcikova, V. (1978) Die Nannofossilien des Badenien. 8.1 Das Nannoplankton in der Tschechoslovakei. In *Chronostratigraphie und Neostratotypen, Miozän M₄ Badenien*, ed. A. Papp, I. Cicha, J. Senes & F. Steininger, pp. 481–6. Bratislava: Slovak Academy of Sciences

Martini, E. (1971) Standard Tertiary and Quaternary calcareous nannoplankton zonation. In *Proceedings of the First Planktonic Conference*, ed. A. Farinacci, pp. 739–85. Roma: Technoscienza

Martini, E. (1981) Nannoplankton in der Ober-Kreide, im Alttertiär und im tieferen Jungtertiär von Süddeutschland und dem angrenzenden Österreich. *Geol. Bavaria*, **82**, 345–56

Martini, E. & Müller, C. (1975a) Calcareous nannoplankton and silicoflagellates from the type Ottnangian and equivalent strata in Austria (Lower Miocene). *Proc. VIth Congr. Reg. Comm. Mediterr. Neog. Strat.*, 1, 121–3

Martini, E. & Müller, C. (1975b) Calcareous nannoplankton from the Karpatian in Austria (Middle Miocene). *Proc. VIth Congr. Reg. Comm. Mediterr. Neog. Strat.*, 1, 125–7

McGowran, B. (1979) Some Miocene configurations from an Australian standpoint. *Ann. Géol. Pays Hellén., hors sér.*, 2, 767–79

Mein, P. (1975) Résultats du Groupe de Travail des Vertébrés. In *Report on the Activity of R.C.M.N.S. Working Groups*, ed. J. Senes, pp. 78–81. Bratislava: Slovak Academy of Sciences

Mein, P. (1979) Rapport d'activité du groupe de travail vertébrés mise à jour de la biostratigraphie du Néogène basée sur les mammifères. *Ann. Géol. Pays Hellén., hors sér.*, 3, 1367–72

Mein, P. (1981) Mammal zonations: introduction. *Ann. Géol. Pays Hellén., hors sér.*, 4, 83–8

Mein, P., Bizon, G., Bizon, J. J. & Montenat, C. (1973) Le gisement de mammifères de La Alberca (Murcia, Espagne méridionale). Corrélations avec les formations marines du Miocène terminale. *C.R. Acad. Sci. Paris, Sér. D*, 276, 3077–80

Mottl, M. (1957) Bericht über die neuen Menschenaffenfunde aus Österreich, von St. Stefan im Lavanttal, Kärnten. *Carinthia II, Mitt. Naturwiss. Ver. Kärnten*, 67, 39–84

Mottl, M. (1970) Die Jungtertiären Säugetierfaunen der Steiermark Südost Österreichs. *Mitt. Geol. Paläont. Bergb., Landesmus. Joanneum*, 31, 79–168

Papp, A. & Steininger, F. F. (1979) Paleogeographic implications of Late Miocene deposits in the Aegean region. *Ann. Géol. Pays Hellén.*, 2, 955–9

Paramonova, N. P., Ananova, E., Andreeva-Grigorovic, A. S., Belokrys, L. S. & Gabunia, L. K. (1979). Paleontological characteristics of the Sarmatian s.l. and Maeotian of the Ponto-Caspian area and possibilities of correlation to the Sarmatian s.str. and Pannonian of the Central Paratethys. *Ann. Géol. Pays Hellén., hors sér.*, 2, 861–971

Rabeder, G. (1978) Die Säugetiere des Badenien. In *Chronostratigraphie und Neostratotypen, Miozän M₄ Badenien*, ed. A. Papp, I. Cicha, J. Senes & F. Steininger, pp. 467–480. Bratislava: Slovak Academy of Sciences

Rabeder, G. & Steininger, F. (1975) Die direkten biostratigraphischen Korrelations-möglichkeiten von Säugetierfaunen aus dem Oligo/Miozän der Zentralen Paratethys. *Proc. VIth Congr. Reg. Comm. Med. Neog. Stratig. Bratislava*, 1, 177–83

Rehakova, Z. (1977) Marine planktonic diatom zones of the Central Paratethys Miocene and their correlations. *Vest. Ustred. Ustav. Geog.*, 52, 147–57

Rögl, F., Hochuli, P. & Müller, C. (1979) Oligocene–Early Miocene stratigraphic correlations in the Molasse basin of Austria. *Ann. Géol. Pays. Hellén., hors sér.*, 1045–9

Rögl, F. & Steininger, F. F. (1983) Vom Zerfall der Tethys zu Mediterran und Paratethys. Die neogene Palaeogeographie und Palinspastik des zirkummediterranen Raumes. *Ann. Naturhist. Mus. Wien*, 85A, 135–63

Semenenko, V. N. (1979) Correlation of Mio-Pliocene of the Eastern Paratethys and Tethys. *Ann. Géol. Pays Hellén., hors sér.*, 3, 1001–111

Semenenko, V. N. & Ljulieva, S. A. (1978) [Versuch einer direkten Mio-Pliozän-Korrelation der östlichen Paratethys und Tethys.] *Wiss. Unters. Geol. Inst. Dnjepropetrovs, DGU*, 95–105. (In Russian)

Semenenko, V. N. & Pevsner, M. A. (1979) [A correlation of Miocene and Pliocene of the Pont-Caspian on the biostratigraphic and paleomagnetic data.] *Proc. USSR Acad. Sci., Geol. Ser.*, 1, 5–9

Steininger, F. F. & Papp, A. (1979) Current biostratigraphic and radiometric correlations of Late Miocene Central Paratethys stages (Sarmanian s.str., Pannonian s.str. and Pontian) and Mediterranean stages (Tortonian and Messinian) and the Messinian Event in the Paratethys. *Newslett. Stratigr.*, 8, 100–10

Steininger, F. F., Rabeder, G. & Rögl, F. (1985) Land mammal distribution in the Mediterranean Neogene – A consequence of geokinematic and climatic events. In *Geological Evolution of the Mediterranean*, ed. D. J. Stanley & F. C. Wezel, pp. 559–71. New York: Springer

Steininger, F., Rögl, F. & Martini, E. (1976) Current Oligocene/Miocene biostratigraphic concept of the Central Paratethys (Middle Europe). *Newslett. Stratigr.*, 4, 174–202

Stradner, H. & Fuchs, R. (1978) 8. Die Nannofossilien des Badenien–8.3. Das Nannoplankton in Österreich. In *Chronostratigraphie und Neostratotypen, Miozän M4 Badenien*, ed. A. Papp *et al.*, pp. 489–97. Bratislava: Slovak Academy of Sciences

Szalay, F. S. & Delson, E. (1979) *Evolutionary History of the Primates*. New York: Academic Press

Taner, G. (1982) Die Molluskenfauna und Pliocene stratigrafie der Halbinsel Gelibolou. *Comm. Fac. Sci. Univ. Ankara, ser. C., Geol.*, 25, 7 pp.

Thenius, E. (1959) *Wirbeltierfaunen.* Handb. Stratig. Geol. 3/2. Tertiär II. 328 pp. Stuttgart: Enke

Thenius, E. (1972) *Grundzüge der Verbreitungsgeschichte der Säugetiere.* 345 pp. Jena: Fischer Verlag

Thenius, E. (1982) Ein Menschenaffenfund (Primates: Pongidae) aus dem Pannon (Jung-Miozän) von Niederösterreich. *Folia Primatol*, 39, 187–200

Thenius, E. (1983) Zur Paläoklimatologie des Pannon (Jungmiozän) von Niederösterreich. *N. Jb. Geol. Paläontol.*, 11, 692–704

Thomas, H. (in press) The Lower and Middle Miocene Land Connection of the Afro-Arabian Plate and Asia: a major event for hominoid dispersal? In *Paleoanthropology: The Hard Evidence*, ed. E. Delson. New York: Alan R. Liss

Vass, D. & Bagdasarjan, G. P. (1978) A Radiometric Time Scale for the Neogene of the Paratethys Region. In *Contributions to the Geologic Time Scale.* Stud. Geol. No. 6, ed. G. V. Cohee, M. F. Glaessner & H. D. Hedberg, pp. 179–203. Tulsa: Am. Assoc. Petrol. Geol.

Vass, D., Bagdasarjan, G. P. & Steininger, F. (1978) The Badenian Radiometric Ages. In *Chronostratigraphie und Neostratotypen*, ed. A. Papp *et al.*, pp. 35–45. Bratislava: Slovak Academy of Sciences

Weber, L. & Weiss, A. (1983) Bergbaugeschichte und Geologie der Österreichischen Braunkohlenvorkommen. *Arch. Lagerstättenforsch. Geol. Bundesanst.*, 4, 1–317

Zapfe, H. (1956) Die geologische Altersstellung österreichischer Kohlenlagerstätten nach dem gegenwärtigen Stand der Kenntnis. *Berg-u. Hüttenmänn. Mitt. N.F.*, 1, 1–5

Zapfe, H. (1961) Ein Primatenfund aus der miozänen Molasse von Oberösterreich. *Z. Morphol. Anthropol.*, 51, 247–67

Zapfe, H. (1969) Primates. *Catal. Foss. Austriae*, 1–16

I.7

The Arabian Miocene: rocks, fossils, primates and problems

P. J. WHYBROW AND M. A. BASSIOUNI

Introduction

The Miocene rocks found in the coastal region of eastern Saudi Arabia are a relatively thin sequence of about 270 m. Deposited on an almost flat shelf (dip about 1° NE) of pre-Neogene rocks are continental sediments that in part are overlain by a transgressive 'wedge' of marine deposits, mainly carbonates. In the southern part of the State of Qatar, about 90 m of mainly marine Miocene strata unconformably lie on pre-Neogene rocks. At its top, this sequence is terminated by a thin evaporite bed that in turn is disconformably overlain by continental sandstones and conglomerates. In the neighbouring United Arab Emirates some 60 m of continental sediments outcrop near the modern coastline. Both terrestrial and marine vertebrate fossils have been collected from these eastern Arabian deposits. In this region, because no rocks exist that may be used for radiometric dating and owing to its geographical distance from mammalian biochronologic schemes of the European Neogene, only two methods have been used to date the faunas. They are: (1) comparison with other faunas of a 'known' age, mainly from Africa; and (2) a direct lithostratigraphic link with the local marine record.

In contrast, K–Ar whole-rock dates of the volcanic rocks of the coastal Red Sea rift in southwestern Saudi Arabia have helped date an anthracothere jaw fragment recovered from tuffaceous lake-bed facies.

Saudi Arabia

The Miocene of the eastern region

Three units (strictly phases of deposition), each of varying thickness (20–120 m), have been formally defined (Steineke *et al.*, 1958). The oldest beds, continental sandstones and clays of the Hadrukh Formation, are found up to 200 km from the modern coastline and were deposited with slight angular unconformity on Middle and Lower Eocene limestones. This pre-Neogene unconformity is found in Qatar, Kuwait and western Iraq. Rocks of Oligocene age have not yet been recognised. Marine limestones and marls of the Dam Formation in part overlie the Hadrukh up to about 120 km inland to show the most western limit of a marine transgression from the Indian Ocean (Adams, Gentry & Whybrow, 1983). Deposits of the Dam Formation are succeeded by continental sandstones, marls and some conglomerates of the Hofuf Formation. Overall, where the marine deposits of the Dam Formation disappear inland, continental rocks of the Hadrukh cannot usually be separated from the continental Hofuf Formation (Powers et al., 1966).

Dating the primates and the fossil localities

Five dryopithecine specimens consisting of a partial left maxilla and four isolated teeth were collected in 1974 from continental equivalents of the Dam Formation located near a bored water well called Ad Dabtiyah (Hamilton, Whybrow & McClure, 1978). Andrews had difficulty in assigning these specimens to any dryopithecine taxon. He did not name them and suggested that they may 'represent a primitive branch of the Dryopithecinae that was not related to any of the later pongid lineages' (Andrews, Hamilton & Whybrow, 1978). The importance of these fossils lies not only in their enigmatic phylogenetic relationships (they are now being re-studied by Andrews and Martin), but also in their age and location. They appear to be the earliest occurrence of dryopithecines found at any distance from the East African early Miocene sites and their habitat seems to have been near to the tropical shores of the Tethys epi-continental sea.

The vertebrate-bearing sediments at Ad Dabtiyah (Fig. 1) are stratigraphically close to the margin of the Dam marine transgression. Although some fossils were found in an area of about 6 km², the dryopithecines together with other vertebrates occurred in a 2 km² localised area of unbedded, white calcareous grit. Freshwater algal bioherms were found close to the vertebrates and algal encrustations covered both a rhinoceros skull and the in situ boles and 'fallen' trunks, now silicified, of palm trees. No in situ marine fossils were found.

The fauna associated with the primates (it includes several enigmatic taxa some of which are now being described by A. W. Gentry) consisted of a trilophodont mastodon, two rhinoceros species, tragulids, bovids, a giraffoid, suids, chelonian and crocodilian remains, and teeth and incomplete skulls of cyprinid and centropomid fish.

A similar fauna to that from Ad Dabtiyah but with more taxa (27 mammal species), was collected by Thomas and his colleagues from the Al-Sarrar region, about 80 km north of Ad Dabtiyah. A well-preserved lateral incisor which 'may belong to a primate' and the distal end of a tibia 'only doubtfully referred to a primate' were collected (Thomas *et al.*, 1982).

At present, unequivocal identifications to species level of both the Ad Dabtiyah and Al-Sarrar faunas have not been published. Parts of the fauna, especially the rodents, may be new at both generic and specific levels. Of the 22 terrestrial mammals recorded from Al-Sarrar, the only species identified with certainty is the felid *Pseudaelurus turnauensis*. Of the remainder some appear to have affinity with either African or European taxa. Despite these current taxonomic problems, a 15–17 million year age for both faunas has been suggested (Hamilton *et al.*, 1978; Thomas *et al.*, 1982).

As dating the faunas relies at present on the taxonomic comparison with geographically distant faunas, it is useful to examine the lithostratigraphic proximity of the fossil-bearing sediments to the marine record.

Both localities are stratigraphically close to the basal deposits of the marine Dam Formation. In previous publications, the Ad Dabtiyah locality was wrongly stated to lie *within* the Dam Formation (Hamilton *et al.*, 1978; Andrews *et al.*, 1978). As formally defined, contact of the

Fig. 1. Geological section around the bored water well at the Ad Dabtiyah fossil locality to another bored well to the east near Jabal Qidam, Saudi Arabia, to show the Miocene succession from the pre-Neogene unconformity, the vertebrate horizon, the stratigraphical position of the marine Dam Formation and its basal Button bed. Adapted from unpublished oil company information, aerial photographs, U.S.G.S. map I-208A (Steineke *et al.*, 1958) and field notes.

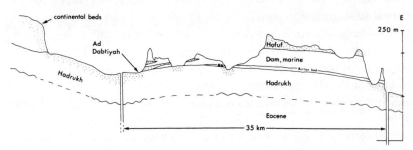

base of the Dam with the underlying clays and sandstones of the Hadrukh is recognised by a regionally widespread, thin (about 1 m) limestone marker bed packed with the small echinoid *Fibularia damensis* and known locally as the Button bed (Steineke *et al.*, 1958; Powers *et al.*, 1966). Significantly this bed does not occur at the fossil localities but is found about 10 km to the east. However, the oyster *Ostrea latimarginata* occurs in shales in the lower parts of some sections at Al-Sarrar. At Ad Dabtiyah it was seen but not found *in situ*. Above the shales at Al-Sarrar lay continental sediments with vertebrates. Above them lay marine rocks consisting of shelly limestones with coral fragments and sirenian bones (Thomas *et al.*, 1982).

Recent studies by us of the Dam Formation in the State of Qatar indicate the following. About 10–15 m of Miocene claystones and shales containing *O. latimarginata* unconformably lie on Eocene limestones – the pre-Neogene unconformity. Within these clastics, subaerial conditions are suggested by the presence of mud cracks and ferruginous structures resembling roots. At the top of this sequence the Button bed occurs and marks the beginning of a mainly non-clastic, marine carbonate environment. At the top of the carbonates lies a thin bed of evaporites that in turn are disconformably overlain by sandstones and conglomerates of the basal part of the Hofuf Formation. The marine limestones in Qatar can be easily correlated with the Dam limestones in Saudi Arabia as, besides the Button bed, they share the same Burdigalian-aged echinoderms (Kier, 1972). However, the lowermost clastics cannot be so easily correlated as, stratigraphically, they appear to be in part coeval with the continental Hadrukh. In a small coastal area of Saudi Arabia, Powers *et al.* (1966) record poorly preserved marine molluscs and *Ostrea latimarginata* at the top of the Hadrukh. For the whole of the Hadrukh they suggest an early Miocene age (Powers *et al.*, 1966).

Recently, Adams *et al.* (1983) when reviewing the Oligocene and Miocene stratigraphy of the Middle East, showed the top of the Hadrukh and all of the Dam Formation to be Burdigalian (marine chronostratigraphy), which is 16–19 million years old. Similarly, *O. latimarginata* is considered to be of Burdigalian age (Cox, 1936). Interestingly, Thomas (in press) comments in his paper on land connections for hominoid dispersal between Afro-Arabia and Asia, that the disconnection of Tethys at about 18 ± 1 million years ago has been best dated by Adams *et al* (1983) (see also Whybrow, 1984).

In summary, the basal Miocene non-continental sequence in eastern Arabia is characterised by shales and claystones containing *Ostrea latimarginata*, the presence of which is probably facies-controlled (? lagoonal). This sequence is overlain by marine carbonates containing age-diagnostic echinoderms. At both the Al-Sarrar and Ad Dabtiyah localities the base of the marine carbonate sequence lies stratigraphically higher than the continental, vertebrate-bearing sediments. As the lithostratigraphic link with the marine record is strong, we suggest that the vertebrate faunas can be dated at 16–19 million years ago.

The southwestern Saudi Arabian Miocene

Notably absent, as yet, from the eastern Arabian Miocene collections are anthracotheres. In 1982, Dwight Schmidt, United States Geological Survey, collected an anthracotheriid lower jaw fragment with M_3 from the Baid formation located in the Red Sea rift. The Baid formation consists of laminated siliceous tuffs deposited in freshwater lakes and is part of the sandstones and volcanic rocks that form the Jizan group. Intruding into the Jizan group, including the Baid sediments, are a granophyre and a gabbro which have been K–Ar whole-rock dated at 20–23 million years old (Coleman *et al.*, 1979). Based on the presence of the anthracothere *Masritherium*, the fossil locality in the Baid formation has been dated at 21–25 million years ago (Madden *et al.*, 1983).

The United Arab Emirates

Miocene sediments outcrop over a distance of about 250 km in the coastal region known as the Baynunah plateau. Although no primate fossils have yet been found, a small fauna has been collected. A proboscidean tooth was first collected by Glennie & Evamy (1968) who thought the animal had died in desert sands close to water-transported conglomerates. Later, Whybrow & McClure (1981) collected a crocodilian vertebra and a bovid radius, possibly of an early caprine, and suggested that root horizons might be preserved mangroves. They further stated the deposits to be not later than 'Vindobonian' equivalent age and probably coeval with the Hofuf Formation of Saudi Arabia.

Recent field studies by us show the fauna to consist of a hexaprotodont hippopotamid, the boselaphine *Miotragocerus*, *Hipparion* sp., a suid, crocodilian and chelonian remains, bagrid and clariid catfish bones, freshwater Unionacea molluscs and numerous fragments of *in situ* ostrich egg shell.

Madden *et al.* (1982) identified the proboscidean as *Stegotetrabelodon grandincisivum* and suggested an age of 8–12 million years for the deposits. The presence of *Hipparion* suggests a similar age.

The deposits are mapped as Tertiary, undifferentiated (Bramkamp & Ramirez, 1961) lateral equivalents of the Dam and Hofuf formations of Saudi Arabia. Although both these formations thicken considerably in this region, the Rub al 'Khali basin, they are only found at depth. Consequently, because of its presumed age, the Miocene of the coastal United Arab Emirates may be coeval with the Mishan or Agha Jari Formations of southwestern Iran. These are mainly brackish water or continental deposits (James & Wynd, 1965; Adams *et al.*, 1983) and, if shown to be contiguous with the UAE deposits, would suggest that there was free passage for animals in the southern parts of the Arabian Gulf during the late Neogene.

Acknowledgements

We are most grateful to Dr Omar Abdel Rahman, Scientific and Applied Research Centre, University of Qatar, for the invaluable assistance granted to us during two field seasons. We also thank Dr A. W. Gentry for some preliminary identifications.

References

Adams, C. G., Gentry, A. W. & Whybrow, P. J. (1983) Dating the terminal Tethyan event. *Utrecht Micropal. Bull.*, **30**, 273–98

Andrews, P. J., Hamilton, W. R. & Whybrow, P. J. (1978) Dryopithecines from the Miocene of Saudi Arabia. *Nature*, **274**, 249–51

Bramkamp, R. A. & Ramirez, L. F. (1961) Geologic map of the Central Persian Gulf quadrangle Kingdom of Saudi Arabia. *Miscellaneous Geologic Investigations*, Map I-209A (Washington, D.C.)

Coleman, R. G., Hadley, D. G., Fleck, R. J., Hedge, C. E. & Donato, M. M. (1979). The Miocene Tihama Asir ophiolite and its bearing on the opening of the Red Sea. In *Evolution and Mineralization of the Arabian–Nubian Shield*, Vol. 1, pp. 173–86. Oxford & New York: Pergamon Press

Cox, L. R. (1936). Fossil Mollusca from southern Persia (Iran) and Bahrein Island. *Mem. Geol. Surv. India, Palaeontol. indica*, N.S., **22**(2), 1–69

Glennie, K. W. & Evamy, B. D. (1968) Dikaka: plants and plant-root structures associated with aeolian sand. *Palaeogeogr., Palaeoclimatol., Palaeoecol.*, **4**, 77–87

Hamilton, W. R., Whybrow, P. J. & McClure, H. A. (1978) Fauna of fossil mammals from the Miocene of Saudi Arabia. *Nature*, **274**, 248–9

James, G. A. & Wynd, J. G. (1965) Stratigraphic nomenclature of Iranian oil consortium agreement area. *Bull. Am. Assoc. Pet. Geol.*, **49**(12), 2182–245

Kier, P. (1972) Tertiary and Mesozoic echinoids of Saudi Arabia. *Smithsonian Contrib. Paleobiol.*, **18**, 1–242

Madden, C. T., Glennie, K. W., Dehm, R., Whitmore, F. C., Jr, Schmidt, D. L., Ferfoglia, R. J. & Whybrow, P. J. (1982) *Stegotetrabelodon* (Proboscidea, Gomphotheriidae) from Miocene of Abu Dhabi. *U.S. Geol. Surv. Saudi Arabian Project Report*, 1–22

Madden, C. T., Schmidt, D. L. & Whitmore, F. C. (1983) *Masritherium* (Artiodactyla, Anthracotheriidae) from Wadi Sabya, southwestern Saudi Arabia: an earliest Miocene age for continental rift-valley volcanic deposits of Red Sea margin. *Open-file report USGS-OF-03-61.* Jeddah, Saudi Arabia: Ministry of Petroleum and Mineral Resources

Powers, R. W., Ramirez, L. F., Redmond, C. D. & Elberg, E. L., Jr (1966) Sedimentary Geology of Saudi Arabia. *Prof. Pap. U.S. Geol. Surv.*, **560**-D, 1–127

Steineke, M. Bramkamp, R. A. & Sander, N. J. (1958) Stratigraphic relations of Arabian Jurassic oil. In *Habitat of Oil*, ed. L. G. Weeks, pp. 1294–329. Oklahoma: American Association of Petroleum Geologists

Steineke, M., Harriss, T. F., Parsons, K. R. & Berg, E. L. (1958) Geology of the western Persian Gulf quadrangle, Kingdom of Saudi Arabia. *Miscellaneous Geologic Investigations* Map I-208A. (Washington, D.C.)

Thomas, H. (in press) The Lower and Middle Miocene land connection of the Afro-Arabian plate and Asia: a major event for hominoid dispersal? In *Paleoanthropology: The Hard Evidence*, ed. E. Delson. New York: Alan R. Liss, Inc.

Thomas, H., Sen. S., Khan, M., Battail, B. and Ligabue, G. (1982) The lower Miocene Fauna of Al-Sarrar (Eastern Province, Saudi Arabia). *ATLAL, The Journal of Saudi Arabian Archaeology*, **5**, 109–36

Whybrow, P. J. (1984). Geological and faunal evidence from Arabia for mammal 'migrations' between Asia and Africa during the early Miocene. *Cour. Forsch. Inst. Senckenberg*, **69**, 189–98

Whybrow, P. J. & McClure, H. A. (1981) Fossil mangrove roots and palaeoenvironments of the Miocene of the eastern Arabian peninsula. *Palaeogeogr., Palaeoclimatol., Palaeoecol.*, **32**, 213–25

I.8

A review of the chronology of Siwalik hominoids

J. C. BARRY

Introduction

Fossil hominoids were first reported from the Indian Subcontinent in 1837 by Falconer and Cautley and in the years since they have excited considerable interest and controversy. The past decade in particular has seen renewed activity with field projects in Pakistan, India, and Nepal, the goals of which are not just recovering additional specimens but, more importantly, studying the hominoids within their faunal and sedimentary context. Hominoids are now known from several separate regions on the Subcontinent, including Sind, Kashmir, Nepal, and northern India and Pakistan (Sahni, Kumar & Srivastava, 1974; Dutta, Basu & Sastry, 1976; Pilbeam et al., 1980; Gupta, Verma & Tewari, 1982; Johnson et al., 1983; Munthe et al., 1983; Raza et al., 1984). Among other advances, considerable progress has been made in resolving the ages of these localities, a particularly vexing problem which has only been solved with magnetostratigraphic studies. This paper reviews the background to the dating of the Siwalik hominoids and presents a compilation and discussion of their ages as currently known.

The systematics of fossil hominoids are currently unsettled. Throughout this paper, therefore, for convenience I use 'large hominoids' informally to designate a group that includes species usually referred to as *Sivapithecus* (here including *Ramapithecus*) and *Gigantopithecus*. This contrasts to my use of 'small hominoids', which are much smaller species of possible gibbon ancestry. In deference to published references, I also use *Gigantopithecus* '*bilaspurensis*', which is widely regarded as a junior synonym of *G. giganteus*. Both species are known only from single specimens.

Stratigraphic setting

Neogene terrestrial sediments, which may be loosely referred to as 'the Siwaliks', are found in widely separated areas throughout the Indian Subcontinent, where they are associated with young active mountain belts and contain a characteristic fauna in addition to the hominoids. The Siwaliks are structurally related to the collision of India with Asia and the resulting uplift of the Himalayas and other ranges. Typically composed of large and small channel sands and associated fine-grained overbank deposits, they are of fluvial origin and formed as either coalescing piedmont fans in subsiding troughs fronting the rising mountains or as infillings of smaller inter-montane basins. In northern Pakistan and India the fluvial Miocene sediments invariably lie on a low-relief erosional surface developed on Eocene limestones or older rocks, and there is therefore a long hiatus at the base of the terrestrial sequence. In the south, this hiatus is partly filled by marine Oligocene and Lower Miocene sediments that grade upward into the terrestrial sequence. Contemporaneous rocks are also found in Afghanistan and Burma, but because either the tectonic setting or fauna differ these are not now considered a part of the Siwaliks even in the widest sense of the term.

Exposures of the Siwaliks are typically continuous bands of outcrop separated from other similar exposures by tens or hundreds of kilometers. Regardless of the local tectonic setting the sediments are unusually thick, as for example near Khaur on the Potwar Plateau. There, up to 5000 m deposited over more than 10 million years (MY) are exposed in a broad band of outcrop which extends for over 60 km along the Soan and Sil Rivers. Stratigraphic sections have been measured along this band and correlated by laterally tracing marker beds so as to construct a local lithostratigraphic/chronostratigraphic framework. Individual fossil sites can also be traced into the local lithologic sections, so that within the Khaur area their relative stratigraphic positions are established using only the field evidence of superposition (Pilbeam *et al.*, 1979; Barry, Behrensmeyer & Monaghan, 1980). Similar exposures are found elsewhere in Kashmir, Punjab, Sind, Nepal, and northern India (Dutta *et al.*, 1976; Keller *et al.*, 1977; Opdyke *et al.*, 1979; N. M. Johnson *et al.*, 1982, 1985; G. D. Johnson *et al.*, 1983; Munthe *et al.*, 1983; Raza *et al.*, 1984) and within each area it is possible to establish a local stratigraphic framework based on lithologic sections and correlations of fossil sites.

Formations can be differentiated within the Siwalik sequences, but all preserve the same basic variety of paleoenvironments typical of large and small river systems, including channels, point bars, levees, soils and, occasionally, ponds. The abundance of fossils varies from formation to formation. Those with the most heterogeneous mixture of lithologies are usually the most fossiliferous, but all have at least an occasional scattering of poorly preserved bones and teeth. Pollen and other plant fossils are unfortunately extremely rare, although poorly preserved wood is common and a few leaf and grass impressions have recently been found. The vertebrate fossils have two modes of occurrence: (1) as rich, but small and local concentrations; and (2) as an ubiquitous background scatter of isolated specimens. My concept of a locality and its application to the collections in the Geological Survey of Pakistan (GSP), Yale Peabody Museum, and American Museum of Natural History has been discussed elsewhere (Barry *et al.*, 1980). It is important, however, to understand that the localities or sites are concentrations of fossils found in small areas of outcrop (typically 500 m² or less) and, while there may have been transport and reworking of the faunal remains, the specimens at most localities probably all lived and were entombed within an interval of time not more than 20000 years and possibly much less (Behrensmeyer, 1982).

Correlations within the Siwaliks

Because of the lack of physical continuity between areas and the variable lithostratigraphy, correlation of Siwalik sediments between disjunct regions can presently be done only with biostratigraphic or magnetostratigraphic methods. G. E. Pilgrim was the first to attempt such correlations in any detail, having recognized from the faunal evidence that rocks at Chinji, Dhok Pathan, and Hari Talyangar were of different ages. In the early part of this century he developed a Siwalik zonation (Pilgrim, 1913) based on a combination of lithologic homotaxis and biostratigraphy, which, with its familiar Chinji, Nagri, and Dhok Pathan Zones, became widely accepted and used. Pilgrim's zones, however, were too vaguely defined to allow even the general correlations he sought and have always been unsatisfactory. In recent years Siwalik biostratigraphic and chronostratigraphic units have been revised (Barry, Lindsay & Jacobs, 1982), but even with our new interval-zones the minimum level of time resolution is of the order of 1 MY, which is far from satisfactory.

With magnetostratigraphy it is now possible to correlate between the separate areas of the Siwaliks with an accuracy and degree of resolution unavailable before. To a certain extent then, biostratigraphic correlations have become obsolete, except in cases where the

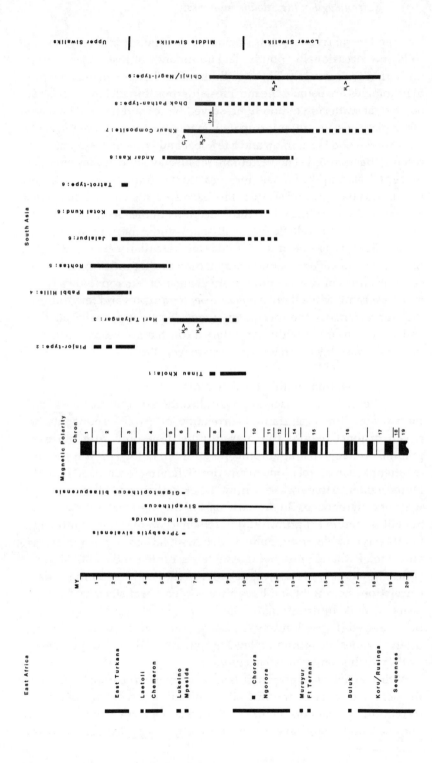

local sections are too incomplete or structurally complex to give reliable correlations, as at Tatrot and Dhok Pathan. Magnetostratigraphic correlations between areas can be made either directly (N. M. Johnson et al., 1982) or, if there is little or no overlap between the local sections, indirectly by matching the polarity zonations of each local section independently to the geomagnetic polarity time scale and thus implicitly to each other. Whether direct or indirect, such correlations have the important advantage of indicating precisely the degree of overlap or lack of it. Furthermore, with a secure chronostratigraphic framework it is now possible to construct and test new biostratigraphic zonations with proven isochroneity. Such zonations have the potential to be very powerful when combined with magnetostratigraphy and other correlative tools and might eventually allow chronostratigraphic correlations with a precision close to 100 000 years. If free of biostratigraphic assumptions, such precise correlations would give a radical new perspective to our studies of faunal dynamics.

With the results of a decade of magnetostratigraphic work in Pakistan (see Tauxe and Opdyke, 1982; N. M. Johnson, et al., 1982, 1985), Nepal (Munthe et al., 1983), and India (Yokoyama, 1981; Azzaroli & Napoleone, 1982; G. D. Johnson et al., 1983), it is now possible to demonstrate the time relationships of many of the key Siwalik exposures (Dera Bugti, the Manchars, and Ramnager being critical exceptions) and I have summarized these relationships in Fig. 1. This summary includes faunas attributed to the Kamlial through Boulder Conglomerate Zones and from the figure it is possible to construct a single composite section spanning the whole of the Siwalik sequence. As far as is known there are no major hiatuses in this composite sequence, although several of the local sections have significant breaks and only three span the Middle to Upper Siwalik transition.

Fig. 1. Correlation of Siwalik stratigraphic sections to geologic time scale and a generalized East African sequence. Parts of Siwalik stratigraphic sections shown as dashed lines are of uncertain age. H_1: oldest small hominoid; H_2: oldest large hominoid; H_3: youngest *Sivapithecus* on Potwar Plateau; H_4: youngest *Sivapithecus*; H_5: horizon of *Gigantopithecus bilaspurensis* type; C_1 oldest monkey. Sources for paleomagnetic columns: (1) Munthe et al., 1983; (2) Azzaroli & Napoleone, 1982; (3) G. D. Johnson et al., 1983; (4) Keller et al., 1977; (5) Opdyke et al., 1979; (6) N. M. Johnson et al., 1982; (7) Tauxe & Opdyke, 1982; (8) Barry et al., 1982; (9) N. M. Johnson et al., 1985. The position of the Tatrot follows Barry et al. (1982).

Correlation to the geological time scale

Except for a local bentonitic clay near Qadirpur and some impressive Late Pliocene ashes (G. D. Johnson *et al.*, 1982), there are no volcanics in the Siwaliks that have much potential for isotopic dating. (Other bentonites of very local occurrence are known, but those investigated so far have all proved to be reworked and contaminated or else lack suitable minerals). Thus the only way to relate the Siwaliks to an absolute time scale is by biostratigraphic or magnetostratigraphic correlations to other calibrated faunal or lithological sequences.

In southern Pakistan the fluvial Miocene conformably overlies marine strata. The fossils of these sediments, however, have not recently been studied and, as a shallow shelf macrofossil assemblage, might be difficult to relate to any of the standard microfossil zonations. Otherwise, none of the various Siwalik sequences has any direct relationship to marine rocks and the only possible biostratigraphic correlations are to the isotopically dated mammal faunas of East Africa or else to the European mammal sequence which can be tied in part to Tethyan marine rocks. The precision of both correlations is disappointing, approximating only about 2 MY. In both cases the problem is the provinciality of Siwalik and other Miocene faunas (Bernor, 1983; Brunet & Heintz, 1983). The history of the Siwalik province (a forerunner of the modern Indo-Malayan Province?) can be seen as an alternation of exchanges with neighboring provinces and what may have been long periods of isolation. During periods of isolation faunal developments within the provinces must have been largely controlled by local tectonic and regional climatic events, and thus decoupled from developments in other regions.

Correlation of 12 local Siwalik magnetic polarity sections to the geomagnetic polarity time scale is shown in Fig. 1. Although there is still uncertainty over the exact ages of the polarity transitions (see Ness, Levi & Couch, 1980), within the time range of interest here, disputed ages for individual polarity transitions differ at most by only about 0.4 MY. Thus the precision of magnetostratigraphic correlations of the Siwaliks to the geological time scale is much superior to biostratigraphic correlations and is generally comparable to the analytic precision of middle Miocene isotopic dates. The results indicate that the base of the Siwalik sequence on the Potwar Plateau is older than 18 MY (Johnson *et al.*, 1985), while the youngest horizons are less than 0.4 MY old (Keller *et al.*, 1977).

The correlation to the geological time scale makes it possible to compare the Siwaliks to the isotopically calibrated mammal faunas of East Africa, as is also shown on Fig. 1. The implications of this are of some interest in interpreting hominoid history and relating it to faunal exchanges between Asia and Africa.

Ages of the hominoids

Table 1 contains estimated dates for selected localities with primates on the Potwar Plateau, plus Hari Talyangar in India and Tinau Khola in Nepal. Hominoids and other primates are of course known from localities in other regions (including the Manchars and Trans-Indus in Pakistan and various places in northern India), but the chronostratigraphic control for these other localities (including all of the specimens in collections made before c. 1930) is currently too poor to allow meaningful estimates of their dates. All of these dates are based on interpolations into local magnetic polarity sections and correlations of the sections to the geomagnetic polarity time scale. The stratigraphic positions and dates were compiled from published and unpublished sources, as noted in Table 1. In the latter cases, these studies are still in progress and for that reason the dates are given as possible ranges and should be regarded as being tentative. The locality listings can be used to assign dates to individual fossil specimens by cross referencing (Pilbeam *et al.*, 1980; Johnson *et al.*, 1983; Badgley *et al.*, 1984). For completeness Table 1 also includes dates for non-hominoid primates.

The dates in Table 1 are given to the nearest 100000 years, but this may be an overestimate of the precision of some and the reader should be aware of two qualifications. The first is that while, as previously noted, I have used the Mankinen & Dalrymple (1979) revised polarity time scale, there are alternatives (Ness *et al.*, 1980) and there is yet no firm consensus on which of these is best. If an alternative is eventually adopted, adjustments to the dates of Table 1 will have to be made. These adjustments could range from 0.1 to 0.5 MY, but will not be constant for all dates. The correlations of local magnetostratigraphic sections to the geomagnetic polarity zonations will, of course, remain unchanged.

A second qualification is related to the problems of correlating laterally equivalent strata in fluvial sections, for small erosional and non-depositional hiatuses make it difficult to establish exact super-positional relationships for nearly contemporaneous localities.

Table 1. *Ages of Siwalik primate localities*

Locality	Chron	Age(MY)[a]	Taxa	Source[b]
Pakistan				
Y 137	upper 8	8.0	*Sivapithecus*	1,2
Y 182	upper 8	8.1	Lorisid,	1,2
			Sivapithecus	
Y 191	upper 8	8.1	*Sivapithecus*	1,2
Y 207	upper 8	8.1	*Sivapithecus*	1,2
Y 211	upper 8	8.1	*Sivapithecus*	1,2
Y 221	upper 8	8.1	*Sivapithecus*	1,2
Y 224	upper 8	8.2	*Sivapithecus*	1,2
Y 226	upper 8	8.1	*Sivapithecus*	1,2
Y 227	upper 8	8.2	*Sivapithecus*	1,2
Y 230	upper 8	8.1	*Sivapithecus*	1,2
Y 251	upper 9	8.9	*Sivapithecus*	1,2
Y 259	mid 9	9.3	Lorisid,	1,2
			Sivapithecus	
Y 260	upper 8	8.1	*Sivapithecus*	1,2
Y 261	lower 8	8.5	*Sivapithecus*	1,2
Y 309	upper 8	8.2	*Sivapithecus*	1,2
Y 310	upper 8	8.1	*Sivapithecus*	1,2
Y 311	upper 9	8.8	*Sivapithecus*	3,4
Y 314	upper 8	8.1	*Sivapithecus*	1,2
Y 317	upper 8	8.1	*Sivapithecus*	1,2
Y 327	upper 8	8.1	*Sivapithecus*	1,2
Y 328	upper 8	8.1	*Sivapithecus*	1,2
Y 350	upper 8	8.2	*Sivapithecus*	1,2
Y 363	mid 7	7.2–7.1	*Nycticeboides*	1,2
			simpsoni	
Y 370	lower 6	6.3	*?Presbytis*	1,2
			sivalensis	
Y 409	upper 8	8.1	*Sivapithecus*	1,2
Y 410	upper 8	8.2	*Sivapithecus*	1,2
Y 414	upper 8	8.1	*Sivapithecus*	1,2
Y 416	upper 8	8.1	*Sivapithecus*	1,2
Y 442	mid 7	7.4	*Sivapithecus*	1,2
Y 450	mid 9	9.1	Lorisid	3,4
Y 463	upper 8	8.0	*Sivapithecus*	1,2
Y 494	lower 11	11.8	*Sivapithecus*	5

Locality	Chron	Age(MY)[a]	Taxa	Source[b]
Pakistan (Cont.)				
Y 495	mid 10	10.7–10.2	*Sivapithecus*	5
Y 496	lower 11	11.8	*Sivapithecus*	5
Y 498	between 12 & 9	11.8–10.0	*Sivapithecus*	5
Y 499	between 12 & 9	11.8–10.0	*Sivapithecus*	5
Y 500	between 12 & 9	11.8–10.0	*Sivapithecus*	5
Y 504	lower 10	11.2–10.7	*Sivapithecus*	5
Y 592	upper 16	16.1	*Sivaladapis* sp., small hominoid	5
Y 604	mid 7	7.4	*Sivapithecus*	5
Y 663	between 12 & 9	11.8–10.0	*Sivapithecus*	5
L 21	between 12 & 9	11.8–10.0	*Sivapithecus*	5
L 28	between 12 & 9	11.8–10.0	*Sivaladapis palaeindicus*	5
L 81	10	11.2–10.0	*Sivapithecus*	3,4
L 94	mid 9	9.1	*Sivapithecus*	3,4
India				
L 35	mid 7	7.6–7.2	*Indraloris himalayensis*, *Sivapithecus*	6
Quarry D	mid 7	7.4	small hominoid	6,7
Unnumbered localities	mid 7	7.8–7.2	*Sivapithecus*	6
Unnumbered locality[c]	lower 6	6.3	*Gigantopithecus* 'bilaspurensis'	6
Nepal				
Tinau Khola	mid 9	9.5–9.0	*Sivapithecus*	8

[a] Based on Mankinen & Dalrymple (1979).
[b] (1) Barry *et al.*, 1980; (2) Tauxe & Opdyke, 1982; (3) N. M. Johnson *et al.*, 1982; (4) Barry *et al.*, 1982 (5) N. M. Johnson, personal communication; (6) G. D. Johnson *et al.*, 1983; (7) Ciochon, 1983; (8) Munthe *et al.*, 1983.
[c] There is considerable doubt about the exact locality of the type of *Gigantopithecus* 'bilaspurensis'. The horizon from which it is said to come is 6.3 MY.

Behrensmeyer & Tauxe (1982) and Behrensmeyer (1982) have discussed this and related problems and their conclusions indicate that, in the absence of detailed analysis of lateral facies, 0.1 MY is a reasonable level of resolution to expect in fluvial systems. Thus for localities that lie in a single stratigraphic section or adjacent sections, such as Y350, Y182, and Y137, the differences in age (8.2, 8.1, and 8.0 MY) are meaningful. For more widely separated localities, such as the 'U-level' localities Y310 (8.1 MY) and Y410 (8.2 MY), the situation is equivocal and the level of resolution is probably no better than 0.2 MY.

A prime objective of our research in the Siwaliks is to determine the temporal ranges of the various hominoid and other mammal species. This is done, of course, by attempting to find the oldest and youngest specimens, but the simplicity of the field procedure masks a more difficult statistical sampling problem (Hay, 1972). For instance, on the Potwar Plateau the oldest and youngest large hominoids are 11.8 and 7.4 MY, respectively, but they have been found at only 39 fossil localities out of a total of over 750. That is, only 5% of all Potwar localities have yielded large hominoids and out of these 39 localities, 24 are at the 'U-level', a short interval representing about 0.3 MY within the total time span of 18 MY. It is easy to imagine that if we had only one quarter of the hominoid localities, drawn randomly from the 39, the established or 'observed' stratigraphic range might well be restricted to only the 'U-level' and immediately adjacent horizons. By analogy then the true range might also be much longer than currently established. This sampling problem is of course made more difficult by the non-uniform distribution throughout the section of the most fossiliferous levels and the tendency to concentrate fossil collecting on particular levels because they are richer or more interesting. (Both influences account for the large number of 'U-level' hominoid sites.)

However, although it may be difficult to establish the total range, it is still possible to make some reasonable estimates by using information that indicates the absence of a species where it might be expected (Hay, 1972). While the case is not yet conclusive, it is improbable that the stratigraphic range of the large hominoids extends much below 13 MY, if even that old. This is because there are horizons older than 13 MY in the Chinji Formation in which we have not yet found hominoids, although other fossils are very abundant. Continued collecting should soon settle this question, although the nature of the problem precludes ever proving the assertion.

The upper boundary of the temporal range of the large hominoids is also uncertain. At Hari Talyangar the youngest specimens of

Sivapithecus are 7.2 MY old and, as there are numerous localities at Hari Talyangar and on the Potwar Plateau younger than 7.2 MY without *Sivapithecus* it is likely that it had become locally extinct by then. This extinction, however, may have been slightly diachronous, as there is some evidence that *Sivapithecus* was not present after 7.4 MY on the Potwar Plateau. This evidence comes mainly from the outcrops of the Dhok Pathan Formation near the Dhok Pathan Rest House, which is a very fossiliferous short sequence clearly lacking hominoids. On the basis of fauna and paleomagnetics these outcrops apparently span the interval between 7.4 and 7.0 MY, but as this correlation is somewhat doubtful the question of diachroneity is unsettled. Indeed, as noted by Johnson *et al.* (1983, p. 237). The interpretation of the Hari Talyangar paleomagnetics is itself equivocal and it is possible that the whole of their section lies only in the interval between the top of Chron 9 and the lower part of Chron 7. This alternative interpretation would make all the fossils at Hari Talyangar older than 7.2 MY and the *Sivapithecus* specimens closer to 8 MY. Such a correlation would also be more consistent with Pilgrim's analysis of the fauna.

The type and only specimen of *Gigantopithecus* '*bilaspurensis*' is thought to have come from a horizon 6.3 MY old (Johnson *et al.*, 1983). Fossiliferous rocks of this age are rare throughout the Siwaliks and therefore it is uncertain what the limits of its stratigraphic range are. It seems unlikely, however, that the lower boundary could be much older than about 6.5 MY because of the large number of localities older than 6.5 MY at Hari Talyangar and in the Potwar. If the disjunction between the ranges of *Sivapithecus* and *Gigantopithecus* is real, then *Gigantopithecus* must have been a later immigrant into the region.

As shown on Fig. 1 most of the Siwalik *Sivapithecus* sample comes from three restricted horizons: one at Hari Talyangar between 7.6 and 7.2 MY; one at 8.1 MY in the Khaur region; and one near Chinji at 11.8 MY. This observation is based on recent collections (Table 1), but from our own collecting experience I suspect that the older collections of hominoids in the Geological Survey of India Museum and the British Museum (Natural History) were also largely from the same three horizons. It is important to note, however, that *Sivapithecus* has been found at intermediate levels, which establishes the continuity of the taxon throughout the whole of its stratigraphic range.

If the base of the stratigraphic range of *Sivapithecus* is less than 13 MY, then there are implications that are of some interest. One is that large hominoids must have entered southern Asia separately from, and considerably later than, the small hominoids (known to be present at 16.1 MY). Monkeys also appear to have reached southern Asia separately and, if the dates are to be trusted, after all large hominoids except *Gigantopithecus* had become locally extinct. In Africa, monkeys and large *Sivapithecus*-like hominoids appear by about 18 MY. This is shortly before, or at the same time as, small hominoids dispersed into southern Asia, but long before either monkeys or large hominoids did. It is curious that the barriers between Africa and Asia could so effectively segregate the three groups but allow tragulids, bovids, and similar forms to pass.

On the Potwar Plateau there is a major but diffuse change in the fauna between 7.5 and 7.0 MY (Barry *et al.*, 1982) which sees the extinction of several archaic families, as well as the appearance of larger, higher-crowned bovids and the first true sabertooths and modern hyaenas in southern Asia. This is probably related to climatic change and it is undoubtedly not a coincidence that the large hominoids also became extinct then. Further, just as their local extinction can be linked to climatic events, the appearance of large hominoids sometime between 12 and 13 MY might also be connected to global tectonic or climatic events.

Research in the Siwaliks continues and over the next 10 years I foresee additional progress on topics related to dating the hominoids. A particularly critical priority is the dating and reanalysis of faunas from the older sequences at Dera Bugti and the Lower Manchars. It is now known that there are no primates in the former, while the lowest level of the Manchars does have a small species which may be an ape (Raza *et al.*, 1984). This absence corresponds to a marked difference in the faunas and it may be that the initial dispersal of small hominoids into Asia is documented by the Lower Manchar occurrence.

Finally, a second interesting problem is the persistence of *Sivapithecus* through a major faunal turnover coincident with the appearance of hipparionines in the Siwaliks at 9.5 MY. This faunal change occurs in a time interval that is only moderately well sampled, but it appears to have been an abrupt and nearly complete replacement of the older fauna's dominant suids and ruminants by immigrant species of equids, suids, giraffes, and probably bovids. The taxa involved were mostly herbivores, but they belonged to a wide range of adaptive types and certain closely related forms, such as the tragulids and rhinos, seem to have been unaffected other than by changes in species. In addition a number of archaic types, such as creodonts, chalicotheres, and adapid primates also survived. The oldest true lorisids and herpestines in Asia appeared at this time (Jacobs, 1981; Barry, 1983); both are presumably immigrant African lineages.

Acknowledgments

The efforts of many individuals have provided the basic data for this survey, but those of A. K. Behrensmeyer, S. M. Raza, M. Monghan, M. Pickford, and L. Tauxe need particular notice. I am also indebted to N. Johnson and D. Pilbeam, as well as J. Kelley who has discussed hominoid systematics with me. Support was provided by NSF and Smithsonian Foreign Currency Program grants (BNS 8140818 and FC 30942300).

References

Azzaroli, A. & Napoleone, G. (1982) Magnetostratigraphic investigation of the Upper Siwaliks near Pinjor, India. *Riv. Ital. Paleontol.*, **87**, 739–62

Badgley, C., Kelley, J., Pilbeam, D. & Ward, S. (1984) The paleobiology of south Asian Miocene hominoids. In *The People of South Asia*, ed. J. Lucacs, pp. 3–27. New York: Plenum Press

Barry, J. C. (1983) *Herpestes* (Viverridae, Carnivora) from the Miocene of Pakistan. *J. Paleontol.*, **57**, 150–6

Barry, J. C., Behrensmeyer, A. K., Monaghan, M. (1980) A geologic and biostratigraphic framework for Miocene sediments near Khaur Village, northern Pakistan. *Postilla*, **183**, 1–19

Barry, J. C., Lindsay, E. H. & Jacobs, L. L. (1982) A biostratigraphic zonation of the Middle and Upper Siwaliks of the Potwar Plateau of northern Pakistan. *Palaeogeogr. Palaeoclimatol. Palaeoecol.*, **37**, 95–130

Behrensmeyer, A. K. (1982) Time resolution in fluvial vertebrate assemblages. *Paleobiol.*, **8**, 211–27

Behrensmeyer, A. K. & Tauxe, L. (1982) Isochronous fluvial systems in Miocene deposits of northern Pakistan. *Sedimentol.*, **29**, 331–52

Bernor, R. L. (1983) Geochronology and zoogeographic relationships of Miocene Hominoidea. In *New Interpretations of Ape and Human Ancestry*, ed. R. L. Ciochan & R. S. Corruccini, pp. 21–64. New York: Plenum Press

Brunet, M. & Heintz, E. (1983) Interpretation paleoécologique et relations biogéographiques de la faune de vertébrés du Miocene Supérieur d'Injana, Irak. *Palaeogeogr. Palaeoclimatol. Palaeoecol.*, **44**, 283–93

Ciochon, R. L. (1983) Hominoid cladistics and the ancestry of modern apes and humans: a summary statement. In *New Interpretations of Ape and Human Ancestry*, ed. R. L. Ciochon & R. S. Corruccini, pp. 781–843. New York: Plenum Press

Dutta, A. K., Basu, P. K. & Sastry, M. V. A. (1976) On the new finds of hominoids and additional finds of pongids from the Siwaliks of Ramnager area, Udhampur District, J. and K. State. *Ind. J. Earth Sci.*, **3**, 234–5

Falconer, H. & Cautley, P. T. (1837) On additional fossil species of the Order Quadrumana from the Sewalik Hills. *J. Asiatic Soc. Bengal*, **6**, 354–60

Gupta, S. S., Verma, B. C. & Tewari, A. P. (1982) New fossil hominoid material from the Siwaliks of Kangra District, Himachal Pradesh. *J. Palaeontol. Soc. India*, **27**, 111–15

Hay, W. W. (1972) Probabilistic stratigraphy. *Ecologae Geol. Helv.*, **65**, 255–66

Jacobs, L. L. (1981) Miocene lorisid primates from the Pakistan Siwaliks. *Nature*, **289**, 585–7

Johnson, G. D., Opdyke, N. D., Tandon, S. K. & Nanda, A. C. (1983) The magnetic polarity stratigraphy of the Siwalik Group at Haritalyangar (India) and a new last appearance datum for *Ramapithecus* and *Sivapithecus* in Asia. *Palaeogeogr. Palaeoclimatol. Palaeoecol.*, **44**, 223–49

Johnson, G. D., Zeitler, P., Naeser, C. W., Johnson, N. M., Summers, D. M., Frost, C. D., Opdyke, N. D. & Tahirkheli, R. A. K. (1982) The occurrence and fission-track ages of Late Neogene and Quaternary volcanic sediments, Siwalik Group, northern Pakistan. *Palaeogeogr. Palaeoclimatol. Palaeoecol.*, **37**, 63–93

Johnson, N. M., Opdyke, N. D., Johnson, G. D., Lindsay, E. H. & Tahirkheli, R. A. K. (1982) Magnetic polarity stratigraphy and ages of Siwalik Group rocks of the Potwar Plateau, Pakistan. *Palaeogeogr. Palaeoclimatol. Palaeoecol.*, **37**, 17–42

Johnson, N. M., Stix, J., Tauxe, L., Cerveny, P. F. & Tahirkheli, R. A. K. (1985) Paleomagnetic chronology, fluvial processes and tectonic implications of the Siwalik deposits near Chinji Village, Pakistan. *J. Geol.*, **93**, 27–40

Keller, H. M., Tahirkheli, R. A. K., Mirza, M. A., Johnson, G. D., Johnson, N. M. & Opdyke, N. D. (1977) Magnetic polarity stratigraphy of the Upper Siwalik deposits, Pabbi Hills, Pakistan. *Earth Planet. Sci. Lett.*, **36**, 187–201

Mankinen, E. A. & Dalrymple, G. B. (1979) Revised geomagnetic polarity time scale for the interval 0–5 m.y.B.P. *J. Geophys. Res.*, **84**, 615–26

Munthe, J., Dongol, B., Hutchison, J. H., Kean, W. F., Munthe, K. & West, R. M. (1983) New fossil discoveries from the Miocene of Nepal include a hominoid. *Nature*, **303**, 331–3

Ness, G., Levi, S. & Couch, R. (1980) Marine magnetic anomaly timescales for the Cenozoic and Late Cretaceous: a precis, critique, and synthesis. *Rev. Geophys. Space Phys.*, **18**, 753–70

Opdyke, N. D., Lindsay, E., Johnson, G. D., Johnson, N., Tahirkheli, R. A. K. & Mirza, M. A. (1979) Magnetic polarity stratigraphy and vertebrate paleontology of the Upper Siwalik Subgroup of northern Pakistan. *Palaeogeogr. Palaeoclimatol. Palaeoecol.*, **27**, 1–34

Pilbeam, D. R., Behrensmeyer, A. K., Barry, J. C. & Shah, S. M. I. (1979) Miocene sediments and faunas of Pakistan. *Postilla*, **179**, 1–45

Pilbeam, D. R., Rose, M. D., Badgley, C. & Lipschutz, B. (1980) Miocene hominoids from Pakistan. *Postilla*, **181**, 1–94

Pilgrim, G. E. (1913) The correlation of the Siwaliks with mammal horizons of Europe. *Rec. Geol. Surv. India*, **43**, 264–326

Raza, S. M., Barry, J. C., Meyer, G. E. & Martin, L. (1984) Preliminary report on the geology and vertebrate fauna of the Miocene Manchar Formation, Sind, Pakistan. *J. Vertebrate Paleontol.*, **4**, 584–99

Sahni, A., Kumar, V. & Srivastava, V. C. (1974) *Dryopithecus* (Subgenus: *Sivapithecus*) and associated vertebrates from the Lower Siwaliks of Uttar Pradesh. *Bull. Ind. Geol. Assoc.*, **7**, 54

Tauxe, L. & Opdyke, N. D. (1982) A time framework based on magnetostratigraphy for the Siwalik sediments of the Khaur area, northern Pakistan. *Palaeogeogr. Palaeoclimatol. Palaeoecol.*, **37**, 43–61

Yokoyama, T. (1981) Palaeomagnetic study of Tatrot and Pinjor Formations, Upper Siwaliks, east of Chandigarh, north-west India. *Neogene Quaternary Boundary Field Conference, India, 1979. Proceedings*, 217–20

I.9

Succession and dating of the late Miocene primates of Macedonia

L. DE BONIS, G. BOUVRAIN, G. KOUFOS AND
J. MELENTIS

Introduction

The primates from the late Miocene of Macedonia (Greece) belong to two superfamilies of cercopithecoids and hominoids. The former have been known in Greece since the last century and they belong to the genus *Mesopithecus*. This genus was initially described from specimens coming from the well known locality of Pikermi (Southern Greece). It was later discovered in Macedonia (Arambourg & Piveteau, 1929). Recent field work has yielded several specimens which are cited for the first time in this paper. The hominoids belong to the genus *Ouranopithecus*. This genus is known from a single locality, the 'Ravin de la Pluie', which nonetheless has yielded significant material consisting of several jaws and isolated teeth. Another hominoid primate of the late Miocene deposits of Greece has been described under the name *Graecopithecus*. It comes from the site of Tour la Reine (Pyrgos) and it is known only from the type-specimen. This is a mandibular fragment bearing a very worn M_2, the root of M_1 and a piece of P_3. Although the area of Athens is not within the geographical framework of this study, it seems useful to us to know the geological age of this specimen as it is comparable to the Macedonian *Ouranopithecus* (de Bonis & Melentis, 1984).

Graecopithecus

The site of Tour la Reine was discovered by accident during the construction of a swimming pool and its exploitation seems no longer possible. The fauna discovered along with the remains of the primate thus constitutes the only element for dating. It consists of the following species: *Mastodon pentelici, ?Dicerorhinus orientalis, Hipparion mediterraneum*, bovids undet., *Tragocerus amaltheus, Gazella gaudryi, Helladotherium duvernoyi* and *Giraffa attica*.

This fauna would seem to correspond with that of Pikermi and the age of the site can be taken as Turolian. According to von Koenigswald (1972), the age would not exceed 8.5 million years (m.y.) We were unable to examine the fossils directly but one might make certain reservations in the light of the material used and on the stratigraphic distribution of the species. *Choerolophodon* (='*Mastodon'*) appeared in Europe during the Vallesian and continues throughout all the late Miocene, so it cannot be representative of a particular stage in the late Miocene. The rhinocerotid *D. orientalis*, doubtfully identified on the basis of an ankle bone, is not strong evidence for determining the age of a site. *H. mediterraneum* may be more representative; however, the identification of a species of *Hipparion* is a difficult exercise and the specialists of this group sometimes arrive at quite different results. According to von Koenigswald (1972) the presence of two species of *Hipparion* of different size is sufficient to indicate a later period than that of Pikermi. This could also apply to Tour la Reine, despite the fact that the smaller *Hipparion* does not figure on the list of the fauna. In fact, species of *Hipparion* of different sizes are met during all the late Miocene. The specimens of Tour la Reine almost certainly require a closer examination. The bovid *'Tragocerus' amaltheus* is identified from a fragment of mandible bearing M_1 to M_3. Given the uniformity of the molars of the bovids, this piece would seem to us to be completely insufficient for making an identification. *Gazella gaudryi*, on the list of the fauna, is identified without reference to the elements allowing the recognition of this species; an assessment of the identification is thus impossible. The giraffids are also not very representative. *Helladotherium*, frequent in the Turolian, has also been indicated in Vallesian sites of Turkey and Southern Russia. This is also the case for *Bohlinia* (='*Giraffa'*) *attica*.

In conclusion, lacking a more detailed analysis, it is not possible to determine accurately the stratigraphic period of *Graecopithecus freyburgi*. One can be certain that it is within the late Miocene without being more exact. One can therefore fix the age of this primate as being between 12 and 5.5 m.y.

Ouranopithecus
This primate can be distinguished from the different species of *Sivapithecus* by its dental morphology, in particualr the area of the premolars, and by its dental proportions. The abundant material coming from the 'Ravin de la Pluie' site gives us a good idea of the variation of this species. *Ouranopithecus* is accompanied by a fauna of

mammals of about 20 species: *Adcrocuta eximia leptorhyncha, Plioviver-rops orbignyi, Choerolophodon pentelicus, Hipparion primigenium, H. macedonicum,* rhinocerotid uniden., *Progonomys cathalai,* cf. *Palerinaceus* sp., *Mesembriacerus melentisi, Prostrepsiceros vallesiensis, Samotragus* n. sp., bovid uniden. (large size), *Decennatherium pachecoi, Palaeotragus coelophrys, P.* cf. *rouennii, Bohlinia attica,* and *Ouranopithecus macedoniensis.*

Certain species, *D. pachecoi* and *Progonomys cathalai,* are character-istic of the Vallesian. *A.e. leptorhyncha* is more primitive than the typical form of *Adcrocuta* of Pikermi (de Bonis & Koufos, 1981). *Mesembriacerus* is the most primitive ovibovine known, differing from the genera obtained from the Turolian of China and Samos. Finally, *Samotragus* and *Prostrepsiceros* attain smaller dimensions than those of the species of the Turolian.

If we consider that the appearances of *Progonomys cathalai* is more or less the same for the whole of Europe, one notices its absence in some Vallesian sites which are nonetheless rich in rodents. Such is the case, for example, for Rudabanya in Hungary and for Nombrevilla and perhaps for Can Llobateres in Spain. One may consider that they constitute the earliest period of the Vallesian, between 12 and 11 m.y. ago. The 'Ravin de la Pluie', where *P. cathalai* is present despite the remarkable paucity of rodents in the fauna, would therefore be more recent and might be situated between 11 and 9 m.y. ago.

If we compare these data with those of the Indian sub-continent (Barry, Behrensmeyer & Monaghan, 1980; Chapter I.8, this volume), one notices that *Ouranopithecus* is contemporaneous with certain fossils of the Siwaliks. Indeed in the Khaur area the hominoid primates collected range from about 9.5 to 7.5 m.y. old with the bulk of the discoveries situated between 9 and 8 m.y. old. Furthermore, several specimens have been unearthed from earlier periods (Raza, *et al.,* 1983) near the village of Chinji on the southern part of the Soan synclinorium. The Greek primate corresponds therefore to the earliest forms of the *Sivapithecus* group or ramamorphs (thick-enamelled primates) of the late Miocene.

The genus *Bodvapithecus* also belongs to the ramamorphs and it comes from the Hungarian site of Rudabanya. This site contains a fauna of the early Vallesian: *Hipparion* is found with a fauna, particu-larly of rodents, which is reminiscent of the middle Miocene and which, despite its richness, has never yielded the murid *Progonomys.* Therefore, it would seem to be older than *Ouranopithecus* and dating perhaps from 12 to 11 m.y. ago.

In China, the site of Lufeng (Yunnan) has also yielded ramamorphs, identified as *Sivapithecus* and *Ramapithecus*. The layers of Lufeng might be an equivalent of the early Turolian, between 9 and 8 m.y. old.

Other finds are either too fragmented to yield valuable interpretation or they are without good biostratigraphic evidence to allow for dating or useful comparisons.

Mesopithecus

The Macedonian sites with *Mesopithecus* can be separated into two groups. The first group consists of those sites near the village of Vathylakkos and that of the 'Ravin des Zouaves No: 5' (RZO) near Nea Mesimbria. It is this latter site which has yielded the new remains of *Mesopithecus*. All these sites are located in sandstones, marls, sands or clays of more or less ochre-greyish colour. These layers cover the reddish layers containing the Vallesian fauna. The second group is located stratigraphically above the first group. It is made up of sediments of a similar type but lighter in colour. These sediments extend to the limestone area of Agriossikia on the right bank of the Axios river. Three sites are grouped around the little village of Ditiko.

Ravin des Zouaves No: 5

This site has yielded the following mammalian fauna: *Adcrocuta eximia*, hyaenid uniden., *Ictitherium robustum, Zygolophodon turicensis, Choerolophodon pentelici, Hipparion primigenium, H. concudense, Hipparion* sp. (small size), *Dicerorhinus orientalis, Mesopithecus pentelicus, Microstonyx major, Potamochoerus hyotherioides, Helladotherim duvernoyi, Prostrepsiceros rotundicornis, P. zitteli, Nisidorcas planicornis, 'Miotragocerus' rugosifrons, Palaeoreas zouavei, Gazella* sp., and *?Valerymys* sp.

One finds in this list a number of species also found in the famous site of Pikermi. However some other species seem to indicate a difference in time with regard to the Attica site. According to G. Koufos (unpublished), the *Hipparion* species would correspond to zone 2 and zone 3 (Sen, Sondaar & Staesche, 1978), that is the end of the Vallesian and the beginning of the Turolian, a little earlier than the Pikermi site. *Prostrepsiceros rotundicornis* is smaller than its homologue at Pikermi, which would indicate an earlier period. *Nisidorcas planicornis* is widespread from Yugoslavian Macedonia to the Indian sub continent but is absent in Pikermi. Other sites containing this antelope are also dated as being at the end of the Vallesian and at the beginning of the Turolian. This, for example, is the case for Kayadibi in Asia

Minor. One can thus estimate the age of the Ravin des Zouaves No: 5 as being between 8 and 9 m.y.

Ditiko

The three sites of Ditiko (DTK, DIT and DKO) incorporate a fauna which is different from that of the group of sites of Vathylakkos and Nea Mesembria. From the stratigraphic point of view, they are located in the layers that terminate the sedimentary range of the late Miocene of the lower valley of the Axios river. The following species can be noted:

	DTK	DIT	DKO
Adcrocuta eximia	+		
Protictitherium crassum			+
Choerolophodon pentelicus	+	+	+
Dicerorhinus orientalis	+		
Hipparion mediterraneum	+		
H. gromovae	+		
H. matthewi	+	+	+
H. periafricanum	+		
Microstonyx major	+		
Bohlinia attica	+	+	
Palaeotragus rouennii		+	
Protragelaphus theodori	+		+
Palaeoreas lindermayeri	+	+	
'Graecoryx cf. *valenciennesi'*	+	+	+
Gazella sp.	+	+	+
Bovid uniden. (large size)	+	+	
Pliocervus pentelicus	+		
Dorcatherium puyhauberti		+	
Mesopithecus pentelicus	+	+	+
Hystrix sp.			+

Except for *Protictitherium crassum*, which constitutes an anachronism within this fauna, the fossils represent a late stage in the Turolian. The *Hipparion* species correspond to zone 4 (Sen *et al.*, 1978), that is to the late Turolian, while Pikermi is placed in zone 3. *Protragelaphus* is larger than the species found in Pikermi and it is more evolved with regard to the reduction of its premolars, by its longer face and the structure of the basioccipital. Similarly *Palaeoreas lindermayeri*, slightly larger than the typical form and with deeper supra-orbital pits, seems to be more recent.

The sites of Ditiko, younger than those of Pikermi, can be dated from the later part of the Turolian. Their age can be placed at between 7 and 5.5 m.y.

Conclusions

The two super-families of catarrhines succeed each other in time in the Macedonian ranges. *Ouranopithecus* relates to the Vallesian and *Mesopithecus* to the Turolian. With our present knowledge the site of 'Tour la Reine' (Pyrgos), which has furnished *Graecopithecus freybergi*, cannot be accurately dated.

One can surmise that the succession in Macedonia of two types of primates, hominoid and cercopithecoid, corresponds to a climatic change and to a modification of the paleoenvironment. Ever since the classic study of Gaudry, the fauna of Pikermi has been considered as a typical savannah fauna. The diversity of antelopes and giraffes, and the morphology of *Hipparion's* limb bones point to an open landscape, similar perhaps to some present-day areas of Africa. The skeleton of *Mesopithecus pentelicus* differs from that of recent colobines with regard to some morphological features, implying a less arboreal habitat and therefore adaptations to an open environment. '*M. pentelicus* was a colobine which had begun to converge toward a more terrestrial macaque-like way of life' (Szalay & Delson, 1979). In Western and Central Europe, the Vallesian generally represents a more forested environment. The fauna includes numerous cervids or suids and the sediments often point to a humid if not swampy environment. More or less lignitous sites are common, such as Montredon, Soblay and Rudabanya. With few exceptions, the primates are represented by the genus *Dryopithecus*. This is a forest-dwelling primate, the teeth of which are thinly enamelled. Sometimes it is found with a ramamorph, as in the case of the site at Rudabanya. Its replacement by an open-environment primate such as *Mesopithecus* during the Turolian seems to be completely logical. However this is not the case for the Vallesian of Greece. *Ouranopithecus* is found with a well characterized open-environment fauna as noted from species of giraffes, including *Bohlinia attica*, reminiscent of the genus *Giraffa*. The antelopes are very abundant, especially those with spiralled horns, *Samotragus* and *Prostrepsiceros*. In contrast to recent *Ovibos*, the limbs of which are short, the ovibovine *Mesembriacerus* had limb bones whose proportions recall those of modern antelopes and which show a marked cursorial adaptation. Although the majority of specific taxa are different from those of the Turolian period, the fauna indicates an open environment with many grasslands which should not differ greatly from those indicated by the fauna of Pikermi. The transition from Vallesian to Turolian ought to have occurred without any hiatus. The climate and environment of the Turolian already existed in Greece during the preceding period. But in this case it is difficult to understand the extinction of the large ramamorph primates, which seem to have been well adapted to this environment, and their replacement by the cercopithecoids. It is nonetheless possible that environmental changes such as a slight cooling, for example, might have been sufficient to have impeded their development.

References

Arambourg, C. & Piveteau, J. (1929) Les Vertébrés du Pontien de Salonique. *Ann. Paleontol., Paris*, **18**, 59–138

Barry, J., Behrensmeyer, A. K. & Monaghan, M. (1980) A geologic and biostratigraphic framework for Miocene sediments near Khaur village, northern Pakistan. *Postilla*, **183**, 1–19

Bouvrain, G. (1978) *Protragelaphus theodori* n. sp. (Mammalia, Artiodactyla, Bovidae) du Miocène de Macédoine (Grèce). *Géol. Médit.*, **5**(2), 229–36

Bouvrain, G. (1979) Un nouveau bovidé de la fin du Miocène. *Bull. Soc. Géol. France*, **7**, 507–11

Bouvrain, G. (1980) Le genre *Palaeoreas* (Mammalia, Artiodactyla, Bovidae), systématique et extension géographique. *Paläontol. Z.*, **54**, 55–68

Bouvrain, G. (1982) Révision du genre *Prostrepsiceros* Major 1891 (Mammalia, Bovidae). *Paläontol. Z.*, **56**, 113–24

de Bonis, L. & Koufos, G. (1981) A new Hyaenid (Carnivora, Mammalia) in the Vallesian (Late Miocene) of northern Greece. *Sci. Annals, Fac. Phys. Math. Univ. Thessaloniki*, **21**, 79–94

de Bonis, L. & Melentis, J. (1977) Les Primates hominoïdes du Vallésien de Macédoine (Grèce). Etude de la mâchoire inférieure. *Géobios*, **10**(6), 849–85

de Bonis, L. & Melentis, J. (1978) Les Primates hominoïdes du Vallésien de Macédoine (Grèce). Etude de la mâchoire supérieure. *Ann. Paleontol. (Vert.)*, **64**(2), 177–94

de Bonis, L. & Melentis, J. (1984) Position phylétique du genre *Ouranopithecus*. *Mem. von Koenigswald, Cour. Forsch. Inst. Senckenberg*, **69**, 13–23

Gaudry, A. (1862–1867) *Animaux Fossiles et Géologie de l'Attique*. Paris: Savy

Geraads, D. (1978) Les Paleotraginae (Giraffidae, Mammalia) du Miocène supérieur de la région de Thessalonique (Grèce). *Geol. Médit.*, **5**, 269–76

Geraads, D. (1979) Les Giraffinae (Artiodactyla, Mammalia) du Miocène supérieur de la région de Thessalonique (Grèce). *Bull. Mus. Natl Hist. Nat., Paris*, **4**, 377–89

Koenigswald, G. H. R. von (1972) Ein Unterkiefer eines fossilen Hominoiden aus dem unter Pliocän Griechenlands. *Proc. K. Ned. Akad. Wet.*, **75**(5), 385–94

Koufos, G. (1980) [Palaeontological and stratigraphical study of the continental Neogene sediments of the Axios valley.] Thesis, University of Thessalonika. (In Greek)

Koufos, G. (1984) A new *Hipparion* (Mammalia, Perissodactyla) from the Vallesian (Late Miocene) of Greece. *Paläont. Z.*, **58**, 307–17

Melentis, J. (1967) Die Pikermi fauna von *Halmyropotamus* (Euböa, Griechenland). 1 – Ondontologie und Kraniologie. *Ann. Géol. Pays Hell.*, **19**, 283–411

Raza, S. M., Barry, J. C., Pilbeam, D., Rose, M. D., Ibrahim, S. M. & Ward, S. (1983) New hominoid primates from the Middle Miocene Chinji Formation, Potwar Plateau, Pakistan. *Nature*, **306**(5938), 52–4

Sen, S., Sondaar, P. Y. & Staesche, V. (1978) The biostratigraphical applications of the genus *Hipparion* with special references to the Turkish representatives. *Proc. K. Ned. Akad. Wet.*, *B*, **81**(3), 370–85

Szalay, F. & Delson, E. (1979) *Evolutionary History of the Primates.* New York: Academic Press

I.10

Age of the early Javanese hominids: a review

S. MATSU'URA

Introduction

The island of Java has yielded many fossil remains of early Asian hominids. For decades the mammalian faunas have been believed to be decisive for the dating of the Plio–Pleistocene strata in Java. However recent studies (Sartono *et al.*, 1981; De Vos *et al.*, 1982; Bartstra, 1983; Aimi & Aziz, in press; Braches & Shutler, in press) have called for reconsideration of the validity of the Javanese faunal sequence, and at least have shown that the distinction of the fossil faunas, e.g. Jetis fauna and Trinil fauna, is 'not so clear as has been suggested' (Aimi & Aziz, in press) in the literature. Thus, time correlations of strata according to the 'established' Javanese vertebrate stratigraphy would best be dismissed at present.

Of late, new data have become available concerning the stratigraphy and age of the human fossil bearing formations. Still, hominid remains of Java have bad histories of collection; this has been a serious obstacle to a sensible appreciation of the antiquity of these specimens. None of the fossil finds of the early hominids from Java was obtained *in situ* through controlled excavations, and in most cases the adequate context for provenance or even the spot of the find is unknown. For this reason, locating the original source horizons of hominid fossils by some geochemical approach is fundamental to the construction of their chronology, relative or absolute. Such detective work was done, using the fluorine dating technique, by Matsu'ura (1982) on Sangiran specimens, for which a chronological framework has been developed.

This communication is a note on the age estimates and their implications for the early Javanese hominids, on the basis of an examination and rating of both past and new data.

Sangiran

The main part of the late Cenozoic rock group exposed in the Sangiran anticline area is subdivided into the Kalibeng, Pucangan, Kabuh and Notopuro formations, in ascending order. The stratigraphy and geological structure of this area have been investigated in detail by Itihara *et al.*, (in press) under the Indonesia–Japan Joint Research Project CTA-41.

One of the most important findings so far available involving the age of the fossil-bearing formations of Sangiran is the provenance of Javan tektites which have been well dated at 0.7 million years (Myr) (e.g. Isaac, 1972; Suzuki *et al.*, in press). The CTA-41 research team collected two tektite specimens *in situ* from two sites separated by about 6 km. The stratigraphic positions are in agreement with each other, between the Upper and the Middle Tuff of the Kabuh formation (see Matsu'ura, 1982; Itihara, personal communication). This horizon should correlate to the Brunhes/Matuyama boundary of the worldwide geomagnetostratigraphy. The palaeomagnetic data given by Shimizu *et al.*(in press) are compatible with the above.

Furthermore, scrutiny of reported dating results of the sediments in Sangiran (Matsu'ura, 1982) suggests the following age estimates: Pucangan/Kalibeng boundary = 2 Myr; Kabuh/Pucangan boundary = 1 Myr; uppermost part of Kabuh = 0.5–0.6 Myr.

Discoveries of hominid fossils in Java, especially those after World War II, have centred on the Sangiran area. The Sangiran remains of early man were found, however, by chance by the local inhabitants, and the source horizons of the fossil specimens are difficult to locate, as mentioned before. To solve the allocation problems, Matsu'ura (1982) applied the fluorine dating method to seven key hominid specimens.

Fig. 1. Localities of the early Javanese hominids (small dots).

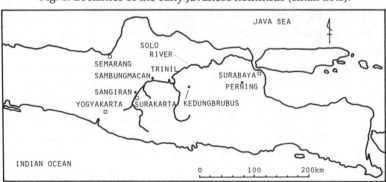

Fluoride ions, taken up by buried bone (or tooth) from surrounding soils and groundwater, accumulate over a period of time at the cost of hydroxyl ions in apatite crystals, and consequently the fluorine content of fossil bone increases with geological time. The rate of fluorine accumulation is, however, dependent on the burial environment so that it is not possible to determine the absolute age of a bone merely from its fluorine measurement. Still, the fluorine analysis provides relative dating information on bone remains from similar sedimentary matrices, or an 'identification' for the bone sources. When a human skeletal element happens to have been washed out of a deposit, a comparison of its fluorine content with that of a series of animal bones from known horizons at the same or neighbouring sites allows an inference of the original stratigraphic provenance of the specimen in question to be made, provided the fluorine content shows significant differences between horizons. It may be remarked here that the cancellous regions of a bone are liable to introduction of adventitious mineral grains or soil particles. This contamination should be compensated for through phosphate determination, which gives a convenient measure of the apatite present in the bone sample. For a more detailed account of this dating method the reader is referred to Oakley (1980) and Matsu'ura (1982).

A series of comparative standard data for the fluorine dating of the Sangiran hominids was obtained (Matsu'ura, 1982) by analysing a large number of vertebrate bones collected *in situ* from various known horizons in this area during excavations by the CTA-41 project (1977– 79). The provenance of Sangiran hominids is suggested (or, the reported and alleged associations of hominid specimens with particular beds are checked) by the fluorine approach as follows:

> Sangiran 3 (*Pithecanthropus* III), 12 (*Pithecanthropus* VII) and 17 (*Pithecanthropus* VIII) derive from an upper horizon of the lower part of the Kabuh formation, having an age of around 0.8 Myr.

> Sangiran lb (*Pithecanthropus* B), 2 (*Pithecanthropus* II), 4 (*Pithecanthropus* IV) and 6 (holotype of *Meganthropus palaeojavanicus*) come probably from Grenzbank (that is, the basal layer of the Kabuh) or, in the case of Sangiran lb and 4, possibly from the uppermost part of the Pucangan formation; all assignable to a period of c. 1.0–1.1 Myr.

> Sangiran 5 (holotype of *Pithecanthropus dubius*) derives from Grenzbank or the upper part of the Pucangan formation, being c. 1.0–1.3 Myr old.

The age span inferred for these hominids is found to be not as long as hitherto guessed.

Sambungmacan

An adult calotte of a fossil hominid was encountered near Sambungmacan in 1973 in the course of canal-digging operations. The fluviatile sediments in which the specimen was recovered were assigned to the lower part of the Kabuh formation (e.g. Indonesia–Japan Research Cooperation Programme – CTA-41, 1979; Kumai, personal communication). Another view, by Sartono (1979) and Bartstra (1982a), is that the parent-sediments are the Solo river terrace fills which are younger than the Kabuh beds. In either case, the hominid is less than 1 Myr old.

Trinil

Dubois' Layer D (see Dubois, 1896) that contained Trinil 2 (*Pithecanthropus* Skull I) and 3 (Femur I) has been referred to a lower part of the Kabuh formation by Itihara *et al.* (Indonesia–Japan Research Cooperation Programme – CTA-41, 1979).

Recently there has again arisen some doubt about the contemporaneity of the Trinil femora with the Trinil calotte (Day & Molleson, 1973; Kennedy, 1983). The association of the primitive skullcap and the evolved thighbones has been questioned since the first reports. Later Bergman & Karsten (1952) supported the alleged synchronism of the human remains through fluorine analysis of bones; this reinforcement has been widely accepted. However, the samples analysed in that study, I believe, may have suffered from contamination by varying amounts of extraneous matter such as silt, infiltrated minerals and preservative (glue) (see Day & Molleson, 1973). The conclusion of Bergman & Karsten (1952) may also have suffered from the lack of adequate comparative data. Geochemical reconsideration is currently under way. In this connection. Bartstra (1982b, 1983) has indicated that the Dubois collection of vertebrate remains from Trinil could be a mixture of fossils from the Kabuh formation and from the upper terrace sediments, though this possibility is under discussion (Sondaar, De Vos & Leinders, 1983).

Kedungbrubus

A juvenile mandible designated as *Pithecanthropus* A was found in 1890 by E. Dubois at Kedungbrubus. No detailed reports of the stratigraphic context involved are available. It is generally supposed that the specimen has its origin in the Kabuh formation (e.g. Oakley, Campbell & Molleson, 1975). Yet the stratigraphic positioning of the vertebrate fossils collected by Dubois at this locality is in dispute (Bartstra, 1983; Hooijer, 1983; Sondaar *et al.*, 1983).

Perning

Perning, near Mojokerto, is the site of the surface find of the *Homo modjokertensis* infant skull (Perning 1). A pumice tuff sample collected around the site of discovery has a K–Ar date of 1.9 ± 0.4 Myr (Jacob & Curtis, 1971); this has been a supporting factor of the supposed occurrence of Javanese hominids in the time comparable to that of *Australopithecus* or early *Homo* in Africa. This date with a large error, however, is of poor quality due to the very high atmospheric argon content (Curtis, 1981). Additionally, the provenance of the tuff sample is unreliably reported and thus there is doubt about its content. For example, the following localities are mentioned:

1. underlying the site of the 1952 specimen of *Meganthropus* (Jacob & Curtis, 1971) (the *Meganthropus* specimen was found in the Sangiran area, but they reported it in error as deriving from near Mojokerto);
2. a few metres below the *modjokertensis* site at Perning (Jacob, 1972);
3. some 50 m below the *modjokertensis* infant site (Curtis, 1981);
4. approximately 400 m below the Notopuro formation (Curtis in Pope, 1983).

This date has little or no significance for the chronology of any of the Javanese hominids.

Lately Sartono *et al.* (1981) and Pope (1983) have also commented that the assignment of 1.9 Myr to Perning 1 is impeded by the lack of trustworthy sampling reports. Pope (1983) adds that Perning 1 cannot be attributed to an age over 1 Myr.

Because of the differences in rock facies and the distance, it is difficult to make a good geological correlation of the Perning site with the fairly well-dated Sangiran sequence. Thus we need absolute dating of the primary minerals from tuffs of known horizon at the site, as well as relative dating of the hominid find by geochemical methods.

Remarks

A multiplicity of specific names or nomenclature has been assigned to the fossil hominid specimens from Java (see Matsu'ura, 1982) on the basis of unclear morphological and/or chronological reasons; this has caused confusion and prolific complications. There seem to be no reasonable doubts that all of the early Javanese hominids including *Meganthropus* represent a single species, *Homo erectus* (Lovejoy, 1970; Le Gros Clark, 1978; Pope, 1983).

Here I suggest a date of c. 1.0–1.1 Myr or possibly c. 1.3 Myr for the earliest known hominid remains of Java. Pope (1983) independently comes to similar conclusions, and further implies that the fossil hominid material found so far in Asia, including China, should be assigned an age less than 1 Myr. As Shutler & Braches (in press) also think, the probability must now be admitted that *Homo erectus* first appeared in East Africa, which has provided fossils from this taxon dated as early as 1.6 Myr ago.

Acknowledgements

I wish to express my thanks to Dr M. Pickford of the National Museums of Kenya for suggesting this contribution and for his interest. I also thank Miss A. Nakatsuka for manuscript preparation.

References

Aimi, M. & Aziz, F. (in press) Vertebrate fossils from the Sangiran dome, Mojokerto, Trinil and Sambungmacan areas. In *Special Publication of the Geological Research and Development Centre*, No. 4, ed. N. Watanabe & D. Kadar. Indonesia: GRDC

Bergman, R. A. M. & Karsten, P. (1952) The fluorine content of *Pithecanthropus* and of other specimens from the Trinil fauna. *Proc. K. Ned. Akad. Wet., Ser. B.*, **55**, 150–2

Bartstra, G.-J. (1982a) *Homo erectus erectus:* the search for his artifacts. *Curr. Anthropol.*, **23**, 318–20

Bartstra, G.-J. (1982b) The river-laid strata near Trinil, site of *Homo erectus erectus*, Java, Indonesia. In *Modern Quaternary Research in Southeast Asia*, vol. 7, ed. G.-J. Bartstra & W. A. Casparie, pp. 97–130. Rotterdam: A. A. Balkema

Bartstra, G.-J. (1983) Comment I: The vertebrate-bearing deposits of Kedungbrubus and Trinil, Java, Indonesia. *Geol. Mijnb.*, **62**, 329–36, 342–3

Braches, F. & Shutler, R., Jr (in press) Von Koenigswald's Cijulang fauna reconsidered. *Proc. 6th Int. Symp. on Asian Studies*, 1984, Hong Kong.

Curtis, G. H. (1981) Establishing a relevant time scale in anthropological and archaeological research. *Phil. Trans. R. Soc. B*, **292**, 7–20

Day, M. H. & Molleson, T. I. (1973) The Trinil femora. In *Human Evolution, Symp. S.S.H.B.* **11**, ed. M. H. Day, pp. 127–54. London: Taylor & Francis Ltd.

De Vos, J., Sartono, S., Hardja-Sasmita, S. & Sondaar, P. Y. (1982) The fauna from Trinil, type locality of *Homo erectus*; a reinterpretation. *Geol. Mijnb.*, **61**, 207–11

Dubois, E. (1896) *Pithecanthropus erectus*, eine Stammform des Menschen. *Anat. Anz.*, **12**, 1–22

Hooijer, D. A. (1983) Comment II: Remarks upon the Dubois collection of fossil mammals from Trinil and Kedungbrubus in Java. *Geol. Mijnb.*, **62**, 337–8, 342–3

Indonesia–Japan Research Cooperation Programme – CTA-41 (1979) Progress report of the Indonesia–Japan joint research project on geology of human fossil bearing formations in Java (I). *Bull. Geol. Res. Devel. Centre (Indonesia)*, No. 1, 47–60

Isaac, G. Ll. (1972) Chronology and the tempo of cultural change during the Pleistocene. In *Calibration of Hominoid Evolution*, ed. W. W. Bishop & J. A. Miller, pp. 381–430. Edinburgh: Scottish Academic Press

Itihara, M. *et al.* (in press) Geology and stratigraphy of the Sangiran area. In *Special Publication of the Geological Research and Development Centre*, No. 4, ed. N. Watanabe & D. Kadar. Indonesia: GRDC

Jacob, T. (1972) The absolute data of the Djetis beds at Modjokerto. *Antiquity*, **46**, 148

Jacob, T. & Curtiss [sic], G. H. (1971) Preliminary potassium–argon dating of early man in Java. *Univ. Calif. Archaeol. Res. Facility Contrib.*, No. 12, 50

Kennedy, G. E. (1983) Some aspects of femoral morphology in *Homo erectus. J. Hum. Evol.*, **12**, 587–616

Le Gros Clark, W. E. (1978) *The Fossil Evidence for Human Evolution – an Introduction to the Study of Palaeoanthropology*, 3rd edn. Chicago: University of Chicago Press

Lovejoy, C. O. (1970) The taxonomic status of the 'Meganthropus' mandibular fragments from the Djetis beds of Java. *Man.*, N.S., **5**, 228–36

Matsu'ura, S. (1982) A chronological framing for the Sangiran hominids – Fundamental study by the fluorine dating method. *Bull. Natl Sci. Mus., Tokyo., Ser. D* (Anthropol.), **8**, 1–53

Oakley, K. P. (1980) Relative dating of the fossil hominids of Europe. *Bull. Br. Mus. Nat. Hist., Geol.*, **34**, 1–63

Oakley, K. P., Campbell, B. G. & Molleson, T. I. (1975) (eds) *Catalogue of Fossil Hominids, Part III*. London: British Museum (Natural History)

Pope, G. G. (1983) Evidence on the age of the Asian Hominidae. *Proc. Natl Acad. Sci. USA*, **80**, 4988–92

Sartono, S. (1979). The stratigraphy of the Sambungmacan site, Central Java. In *Modern Quaternary Research in Southeast Asia*, vol. 5, ed. G.-J. Bartstra & W. A. Casparie, pp. 83–8. Rotterdam: A. A. Balkema

Sartono, S., Semah, F., Astadiredja, K. A. S., Sukendarmono, M. & Djubiantono, T. (1981) The age of *Homo modjokertensis*. In *Modern Quaternary Research in Southeast Asia*, vol. 6, ed. G.-J. Bartstra & W. A. Casparie, pp. 91–101. Rotterdam: A. A. Balkema

Shimizu, Y., Mubroto, B., Siagian, H. & Untung, M. (in press) A paleomagnetic study in the Sangiran area. In *Special Publication of the Geological Research and Development Centre*, No. 4, ed. N. Watanabe & D. Kadar. Indonesia: GRDC

Shutler, R., Jr & Braches, F. (in press) The migration of the Pithecanthropines to Java. *Proc. 6th Int. Symp. on Asian Studies*, 1984, Hong Kong.

Sondaar, P. Y., De Vos, J. & Leinders, J. J. M. (1983) Reply: Facts and fiction around the fossil mammals of Java. *Geol. Mijnb.*, **62**, 339–43

Suzuki, M., Wikarno, Budisantoso, Saefudin, I. & Itihara, M. (in press) Fission track ages of pumice tuff, tuff layers and javites of hominid fossil bearing formations in Sangiran, Central Java. In *Special Publication of the Geological Research and Development Centre*, No. 4, ed. N. Watanabe & D. Kadar. Indonesia: GRDC

I.11

Geochronology of the Hominoidea: a summary

M. PICKFORD

Introduction

The timing of events in the hominoid fossil record is central to any detailed scenario concerning the evolution of higher primates. Whilst bio-molecular methods can provide a sense of relatedness among living primates, including in some cases a reasonably confident but partial view as to the sequence of events, it can tell us very little about when dichotomies occurred and almost nothing about extinct species. In order to arrive at estimates of the timing of events in hominoid evolution it is necessary to recognise the usefulness of the fossil record, albeit a record which currently contains numerous information gaps and other lacks which are the source of much debate.

This paper summarises the results of the contributions to this section on Dating the Fossil Primate Record. Between these papers, the period from the Eocene to the Pleistocene has been spanned, and many of the areas where hominoids are found have been discussed. The papers are by nature review articles that present the currently held ideas about the ages of hominoids from various parts of the world. While there are a few discrepancies between the papers, there is generally a remarkable agreement, and I shall attempt to provide a broad picture of hominoid distributions in time and space during the past 32 million years (m.y.).

Immediately noticeable are various gaps in the record (Fig. 1). The African record begins with primates which are barely catarrhine at the Fayum in Egypt (Fleagle et al., Chapter I.1). After this brief glimpse of early primate communities. There is a tremendously long and frustrating gap in excess of 10 m.y. from which nothing is known. This is the more frustrating because it was during this period, the entire Oligocene era, that the first major radiation of the catarrhines took place. When the fossil record improves abruptly at the beginning of the Miocene in Kenya (Pickford: Chapter I.2), the higher primates are represented by diverse and abundant taxa some of which, e.g. *Proconsul*, have already reached the status of hominoid, at least in derived characters of the post-cranial skeleton. In Eastern Africa the primate fossil record is more or less continuous from the lower Miocene to the present day but there is one major period (13–4 m.y. ago) when the record is very sparse, fewer than two dozen fossil hominoids having been collected from this 9 m.y. time span. Plio–Pleistocene African fossil hominoids are relatively abundant from 4 m.y. ago to the present day.

In Europe, no higher primates have been collected prior to 17 m.y. ago (Mein: Chapter I.5). The hominoid record is then continuous until 9 m.y. ago (Ginsburg: Chapter I.4) when the European Primate record abruptly stops, after which nothing is known of higher primates until the arrival on the scene of *Homo* in the Pleistocene period.

In Asia, there is likewise a vacant hominoid record prior to about 16 m.y. ago (dating uncertain). The earliest hominoids from Asia are from China (Wu *et al.*, 1982), Saudi Arabia (Whybrow and Bassiouni: Chapter I.7) and Pakistan (Barry: Chapter I.8) and the record continues with gaps until about 6.5 m.y. ago after which there is a 5 m.y. period from which no hominoids are known. Hominoids were presumably present in Asia during this period since *Sivapithecus* seems to represent a plausible ancestor for *Pongo* which still survives there. The Asian hominoid record picks up again during the Pleistocene with abundant *Homo*, *Pongo* and *Gigantopithecus* specimens.

Fig. 1 not only provides a useful summary of the current state of our knowledge of the hominoid fossil record but also raises a few questions. The Oligocene gap in Africa is presumably due to the fact that sediments of that age are very scarce in Africa. A concerted effort should be made to identify sediments of that age, particularly in Northern Kenya and Ethiopia where radio-isotopic dates suggest the presence of an Oligocene stratigraphic record (Piccirillo *et al.*, 1979; Zanettin *et al.*, 1978).

The pre-middle Miocene paucity of hominoids in Europe and Asia is more likely to be due, in the main, to the probability that there were no hominoids in those continents at that time. The European Oligocene and lower Miocene, in particular, have been extensively studied during the last century without the recovery of a single higher primate fossil, suggesting that the absence is real. The abrupt end of the higher primate fossil record in Europe about 9 m.y. ago probably

Fig. 1. Geographic and chronologic distribution of the Hominoidea.

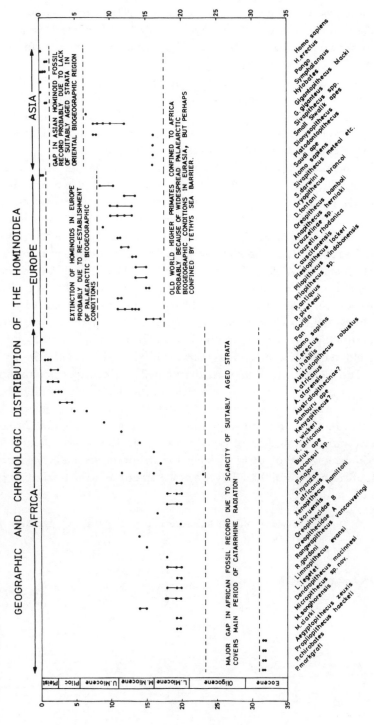

indicates the local European extinction of the order. Younger strata abound in Europe and have been well studied; the lack of hominoid fossils suggests a real absence of hominoids from Europe for most of the Upper Miocene and Pliocene.

In Asia, the dearth of hominoid fossils younger than 6.5 m.y. is more likely to be due to vagaries of the fossil record than to a real absence of hominoids from the continent, especially its more tropical parts. Concerted efforts to identify strata of Upper Miocene and Pliocene Age in Southern Asia would, in my view, well repay the effort. At least two lineages of hominoid (*Gigantopithecus giganteus* to *G. blacki*; *Sivapithecus indicus* to *Pongo*) and possibly four if we include *Symphalangus* and *Hylobates*, probably spanned the Upper Miocene to the Pliocene in Asia, and presumably left a fossil record somewhere.

The hominoid fossil records of both Europe and Asia start up again rather abruptly in the Pleistocene, with the widespread introduction of *Homo*. In Africa, the *Homo* and pre-*Homo* fossil records, when compared with those of Eurasia, suggest strongly that sub-Saharan Africa was the main arena for the evolution of man in late Miocene to Pliocene times. Unfortunately, it is principally in the Upper Miocene period that the African hominoid fossil record is so poor, having so far yielded only two specimens (Pickford, 1975; Ishida *et al.*, 1984).

The distribution pattern seen in Fig. 2 may be explained in biogeographic terms. Modern primates, particularly the hominoids, are inhabitants largely of tropical to sub-tropical environments. If we examine the European sequence closely it is plausible that the southern and central parts of Europe, which in the Oligocene and lower Miocene were of proto-Palaearctic affinities, became warmer and more sub-tropical than they are now sometime in the beginning of the

Fig. 2. Geographic distribution of primates at 18 m.y. ago, 12 m.y. ago and at present.

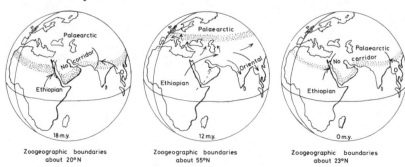

Zoogeographic boundaries about 20°N   Zoogeographic boundaries about 55°N   Zoogeographic boundaries about 23°N

middle Miocene period and remained sub-tropical in parts until about 9 m.y. ago when they reverted to being Palaearctic. For the relatively brief period 16–9 m.y. ago, hominoids and a variety of other proto-Ethiopian mammals were able to survive in southern, and parts of central, Europe leaving behind a scant fossil record of their former presence.

In Asia, however, there have been long-established tropical and sub-tropical environments in the more southerly regions, and Palaearctic conditions have prevailed in the more northerly latitudes. However, the boundary zone between the Palaearctic and Oriental zoogeographic regions has oscillated northwards and southwards in the past, driven by global climatic changes. These north/south oscillations would more or less have coincided with those in Europe.

Fig. 1 shows that the earliest known record of hominoids in Europe coincides rather closely with the earliest Asian records at about 16 m.y. ago. It is my contention that prior to 16 m.y. ago Europe and large parts of Asia (southwards to 20°N latitude) were proto-Palaearctic in their affinities and were therefore unsuitable for the survival of primates. The southern parts of Asia, including India, would have been suitable for primates but there was no corridor through the intervening proto-Palaearctic land mass (the Middle East, Arabia, Afghanistan, China) by way of which the primates may have travelled from Africa where they abounded.

About 16 m.y. ago, at the beginning of the middle Miocene, the boundary zone between proto-Palaearctic and proto-Ethiopian zoogeographic regions moved northwards from about 30°N to about 40°N, so that southern Europe and much of Eurasia now became part of the proto-Ethiopian zoogeographic region, allowing primates easy access to large parts of southern Eurasia including the subtropical and tropical Oriental zoogeographic region.

About 9 m.y. ago, at the beginning of the Turolian Land Mammal Age, the boundary between the zoogeographic regions moved southwards again to about latitude 23°N, so that all of Europe and much of Asia was once again proto-Palaearctic in its zoogeographic affinities.

The Indian subcontinent remained sub-tropical to tropical for somewhat longer, at least until 6.5 m.y. ago at the latitude of the Siwaliks of Pakistan (23°N).

Primates thereafter were no longer able to survive over much of the northern parts of their Middle Miocene range, and their areas of distribution consequently shrank equatorwards. The southerly zoogeographic boundary shift would effectively have cut the African and Asian hominoid populations off from one another, encouraging separate evolutionary pathways to be followed by the now allopatric populations. The southern zoogeographic boundary shift was great enough that all of Europe once again became proto-Palaearctic and primates could no longer survive there.

Throughout the Neogene, Africa (at least sub-Saharan Africa) was of proto-Ethiopian zoogeographic affinities and was therefore suitable for primates all the time, as evidenced by the more or less continuous fossil record.

This symposium has therefore not only documented the chronologic and geographic distribution of Old World higher primates but has also led to the generation of some interesting ideas and questions.

We need to explain or to try to fill the gaps in the fossil record as depicted in Fig. 1. Some of these gaps are theoretically fillable, in the sense that primates were probably present during the gaps in certain areas such as southern Asia, even though no fossils are known. Other gaps such as those in Europe are less likely to be filled, and I present an explanation as to why I think so.

Finally, although I have not entered into the question, the hominoid geochronology summarised in Fig. 1 puts restraints on evolutionary scenarios of the hominoids. The time ranges of some taxa are now well enough documented to permit reasonable estimates of evolutionary pathways to be constructed for some of the hominoids.

It also provides the raw chronological data upon which estimates of the timing of some of the dichotomies among the Hominoidea may be made.

References

Ishida, H., Pickford, M., Nakaya, H. & Nakano, Y. (1984) Fossil anthropoids from Nachola and Samburu Hills, Samburu District, Kenya. *Afr. Studies Monogr. Suppl., Issue* 2, 73–85

Piccirillo, E. M., Justin-Visentin, E., Zanettin, B., Joron, J. L. & Trevil, M. (1979) Geodynamic evolution from Plateau to rift: major and trace element geochemistry of the central eastern Ethiopian plateau volcanics. *N. Jahrb. Geol. Palaeontol. Abh.,* **158**, 139–79

Pickford, M. (1975) Late Miocene sediments and fossils from the Northern Kenya Rift Valley. *Nature,* **256**, 279–84

Wu, R., Han, D., Xu, Q., Qi, G., Lu, Q., Pan, Y., Chen, W., Zhang, X. & Xiao, M. (1982) More *Ramapithecus* skulls found from Lufeng, Yunnan. Report on the excavation of the site in 1981. *Acta Anthropol. Sinica,* **1**, 106–8

Zanettin, B., Justin-Visentin, E. & Piccirillo, E. M. (1978) Volcanic succession, tectonics and magmatology in Central Ethiopia. *Mem. Accad. Patavina, SS. LL. AA.,* **90**, 1–19

Part II

Issues in higher primate evolution

Introduction *J. G. Fleagle*

The papers in this section illustrate the diversity of current research problems and techniques that characterize studies of primate evolution today. These papers are not intended to provide the definitive word on any of the topics covered; rather, most of them offer a brief description of research activities in progress or recently completed, and a statement of current hypotheses remaining to be tested on important issues in higher-primate evolution. It is surely the sign of an active discipline that every new find or new answer raises a dozen new questions that had never been anticipated.

If the papers in this section have a theme, it is Africa, a reflection of both the site of the IPS meetings in Nairobi and the overwhelming role that Africa plays in our knowledge of primate evolution. The authors deal with the entire temporal span of the higher-primate fossil record in Africa, with the exception of the Pleistocene, and many of the papers find on that continent evidence for both the origin of major phyletic groups and important changes in primate evolution.

The articles have been arranged in rough chronological order, according to the relative age of the fossil primates under discussion. The first paper reviews a number of recent findings about the early primates and rodents from the Oligocene of Africa and South America that bear on the issue of the origin of platyrrhine monkeys. All the new evidence supports the theory that the New World monkeys (and caviamorph rodents) are derived from African ancestors.

The next three papers discuss the numerous fossil apes from the Miocene of Africa and Eurasia. Walker, Teaford and Leakey (Chapter II.2) describe the results of their recent excavations on Rusinga Island where they recovered additional skeletal material of a juvenile individual of *Proconsul africanus*, the most complete skeleton of any African fossil ape. They review the long history of recovery of bones from this single individual, they discuss the geology of the locality, and they speculate on the origin of the unique depositional situation that led to such a complete find. Senut (Chapter II.3) discusses another fossil ape bone from Rusinga Island, a fossil humerus, and compares it with similar-aged fossils from Asia. She finds that this part of the limb skeleton was strikingly similar in the African and Asian Miocene apes and that both resemble extant African apes rather than either the Asian orangutan or humans. She speculates on what these similarities may mean for our interpretation of ape biogeography and the evolution of pongid locomotor behaviour. Pickford (Chapter II.4) summarizes new knowledge on the dental morphology of *Kenyapithecus*, an African fossil ape from the middle Miocene that is now known from hundreds of dental remains. He shows that *Kenyapithecus* is not very much like later hominids, as had been previously suggested, and retains many primitive features in common with *Proconsul* from the early Miocene, rather than showing derived similarities linking it with *Sivapithecus* from the middle and later Miocene of Asia. He outlines a series of possible phylogenetic relationships for *Kenyapithecus* with respect to other fossil and living apes that can only be tested by the recovery of additional fossils.

The next three papers report a variety of more anatomical studies aimed at reconstructing the behavior and phylogeny of monkeys and early hominids from the Plio–Pleistocene of Kenya and Ethiopia. Jablonski (Chapter II.5) discusses the anatomy of the hand of *Theropithecus brumpti*, an unusual Pliocene baboon related to the living gelada. She shows that the hand of this 3 million year old species had the same unusual proportions as that of the living gelada, with a relatively long thumb and short fingers. She suggests that these morphological adaptions for grasping small objects such as grass seeds probably characterized the entire radiation. Tardieu (Chapter II.6) uses dissections of living primates to reconstruct the evolution of the lateral meniscus in the knee throughout the order of primates. She is then able to demonstrate from the bony morphology of the tibia that the unique condition of the human lateral meniscus has evolved since the first appearance of early hominids in the Pliocene of Ethiopia. Some individuals (or species) of Plio–Pleistocene hominids show the primitive ape condition, while others show the derived human morphology. Lucas, Corlett and Luke (Chapter II.7) use physiological studies of human chewing and computer simulations to evaluate the relation between absolute tooth size and aspects of the diet such as particle size, particle hardness and food consistency. They then speculate on what types of foods in the diet of early hominids might have selected for differences in tooth size that characterize different species or lineages. The paper by Marzke (Chapter II.8) identifies morphological features in the hand for effective manipulation of tools and discusses the importance of a stable bipedal posture for exploiting trunk leverage during tool use.

The final paper by Conroy and Vannier (Chapter II.9) describes an exciting new development in radiographic imaging that allows investigators to examine the three-dimensional anatomy of living and fossil skulls without sectioning them or even removing encasing matrix. Their technique allows an investigator to section, prepare and measure three-dimensional cranial structures electronically. They give several examples of how this technique can be applied to problems normally addressed by physical anthropologists and paleontologists.

II.1

Early anthropoid evolution in Africa and South America

J. G. FLEAGLE

Introduction

Some of the most fascinating problems in primate evolution are those surrounding the early evolution and dispersal of higher primates (e.g. Ciochon & Chiarelli, 1980). The unresolved problems about this episode in primate and human evolution involve a series of alternative theories of both phylogeny and biogeography. The major phylogenetic issues are whether the higher primates are a monophyletic group and which group (or groups) of prosimian primates gave rise to the earliest anthropoids. Most current authorities seem to agree that anthropoid primates are, indeed, a monophyletic group; that is, the higher primates of the Neotropics (platyrrhines) and those of the Old world (catarrhines) are descended from a common ancestor that was itself a higher primate (e.g. Ciochon & Chiarelli, 1980; Delson & Rosenberger, 1980). There remains considerable disagreement regarding which group of fossil (or living) prosimians most closely represents that which gave rise to anthropoids (e.g. Rosenberger & Szalay, 1980; Dawson & Krishtalka, 1984; Gingerich, 1985).

The major biogeographic question concerns the origin of platyrrhine monkeys in South America. Except for a connection with Antarctica, South America was an island continent with its own largely endemic mammalian fauna until the rise of the Panama land bridge in the Pliocene. Despite a fairly good fossil record from the southern part of the continent for much of the Paleogene, primates are unknown prior to the Oligocene. They seem to appear abruptly, along with hystricomorph rodents (e.g. Hoffstetter, 1972) in deposits of Deseadan and Colhuehuapian age in Bolivia and Argentina. Virtually all authorities agree that the appearance of these two groups is probably the result of an immigration from either North America or Africa, but opinions are about equally divided as to which continent is the more likely source area (e.g. Simpson, 1980; Fig. 1). Most North American paleontologists favor North America as the more likely source area (e.g. Gingerich, 1980; Rosenberger & Szalay, 1980) and most Europeans seem to favor Africa (e.g. Ciochon & Chiarelli, 1980; Hoffstetter, 1980; Lavocat, 1980).

The purpose of this paper is to report several recent discoveries about Oligocene mammalian evolution in Africa and South America that have become available since the last major review of this topic (Ciochon & Chiarelli, 1980). This new information appears to strengthen the argument for an African origin of platyrrhines (and South American hystricomorph rodents).

New fossil platyrrhines

The major impediment to our understanding of early anthropoid evolution in South America is the meager fossil record of platyrrhines (e.g. Rose & Fleagle, 1981). There are fewer than a dozen fossil primate species known from the last 30 million years in Central and South America, and all of the fossils could easily fit into a single

Fig. 1. The biogeographic origin of platyrrhine monkeys is a major issue in higher primate evolution. Some authors favor an origin by rafting from North America while others favor rafting from Africa.

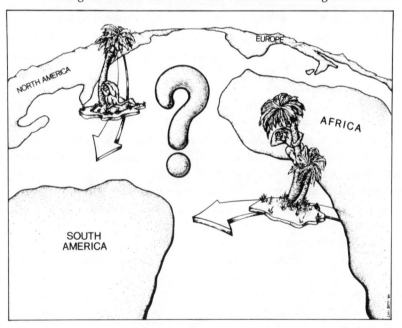

shoebox. Most are known from only a few specimens. In the past few years there have been a number of new fossil finds that add to our knowledge of platyrrhine evolution.

The most complete fossil platyrrhines and those which seem to be most clearly related to extant genera or subfamilies are those from the middle-to-late Miocene La Venta Formation in Colombia (Stirton, 1951). Recent paleontological work by scientists from Kyoto University has produced considerable numbers of new specimens and several new taxa of fossil monkeys. These suggest that by middle-to-late Miocene times there was a great diversity (eight or nine genera) of platyrrhines, all of which seem to be closely related to living taxa (Setagouchi & Rosenberger, in press).

The earliest fossil platyrrhine is *Branisella boliviana* from the Deseadan Land Mammal Age in Bolivia. Originally described on the basis of a single maxillary specimen with three teeth, this species is now known from four specimens, all possibly from the same individual (Rosenberger, 1981; Wolff, 1984). The new specimens of *Branisella* confirm the presence of characteristic platyrrhine features such as a reduced M3 and absence of a paraconid that could not be determined from earlier material.

There has been considerable debate over the phyletic relationships of two fossil platyrrhines, *Tremacebus* and *Dolichocebus*, from slightly younger Colhuehuapian deposits in Argentina. Both taxa are known from relatively complete, but distorted and largely edentulous skulls. Some workers have argued that they are closely related to extant taxa and suggest an early radiation of essentially modern platyrrhines (e.g. Rosenberger, 1979, 1982; Fleagle & Rosenberger, 1983) while others have argued that they are too divergent to have a close relationship with any modern forms (Hershkovitz, 1974, 1982).

Fleagle & Bown (1983) recently described the first dental material of *Tremacebus* and *Dolichocebus*. Although the new material contributes little to the issue of their phyletic relationships with living species, it provides new documentation of the dental morphology of relatively early platyrrhines. In general, the teeth of *Dolichocebus* and *Tremacebus* support theoretical reconstructions of the primitive platyrrhine dental morphology based on analysis of living species (e.g. Delson & Rosenberger, 1980; Kay, 1980). In addition, the new material of *Dolichocebus* demonstrates striking similarities to early catarrhines from the Oligocene of Africa (Fig. 2). Such features as large canines with a prominent mesial groove and upper molars with a well-developed paraconule and a large lingual cingulum are rare among extant platyrrhines, but were apparently common to both early catarrhines and early platyrrhines. These detailed dental similarities between the earliest members of both major groups of living anthropoids support a common ancestry for the two.

Fossil rodents from the African Oligocene

The phyletic and biogeographic issues surrounding the early evolution and distribution of higher primates are paralleled by those concerning the evolution of hystricomorph rodents. Both groups, primates and rodents, appear for the first time in the Oligocene of South America. As with primates, there is a debate as to whether the South American hystricomorph rodents came from North America, where the group is unknown, or from Africa, where there are similar, presumably related taxa both living and fossil. As with the primates, most North American paleontologists (e.g. Wood, 1980) have argued for a North American origin of the South American hystricomorphs and have suggested that the similarities to African forms are the result of parallelisms. Others (e.g. Hoffstetter, 1980; Lavocat, 1980) have argued that rodents, like primates, reached South America by rafting from Africa.

The earliest known hystricomorph rodents in Africa are the five genera and eight species of phiomyids from the Fayum of Egypt. They have generally been regarded as most closely related to the livng Petromuridae of Southwest Africa, but have also been considered to be suitably primitive to represent the ancestral hystricomorphs (Lavocat, 1980). The systematics of these rodents have not been closely studied in over 15 years. However, Schneider (1984) recently examined

Fig. 2. Left upper molars of (a) *Aegyptopithecus zeuxis* from the early Oligocene of Egypt and (b) *Dolichocebus gaimanensis* from the late Oligocene of Gaiman Argentina. Not to scale.

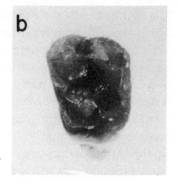

the limb skeleton of the phiomyids from the Egyptian Oligocene for information that might be useful in reconstructing the paleoenvironment of the Fayum deposits. Her studies showed that the most common of the Fayum rodents, *Metaphiomys beadnelli*, and probably several others, was an arboreal quadruped that presumably lived in a forested habitat (e.g. Bown *et al.*, 1982).

In its skeletal anatomy, *Metaphiomys* shows greatest similarities with the Southwest African *Petromus* and the Neotropical spiny rat *Echimys*. Schneider's study documented numerous osteological similarities among the three genera *Metaphiomys*, *Petromus*, and *Echimys* in detailed osteological features of the ulna, femur, tibia, pelvis, and astragalus that are characteristic of many hystricomorph rodents but are not found in other suborders. For example, the femora are strikingly similar (Fig. 3). In each there is a very short, dorsoventrally flattened femoral shaft with a spherical head set on a small neck and the third trochanter is present only as a crest rather than a prominence.

Fig. 3. Femora of extant and fossil hystricomorph rodents: (a) *Echimys*; (b) *Metaphiomys beadnelli*; (c) *Petromus*; (d) *Proechimys*; (e) *Octodon*. Note similarities in the shape and orientation of the head and neck, the lack of a pronounced third trochanter, and the flattened shaft among a,b,c, and d.

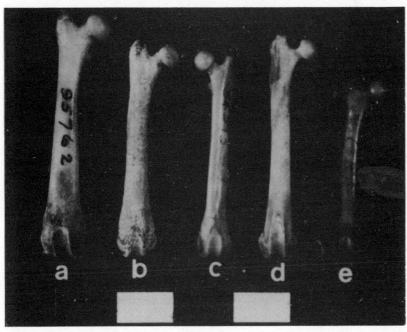

Anatomical similarities between the Petromuridae and various South American taxa have been noted before by many authors (e.g. Woods, 1972). The most likely interpretation of these detailed skeletal similarities among such biogeographically and temporally removed genera of hystricomorphs is that these features are primitive hystricomorph characters which have been retained in the Petromuridae and many extant New World hystricomorphs. They support a monophyletic, African origin for African and Neotropical hystricomorphs.

The age of African and South American Oligocene faunas

Both the early catarrhines from Egypt and the early platyrrhines from Bolivia and Argentina have generally been recognized as Oligocene in age (e.g. Savage & Russell, 1983). Until recently, the best available radiometric age for the Oligocene fossil anthropoids and rodents from Egypt was older than 25–27 million years BP (Simons, 1967). The Deseaden Land Mammal Age in South America has been dated at between 27 and 35 million years (Marshall, 1982). On the basis of these dates, the fossil higher primates (and rodents) from South America seemed to be considerably older than those from Africa. Thus, regardless of any morphological similarities between African and South American taxa, the relative ages argued against any of the known African forms being ancestral to South American groups and the relative antiquity of the South American forms made parallel evolution a likely interpretation. In the case of the rodents, the presence of a substantial adaptive radiation in South America 10 million years earlier than the relatively more restricted African fauna made an African origin of the South American radiation most suspicious (Wood, 1983).

In the past year, the ages of both the African and South American early primate localities have been revised as a result of new geological studies. The new results indicate that the relative ages of early anthropoids (and rodents) on the two continents are the reverse of what has been accepted previously. The Jebel Qatrani formation in Egypt now has a radiometrically determined age of greater than 31.0 ± 1.0 million years BP. This minimum age accords well with faunal correlations which indicate that the Fayum fauna is most likely to be early Oligocene or older (Fleagle *et al.*, Chapter I.1). Recent work in Bolivia (MacFadden *et al.*, 1985) has revised the age of the Deseaden deposits in the Salla-Luribay Basin that yielded the earliest fossil platyrrhine, *Branisella boliviana*. The quarry from which the monkey was recovered now appears to have an age of between 24 and 28 million years, rather than the 35 million years previously cited (e.g. Ciochon & Chiarelli 1980). Thus, the African higher primates (and rodents) are probably as much as 10 million years older than the earliest South American primates and rodents.

Discussion and conclusions

The new discoveries about early primate (and rodent) evolution in Africa and South America provide added support for the theory that platyrrhine monkeys had an African origin, by demonstrating additional morphological similarities between the primates and rodents of the two continents. As the number of detailed morphological similarities linking platyrrhines and early catarrhines (or New World and Old World hystricomorphs) increases, the likelihood that they are the result of parallel evolution decreases (e.g. Lavocat, 1980). The morphological link between African higher primates and those of South America seems to be proved beyond any reasonable doubt. Furthermore, the new radiometric ages for the Fayum fauna in Africa and the Deseaden fauna from Bolivia eliminate the often cited problem that the New World forms were the result of a much older radiation than their postulated African relatives (e.g. Wood, 1983).

The major remaining difficulty in postulating an African origin for South American monkeys and rodents concerns the mechanism of how the animals reached South America. Many authors have questioned whether long-distance rafting is a possible means of dispersal for primates. However, as Hoffstetter (e.g. 1972, 1980) has repeatedly emphasized, the island status of South America throughout the Paleogene means that the primates and rodents must have crossed a substantial water barrier from any source area (except possibly Antarctica). It is worth noting that the largest worldwide drop in sea level recorded for the entire Tertiary apparently occurred about 29 million years ago (Vail & Hartenbol, 1979). With the new dating of early anthropoids in Africa and South America, this event is after the Fayum deposits and before the first appearance of platyrrhines in Bolivia. A major drop in sea level would facilitate intercontinental dispersal of any sort.

The argument for an African rather than a North American origin for the rodents and monkeys is based on the presence of similar animals on that continent and the absence of any evidence for undoubted hystricomorphs or higher primates in other continents. Obviously, the negative aspects of this argument could easily be overturned by recovery of suitable fossils in Asia or North America. Until such evidence is available to support the presence of early anthropoids outside Africa, an African origin for platyrrhines must be considered the most reasonable hypothesis.

Acknowledgments

This work was supported in part by research grants BNS 8210949 and BNS8209937 from the National Science Foundation and 2440-82 from the National Geographic Society, and a Fellowship from the John Simon Guggenheim Memorial Foundation. I am grateful to Thomas Bown, Elwyn Simons, Eileen Schneider, Bruce MacFadden, and Alfred Rosenberger for permission to discuss their work in this contribution. I thank D. W. Krause for his comments and suggestions on the manuscript.

References

Bown, T. M., Kraus, M. J., Wing, S. L., Fleagle, J. G., Tiffney, B. H., Simons, E. L. & Vondra, C. F. (1982) The Fayum Primate Forest revisited. *J. Hum. Evol.*, **11**, 603–32

Ciochon, R. L. & Chiarelli, A. B. (1980) Paleobiogeographic perspectives on the origin of the Platyrrhini. In *Evolutionary Biology of the New World Monkeys and Continental Drift*, ed. R. L. Ciochon and A. B. Chiarelli, pp. 459–73. New York: Plenum Press

Dawson, M. R. & Krishtalka, L. (1984) Fossil history of the families of Recent mammals. In *Orders and Families of Recent Mammals of the World*, ed. S. Anderson & J. K. Jones, pp. 11–58. Chichester: John Wiley & Sons

Delson, E. & Rosenberger, A. L. (1980) Phyletic perspectives on platyrrhine origins and anthropoid relations. In *Evolutionary Biology of the New World Monkeys and Continental Drift*, ed. R. L. Ciochon & A. B. Chiarelli, pp. 445–58. New York: Plenum Press

Fleagle, J. G. & Bown, T. M. (1983) New primate fossils from Late Oligocene (Colhuehuapian) localities of Chubut Province, Argentina. *Folia Primatol.*, **41**, 240–66

Fleagle, J. G. & Rosenberger, A. L. (1983) Cranial morphology of the earliest anthropoids . In *Morphologie Evolutive, Morphologenese du Crane et Origine de l'Homme*, ed. M. Sakka, pp. 141–53. Paris: CNRS

Gingerich, P. D. (1980) Eocene Adapidae, paleobiogeography and the origin of South American platyrrhini. In *Evolutionary Biology of the New World Monkeys and Continental Drift*, ed. R. L. Ciochon & A. B. Chiarelli, pp. 123–38. New York: Plenum Press

Gingerich, P. D. (1985) Primate evolution: evidence from the fossil record, comparative morphology, and molecular biology. *Yearb. Phys. Anthropol.*, **27**, 1–16

Hershkovitz, P. (1974) A new genus of Late Oligocene monkey (Cebidae, Platyrrhini) with notes on postorbital closure and platyrrhine evolution. *Folia Primatol.*, **21**, 1–35

Hershkovitz, P. (1982) Supposed squirrel monkey affinities of the late Oligocene *Dolichocebus gaimanensis. Nature,* **298,** 201–2

Hoffstetter, R. (1972) Relationships, origins, and history of the ceboid monkeys and caviomorph rodents: a modern reinterpretation. *Evol. Biol.,* **6,** 323–47

Hoffstetter, R. (1980) Origin and deployment of New World Monkeys emphasizing the southern continents route. In *Evolutionary Biology of the New World Monkeys and Continental Drift,* ed. R. L. Ciochon & A. B. Chiarelli, pp. 103–38. New York: Plenum Press

Kay, R. F. (1980) Platyrrhine origins: a reappraisal of the dental evidence. In *Evolutionary Biology of the New World Monkeys and Continental Drift,* ed. R. L. Ciochon & A. B. Chiarelli, pp. 159–88. New York: Plenum Press

Lavocat, R. (1980) The implications of rodent paleontology and biogeography to the geographical sources and origin of platyrrhine primates. In *Evolutionary Biology of the New World Monkeys and Continental Drift,* ed. R. L. Ciochon & A. B. Chiarelli, pp. 93–102. New York: Plenum Press

MacFadden, B. J., Campbell, K. E., Jr, Cifelli, R. L., Siles, O., Johnson, N., Naeser, C. W. & Zeitler, P. K. (1985) Magnetic polarity stratigraphy and mammalian biostratigraphy of the Deseadan (Late Oliocene–Early Miocene) Salla Beds of northern Bolivia. *J. Geol.,* **93,** 223–50

Marshall, L. G. (1982) Calibration of the age of mammals in South America. *Geobios,* **6** (Suppl.), 427–37

Rose, K. D. & Fleagle, J. G. (1981) The fossil history of nonhuman primates in the Americas. In *Ecology and Behavior of Neotropical Primates,* ed. A. F. Coimbra-Filho & R. A. Mittermeier, pp. 111–67. Rio de Janiero: Academica Brasiliera de Ciencias

Rosenberger, A. L. (1979) Cranial anatomy and implications of *Dolichocebus,* a late Oligocene ceboid primate. *Nature,* **279,** 416–18

Rosenberger, A. L. (1981) A mandible of *Branisella boliviana* (Platyrrhini, Primates) from the Oligocene of South America. *Int. J. Primatol.,* **2,** 1–7

Rosenberger, A. L. (1982) Supposed squirrel monkey affinities of the late Oligocene *Dolichocebus gaimanensis. Nature,* **298,** 202

Rosenberger, A. L. & Szalay, F. S. (1980) On the tarsiiform origins of anthropoidea. In *Evolutionary Biology of the New World Monkeys and Continental Drift,* ed. R. L. Ciochon & A. B. Chiarelli, pp. 139–58. New York: Plenum Press

Savage, D. E. & Russell, D. E. (1983) *Mammalian Paleofaunas of the World.* Reading, Mass.: Addison-Wesley Publishing Company

Schneider, E. (1984) Comparative and functional morphology of the appendicular skeleton in Oligocene Fayum Rodentia. M.S. Thesis, State University of New York: Stony Brook

Setogouchi, T. & Rosenberger, A. L. (in press). *Some New Ceboid Monkeys from the Miocene of Colombia.*

Simons, E. L. (1967) The earliest apes. *Sci. Amer.,* **217,** 28–35

Simpson, G. G. (1980) *Splendid Isolation.* New Haven: Yale University Press

Stirton, R. (1951) Ceboid monkeys from the Miocene of Colombia. *Bull. Univ. Calif. Publ. Geol. Sci.,* **28,** 315–56

Vail, P. R. & Hartenbol, J. (1979) Sea-level changes during the Tertiary. *Oceanus,* **22**(3), 71–9

Wolff, R. (1984) New specimens of the primate *Branisella boliviana. J. Vert. Paleontol.,* **4**(4), 570–4

Wood, A. E. (1980) The origin of the caviomorph rodents from a source in Middle America: a clue to the area of origin of the platyrrhine primates. In

Evolutionary Biology of the New World Monkeys and Continental Drift, ed. R. L. Ciochon & A. B. Chiarelli, pp. 79–92. New York: Plenum Press

Wood, A. E. (1983) The radiation of the Order Rodentia in the southern continents: the dates, numbers and sources of the invasions. *Schriftenr. Geol. Wiss.*, **19/20 S**, 381–394

Woods, C. A. (1972) Comparative myology of jaw, hyoid, and pectoral appendicular regions of New and Old World hystricomorph rodents. *Bull. Am. Mus. Nat. Hist.*, **147**, 119–98

II.2

New information concerning the R114 *Proconsul* site, Rusinga Island, Kenya

A. WALKER, M. F. TEAFORD AND R. E. LEAKEY

Introduction

The R114 early Miocene fossil site was found by T. Whitworth in 1951 (Whitworth, 1953) during a geological survey of the western end of Rusinga Island, Kenya. The site is located at about 34°6′E, 0°20′S on the slopes of Kiakanga Hill. Whitworth described the site as a vertical pipe of bone-filled agglomerate penetrating flaggy sediments. At the time of discovery the major part of a fossil pig skeleton was exposed on the surface. A collecting party from the Coryndon Museum (now National Museum) in Nairobi was sent to the site and bones were excavated by breaking pieces of the hard pipe rock. Parts of a single subadult *Proconsul africanus* skeleton were found beneath the pig bones. Later that same year Dr L. S. B. Leakey visited the site and continued the breaking of the bone-bearing rock. In all, about a meter's depth of pipe rock was removed. Some of the material was taken back to Nairobi for mechanical preparation.

The primate specimen was sent to Sir W. E. LeGros Clark, who passed it on to Dr J. R. Napier for analysis. Napier and his colleague P. R. Davis produced a monograph on the cranial and associated postcranial bones of *Proconsul africanus* and a short account of a reconstruction of the skull of this species (Napier & Davis, 1959; Davis & Napier, 1963). The forelimb skeleton has been very important in all accounts of the evolution of hominoid locomotion.

Much later a block of agglomerate which had been on study-loan with a collection of fossil pigs was returned to Nairobi. This block contained part of the lower leg and foot of the same *Proconsul* individual. This discovery led to a search through all fossils from this site housed in the National Museum of Kenya, and much more of the skeleton was found. An account of these new parts, together with a complete faunal list and paleoenvironmental information is given in Walker & Pickford (1983). In 1984, an expedition funded by the National Science Foundation and the National Museums of Kenya went to Rusinga with the following objectives: (1) to look for missing *Proconsul* bones in all the agglomerate blocks left on Leakey's dumps; and (2) to determine the nature and extent of the pipe. The work of preparing all the bones from the blocks has not yet been completed, so this account of new parts may still have to be modified. Also, as will be seen, work on the pipe will have to be resumed in 1985 since it was impossible to finish it in one season.

New *Proconsul* material

The following new parts of the *P. africanus* KNM-RU 2036 skeleton were found in 1984 (see Fig. 1):

Left maxilla with P3 to M1 and canine alveolus

Lateral half of right clavicle

Right upper canine

Lingual half of left M3 germ

Terminal phalanx right thumb

2 Epiphyses of middle phalanges of right hand

Right metacarpal I

Epiphysis of right metacarpal II

Middle phalanx of right hand

2 Distal phalanges of right hand

Right metacarpal V

Right metacarpal IV (missing epiphysis)

Right triquetrum

Right cuboid

The piece of clavicle was associated with the epiphysis of the right first metacarpal and the canine was associated with the triquetrum. The maxilla was almost totally encased in rock with only a corner of the first molar showing. The bones of the hand, with the exception of the triquetrum, were in a single block but they were not in any obvious anatomical configuration. In fact, the epiphysis of the fifth metacarpal was in close proximity to the distal epiphyseal surface of the fourth metacarpal. The cuboid was recovered during sieving of the surface soil and rock and was almost completely free of matrix. Because rocks broken in 1951 still have fresh surfaces, there has been no subsequent weathering. Therefore, bones without matrix such as the cuboid must have weathered out before the original discovery. It is also clear that the skeleton was partly disarticulated but the parts were not widely separated from each other in the agglomerate matrix.

This single partial skeleton is the most complete of any large-bodied Miocene hominoid. There has only been time since the expedition to remove matrix from the bones and make a superficial analysis. There are a few points of immediate interest, however. The triquetrum of the original left hand skeleton was badly damaged. The right is complete and shows a clear facet for the ulnar styloid process, showing that the derived condition found in living hominoids had not been attained by *P. africanus*. Napier and Davis had to estimate the length of the first metacarpal in 1959. The right metacarpal I is complete in its length

Fig. 1. New parts of *Proconsul africanus* KNM-RU 2036 found in 1984. A. Left maxilla. B. Right upper canine. C. Right cuboid. D. Right clavicle. E. Right metacarpals: I; head of II; IV and V. F. Phalanges of right hand. G. Right triquetrum.

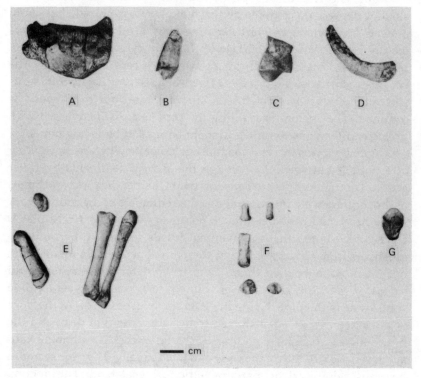

although weathered on its distal lateral surface. Its length is very close to the original estimate of 25 mm. The upper canine, although damaged on its tip, shows a clear strip of wear on the distal crest. Thus, although the root had not yet closed, the crown was in wear. This shows that, in this female individual, the canine had fully erupted even while the third molars were still in their crypts. This confirms evidence from other postcranial specimens that, despite several of the long bone epiphyses not being fused, this individual would have grown very little more had it survived to full maturity.

Sedimentary environment

The whole area around the site was scraped down to bedrock and all surface soil and debris sieved for even the smallest bone fragments. Hundreds of bones of various vertebrates were found. The commonest fossils by far were vertebrae of large pythons and monitor lizards. Only one new taxon was added to the faunal list, a micro-chiropteran bat of the genus *Tadarida* which is known from a complete cranium. The 1951 excavation had finished with about a 4 m wide shallow depression centered on the agglomerate pipe, which is about a meter in diameter and circular in section (see Fig. 2). An obvious feature of the excavated surface of the country rock was a series of planes of slickensides all dipping towards the center of the pipe. The country rock is basically a series of well-bedded grey flaggy tuffaceous silts and sands. Mammal fossils are very rare, but fossil wood is common. The agglomerate filling the pipe is a distinctive grit with green fennite fragments and abundant bones and bone fragments.

Originally it was thought that the agglomerate pipe was an infilling of a pothole cut vertically through the Hiwegi sediments by water action. This naturally led to concerns over whether the rocks and bones of the infilling were the same age as the sediments of the country rock since they could have been much younger. Whitworth (in Napier & Davis, 1959) noted that the mammal fossils seemed to be indistinguishable from Hiwegi ones and therefore that the R114 fossils were not much younger than them. In order to determine the form and extent of the pipe, a wedge of country rock was excavated to the south-west of the pipe during the 1984 season (see Fig. 2). At the close of the season this wedge-shaped trench was over 3 m deep and the pipe showed no signs of ending. The country rock is extremely hard and taxed the strength of the crew and tools equally. The pipe seems to be almost cylindrical, but perhaps getting wider at depth. The junction

Fig. 2. Map of the R114 locality showing the area excavated in 1951 and the deep trench dug in 1984. Contours are every 0.5 m from an arbitrary datum at the edge of the new trench. Small arrows around the 1951 excavation show slickenside directions (observed dips on these range from 39° to 50° but, with allowance for regional dip, all are close to 45°). *Photo inset*: View of the R114 agglomerate pipe from the SW, showing the surface left after the 1951 excavation and the top of the trench excavated in 1984.

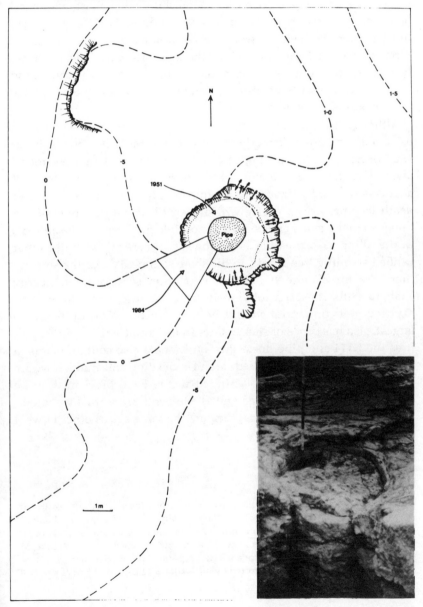

of the pipe and country rocks is weathered with a filling of modern soil between the two. Thus details of the junction are obscure. Horizontal joints and details of grading show that there were about three or four fillings per meter. Bones are seen on the surface facing the trench for the entire depth so far exposed. The details of the stratigraphy of the country rock show that some cylindrical structure was standing when these flood plain deposits were laid down, rather than that a cylindrical hole was cut into previously consolidated sediments. If the latter were the case then the bedding would be continuous on either side of the pipe. As it is, the sediments seen on the southerly wall of the trench are turned up against the pipe rock and those on the northerly wall turned down or horizontal. Several of the horizons also change their clast size and thickness at the pipe.

Although no definitive answers can yet be given, there seems to us to be only one possible mode of formation of the pipe. This is that it was formed by the infilling of a hole left when a large tree rotted away. The standing tree would have been surrounded to a depth of at least 4 or 5 m by floodplain sediments. The tree rotted away after death leaving a deep cavity which then filled with sediments and bones in many small episodes. It is possible that some of the animals in the filling used the hole as a refuge. There are at least three other infilled standing tree trunks in the same sediments near the site and there are three more in Hiwegi Formation sediments on nearby Kiahera Hill. These are obviously trees because they either have exposed roots or natural moulds of bark structure. One of them, the largest, also has cones of slickensides in the country rock centered on it as the R114 site pipe does. Two on Kiahera also contain mammal bones. These examples all need careful excavation and study. If we are correct, then the fauna concentrated in the R114 pipe must all be derived from a localized area and all elements are virtually contemporaneous. It also follows that they are the same age as other Hiwegi mammals.

Acknowledgements

We thank the Government of Kenya for permission to carry out research in Kenya and the Trustees of the National Museums of Kenya. We thank M. Pickford and K. Kimeu for help, advice and useful discussions. Excavations at Rusinga would have been impossible without the assistance of P. Nzube, M. Mulila, M. Kyava, W. Mangao, B. Kyongo and Aila and Solomon ss/o Derekich. The work was supported by the National Musuems of Kenya and NSF Grant BNS 8317849.

References

Davis, P. R. & Napier, J. R. (1963) A reconstruction of the skull of *Proconsul africanus*. *Folia Primatol.*, 1, 20–8

Napier, J. R. & Davis, P. R. (1959) The forelimb skeleton and associated remains of *Proconsul africanus*. *Fossil Mammals of Africa*, 16, 1–69

Walker, A. C. & Pickford, M. (1983) New postcranial fossils of *Proconsul africanus* and *Proconsul nyanzae*. In *New Interpretations of Ape and Human Ancestry*, ed. R. L. Ciochon & R. S. Corruccini, pp. 325–51. New York: Plenum Press

Whitworth, T. (1953) A contribution to the geology of Rusinga Island. *Q. J. Geol. Soc. Lond.*, 109, 75–96

II.3

New data on Miocene hominoid humeri from Pakistan and Kenya

B. SENUT

Introduction

In the last decade *Sivapithecus* and *Ramapithecus* have been widely studied, especially because of new fossils recovered by field expeditions in Pakistan, by the Geological Survey of Pakistan in collaboration with Yale and Harvard Universities, and in China, by the Institute of Vertebrate Palaeontology and Palaeoanthropology of Beijing. Hundreds of new cranial, dental, and postcranial elements have been unearthed, including two almost complete faces of *Sivapithecus*. On the basis of these specimens from China studied by Wu Ru Kang, from Pakistan (e.g. Preuss, 1982; Pilbeam, in press) and from Turkey (e.g. Andrews & Tekkaya, 1980), it is clear that several premaxillary, palate and orbital features of *Sivapithecus* are more similar to *Pongo* than to *Homo* or the African apes. These are interpreted as synapomorphies (Andrews, 1982*a*,*b*; Andrews & Cronin, 1982; Pilbeam, 1984 and in press). However, the postcranial fragments from Pakistan do no exhibit *Pongo*-like features, but more African ape-like features. Recently, Schwartz (1984) has suggested that there is considerable morphological evidence for including *Pongo*, *Homo* and *Sivapithecus* in a single clade. However, several of the features used to support his systematic hypothesis could be the results of convergence. Moreover, after an extensive study of Oligocene and Miocene primates, I have suggested (Senut, 1982*a*, 1983) that the humeral features present in *Homo* and *Pongo* are not derived but primitive, and therefore cannot be taken into account in building phylogenies based on synapomorphies. The possibility that *Pongo* might be a primitive animal has also been suggested by Walker from the new evidence from Buluk in Kenya (in Lewin, 1983; Walker & Herbert, 1984).

In this paper I will focus on fossil humeri from the Miocene of

152   *B. Senut*

Pakistan (GSP 12271, GSP 13606 and GSP 6663) collected from the
Potwar Plateau area of Sethi Nagri (locality 311) and dated at about 10
million years (Pilbeam *et al.*, 1977*a,b*). The other specimen comes from
Rusinga Island In Kenya (Locality R 107) from the Kiahera Formation
(KNM RU 7696) and is probaby at least 17.7 million years old (Pickford,
1981). These fossils will be compared with both living and fossil
hominoids.

Description of the fossils
GSP 12271 (Fig. 1a,b,c)

This specimen, collected in 1979, consists of a fragmentary
right distal humerus, broken in the middle of the *trochlea humeri*.
Several descriptions of the specimen have been published previously
by Pilbeam *et al.* (1980), Morbeck (1983) and Rose (1983).

In anterior view (Fig. 1b), there is a well rounded *capitulum humeri*,
a deep *zone conoidea* and a well expressed anterior lateral trochlear
ridge. The *fossa coronoidea* is separated from the *fossa radialis* by a clear
osseous keel. The *epicondylus lateralis* is set very high and located
largely higher than the *capitulum humeri*. The origin of the lateral
diaphyseal border seems to be rather rectilinear.

In posterior view (Fig. 1a), we note a very deep *fossa olecrani,*

Fig. 1. GSP 12271: (a) posterior view (×0.5); (b) anterior view (×0.5);
(c) lateral view (×0.57). GSP 13606: (d) anterior view (×0.25).
GSP 6663: (e) posterior view (×0.5); (f) anterior view (×0.55).
1: *capitulum humeri*; 2: *zona conoidea*; 3: *trochlea humeri*; 4: *epicondylus
lateralis*; 5: *fossa olecrani*; 6: *fossa radialis*; 7: *fossa coronoidea*.

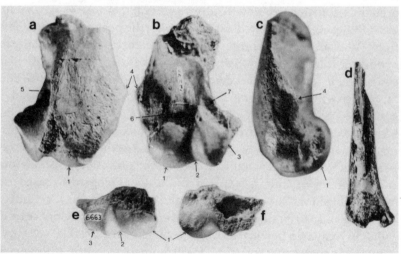

laterally limited by a well expressed crest that continues from the lateral trochlear crest. A facet is clearly present, indicating an articulation with the lateral surface of the *olecranon*.

In lateral view (Fig. 1c), the lateral pillar is antero-posteriorly flattened and the high position of the *epicondylus lateralis* compared to that of the *capitulum humeri* is evident. The *epicondylus lateralis* is not strongly projected anteriorly, but is situated in a prolongation of the lateral border of the *corpus humeri*. The *capitulum humeri* is strongly posteriorly developed and slightly proximo-distally flattened.

In distal view (not shown) the salience of the *capitulum humeri* and of the lateral trochlear crest are on the same level. The posterior extension of the *capitulum* is marked.

GSP 13606 (Fig. 1d)

This right humeral shaft exhibits a clear rectilinear diaphyseal border and deeply depressed *fossa coronoidea* in anterior view (Fig. 1d). Posteriorly, the *fossa olecrani* is deep and laterally limited by a strong crest. The lateral pillar is clearly larger than the medial one. Laterally, there is a distinct lateral diaphyseal flattening.

GSP 6663 (Fig. 1e,f)

This is a distal articular fragment of a right humerus exhibiting the following features: salience of the anterior lateral trochlear crest, large extension of the *capitulum humeri* posteriorly and strong salience of the lateral crest to the *fossa olecrani*.

KNM RU 7696 (Fig. 2)

This right lateral distal end of a humerus was recognized in the miscellaneous collections of the National Museums of Kenya in 1981 by A. Walker. It is broken proximal to the biepicondylar level and half of the *trochlea humeri* is preserved as well as the lateral part of the *fossa olecrani*.

In anterior view (Fig. 2a), the strong salience of the *epicondylus lateralis* can be seen as well as its high position compared to the *capitulum humeri*. The *fossa radialis* is rather depressed and the globular *capitulum humeri* is isolated from the *trochlea humeri* by a deep *zona conoidea*. The two borders of the lateral trochlear crest are asymmetrical; the lateral one is strongly oblique and the more medial one almost flat and horizontal.

In posterior view (Fig. 2b), the lateral pillar to the *fossa olecrani* is well developed and the *capitulum humeri* extends further posteriorly. The *fossa olecrani* is deep and laterally limited by a marked crest which continues the trochlear crest.

In distal view (Fig. 2d), the *capitulum humeri* is extended very posteriorly and the *zona conoidea* is well depressed.

Comparisons

Comparisons have been made with most extant and extinct hominoids. GSP 12271 and KNM RU 7696 are clearly similar in morphology except for one feature, the lateral anterior crest. It shows two equally inclined slopes in the Asian fossil, a condition generally seen in modern African apes, but an almost horizontal medial side in the African fossil.

All the other features are modern African ape-like and probably derived ones (Senut, 1983 and in press). The straightness of the lateral border of the shaft is quite chimpanzee-like. The alignment of the trochlear surface antero-posteriorly is also chimpanzee-, gorilla- and even *Pongo*-like.

Fig. 2. KNM RU 7696: (a) anterior view (×1); (b) posterior view (×1); (c) lateral view (×1.15); (d) distal view (×1.35). 1: *capitulum humeri*; 2: *zona conoidea*; 3: *trochlea humeri*; 4: *epicondylus lateralis*; 5: *fossa olecrani*; 6: *fossa radialis*.

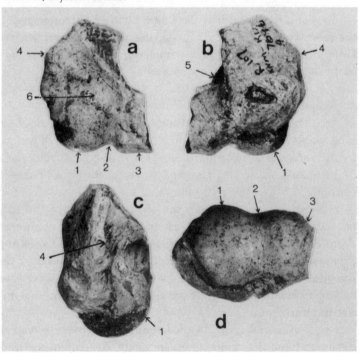

Another Miocene hominoid humerus, KNM FT 2751 from Fort Ternan (Kenya) exhibits two similar features — rectilinearity of the lateral diaphyseal border and high position of the *epicondylus lateralis* relative to the location of the *capitulum humeri*. However, its salience is markedly different and further derived than the condition in the fossils described above.

Previous work (Senut, 1982*b*, 1983) has shown that the salience and the high position of the *epicondylus lateralis* are derived features, as is the strongly salient lateral trochlear crest with two equally inclined slopes. GSP 12271 is more derived than KMU RU 7696 in that feature.

The posteriorly extended *capitulum humeri* is also a derived feature of these fossils that is never observed in Fayum Oligocene specimens or any other Miocene fossils.

Computerized tomography
Methodology

Computerized tomography has been applied to GSP 12271 and GSP 13606. The methodology has been slightly changed from the one described in 1981, as the reference points are not preserved on the specimens. In most modern chimpanzees and gorillas, the tangent line passing through the most salient point of the *capitulum humeri* and the most prominent point on the lateral trochlear crest is parallel to the biepicondylar width. Therefore, GSP 12271 was positioned along a horizontal line that was presumed to be parallel to that used in earlier studies of recent osteological material.

The positioning of GSP 13606 was more problematical and was approximated by comparison with a female gorilla.

The section of KNM RU 7696 was obtained by drawing.

Results (Figs 3,4)

GSP 12271 exhibits a triangular lateral pillar that is similar to that in KNM RU 7696 and in *Gorilla* and *Pan* (for analysis of large sample of modern hominoids, see Senut (1979, 1982*a*)). It shows neither the significant antero-posterior flattening of the shaft seen in *Pongo*, nor the flattening of the lateral pillar. GSP 13606 also exhibits an African ape-like pattern with two triangular-shaped pillars. However, the uncertainty in positioning of that specimen suggests prudence in the interpretation.

The lateral pillar of KNM RU 7696 resembles those of GSP 12271 and African apes. However, the shapes in all the specimens are clearly different from those of *Pongo*.

Interpretations

Thus, it appears from the morphological evidence, albeit fragmentary, that the Asian and African specimens are closely related. We have, then, a challenge. Either we must assume that African ape-like creatures, for which we have no dental evidence, were living in Asia some 10 million years ago; or, the Asian specimens belong to the animals described as *Sivapithecus*. In this case, if *Sivapithecus* is to be linked with *Pongo*, on dental and cranial evidence, we must assume that the ancestor of the orangutan was not a highly suspensory animal, but a more terrestrial one. The features in common between living *Pongo* and *Homo* would be primitive or convergent.

It has been widely accepted that the common ancestor to the great apes was specialized for suspensory locomotion as expressed variously by Keith (1927), Morton (1927), Gregory (1930), and, more recently, by Tuttle (1969) and Tuttle & Basmajian (1974). Some authors

Fig. 3. Drawings of CT scans in fossil hominoids. 1: lateral pillar; 2: medial pillar; 3: *fossa olecrani*; 4: *epicondylus lateralis*; 5: *fossa coronoidea*; ant: anterior; post: posterior; med: medial; lat: lateral; prox: proximal; B: biepicondylar level. Distance between two consecutive sections = 4 mm. KNM RU 7696 (×1); GSP 12271 and GSP 13606 (×0.56). (Thickness of sections = 3 mm.)

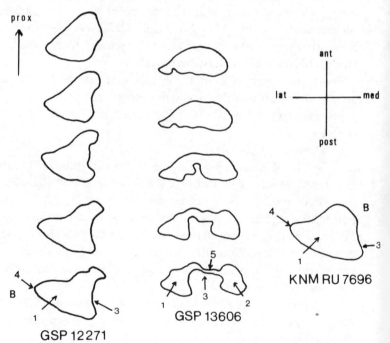

(see especially Washburn, 1968) have also assumed a 'troglodytian' stage in human origins. Susman (1974) has explained carefully the main differences between *Pongo* and *Pan/Gorilla* knuckle-walking. He called it 'facultative knuckle-walking' in the Asian ape.

Tuttle wrote in 1969 that 'On the basis of biomechanical considerations and behavior of living long-handed primates, it may be inferred that the troglodytian ancestors of the African apes probably assumed flexed-finger postures during the initial shift to the terrestriality. The flexed-finger postures of early troglodytians may have been similar to the "fist-walking" or "modified palmigrade" postures of living orangutans.'

Susman (1974) concludes that 'given their secondary nature, terrestrial locomotion modes of *Pongo* might best be viewed as relatively recent adjustments predisposed by quadrupedal locomotor behavior on firm supports in trees'.

Fig. 4. Drawings of CT scans in extant hominoids (×0.45). 1: lateral pillar; 2: medial pillar; 3: *fossa olecrani*; 4: *epicondylus lateralis*; 5: *fossa coronoidea*; 6: *epicondylus medialis*; ant: anterior; post: posterior; med: medial; lat: lateral; prox: proximal; B: biepicondylar level. (Distance between two consecutive sections = 4mm; thickness of sections = 3mm.)

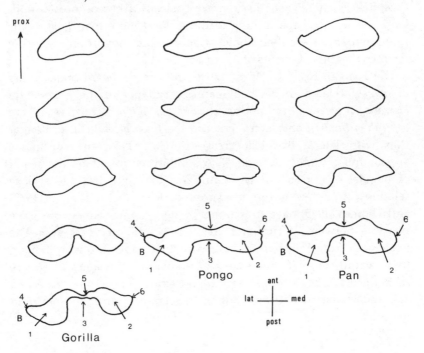

The fossil record does not permit us, at the moment, to hypothesize a suspensory ancestor for any of the great apes. Most of the Miocene hominoids were more or less generalized arboreal quadrupeds (Morbeck, 1976, 1983; Fleagle, 1980, 1983; Rose, 1983; Senut, 1983; Walker & Pickford, 1983).

We cannot solve the problem of evidence of knuckle-walking in the specimens herein studied, as the main features of knuckle-walking occur in the digits; but we can assume that these creatures were at least partially terrestrial. The features pointed out here reveal a strong development of the extensors of the hand, also a marked stabilization of the elbow, evidenced by the lateral crest to the *fossa olecrani*, which is a general quadruped primate feature. There is as well a clear facet for the *olecranon*. The well expressed anterior lateral trochlear crest permits the stabilization of the joint during climbing or suspension. It seems, as also pointed out by Rose (1983), that this joint could be stabilized for terrestrial activities as well as for movements requiring a use of the forelimb for climbing or suspension.

In 1972, both Simons and Pilbeam hypothesized that the brachiating (or so called brachiating) phase in pongid evolution had been preceded by a knuckle-walker phase. In 1982, Pilbeam pointed out that *Sivapithecus* and *Ramapithecus* were basically arboreal forest/woodland species, perhaps coming to the ground more than *Pongo*. The fossil evidence described above supports this suggestion regarding terrestrial habits of the fossil Asian apes.

The Kenyan fossil KNM RU 7696 and the Pakistani material are obviously related in derived features (salience of the *epicondylus lateralis*, high position of the *epicondylus lateralis* relative to the *capitulum humeri*, and lateral crest to the *fossa olecrani* in prolongation with lateral trochlear crest), but the Pakistani specimens appear more highly derived. The similarities might be the result of parallel evolution on two continents or might indicate a close relationship between the two groups. Rögl & Steininger (1983) and Thomas (1985) have shown that biogeographic connections were possible between Africa and Asia 15–14 million years ago. The postcrania from Pakistan described in this paper probably belong to a sivapithecine. If this is so, and if sivapithecines and *Pongo* are related, certain features seen in the postcrania of the modern Asian ape and shared with *Homo* might be retained primitive hominoid features.

Acknowledgments

I would like to deeply thank R. E. F. Leakey (Nairobi), D. Pilbeam (Harvard) and A. C. Walker (Baltimore) for allowing my access to the Miocene hominoids. Dr C. Rumbaugh and B. Chiango are greatly acknowledged for providing facilities for CT scans in the Department of Neuroradiology of Brigham and Women's Hospital in Boston. C. Smeenk (Leiden), P. Napier (London) and Y. Coppens (Paris) have to be thanked for all the facilities that they provided for studying modern *Pongo* and *Homo*. Numerous discussions with the following colleagues have been very helpful for preparing this manuscript: P. Andrews (London), T. Harrison (London), L. Jacobs (Dallas), M. Pickford (Nairobi), M. Le May (Boston), M. Rose (Newark), E. Simons (Durham), A. Walker (Baltimore). The comments and criticism from L. Jacobs (Dallas), P. Tassy (Paris), H. Thomas (Paris) and J. G. Fleagle (Stony Brook) on this manuscript have been greatly appreciated.

I want to thank especially the field expeditions to Potwar Plateau (Pakistan) and Rusinga (Kenya).

The staffs of the following institutions have been helpful in collecting comparative data: The British Museum of Natural History (London), Rijksmuseum van Natuurlijke Historie (Leiden), Laboratoire d'Anthropologie du Muséum National d'Histoire Naturelle (Paris), National Museums of Kenya (Nairobi), Departments of Anthropology and Zoology of Harvard University (Peabody Museum, Cambrige, Mass.).

This work was supported by Muséum National d'Histoire Naturelle and L.A.49 au C.N.R.S. (Prof. Y. Coppens).

References

Andrews, P. (1982a) Hominoid evolution. *Nature*, **295**, 185–6

Andrews, P. (1982b) Un ancêtre pour l'orang-outan. *La Recherche*, **13**, 1211–14

Andrews, P. & Cronin, J. E. (1982) The relationships of *Sivapithecus* and *Ramapithecus* and the evolution of the orang-utan. *Nature*, **297**, 541–6

Andrews, P. & Tekkaya, I. (1980) A revision of the Turkish Miocene hominoid *Sivapithecus meteai*. *Palaeontology*, **23**, 85–95

Fleagle, J. G. (1980) Locomotor behavior of the earliest anthropoids: a review of the current evidence. *Z. Morphol. Anthropol.*, **71**, 149–56

Fleagle, J. G. (1983) Locomotor adaptations of Oligocene and Miocene hominoids and their phyletic implications. In *New Interpretations of Ape and Human Ancestry*, ed. R. L. Ciochon & R. S. Corruccini, pp. 301–24. New York: Plenum Press

Gregory, W. (1930) The origins of man from brachiating stock. *Science*, **71**, 1–7

Keith, A. (1927) *Concerning Man's Origins*. London: Watts & Co.

Lewin, R. (1983) Is the orang-utan a living fossil? *Science*, **222**, 1222–3

Morbeck, M. E. (1976) Problems in reconstruction of fossil anatomy and locomotor behaviour: the *Dryopithecus* elbow complex. *J. Hum. Evol.*, **5**, 223–33

Morbeck, M. E. (1983) Miocene hominoid discoveries from Rudabanya: implications from the postcranial skeleton. In *New Interpretations of Ape and Human Ancestry*, ed. R. L. Ciochon & R. S. Corruccini, pp. 369–404. New York: Plenum Press

Morton, D. J. (1927) Human origins: correlation of previous studies of primate feet and posture with other morphological evidence. *Am. J. Phys. Anthropol.*, **10**, 173–203

Pickford, M. (1981) Preliminary Miocene mammalian biostratigraphy for Western Kenya. *J. Hum. Evol.*, **10**, 73–97

Pilbeam, D. (1972) *The Ascent of Man*. New York: Macmillan Company

Pilbeam, D. (1984) The descent of hominoids and hominids. *Sci. Am.*, April 1984, 60–9

Pilbeam, D. (in press) *The Origin of the Family Hominidae*

Pilbeam, D., Barry, J., Meyer, G. E., Ibrahim Shah, S. M., Pickford, M. H. L., Bishop, W. W., Thomas, H. & Jacobs, L. L. (1977*a*) Geology and palaeontology of Neogene strata of Pakistan. *Nature*, **270**, 684–9

Pilbeam, D., Meyer, G. E., Badgley, C., Rose, M. D., Pickford, M. H. L., Behrensmeyer, A. K. & Ibrahim Shah, S. M. (1977*b*) New hominoid primates from Siwaliks and their bearing on hominoid evolution. *Nature*, **270**, 689–95

Pilbeam, D., Rose, M. D., Badgley, C. & Lipschutz, B. (1980) Miocene hominoids from Pakistan. *Postilla*, **181**, 1–94

Preuss, T. (1982) The face of *Sivapithecus indicus*: description of a new, relatively complete specimen from the Siwaliks of Pakistan. *Folia Primatol.*, **38**, 141–57

Rögl, F. & Steininger, F. F. (1983) Vom Zerfall der Tethys zu Mediterran und Paratethys. Die Neogene Paläogeographie und Palinspastik des zirkummediterranen Raumes. *Ann. Naturhist. Mus. Wien*, **85(A)**, 135–63

Rose, M. D. (1983) Miocene hominoid postcranial morphology. Monkey-like, ape-like, neither, or both? In *New Interpretations of Ape and Human Ancestry*, ed. R. L. Ciochon & R. S. Corruccini, pp. 405–17. New York: Plenum Press

Schwartz, J. H. (1984) The evolutionary relationships of man and orang-utans. *Nature*, **308**, 501–5

Senut, B. (1979) Etude comparative des piliers de la palette humerale. *Cah. Anthropol.*, **3**, 1–8; **4**, 1–20

Senut, B. (1982*a*) Computed tomography of distal humerus in some living hominoid primates. [Abstract of the comm. IXth Congr. Int. Primatol. Soc., Atlanta.] *Int. J. Primatol.*, **3**, 332 (Paper in press in *Current Perspectives in Primate Biology*, New York: Van Nostrand Reinhold)

Senut, B. (1982*b*) Reflexions sur la brachiation et l'origine des Hominides a la lumière des Hominoïdes miocènes et des Hominides plio-pleistocènes. *Geobios*, vol. Jubil, **6**, 335–44

Senut, B. (1983) Nouvelles données sur l'evolution du coude chez les primates hominoïdes. [Round Table of Demokritos Foundation 'Morphogenetik und Evolution', Xanthi, Sept. 83.] *Symposia Thracica*

Senut, B. (in press) Distal humeral osseous anatomy and its implications for hominoid phylogeny. In *Volume Jubilaire du Prof. Jan Jelinek*. Brno.

Simons, E. L. (1972) *Primate Evolution: An Introduction to Man's Place in Nature*. New York: Macmillan Company

Susman, R. L. (1974) Facultative terrestrial hand postures in an orangutan (*Pongo pygmaeus*) and pongid evolution. *Am. J. Phys. Anthropol.*, **40**, 27–38

Thomas, H. (1985) The Early and Middle Miocene land connection of the Afro-Arabian plate and Asia: a major event for hominoid dispersal? In *Ancestors: The Hard Evidence*, ed. E. A. Delson, pp. 42–50. New York: Alan R. Liss

Tuttle, R. H. (1969) Knuckle-walking and the problem of human origins. *Science*, **166**, 953–61

Tuttle, R. H. & Basmajian, J. V. (1974) Electromyography of forearm musculature in *Gorilla* and problems related to knuckle-walking. In *Primate Locomotion*, ed. F. A. Jenkins, Jr, pp. 293–347. New York: Academic Press

Walker, A. C. & Herbert, W. (1984) The living link? *Science News*, Jan. 21, 41
Walker, A. C. & Pickford, M. (1983) New postcranial fossils of *Proconsul africanus* and *Proconsul nyanzae*. In *New Interpretations of Ape and Human Ancestry*, ed. R. L. Ciochon & R. S. Corruccini, pp. 325–51. New York: Plenum Press
Washburn, S. L. (1968) *The Study of Human Evolution*. Eugene, Oregon: Oregon State System of Higher Education

II.4

A reappraisal of *Kenyapithecus*

M. PICKFORD

Introduction

The erection of the genus *Kenyapithecus* by L. S. B. Leakey in 1962 created a great deal of interest, and a large number of papers has been published in the succeeding two decades. Prominent early themes of these papers dealt with two main aspects of the fossils: (1) whether *Kenyapithecus* was a hominid or not; and (2) whether *Kenyapithecus* was a synonym of *Ramapithecus*.

Most of the early debate about *Kenyapithecus wickeri* from Fort Ternan was not to do with the hominid status of the six fossils assigned to this species (most authors agreed with Leakey's original familial assessment), but was instead concerned with its generic status. Leakey (1962, 1967) and Simons & Pilbeam (1965, 1978), although vociferously opposed on the question of synonymy or otherwise of *Kenyapithecus* and *Ramapithecus*, accepted the hominid status of *K. wickeri*, based on a number of features such as: small canines; thick-enamelled molars with no cingulum; parabolic dental arcade reconstruction; canine fossa of *Homo*-type and two-rooted P³. Having accepted *Kenyapithecus/Ramapithecus wickeri* as the earliest known hominid, a number of ramifications was proposed, including the early divergence of hominids from pongids at 14 million years (m.y.) ago or earlier (Leakey, 1970; Uzzell & Pilbeam, 1971) which contradicted early findings in the study of the biochemical relationships of *Pongo*, *Pan*, *Gorilla* and *Homo* (Goodman, 1963) that indicated a considerably later divergence time of *Homo* from the pongids.

In 1967 and 1968, Leakey suggested that *Sivapithecus africanus* was also a *Kenyapithecus* and that hominids had their origins at least as far back as the lower Miocene, 20 m.y. ago. In the ensuing debate, much of Leakey's *Kenyapithecus africanus* hypodigm was found to represent *Proconsul nyanzae*, while only one specimen listed by Leakey, the holotype, was considered to belong to a thick-enamelled hominoid (Pilbeam, 1969). It was generally accepted that *K. africanus* was not a hominid because the upper canine alveolus, partially preserved in the holotype, suggested the former presence of a large canine. Various proposals were made, including: (1) that *K. africanus* was a *Sivapithecus*, as originally published by LeGros Clark & Leakey (1951); (2) that *S. africanus* was a male of *K. wickeri* (Greenfield, 1979); and (3) that the two were not particularly closely related at the generic level (Simons, 1969).

During the long debate about *Kenyapithecus*, several publications appeared dealing with other large hominoid fossils from Fort Ternan (Andrews & Walker, 1976; Shipman, 1977; Simons, 1981) which were generally assigned to *Proconsul nyanzae*. These specimens included a central incisor, some large canines and large third molars. These specimens were excluded from *K. wickeri* because they did not fit into the hominid model which prevailed at the time.

Recently several things have happened to alter the scope of the various debates. These include: (1) the realisation that Pongidae as used by Leakey, Simons & Pilbeam and others during the 1960s to 1970s is a paraphyletic grouping now considered to represent two groups: Pongidae *sensu stricto* (containing *Pongo*, *Sivapithecus* and *Gigantopithecus*) and Panidae, comprising *Pan* and *Gorilla*; (2) the discovery of many additional fossils attributed to *Kenyapithecus* from middle Miocene strata at Maboko, Fort Ternan and Nachola (Ishida *et al.*, 1984); and (3) the suggestion that *Ramapithecus* is probably synonymous with *Sivapithecus* (see Ward & Pilbeam, 1983). Thus the framework in which *Kenyapithecus* was studied has been radically altered, and the material basis of fossils for comparative study has greatly improved.

Various questions remain, since the new collections are rather fragmentary, and crucial skeletal features are missing or are not clear. The expanded hypodigms do, however, reveal some interesting new data which permit a reassessment of *K. wickeri* and *K. africanus*.

More than 100 fossils now attributed to *Kenyapithecus* represent the entire adult upper and lower dentition and some deciduous teeth (Pickford, 1985). Several observations can be made, including: (1) the presence of large and small canines in the collection; (2) many upper and lower molars possess cingula of a simplified type, not similar to those of *Proconsul*; (3) the presence in the collections of large and small individuals of similar morphology; (4) the presence of large third lower molars at all three localities; (5) the molars have low relief dentine-enamel junctions which permit the occlusal surface to wear almost flat before dentine is exposed; (6) upper premolars are antero-posteriorly lengthened compared with those of *Proconsul*; (7) the zygomatic arch in *K. africanus* seems to be low on the face, while that of *K. wickeri* is high; (8) the presence of three roots in P^3 of *K. africanus* and two roots in P^3 of *K. wickeri*; (9) the presence of a shallow arched palate in *K. africanus*; (10) low central lingual pillars in I^1 of both *K. africanus* and *K. wickeri*; (11) the more bilaterally symmetrical lingual outline of I^1's of *Kenyapithecus* compared with those of *Proconsul*; (12) lower canine roots which converge towards the symphyseal midline of the mandible near the genio-glossal fossae; (13) narrow intercanine distance in the mandible; (14) straight cheek tooth rows from C–M_3 in the mandible; (15) tooth rows which are not parabolic but more nearly parallel in arrangement; (16) robust mandibular bodies which contrast with the slim mandibles of *Proconsul*; (17) significant buccal post-canine fossae in mandibles with large canines; (18) the large anteriorly facing wall of the malar portion of the zygomatic arch in *K. wickeri* (morphology not yet known for *K. africanus*); (19) position of the as-cending root of the zygomatic arch over M^1–M^2; (20) the canine alve-olus of *K. wickeri* is nearly vertical with respect to the occlusal surface while that of *K. africanus* slopes strongly upwards and to the rear.

It is now clear that *Proconsul* is not represented in the collections from Maboko Island, a site which has now yielded more than 700 dental remains of higher primates. The possibility is therefore very real that the partial hominoid skeleton (LeGros Clark & Leakey, 1951) hitherto assigned to *Proconsul* belongs instead to *Kenyapithecus africanus*, and thereby acquires a fresh significance.

It is also probable that all specimens from Fort Ternan hitherto assigned to *Proconsul nyanzae* are actually specimens of *K. wickeri*. This is revealed not only by significant differences between these remains and specimens of *P. nyanzae* from Rusinga, the type locality, but also by the morphological compatibility of these fossils with material generally accepted as representing *K. wickeri*. For example all the lower third molars from Fort Ternan previously assigned to *P. nyanzae* have low relief dentine–enamel junctions which allow the teeth to wear almost flat before dentine is exposed, and they have no trace of buccal cingula which so typify *Proconsul* teeth.

It is also probable that all specimens of *Kenyapithecus africanus* hitherto said to come from Rusinga were actually collected at Maboko (Pickford, 1985). *Kenyapithecus* therefore has no reliable basis in the lower Miocene as once thought.

The new data prompt some questions, some of which can be satisfactorily answered, some not. For example are there two or more species of *Kenyapithecus* or only one? Is there any evidence of sexual dimorphism in *Kenyapithecus* species? Are *Kenyapithecus* and *Sivapithecus* (which now includes *Ramapithecus*) representatives of one genus or two? Is *Kenyapithecus africanus* generically the same as *Kenyapithecus wickeri*? Is *Proconsul* likely to have been the ancestral stock from which *Kenyapithecus* arose? Is *Kenyapithecus* a hominid? Could *Kenyapithecus wickeri* have given rise to *Sivapithecus* and thence *Pongo*?

The new collections of *Kenyapithecus* from Maboko and Nachola, as well as the older collections from Fort Ternan, now redefined, indicate that there were individuals with large canines with male morphological characteristics as well as smaller canines of female morphology. Pickford (1985) compared the degree of dimorphism in the Miocene assemblages with that expressed in *Pan* and *Gorilla*, and concluded that it was plausible that both *K. africanus* and *K. wickeri* were sexually dimorphic to a degree comparable to that observed in *Pan* and *Gorilla*.

Comparisons of the *Kenyapithecus* collections from Maboko and Nachola with those of Fort Ternan indicate the following, possibly significant, differences between the two.

Maboko and Nachola	*Fort Ternan*
Many upper and lower molars possess cingula	No known molar cingula
Palate shallow	?Palate deep (not well preserved)
Zygomatic root possibly low	Zygomatic root high
Anterior face of zygomatic slopes forward	Anterior face of zygomatic vertical
P^3 has three roots	P^3 has two roots

These differences, not all of which can be firmly demonstrated because the material is so scanty, are suggestive that two taxa are represented, but it is not yet possible to conclude whether the differences are significant at the specific or the generic level. Pending the recovery of better material I have adopted the view that there are probably two species in the collection, *K. africanus* and *K. wickeri*, and that there may be two genera. Since Nachola is yielding abundant new material, it is considered prudent to wait a while before making a decision on these questions.

The relationships between *Kenyapithecus* and *Sivapithecus* are difficult to evaluate given the limited scope of the Kenyan fossils. There are several morphological features shared by *Kenyapithecus* and *Sivapithecus* but I can identify only one feature which may represent an apomorphic character; that is the vertical anterior face of the zygomatic arch of *K. wickeri* which resembles that of *Sivapithecus* and *Pongo*. The similarities in the teeth of *Kenyapithecus* and *Sivapithecus*, while clearly derived in comparison with *Proconsul*, are primitive for middle Miocene and later hominoids. The elevation of the zygomatic root represents a character shared by *K. wickeri* and *Sivapithecus* but the polarity of this character is difficult to discern since high zygoma also occur in *Homo, Pan* and *Gorilla*. There are, however, several features of *Kenyapithecus* species which differ from *Sivapithecus* and which I expect will eventually indicate generic distinctiveness. These are the morphology of the mandibular symphysis and the strongly convergent roots of the lower canines of *Kenyapithecus*, and the more developed rearward extension of the inferior transverse torus in *Kenyapithecus*. Clearly, however, more complete material of *Kenyapithecus* is required before a proper assessment of the relationship of *Kenyapithecus* to *Sivapithecus* can be made.

Differences between *Kenyapithecus* and *Proconsul* are abundant and marked, yet it is plausible that *Proconsul* gave rise to *Kenyapithecus*. Table 1 summarises some of the major known differences between the two genera, but all morphological characters which define *Kenyapithecus* could be derived from a *Proconsul*-like precursor.

Table 1. *Major known differences between* Proconsul *and* Kenyapithecus

Proconsul	Kenyapithecus
P^{3-4} short antero-posteriorly	P^{3-4} long antero-posteriorly
Upper molar cingula large, inflated	Upper molar cingula reduced, simple
Dentine–enamel junction with high relief	Dentine–enamel junction with low relief
Mandibular body slender	Mandibular body robust
Superior transverse torus larger than inferior transverse torus	Inferior transverse torus larger than superior transverse torus
Palate shallow	Palate shallow in *K. africanus*, but ?deep in *K. wickeri*
Zygomatic root low	Zygomatic root ?low in *K. africanus* but high in *K. wickeri*
Anterior root of zygomatic sloping	Anterior root of zygomatic ?sloping in *K. africanus* but vertical in *K. wickeri*
Differential wear in molars not marked	Marked differential wear in molar series
Asymmetrical I^1 outline with high lingual pillar	More or less symmetrical I^1 outline with low lingual pillar

There is not a single undoubted apomorphic hominid character to be found in the newly expanded hypodigms of *Kenyapithecus africanus* and *K. wickeri*. All the characters formerly taken to be hominid characters were either not truly representative of *Kenyapithecus*, or can be interpreted as plesiomorphic or variable characters. For example the most widely quoted hominid character of *K. wickeri*, the presence of small canines, is here taken to be unrepresentative, since there are large canines at Fort Ternan which probably belong to *Kenyapithecus*. The apparently hominid-like canine fossa of *K. wickeri* is in fact more like that of *Sivapithecus* and *Pongo* in its shape and position relative to the tooth row. The parabolic dental arcade reconstructions were made to support the hominid model, but are probably incorrect. The lower jaw of *Kenyapithecus* from Kaloma (Pickford, 1982) and new specimens from Nachola indicate that the cheektooth row was straight from C to M$_3$. 'Thick-enamelled' cheek teeth, i.e. those with low-relief dentine–enamel junctions which allow the occlusal surface to wear virtually flat before dentine is exposed, are found in *Pongo*, *Sivapithecus*, *Kenyapithecus* and *Gigantopithecus* as well as *Homo*. While these morphological characters are derived with respect to *Proconsul*, they are shared primitive features with respect to *Homo*.

Kenyapithecus wickeri may well have given rise to *Sivapithecus*, but the material basis for comparison is so limited that only one or two possibly apomorphic characters can be identified – the raised root of the zygomatic and the vertical anterior face of the zygomatic. Without additional material it would be hazardous to push the connections too far, and I prefer for the time being to await the recovery of more informative material of *K. wickeri*.

The newly collected material from Buluk has not yet been formally published but has reached the popular press, where it has been publicised as the earliest known *Sivapithecus*. The currently available material does not unequivocally support this viewpoint. The dentition is unlike that of any known *Sivapithecus*, being more reminiscent of, but not exactly similar to, those of *Proconsul* species. The shape and position of the canine fossa is a character shared with *Sivapithecus* but its polarity is not yet clear. The robust mandibular bodies are like those of *Kenyapithecus* and may be plesiomorphic with respect to *Sivapithecus*. The relationship of the Buluk large hominoid to *Xenopithecus hamiltoni* needs examination, for which better material of both is required.

In summary, *Kenyapithecus* as now understood was probably a sexually dimorphic genus, possibly represented by two species. It may be that two genera are represented within the current concept of *Kenyapithecus*. Relationships between *Kenyapithecus* and *Sivapithecus* are difficult to demonstrate and will remain so until more complete material is discovered. It is unlikely that *Kenyapithecus* had achieved the status of hominid, since not a single apomorphic hominid feature can be identified in the expanded hypodigms. Only one possibly apomorphic character links *K. wickeri* with Pongidae *sensu stricto* (i.e. the group of hominoids comprising *Pongo, Gigantopithecus* and *Sivapithecus*), suggesting either that *Kenyapithecus* was not a pongid *sensu stricto* or was a very primitive member of that family. This viewpoint may change with the recovery of more informative material. If these inferences are correct then *Kenyapithecus* probably predates the development of both the Pongidae *sensu stricto* and the Hominidae. The early divergence of hominids at 14 m.y. or earlier is unlikely to be a plausible scenario. Indeed it seems likely that the development of Pongidae *sensu stricto* also occurred later than 14 m.y. These age estimates are based on the Fort Ternan dates which are currently being re-examined with a view to testing their validity.

This reassessment of *Kenyapithecus* is based on more than 100 fossils, most of which were collected at Maboko in the last 3 years – a fossil record which contrasts strongly with the nine specimens that were the source of so much debate. Part of the expanded hypodigm results from reassignment of fossils collected many years ago which were excluded from *Kenyapithecus* because they did not fit the hominid model of *Kenyapithecus/Ramapithecus* prevalent during the 1960s and 1970s.

This view of *Kenyapithecus* is compatible with scenarios currently proposed based on molecular biological methods, in particular with the timing of events in the development of the families Pongidae *sensu stricto* and Hominidae (Goodman *et al.*, 1983). *Kenyapithecus* is not however excluded from a role in the evolution of either family. It just has not evolved a significant quantity of apomorphic characters for it to fit convincingly into either family. In this respect it is a generalised hominoid retaining an appreciable number of plesiomorphic characters from the *Proconsul* stage of evolution. Since *Pan* and *Gorilla* are also rather primitive in many features, being less derived in a number of ways than either *Pongo* or *Homo*, *Kenyapithecus* could also represent the stock from which the Panidae eventually evolved.

Acknowledgements

I thank John Fleagle for encouraging me to participate in the Symposium on Hominoid Evolution of the Xth Congress of the International Primatological Society and to write this contribution to the post-congress proceedings. Fieldwork of Maboko was funded by the LSB Leakey Foundation. I thank the Director/Chief Executive of the Kenya National Museums for permission to study the fossils.

References

Andrews, P. & Walker, A. (1976) The primate and other fauna from Fort Ternan, Kenya. In *Human Origins: Louis Leakey and the East African Evidence*, ed. G. Isaac & E. R. McCown, pp. 279–304. Menlo Park: Benjamin

Goodman, M. (1963) Man's place in the phylogeny of the Primates as reflected in serum proteins. In *Classification and Human Evolution*, ed. S. L. Washburn, pp. 203–34. Chicago: Aldine Press

Goodman, M., Braunitzer, G., Stangl, A. & Schrank, B. (1983) Evidence on human origins from haemoglobins of African apes. *Nature*, **303**, 546–8

Greenfield, L. O. (1979) On the adaptive pattern of *Ramapithecus*. *Am. J. Phys. Anthropol.*, **50**, 527–48

Ishida, H., Ishida, S. & Pickford, M. (1984) Study of the Tertiary hominoids and their palaeoenvironments in E. Africa, 2. *Afr. Study Monogr.*, *Suppl. Issue 2*

Leakey, L. S. B. (1962) A new lower Pliocene fossil primate from Kenya. *Ann. Mag. Nat. Hist.*, **13**, 689–97

Leakey, L. S. B. (1967) An early Miocene member of Hominidae. *Nature*, **213**, 155–63

Leakey, L. S. B. (1968) Lower dentition of *Kenyapithecus africanus*. *Nature*, **217**, 827–30

Leakey, L. S. B. (1970) The relationships of African apes, Man and Old World monkeys. *Proc. Natl Acad. Sci.*, **67**, 746–8

LeGros Clark, W. E. & Leakey, L. S. B. (1951) The Miocene Hominoidea of East Africa. *Fossil Mammals of Africa*, **1**, 1–117

Pickford, M. (1982) New higher primate fossils from the Middle Miocene deposits at Majiwa and Kaloma, Western Kenya. *Am. J. Phys. Anthropol.*, **58**, 1–19

Pickford, M. (1985) A new look at *Kenyapithecus* based on recent discoveries in Western Kenya. *J. Hum. Evol.*, **14**, 113–43

Pilbeam, D. R. (1969) Tertiary Pongidae of East Africa: evolutionary relationships and taxonomy. *Bull. Peabody Mus. Nat. Hist.*, **31**, 1–185

Shipman, P. (1977) Palaeoecology, taphonomic history and population dynamics of the vertebrate fossil assemblage from the Middle Miocene deposits exposed at Fort Ternan. Ph.D. thesis, University of New York

Simons, E. L. (1969) Late Miocene hominid from Fort Ternan, Kenya. *Nature*, **221**, 448–51

Simons, E. L. (1981) Man's immediate forerunners. *Phil. Trans. R. Soc. Lond.*, **B292**, 21–41

Simons, E. L. & Pilbeam, D. R. (1965) Preliminary revision of the Dryopithecinae (Pongidae, Anthropoidea). *Folia Primatol.*, **3**, 81–152

Simons, E. L. & Pilbeam, D. R. (1978) *Ramapithecus* (Hominidae, Hominoidea). In *Evolution of African Mammals*, ed. V. J. Maglio & H. B. S. Cooke, pp. 147–53. Cambridge, Mass.: Harvard University Press

Uzzell, T. & Pilbeam, D. R. (1971) Phyletic divergence dates of hominoid primates: a comparison of fossil and molecular data. *Evolution*, **25**, 615–35

Ward, S. C. & Pilbeam, D. R. (1983) Maxillo-facial morphology of Miocene hominoids from Africa and Indo-Pakistan. In *New Interpretations of Ape and Human Ancestry*, ed. R. L. Ciochon & R. S. Corruccini, pp. 211–38. New York: Plenum Press

II.5

The hand of *Theropithecus* *brumpti*

N. G. JABLONSKI

Introduction

The fossil record of *Theropithecus* is one of the richest and most diverse of any of the higher primates, and phyletic relationships within the genus are now reasonably well understood. *Theropithecus* is distinguished from other cercopithecoids by a complex of derived characters, most of which are functionally interdependent features of the masticatory apparatus (Andrews, 1916; Leakey, 1943; Leakey & Whitworth, 1958; Jolly, 1970, 1972; Maier, 1972 *a,b*; Jablonski, 1981; Eck & Jablonski, 1984, in press). These characters, in turn, appear to be related to an adaptation for chewing large quantities of fibrous vegatation (Jablonski, 1981).

The Pliocene form *Theropithecus brumpti* is an exceptional species in both its morphology and its apparent habitat preference. Its distribution appears to have been spatially and temporally restricted. Remains of the species are known from only two East African formations of the North Turkana Basin – the Shungura and the Kubi Algi – in deposits ranging in age from approximately 2.7 to 1.9 million years (m.y.), and are found in highest densities in those members of the Shungura Formation associated with high proportions of forest and woodland plant communities (Eck, 1977; Eck & Jablonski, in press). *Theropithecus brumpti* is the most highly autapomorphic species of the so-called long-muzzled lineage of *Theropithecus* (Fig. 1) (Eck, 1983; Jablonski, 1983; Eck & Jablonski, 1984, in press). The skull of *T. brumpti*, described at length by Eck & Jablonski (in press), is very distinctive: its robust, anteriorly expanded and laterally flaring zygomatic arches, which supported a massive masseter muscle, are unique amongst mammals.

Behavioral and morphological aspects of the feeding adaptation of the single extant species of *Theropithecus, T. gelada*, are known in some detail (Jolly, 1972; Dunbar, 1977; Iwamoto, 1979; Jablonski, 1981). Geladas are almost exclusively graminivorous, spending large portions of their days throughout the year harvesting various parts of grasses in their montane habitat of central Ethiopia. Geladas are bulk feeders (Dunbar, 1983), but they are not indiscriminate in their choice of food. Preference is shown for the youngest and greenest parts of grass leaves and stems, which are harvested by hand and then conveyed to the mouth. Geladas are extremely adept at 'manual grazing' (Napier & Napier, 1967). Using their thumb and index finger like pincers, they are able to harvest efficiently relatively large quantities of the choicer parts of grasses. A high degree of opposability has been made possible, in part, by relative elongation of the thumb (especially of the pollical metacarpal) and relative shortening of the index finger (especially of the proximal and middle phalanges) (Maier, 1972a; Etter, 1973, 1974). This is reflected, in turn, by the species' opposability index, which is the highest among nonhuman primates (Napier & Napier, 1967; Maier, 1972a; Etter, 1973).

Although the importance of a structurally modified hand in the feeding adaptation of the gelada has been widely recognized, heretofore it has been impossible to determine whether this specialization is

Fig. 1. Hypothesis of phylogenetic relationships among species of *Theropithecus*. See Eck (1983) and Eck & Jablonski (1984) for detailed discussions of this scheme.

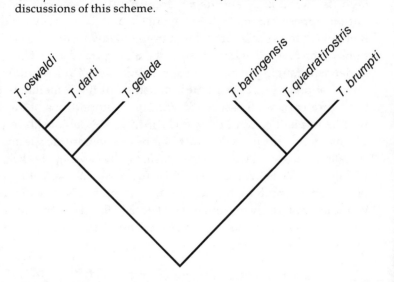

unique to this species or was present in other, earlier species of *Theropithecus* as well. Comparison of the hand skeleton of *Theropithecus gelada* with a partial hand skeleton of *T. brumpti* in the present study permits examination of this question.

Partial hand skeleton of *Theropithecus brumpti*

A partial skeleton of *Theropithecus brumpti* was recovered from silty sediments of Locality 865, Unit 4, Member E of the Shungura Formation by members of the International Omo Research Expedition. Elements of the skeleton of a right hand, designated L865-2 a, b, c, etc., were recovered in direct association with other remnants of the postcranium, the posterior portion of the neurocranium, and a complete mandible. The morphology of the mandible and its contained teeth indicate that the skeleton is that of an old adult male (Eck & Jablonski, in press). The approximate age of the sediments from which the fossil was recovered (based on new decay constants) is 2.22 m.y. (G. G. Eck, personal communication).

The partial hand skeleton is moderately well preserved and comprises elements of the rays of all five digits, including seven sesamoid bones (Fig. 2). No distal phalanges were found. The lengths of the elements present are listed in Table 1.

Fig. 2. Partial hand skeleton of *Theropithecus brumpti* (L865-2).
(A) Dorsal aspect. (B) Ventral aspect. Sesamoid bones are not shown.

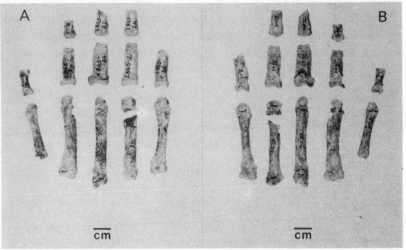

Description

Metacarpals

The preserved portion of metacarpal I (L865-2e) is slender and relatively long. Fracture of the proximal portion of the diaphysis resulted, unfortunately, in loss of the base. (Assessment of the degree of flaring of the proximal diaphysis permitted an estimation of the length of the base and, hence, estimation of the length of the entire bone [see Table 1].) The head of metacarpal I is slightly asymmetric; a prominent tuberosity on the distoradial aspect of the shaft may have been the site of attachment for a portion of *m. flexor pollicis brevis* or *m. opponens pollicis*.

Metacarpal II (L865-2c) is a robust bone with a stout base. Fractured portions of the distoradial aspect of the shaft and the head have been reconstructed, but the distoulnar aspect of the shaft and ulnar aspect of the head are missing. The articular surface of the base is broad and relatively flat: although individual facets for articulation with the trapezoid and capitate are not clearly demarcated, the surface for articulation with the capitate is slightly bevelled in a distoulnar direction and is interrupted by a relatively large, triangular fossa for ligamentous attachment.

Metacarpal III (L865-2d) is relatively slender. Although displacing fractures of the head, base, and midshaft necessitated reconstruction, the bone is essentially complete. Pronounced asymmetry of the head corresponds to an asymmetry of the adjacent articular surface of the proximal phalanx, and may be due to antemortem injury or another pathological condition. The base is robust, but is compressed in a radioulnar direction. The facet for articulation with the capitate is narrow, but its detail is obscured by cracking and flaking of the bone. A prominent crest on the ventroulnar surface of the proximal shaft may have afforded attachment to a portion of the contrahens tendon.

Table 1. *Lengths (in mm) of the elements of the partial hand skeleton of* Theropithecus brumpti *(L865-2)*

	Metacarpal	Proximal phalanx	Middle phalanx
Digit I	42[a]	15.30	–
Digit II	47.35	22.20	10.50
Digit III	52.35	25.40	15.20
Digit IV	47[a]	25.35	15.60
Digit V	45.50	22.65	absent

[a] Estimated, due to damage

Fractures to metacarpal IV (L865-2b) have resulted in irreparable displacement of the head. Although the head and shaft are now separated, relatively little of the intervening bone has been lost. The base is compressed in a radioulnar direction; its articular surface with the hamate is flat and ventrodorsally bevelled. A deep, narrow groove for ligamentous attachment is seen on the ulnar aspect of the base. The ventral surface of the shaft just distal to the base bears a prominent tuberosity, which may have served as an attachment for one of the *mm. interossei palmares.*

Metacarpal V (L865-2a) is stout and is marked by prominent crests and rugosities. Although crushing of the dorsoulnar aspect of the distal shaft has obscured some detail, a strong crest for attachment of *m. opponens digiti minimi* is easily defined. A small tuberosity just proximal to the head on the radial side may mark the insertion of one of the *mm. contrahentes manus.* The base is wide and projects in a ventroradial, rather than a ventroulnar, direction. The facet for articulation with the hamate is saddle-shaped, but bears a flat, rectangular extension onto the dorsoulnar surface of the base.

Phalanges
Proximal phalanx I (L865-2m) is a small, stout bone. The base, although somewhat distorted by crushing, appears to have been large and flared. Proximal phalanges II, III, IV, and V (L865-2g, h, i, and f, respectively) are stout bones with relatively broad shafts and flattened volar surfaces. All are slightly convex dorsally. Asymmetry of the articular surface of the base of proximal phalanx III, as mentioned in the description of the head of metacarpal III, may be attributable to a pathological condition. The distal end of proximal phalanx V deviates slightly to the ulnar side.

Middle phalanges II, III, and IV (L865-21, j, and k, respectively) are short bones with flattened volar surfaces. Middle phalanx II appears particularly abbreviated. Middle phalanges III and IV are slightly convex dorsally.

Comparative analysis

Visual comparison of the partial hand skeleton of *Theropithecus brumpti* (Fig. 2) with a hand skeleton of an adult male gelada (Fig. 3) permits recognition of telling morphological similarities between the two species. The relative sizes of the digits and their respective elements are remarkably similar in *T. brumpti* and *T. gelada*, although the hand skeleton of *T. brumpti* is slightly larger, more robust, and more strongly marked than that of the gelada. Of particular

Table 2. *Calculation of an estimated opposability index of* Theropithecus brumpti *(L865-2), using the formula of Napier & Napier (1967)*

	Digit I Length (mm)	Digit II Length (mm)
Metacarpal	42[a]	47.35
Proximal phalanx	15.30	22.20
Middle phalanx	–	15.20
Distal phalanx[b]	11[a]	12
Estimated total length of ray	68.3	96.8

$$\text{Opposability index} = \frac{\text{thumb length} \times 100}{\text{index ray length}} = 70.6 \text{ (estimate)}$$

[a] Estimated, due to damage
[b] Estimated lengths, based on figures reported by Etter (1973) for several species of large cercopithecoids

Fig. 3. Hand skeleton of an adult male specimen of *Theropithecus gelada* (HKU 0231). (A) Dorsal aspect. (B) Ventral aspect.

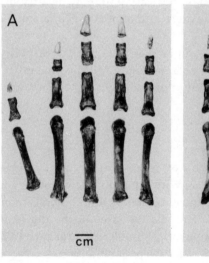
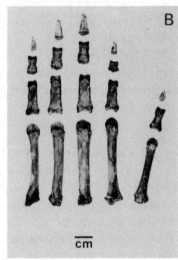

interest are similarities between the species in the morphology of digits I and II. In both *T. brumpti* and *T. gelada* the pollical metacarpal is relatively long and slender and the phalanges of digit II (especially the middle phalanx) are relatively short. These similarities become more striking when digits I and II of *T. brumpti* and *T. gelada* are compared to those of *Macaca mulatta* (Fig. 4).

The similarity of the hand skeletons of *Theropithecus brumpti* and *T. gelada* is further borne out by comparison of the opposability indices of the two species. Although damage to the pollical metacarpal and absence of the distal phalanges in the hand skeleton of *T. brumpti* permits calculation of only a rough estimate of the opposability index of the species (Table 2), that figure compares favorably with the

Fig. 4. Dorsal aspect of the bony elements of digits I and II of *Theropithecus brumpti* (L865-2), *T. gelada* (HKU 0231), and *Macaca mulatta* (HKU 0110). Note especially the differences in the relative sizes of the pollical metacarpal and the phalanges of digit II between *M. mulatta* and the two species of *Theropithecus*.

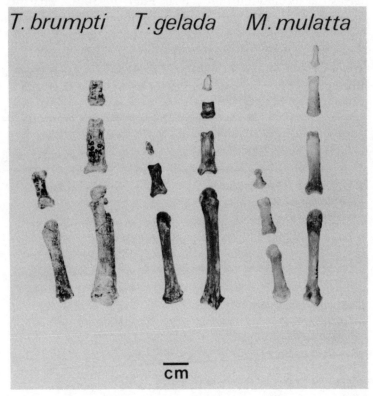

opposability indices calculated for samples of *T. gelada* by Maier (1972*a*) and Etter (1973) (Table 3). The indices for both species of *Theropithecus* are significantly higher than those reported for other cercopithecoid species.

Discussion and conclusions

The structural similarities between the remains of the hand skeleton of *Theropithecus brumpti* and the corresponding elements of the hand of *T. gelada* are indicative of comparable functional capabilities in the hands of the two species. Although the hand of *T. brumpti* was more powerfully built than is that of the gelada, it appears to have been capable of the same high degree of precise opposition of the thumb and index finger. There seems little doubt that this specialized pincer mechanism served *T. brumpti* in much the same way as it serves the gelada today – in the harvesting of edible vegetation. Special note should be taken, however, of one interesting difference between the hands of the two species. Although the hand skeletons of *T. brumpti* and *T. gelada* bear the hallmarks of an adaptation for terrestrial locomotion (Jolly, 1970; Etter, 1973), the phalanges of *T. brumpti* are slightly curved, whereas those of the gelada are not.

Table 3. *Comparison of the estimated opposability index of* Theropithecus brumpti *with the opposability indices reported for* T. gelada *and other extant cercopithecoids*

	N	Opposability index
Theropithecus brumpti (L865-2)	1	70.6
T. gelada	5	69.6[a]
T. gelada	3	70[b]
Papio hamadryas hamadryas	12	60.0[a]
P. h. cynocephalus	8	52.8[a]
P. h. subsp.	13	57[c]
P. h. subsp.	10	60[b]
Macaca mulatta	15	53.2[a]
Macaca sp.	18	54[c]
Cercopithecus aethiops	12	49.2[a]
Cercopithecus sp.	11	53[c]

[a] Reported by Etter (1973)
[b] Reported by Maier (1972*a*)
[c] Reported by Napier & Napier (1967)

Curved phalanges are commonly found in arboreal mammals and their suggestion in the hand of *T. brumpti* may indicate a more arboreal habit for this species than that which characterizes *T. gelada*. This morphological evidence accords with the apparent preference of the fossil species for woodland or forest habitats (Eck & Jablonski, in press). Future examination of the preserved tarsal bones of skeleton L865 (calcaneum, navicular, and talus) may shed further light on this issue.

It is reasonable to suggest that the traits of the hand skeleton shared by *T. brumpti* and *T. gelada* are heritage traits that were present in the common ancestor of the respective lineages of the two species. In light of the hypothesis of phyletic relationships within *Theropithecus* presented in Fig. 1, this suggestion implies that the specialized hand morphology seen in both *T. brumpti* and *T. gelada* is primitive for the genus as a whole. The cranial and postcranial elements of the feeding apparatus of *Theropithecus* thus appear to have evolved in concert.

The great evolutionary success enjoyed by *Theropithecus* throughout most of the Pliocene and Pleistocene was correlated to a large extent with evolution of feeding and locomotor apparatuses, which permitted invasion of relatively open habitats (Jolly, 1972; Jablonski, 1981; Eck & Jablonski, in press) and utilization of food resources similar to those exploited in the same areas by ungulates. *Theropithecus brumpti* is the only species of the genus which appears to have retreated to a life amongst the trees.

Acknowledgements

I thank F. Clark Howell for permitting me to borrow specimen L865-2 for study. Samuel K. O. Hui is very gratefully acknowledged for his expert assistance in the preparation of Figs 2, 3, and 4. Fig. 1 was drawn by Doris S. P. Chan. This research was supported in part by a grant from the Pauline Chan Medical Research Fund of the University of Hong Kong.

References

Andrews, C. W. (1916) Notes on a new baboon (*Simopithecus oswaldi*, gen. et sp. nov.) from the (?) Pliocene of British East Africa. *Annals Mag. Nat. Hist.*, **18**, 410–19

Dunbar, R. I. M. (1977) Feeding ecology of gelada baboons: a preliminary report. In *Primate Ecology: Studies of Feeding and Ranging in Lemurs, Monkeys, and Apes*, ed. T. H. Clutton-Brock, pp. 251–73. London: Academic Press

Dunbar, R. I. M. (1983) Theropithecines and hominids: contrasting solutions to the same ecological problem. *J. Hum. Evol.*, **12**, 647–58

Eck, G. G. (1977) Diversity and frequency distribution of Omo Group Cercopithecoidea. *J. Hum. Evol.*, **6**, 55–63

Eck, G. G. (1983) The six species of *Theropithecus*. *Am. J. Phys. Anthropol.*, **60**, 190–1 (abstract)

Eck, G. G. & Jablonski, N. G. (1984) A reassessment of the taxonomic status and phyletic relationships of *Papio baringensis* and *Papio quadratirostris* (Primates: Cercopithecidae). *Am. J. Phys. Anthropol.*, **65**, 109–34

Eck, G. G. & Jablonski, N. G. (in press) The skull of *Theropithecus brumpti* compared with those of the other species of the genus *Theropithecus*. In *Paléobiologie du Bassin de l'Omo (Ethiopie)*. Paris: CNRS

Etter, H. F. (1973) Terrestrial adaptations in the hands of Cercopithecinae. *Folia Primatol.*, **20**, 331–50

Etter, H. F. (1974) Morphologisch- und metrisch-vergleichende Untersuchung am Handskelet rezenter Primaten. *Gegenbaurs Morphol. Jahrb.*, **120**, 457–84

Iwamoto, T. (1979) Feeding ecology. *Contrib. Primatol.*, **16**, 279–330

Jablonski, N. G. (1981) Functional analysis of the masticatory apparatus of *Theropithecus gelada* (Primates: Cercopithecidae). Ph.D. dissertation, University of Washington, Seattle

Jablonski, N. G. (1983) Evolution of a novel masticatory apparatus in a lineage of cercopithecoid primates. *Am. Zoologist*, **23**, 1009 (abstract)

Jolly, C. J. (1970) The large African monkeys as an adaptive array. In *Old World Monkeys*, ed. J. R. Napier & P. H. Napier, pp. 139–74. New York: Academic Press

Jolly, C. J. (1972) The classification and natural history of *Theropithecus* (*Simopithecus*) (Andrews, 1916), baboons of the African Plio–Pleistocene. *Bull. Br. Mus. Nat. Hist. (Geol.)*, **22**, 1–123

Leakey, L. S. B. (1943) Notes on *Simopithecus oswaldi* Andrews from the type site. *J. E. Afr. Nat. Hist. Soc.*, **17**, 39–44

Leakey, L. S. B. & Whitworth, T. (1958) Notes on the genus *Simopithecus*, with a description of a new species from Olduvai. *Coryndon Mem. Mus. Occ. Papers*, **6**, 3–14

Maier, W. (1972a) Anpassungstyp und systematische Stellung von *Theropithecus gelada* Rüppell, 1835. *Z. Morphol. Anthropol.*, **63**, 370–84

Maier, W. (1972b) The first complete skull of *Simopithecus darti* from Makapansgat, South Africa, and its systematic position. *J. Hum. Evol.*, **1**, 395–405

Napier, J. R. & Napier, P. H. (1967) *A Handbook of Living Primates*. London: Academic Press

II.6

Evolution of the knee intra-articular menisci in primates and some fossil hominids

C. TARDIEU

Introduction

The knee joint of primates and other mammals contains two fibrocartilaginous menisci, an internal one and an external one. The internal meniscus is very similar in all primates; it is crescent-shaped with two tibial insertions. In contrast, the external meniscus is more variable in shape and in the number of tibial insertions. Dissections of primate knee joints by Retterer (1907), Vallois (1914) and more recently by myself have shown that the external meniscus displays three distinct morphologies in extant primates (Fig. 1).

A crescent-shaped external meniscus with one tibial insertion anterior to the external tibial spine (Fig. 1A) is found in all lemuriforms, in *Tarsius*, in platyrrhines, and in the orangutan. This type of meniscus is also found in *Tupaia* and many insectivores (de Fenis, 1918) and probably represents the primitive mammalian morphology for this structure.

A crescent-shaped meniscus with two tibial insertions, one anterior and one posterior to the external spine (Fig. 1C) is found in *Homo sapiens* and is a unique condition among living mammals.

Fig. 1. The three morphologies of the external meniscus in extant primates. (A) Crescent-shaped meniscus with a single tibial insertion. (B) Ring-shaped meniscus with a single tibial insertion. (C) Crescent-shaped meniscus with two tibial insertions.

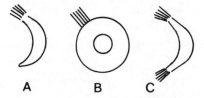

A   B   C

A ring-shaped meniscus with one insertion anterior to the external spine (Fig. 1B) is found in cercopithecoids, gibbons, chimpanzees, and gorillas.

In this paper I discuss some possible phylogenies for the evolution of the different morphologies found in the external meniscus, evidence for meniscal morphology in some fossil hominids, and the functional significance of differences in the shape and number of attachments of the lateral meniscus.

Materials

This study is based on the following sample of living primates:

Tarsiiforms	1 *Tarsius*		
Lemuriforms	2 *Daubentonia*	1 *Nycticebus*	
	3 *Lemur*	1 *Perodicticus*	
	1 *Galago*	2 *Loris*	
Platyrrhines	2 *Callithrix*	2 *Cebus*	
	2 *Saguinus*	2 *Saimiri*	
	2 *Aotus*	2 *Ateles*	
	2 *Alouatta*		
Cercopithecoids	4 *Papio*	5 *Colobus*	
	3 *Macaca*	3 *Semnopithecus*	
	7 *Cercopithecus*	8 *Erythrocebus*	
	1 *Cercocebus*		
Hominoids	4 *Hylobates*	3 *Gorilla*	
	4 *Pongo*	18 *Homo*	
	5 *Pan*		

The evolution of the lateral meniscus

Several phylogenies can be constructed from the distribution of meniscal morphologies described above. One phylogenetic hypothesis, based on commonality and comparisons with insectivores and *Tupaia*, would be the following:

1. There has been a retention of the primitive crescent-shaped morphology during primate evolution.
2. There was a slight modification in man, with the addition of the second posterior insertion.
3. Appearance of the ring-shaped meniscus occurred on the divergent line joining cercopithecoids, gorilla, chimpanzee and gibbon.

This hypothesis is inconsistent with the recognized phylogeny of primates and will not be considered further.

Alternatively, we can propose two different hypotheses that are more consistent with current views on primate phylogeny.

The first hypothesis (Fig. 2) involves a transition from the crescent shape to the ring shape during catarrhine evolution. It suggests:

1. The ring-shaped meniscus developed in the last common ancestor of cercopithecoids and hominoids.
2. There were two reversions to the more primitive condition in orangutan and man.
3. There is one autapomorph human feature with the formation of the posterior tibial insertion.

The second hypothesis (Fig. 3) supposes the retention of the primitive crescent-shape during the primate evolution and suggests:

1. There have been three convergences of the ring type, occurring separately in cercopithecoids, gibbon, and chimpanzee and gorilla.
2. There was one change in man, with the addition of a posterior tibial insertion.

Neither of these two hypotheses is totally satisfying, but the first one seems to me more probable.

The first hypothesis raises the problem of the infantile and embryological development of the external meniscus in man. Does the external meniscus present a ring-shaped stage in its development?

Fig. 2. First phylogenetic hypothesis based on the morphology of the external meniscus in extant primates. ●: two modifications of the primitive condition; 1, 2: two reversals to the primitive condition.

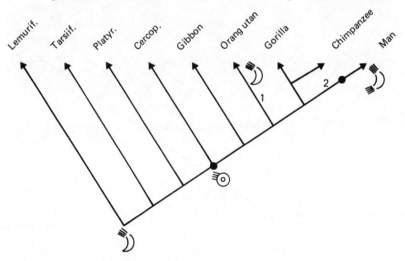

On a sample of 10 skeletons of infants from 0 to 12 months of age (collection of the Musée de l'Homme, Paris), I observed the presence of a ring-shaped meniscus on one specimen. The occasional occurrence in man of a ring-shaped meniscus is consistent with the first hypothesis. It would represent the reappearance of an ancestral feature. This observation needs further investigations in human infants and adults.

My only data on embryology are from the literature, which is very poor. One author (Kaplan, 1957) reported no ring-shaped stage in the embryological development of the external meniscus in man. These ontogenetic results would *not* support our first hypothesis. However, I think this single embryological study is insufficient to conclude definitively. A very precise dissection, including precartilaginous stages and histological study, on a large number of human embryos would be necessary to observe the priority of appearance of each insertion of the meniscus. Perhaps the anterior one develops very early and the posterior one very late as the result of the retraction of a cartilaginous process directed towards the anterior horn of the meniscus.

The second hypothesis presented above has the inconvenience of showing morphological convergences between primates whose type of locomotion, and presumed knee function, is quite different, such as

Fig. 3. Second phylogenetic hypothesis based on the morphology of the external meniscus in extant primates. ●: one modification of the primitive condition; 1, 2, 3: three convergences.

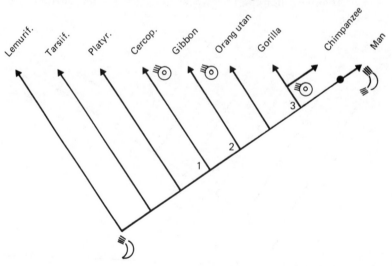

gibbons and cercopithecoids. In addition, different morphologies are present in primates with similar locomotion, such as *Ateles* and *Hylobates*.

I should note that the crescent-shaped meniscus of the orangutan is very closed. This may be indicative either of a ring shape recently reopened, or of a crescent shape in the process of closing.

Interpretation of fossil hominid tibias

Fossil tibias are always without menisci. However, on the dry tibia we can detect the presence of one or two tibial insertions of the external meniscus (Tardieu, in press). In man, there are two areas of insertion, which set free the external spine. The posterior border of the external plateau is long, discontinuous, and notched by the posterior insertion of the meniscus. In African apes, there is one area of insertion of the external meniscus. The posterior border of the external plateau is short, continuous and abrupt.

On the right tibia KNMER 1481 B from East Turkana, the posterior border is long, discontinuous, and notched by the posterior insertion of the external meniscus. This suggests that the meniscus was crescent-shaped with two insertions as in modern man.

In contrast, on the right tibia AL 129 1b (and AL 288 1 AQ) from Hadar, the posterior border of the external plateau is short, continuous and abrupt. This fossil presumably had an external meniscus with a single tibial insertion, anterior to the external spine. On the left tibia AL 333 × 26 from Hadar as in AL 129, there was no posterior insertion of the external meniscus.

Thus the fossil record of hominids provides evidence that the evolution from a single insertion of the lateral meniscus, as found in all other primates, to the double insertion found in *Homo sapiens* has occurred within hominid evolution, rather than in a prehominid ancestor. The Plio–Pleistocene hominids give some very representative specimens of each type. The common presence of a single insertion in AL 333 × 26 and in AL 129 1b cannot constitute an argument for placing these two fossils in the same species, as proposed by some authors (Johanson & White, 1979) since it is a common *primitive* feature and not a common *derived* one.

The tibias of the Middle Miocene fossils *Pliopithecus vindobonensis* and *Oreopithecus bambolii* show the primitive pattern of one single anterior insertion of the external meniscus. However, the crescent shape or ring shape of the meniscus cannot be distinguished on the dry tibia and consequently on the fossil tibia we studied.

Elements of morphofunctional analysis

The external meniscus is always more opened than the internal one in primates, except in slow climbers. The crescent-shaped meniscus with one single insertion presents variations in primates (Fig. 4). It is very open in leapers, such as *Galago* and *Tarsius*, and is very closed in slow climbers such as *Perodicticus* and *Nycticebus*. It is intermediate in *Lemur*. In primates other than man, it seems clear that the closure of the meniscus occurs with an increase in knee rotation movement. For example, knee rotation movements appear to be important in the locomotion of slow climbers.

In man, the presence of a second, more posterior tibial insertion corresponds to a very different type of knee function. It limits the mobility of the meniscus on the tibial plateau. In Fig. 5 one can observe the displacements of the menisci in man. In extension (B), the menisci go forwards; in flexion (C) they go backwards; in external rotation of the femur about the tibia (D), the external meniscus is pulled backwards strongly; and in internal rotation of the femur about the tibia (E) the movements of the menisci are reversed. Thus, the second posterior insertion in man contributes to prevent the external meniscus from an extreme forwards gliding during frequent extension and limits the amplitude of rotation of the knee.

I have shown in previous work that the amplitude of rotation of the femur about the tibia, especially internal rotation, is very weak in man

Fig. 4. Superior view of the right proximal tibia with the menisci in three lemuriform primates: (A) *Galago*; (B) *Nycticebus*; (C) *Lemur catta*. Notice the variable shape of the external meniscus.

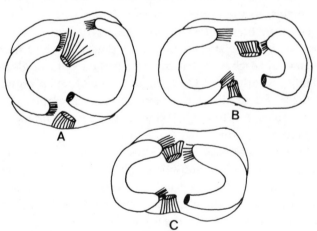

in comparison with the chimpanzee. The absence of a posterior insertion in chimpanzee permits the very high amplitude of internal rotation. In fact, the mode of insertion of the meniscus determines its mobility, which thus determines the amplitude of knee rotation. So we observe more knee stability in man and less knee stability in chimpanzee and most other primates (except leapers).

Conclusions
In conclusion, the number of tibial insertions of the external meniscus has a simple phylogenetic history in primates. The dual insertion that is unique to *Homo sapiens* among living species appears to have evolved within the hominid lineage. I feel that the shape of the meniscus also has an interpretable evolutionary pattern, as suggested in the two hypotheses presented above. However, this feature is more variable because it is linked to many different interrelated functional factors such as weight, pressure, and rotation, that are difficult to measure and isolate at the moment. Further work will be needed to confirm these results and to evaluate the phylogenetic hypotheses that have been suggested. In particular, the occasional observations (by Vallois (1914) and by myself) of intermediate morphologies between the ring-shaped and the crescent-shaped meniscus in some platyrrhines and cercopithecoids need further investigation.

Fig. 5. Diagrammatic representations of the movement of the right medial and lateral menisci in humans (from Langa, 1963): (A) normal; (B) extension; (C) flexion; (D) external rotation of the femur on the tibia; (E) internal rotation of the femur on the tibia.

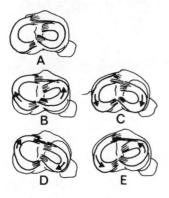

Acknowledgements

I wish to thank Professor J. Anthony and Professor Y. Coppens, Paris, for access to their primate and human collections and for practice of primate dissections; R. E. F. Leakey, Nairobi, and Dr D. C. Johanson, Berkeley, for their kind permission to study the original fossils in their care; and M. Godinot and P. Tassy, Paris, and P. W. Luckett, Puerto Rico, for their scientific advice. This work has been supported by the E.R. CNRS 246 'Locomotion animale', associée au Museum National d'Histoire Naturelle.

References

de Fenis, F. (1918) Note sur la formation et la disparition des menisques intra-articulaires du genou. *Bull. Mem. Soc. Anthropol., Paris*, **9**, 19–32

Johanson, D. C. & White, T. D. (1979) A systematič assessment of Early African hominids. *Science*, **203**, 321–30

Kaplan, E. B. (1957) Discoid lateral meniscus of the knee-joint. Nature, mechanism, and operative treatment. *J. Bone Joint Surg.*, **39A**, 77–87

Langa, G. S. (1963) Experimental observations and interpretations of the relationship between the morphology and function of the human knee-joint. *Acta Anat*, **55**, 16–38

Retterer, Ed. (1907) De la forme et des connexions que présentent les fibro cartilages du genou chez quelques singes d'Afrique. *C.R. Soc. Biol.*, **63**, 20 juillet 1907

Tardieu, C. (in press) Knee-joint in three hominoid primates. Osteology, meniscal dissections, rotation measurements. Application to plio-pleistocene hominids. Evolutionary implications. In *Proceedings of the IXe Congress of the International Primatological Society*, vol. 2, *Current Perspectives in Primate Biology*, ed. D. M. Taub & F. A. King. New York: Van Nostrand Reinhold

Vallois, H. (1914) *Etude Anatomique de l'Articulation du Genou chez les Primates.* Montpellier: Impr. Coop. ouvrière 'l'Abeille'

II.7

A new approach to postcanine tooth size applied to Plio–Pleistocene hominids

P. W. LUCAS, R. T. CORLETT AND D. A. LUKE

Introduction

Most taxonomic assessments are accompanied and assisted by dental measurements. These are more critical for studies of fossils because teeth usually form the bulk of reported finds. Yet tooth size is not well understood in relation to ecological adaptation. We present here, in abbreviated form, a model of food characteristics that can help in unravelling the relation between teeth and diet.

Our approach to this relation stems from experiments on modern man. Though the word 'mastication' may connote images of electromyography, neurophysiology and bone-strain, the mechanics of mastication to which we refer are intra-oral, at the tooth–food–tooth interface. This is the working end of the process where the food breakdown, from which the dictionary definition of the word 'mastication' arises, takes place. The rate at which the process runs is probably critical to an animal and depends on the rate at which it chews. Little is yet known about chewing rates and our analysis is limited to a consideration of the rate of food breakdown as per chew.

This rate of breakdown depends on two variables: the first is the chance that any particle has of being broken; the second is the manner of fragmentation of the particle on being hit. These are distinct. For example, equal-sized particles of carrot and peanut may have equal probabilities of being broken, although carrot fragments into a few pieces while peanut shatters into many. This introduces a key issue into the present discussion, which is that food particles behave in a statistical manner. The soft tissues guide particles but cannot rigidly control their movements. They merely influence what particle positions are likely. However, given a constant repetition of such movements as is inherent in the cyclical nature of the process, the particle size distribution after many cycles becomes predictable. These variables have been defined in mathematical terms by Lucas & Luke (1983).

Bearing this general framework in mind, it is possible to abstract general conclusions from chewing experiments in modern man and apply these to a comparative analysis of what food types could cause problems to the rate of oral processing. We hypothesise that, of all the factors that could affect the probability of food fracture, the most obvious is tooth size. This is the factor that is correlated best with the rate of food processing in man (Manly, 1951; Fig. 1). Any adaptation other than this would be unlikely to increase the proportion of food particles by volume (or weight) that are broken per chew unless postcanine tooth area were also increased. Tooth size cannot be

Fig. 1. The median size of raw carrot particles produced by 32 human subjects after 30 chews is significantly correlated ($p<0.001$) with their postcanine tooth area ($\bullet$ = males, $\bigcirc$ = females). Tooth area was estimated from dental casts. The mean ability to reduce particle size did not differ between males and females, though the females had significantly smaller tooth dimensions ($t = 3.22$, $p<0.01$).

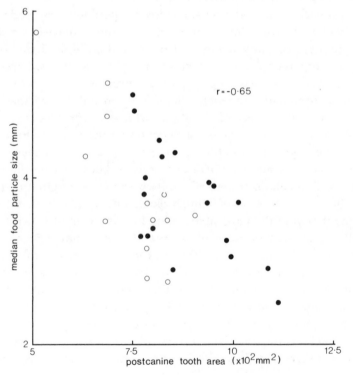

estimated in absolute terms and we suggest that it is best estimated as the proportion of available intra-oral surface that is allotted to the postcanine occlusal surfaces. If this proportion were increased or decreased, then the probability of particle fracture would alter in accordance.

Masticatory input

As a primate acquires a food, it has a potential input for mastication. The rate of comminuted output depends on the form of the input. We assume a batch form of mastication rather than a continual feed of particles as on a conveyor-belt. This allows the use of the term 'mouthful' to describe a given quantity of food in the mouth. This mouthful is best understood as the degree to which intra-oral volume is filled with food. (Therefore both tooth size and the mouthful of food are dimensionless quantities.) We now suggest a new and comprehensive categorisation of the mouthful (Fig. 2).

External physical characteristics

These are properties of the external surface of food particles and include particle size, shape, volume, stickiness and abrasiveness. The roughness (rugosity) is another such feature which must cause problems with grip, but it is not dealt with here.

1. Food particle size is very important to the likelihood of the particle being fractured. The smaller the particle, the less likely it is to be hit and therefore the slower the rate that particle size is reduced per chew (Lucas & Luke, 1983). Why would ingesting small particles cause any problem to an

Fig. 2. A categorisation of the process of mastication with a definition of the input (see text).

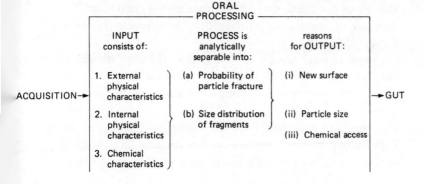

animal? If the purpose of making them small is to increase their surface area or to reduce them to below the size that they can be swallowed, then the smaller that they are to begin with, the closer that they are to the desired objective. The only reason for dental changes following an adaptation to small objects is that if they remained unbroken then they would be impervious to digestion. This is only clear if the behaviour of food particles in the mouth is treated in a statistical way. The importance of particle size for swallowing, or surface area for digestion, depends only on the average particle. Chemical access, in contrast, demands that all particles be broken. Treating particles as possessing a probability of being broken implies that, for a given group of such particles, they must be kept in the mouth until all are (probably) broken. The critical assumption is that of limited sensory feedback to the central nervous system about the size and position of particles in the mouth. If only one such particle is ingested then it is clear that the tongue can manoeuvre it towards the teeth for them to break it in the first chew. However, even for a small group of particles, this ability would be much diminished. Therefore, for numbers of small particles above one or two, their rate of processing is hampered by the possession of a chemically defended outer coat.

2. The volume of food taken into the mouth markedly affects the rate of oral processing. An increase in the amount ingested decreases the rate exponentially, presumably because the probability of fracture of all particles is correspondingly reduced (Lucas & Luke, 1984). However, when equal volumes are compared, the processing of large volumes is more rapid. There is a little evidence in man that the rate of production of total surface area is greater and the number of chews per unit volume is reduced (Lucas & Luke, 1984).

Small objects are likely to be taken into the mouth in smaller quantities than larger ones given a similar rate of acquisition in terms of number of particles per unit of time.

3. The shape of a particle must be important initially to the masticatory process because tooth surfaces act on food surfaces and the presentation of food surface depends on

its shape. Furthermore, the rate of production of new surface depends on shape. Three extremes of shapes can be envisaged – a sheet, a rod and a sphere. These extremes are useful because, for example, leaves are sheets, rhizomes are rods and many fruits and seeds are approximately isodiametric. The smallest dimension of each of these objects will determine the amount of new surface exposed by a crack. The initial advantage that a leaf might present by virtue of its large initial surface area will quickly be lost in comparison to a seed of equal volume whose fracture exposes a greater new area. For these reasons particle size is probably best estimated by individual volume. Thus leaves are effectively small objects.

4. The stickiness of a food particle affects bolus formation. Reviews of swallowing usually refer to a bolus (Miller, 1982) but the success of the soft tissues of the mouth in collecting the food particles together does not mean that they are cohering. An example of a human food that does not form a bolus in this sense is carrot (Lucas & Luke, in press). The human tongue can collect comminuted carrot particles together (they are spat out in tests as such) but they are always free to disperse. Few good reasons can be found in the literature for the relative advantages of a molar being somewhat buccolingually narrow and mesiodistally long rather than vice-versa. We suggest the former tooth shape would be appropriate for a non-bolus-forming food since the food particles are likely to be dispersed within the mouth following each chew. A sticky bolus, however, is probably thrown laterally as a ball by the tongue. The occlusal surface in the centre of the tooth row would be expected to receive and break most of the food particles. The direction of tongue movement would put a premium on the evolution of a wide short tooth row when the diet consists largely of sticky foods.

5. Wear results from the abrasiveness of food and, also, from the inevitable tooth-tooth contacts of the teeth (Osborn & Lumsden, 1978; Teaford & Walker, 1983). The abrasiveness of food acts over time for its effect. Nevertheless, it can be considered along with other surface properties because the chances of continuing to break food particles are jeopardised by wear.

All these food properties are associated with only one of the two aspects of mastication as we have defined it – the probability of fracture. We argue that the evidence from human studies suggests that a logical evolutionary response would be to increase postcanine tooth area if the rate of oral processing is too low. Thus the ingestion of small volumes of small particles (in numbers greater than one), needing to be processed for chemical access, require large teeth. If the food is sticky, then occlusal area should be concentrated in the centre of the postcanine row. If food is not sticky, then the tooth row can be of equal width along its length.

Abrasive foods require larger teeth. This is most easily argued by imagining food to be broken at sites along the tooth row. The more sites that are available, the less often will a food particle be broken at any one site and, therefore, the more wear-resistant will be the dentition.

Internal physical characteristics

By these we mean deformability, toughness and strength. Little is still known about the distribution of these properties in food objects. However, none of them affects the probability of hitting a particle since they are, by definition, not exposed to the surface. In complete contrast to surface properties they affect only the fragmentation of the particle, which can be measured as the size distribution of fragments. Luke & Lucas (1983) predicted that particular postcanine tooth shapes were adapted for masticating certain combinations of these properties. Stiff, strong (in compression) but brittle foods would best be processed by 'pestle and mortar' structures. There is now evidence that the molar teeth of peccaries (Kiltie, 1982) and certain primates such as *Cebus* (Izawa & Mizuno, 1977), *Cercocebus* (Kay, 1981) and savanna woodland populations of *Pan troglodytes* (Suzuki, 1969) may often be used to break such food types.

Chemical characteristics

These include the detailed chemical structure of the foodstuff, including structural compounds, nutrients and (for plant foods) defence chemistry (Waterman, 1984). These are clearly relevant to tooth design, since gaining access to a foodstuff must be one function of mastication. This is likely to be particularly important for foods that are shaped like sheets (e.g. leaves) since it is difficult to see any other benefit from breaking them. It is hard to create hypotheses about chemical structures and relate them to highly physical processes like mastication. This is particularly true because mastication is followed by chemical processing in the gut. However, Sheine (1979) has found strong evidence to link cellulose content of foods to molar design in prosimians, and Waterman (1984) reviews evidence which suggests that some anthropoid primates select foods on the basis of fibre content.

Application to Plio–Pleistocene hominids

Plio–Pleistocene hominids are examples of mammals that are closely related and have broadly similar tooth shapes but very dissimilar dental proportions and sizes. It is widely agreed now that, by the early Pleistocene, at least two lineages of hominids co-existed (Andrews, 1984). Robust australopithecines possessed very large molar teeth with greatly expanded premolars compared to early *Homo* ('*Homo habilis*'). The lineage leading to early *Homo sapiens* is marked by a progressive decline in tooth size, particularly in the distal molars. Thus, in *Homo sapiens*, most of the postcanine area is in the centre of the row.

Jolly (1970) proposed that early hominids fed on 'small hard spherical objects'. Provided that this argument is transferred only to robust australopithecines (e.g. Wolpoff (1973), who also applied the argument to gracile australopithecines), we support his suggestion. Particle shape is probably the least important part of his dietary definition. Peters (1981) refers to very tough and dry foods. Grine (1981) emphasizes hard and tough objects which were probably small. The emphasis on toughness may arise from confusion about its definition, which is the energy needed to make unit area of new cracked surface. It is independent of the force required to initiate the crack and refers solely to the resistance of a crack to being propagated. A food, therefore, can be very strong under a compressive load but very brittle (the opposite of tough). Peters (1981) assumes that processing time was a crucial factor in the ecological adaptation of hominids which is the same as proposed here. However, his estimates of processing time are based on experiments with naturally occurring foods and are those necessary to swallow an undefined volume of food. It is therefore difficult to compare his approach with ours, where the volume of food in the mouth is crucial. Peters (1981) and Grine (1981) both imply that the robust australopithecines were eating foods of exceptional strength. Walker (1981), however, suggests that the larger muscle force of robust australopithecines is an adaptation to processing very large volumes of food in the mouth. In contrast, our argument is that larger teeth are, somewhat paradoxically, adapted to a decrease in input volume and therefore must support Peters and Grine in saying that compressive strengths of some foods in the diet were very high.

Arguing further, the selection of large teeth in robust australopithecines for breaking small amounts of food suggests a high probability of many empty contacts between teeth during mastication. It is reasonable to assume that such contacts could substantially wear the teeth. Since Teaford & Walker (1983) have shown that tooth–tooth wear tends to leave smooth enamel surfaces, it is possible that some of the microwear evidence for the comminution for abrasive food items could be lost. Walker (1981) showed that *Australopithecus boisei*, from East Africa, possessed smooth polished surfaces on the molar teeth despite incurring heavy wear (Wolpoff, 1973). We tentatively suggest that much of the microwear from abrasive foods might be erased by tooth–tooth wear. This has been argued to explain wear during Phase I in herbivorous mammals by Fortelius (1981). Grine (1981) has found that Phase I wear facets of australopithecines are smoother than Phase II facets.

The comparatively small size of the premolars in *Homo* and the progressive reduction of the distal molar teeth through time suggest a masticatory input of large volumes of large particles that consisted largely of sticky but relatively unabrasive food. A coherent bolus could not be easily distributed along the mesiodistal length of the tooth row. Thus, placing most of the occlusal area in the centre of the row does not affect the rate of food processing and probably saves tissue by reducing the consequences of many empty tooth contacts. Although the hypothesis is tenuous, it is, however, difficult to suggest a selective advantage for the reduction of structures during evolution. The behaviour of food particles in the mouth must be pertinent to the interpretation of dental changes and it is therefore worth consideration.

We assume both hominid lineages inhabited a mosaic of woodland, edaphic grassland and riverine forest, although Behrensmeyer (1978) provides possible evidence for different habitat preferences. Within this mosaic a wide range of potential (i.e. digestible) food items would have been at least seasonally available, but only a few in sufficient abundance to be dietary staples. Most abundant are the leaves of grasses and other plants. Mature leaves can probably be ruled out by their high content of undigestible fibre, but young leaves are more palatable and nutritious. Grass leaves form a major part of the wet season diet of savanna baboons which, like hominids, lack digestive specialisations for utilising cellulose and must rely on efficient mastication to extract maximum food value (Dunbar, 1976; Iwamoto, 1979). During the later part of the wet season, grass seeds are abundantly available at open sites and provide a concentrated food source for any animal which can harvest them efficiently. During the dry season the leguminous trees, which dominate vast areas of savanna and woodland in Africa today, produce large quantities of highly nutritious pods and seeds. Other non-leguminous species in the woodland and riverine forest produce seeds and fruits at various times of the year. Particularly during the dry season, roots and storage organs of grasses and herbs provide another potential staple. Finally, invertebrate and vertebrate animal life provides the most concentrated food supply for animals able to acquire it.

If our earlier arguments are correct, the peculiar (for a primate) dentition of the robust australopithecines suggests a diet in which small, hard, brittle objects were a major component.

The seeds of grasses, legumes and a variety of other species not only fit this description but also occur with sufficient abundance and uniform distribution to make it energetically worthwhile for a large animal to specialise on them. A diet of small objects harvested individually requires that feeding should be almost continuous to ensure adequate intake, as it is in the graminivorous baboons (Altmann & Altmann, 1970; Iwamoto, 1979). Shallow-lying roots and storage organs (e.g. grasses and sedges) are another possible seasonal staple which broadly fit the properties predicted. Young leaves of grasses and other plants may have been an important food item in the early wet season. Such leaves are, from our analysis, small objects but are certainly not hard. Treating leaves as small objects, chewed in small amounts, might make some sense of the fact that leaf-eating primates generally have large molars (Kay, 1975, 1978; Pirie, 1978).

Early *Homo* was probably capable of eating most, if not all, of the food items listed above. Hard dry seeds dominate the dry season diet of savanna chimpanzees (Suzuki, 1969) which lack the extreme developments of the masticatory systems seen in the robust australopithecines. However, the trend to molar reduction in the *Homo* lineage is not compatible with specialisation on small hard objects. We believe they concentrated on larger food items, compensating for their more limited masticatory abilities by postcranial, behavioural and technological adaptations. There is convincing evidence for the use of stone tools in the processing of meat, however acquired (Isaac & Crader, 1981), although this evidence is not directly linked to early *Homo*. The less sophisticated technology of the digging stick would have given access to the large, deeply buried storage organs which form such an important item in the diet of modern hunter-gatherers. A wide range of seeds, fruits and vegetative parts of plants may also have been consumed. The possibility of considerable extra-oral processing reduces our expectation of direct teeth–diet correlations and makes firm conclusions impossible to reach.

We conclude, therefore, that the robust australopithecines were basically specialised seed-eaters with perhaps a fairly large component of roots, storage organs and young leaves in their diet. The diet of early *Homo* was certainly different but cannot be determined from dental evidence alone. The results of our analysis differ far less from those of other authors than the analysis itself, which is addressed directly to the rate of processing and how it can be affected. Different types of approach to reconstructing hominid diets can produce different types of information. We hope that postcanine tooth size can attain the prominence in functional studies that it has in taxonomy.

Acknowledgements

Many thanks to Professor W. C. Wong and A. N. Rao for their total support and encouragement, S. E. Gerrard for indispensable help with acquiring the literature, Dr J. G. Fleagle, Professor J. W. Osborn and Professor Dr H. Preuschoft for their comments and the last-named for his invitation.

References

Altmann, S. A. & Altmann, J. (1970) *Baboon Ecology.* Chicago: University of Chicago Press

Andrews, P. (1984) The descent of man. *New Scientist,* 3 May, 24–5

Behrensmeyer, A. K. (1978) The habitat of Plio–Pleistocene hominids in East Africa: taphonomic and microstratigraphic evidence. In *Early Hominids of Africa,* ed. C. J. Jolly, pp. 165–89. London: Duckworth

Dunbar, R. I. M. (1976) Australopithecine diet based on a baboon analogy. *J. Hum. Evol.,* 5, 161–7

Fortelius, M. (1981) Functional aspects of occlusal cheek-tooth morphology in hysodont, non-ruminant ungulates. *Int. Symp. Concepts and Methods in Paleontology, Barcelona* 1981, 153–62

Grine, F. E. (1981) Trophic differences between 'gracile' and 'robust' australopithecines: a scanning electron microscope analysis of occlusal events. *S. Afr. J. Sci.,* 77, 203–30

Isaac, G. L. & Crader, D. S. (1981) To what extent were early hominids carnivorous? An archaeological perspective. In *Omnivorous Primates,* ed. R. S. O. Harding & G. Teleki, pp. 37–103. New York: Columbia University Press

Iwamoto, T. (1979) Feeding Ecology. In *Ecological and Sociological Studies of Gelada Baboons,* ed. M. Kawai, pp. 279–335. Basel: Karger

Izawa, K. & Mizuno, A. (1977) Palm-fruit cracking behaviour of wild black-capped capuchin (*Cebus apella*). *Primates,* 14, 773–92

Jolly, C. J. (1970) The seed-eaters: a new model of hominid differentiation. *Man. (n.s.)*, **5**, 1–26

Kay, R. F. (1975) The functional adaptations of primate molar teeth. *Am. J. Phys. Anthropol.* **43**, 195–216

Kay, R. F. (1978) Molar structure and diet in extant cercopithecoids. In *Development, Function and Evolution of Teeth*, ed. P. M. Butler & K. A. Joysey, pp. 309–39. London: Academic Press

Kay, R. F. (1981) The nut-crackers – a new theory of the adaptations of the Ramapithecinae. *Am. J. Phys. Anthropol.*, **55**, 141–51

Kiltie, R. A. (1982) Bite force as a basis for niche differentiation between rain forest peccaries. *Biotropica*, **14**, 188–95

Lucas, P. W. & Luke, D. A. (1983) Methods for analysing the breakdown of food in human mastication. *Arch. Oral. Biol.*, **28**, 813–19

Lucas, P. W. & Luke, D. A. (1984) Optimum mouthful for food comminution during human mastication. *Arch. Oral Biol.*, **29**, 205–10

Lucas, P. W. & Luke, D. A. (in press) Is food particle size a criterion for the initiation of swallowing? *J. Oral Rehabil.*

Luke, D. A. & Lucas, P. W. (1983) The significance of cusps. *J. Oral Rehabil.*, **10**, 197–206

Manly, R. S. (1951) Factors affecting masticatory performance and efficiency in young adults. *J. Dent. Res.*, **30**, 874–82

Miller, A. J. (1982) Deglutition. *Physiol. Rev.*, **62**, 129–84

Osborn, J. W. & Lumsden, A. G. S. (1978) An alternative to "thegosis" and a re-examination of the ways in which mammalian molars work. *N.Jb. Geol. Palaeont. Abh.*, **156**, 371–92

Peters, C. R. (1981) *Australopithecus* vs. *Homo* dietary capabilities: the natural competitive advantage of the megadonts. In *Perceptions of Human Evolution*, ed. L. L. Mai, E. Shanklin & R. W. Sussman, vol. 7, pp. 161–81. Los Angeles: UCLA

Pirie, P. L. (1978) Allometric scaling in the postcanine dentition with reference to primate diets. *Primates*, **19**, 583–91

Sheine, W. S. (1979) The effects of variations in molar morphology on masticatory effectiveness and digestion of cellulose in prosimian primates. Ph.D. thesis, Duke University, North Carolina

Suzuki, A. (1969) An ecological study of chimpanzees in a savanna woodland. *Primates*, **10**, 103–48

Teaford, M. F. & Walker, A. C. (1983) Dental microwear in adult and still-born guinea-pigs *(Cavia procellus)*. *Arch. Oral Biol.*, **28**, 1077–81

Walker, A. C. (1981) Diet and teeth: dietary hypotheses and human evolution. *Phil. Trans. Soc. Lond.*, **B292**, 57–64

Waterman, P. G. (1984) Food acquisition and processing as a function of plant chemistry. In *Food Acquisition and Processing in Primates*, ed. D. J. Chivers, B. A. Wood & A. Bilsborough, pp. 177–211. New York: Plenum Press

Wolpoff, M. H. (1973) Posterior tooth size, body size and diet in South African gracile australopithecines. *Am. J. Phys. Anthropol.*, **39**, 375–94

II.8

Tool use and the evolution of hominid hands and bipedality

M. W. MARZKE

Introduction

Morphological features which distinguish hominid hands from those of nonhuman primates have been attributed to the demands of tool use for power and precision in the gripping of objects (Washburn, 1959; Napier, 1962; Lewis, 1977; Marzke, 1983). Bipedality also has been linked to tool use, indirectly through its release of the hands from locomotor demands (Darwin, 1874; Washburn, 1959). The functional analysis of tool-using behavior reported here was undertaken for the purpose of identifying more precisely morphological features in hominids which might be related to the effective control of objects by the palm and fingers, stabilization of the hand against forces which accompany the wielding of tools, and exploitation of trunk movements in throwing, digging and clubbing. Films were made of an archeologist using tools, showing movements of the forelimb, trunk and hindlimb, gripping postures, and the direction of forces sustained by the hand. Through dissections and radiographs, morphological features were identified which appear to be in positions to stabilize the hand during these activities and to facilitate the postures and movements involved in tool use. Morphological features of *Australopithecus afarensis* were then interpreted in the light of findings from these experiments.

Materials and methods

Hand postures and movements of the body during the manipulation of stones and sticks in pounding nuts, butchering chickens, cutting vegetation, digging, and throwing were recorded with a Canon Super 8 camera and analyzed with a stop action projector.

Dissections of eight human hands (which had been frozen) were focused primarily on joint complexes of the carpometacarpal region. Before the removal of skin, and progressively during the dissection as tissues were cut, segments were moved at joints and the range of movement was observed. Attachments of muscles and ligaments were carefully noted and in some regions (for example, at the base of the third metacarpal) their angle of approach to insertion was measured. These hands were compared with a large sample of nonhuman primate hands, described in Marzke (1983), and with anthropoid hand skeletons from collections at Arizona State University, the University of California, Santa Cruz (collection of A. Zihlman), the Cleveland Museum of Natural History, and the Museum of Comparative Zoology at Harvard University.

Radiographs of a human hand in various gripping postures were made in the Arizona State University Anthropology Department X-ray laboratory. Each posture was filmed twice, first at rest and then with full force of the digits on the object.

Magnetic resonance images of human hands in gripping postures were obtained in three planes, again with the hand at rest and then with a tight grip on the enclosed object. These images provided information for the biomechanical analysis of the joint between the capitate and third metacarpal, including the location of muscles relative to the joint center and the angle of their approach to insertion.

The wrist and hand bones of *Australopithecus afarensis* were examined at the Cleveland Museum of Natural History.

Results and discussion
Morphological basis of tool using

The films revealed a preference for two grips when stones were used to hammer, pound, cut, dig and throw. One was a pad-to-side pinch* of the stone between the thumb and side of the index finger, bolstered by the remaining fingers when the stone was large. The other was a three-jaw chuck grip involving the thumb, index finger, and medius (Fig. 1). The film showed a preponderance of blows whose reaction forces were directed toward the distal end of the central part of the palm, in the vicinity of the head of the third metacarpal.

There are two sets of derived features in the modern human hand which seem to find an explanation in requirements for control of these grips and in the forces endured by the palm of the hand during these

* Names of gripping postures come from Long (1981).

activities. The first set involves the index finger and thumb. The configuration of joints between the second metacarpal base and the capitate and third metacarpal apparently facilitates pronation and abduction of the index finger (Lewis, 1977; Marzke, 1983). A radial protrusion on the second metacarpal head gives the overlying first dorsal interosseus tendon a favorable angle of approach to its insertion on the proximal phalanx, enhancing its function as an abductor of the phalanx (Koebke, 1983). It also tenses the radial collateral ligament, causing the proximal phalanx to pronate with flexion (Lewis, 1977). These movements together bring the radial side of the index finger in line with the palmar tip of the thumb and secure the pad-to-side pinch of objects. A strong anterior oblique ligament between the trapezium and first metacarpal prevents dorsal displacement of the base of the thumb metacarpal during the pinch grip (Eaton & Dray, 1982). The same features of the second metacarpal also facilitate alignment of the palmar surface of the index finger with spherical objects in the three-jaw chuck grip, enhancing the force of the grip and control of the object when it is thrown or used in pounding.

The second set of features involves the third finger. The base of the third metacarpal is braced dorsally by a styloid process on the radial corner which abuts against the capitate, and on the palmar aspect by an extension of the pisometacarpal ligament which runs to the third metacarpal (Fig. 2). An analysis was undertaken of forces in this region which accompany the firm grip of tools and their use in pounding (Marzke, 1984; M. W. Marzke & R. Marzke, unpublished). It was found that forces generated by the flexor muscles and the reaction forces of the tool on the joints of the third ray increase from the fingertip to the base of the third metacarpal and tend to hyperextend the metacarpal

Fig. 1. Pad-to-side grip (left); three-jaw chuck grip (right).

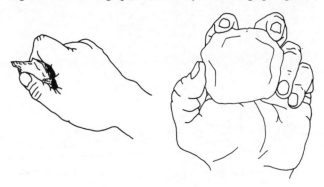

and to displace the base forward. The pisometacarpal ligament (together with a ligament from the trapezium to the palmar base of the third metacarpal) is in a position to resist hyperextension of the metacarpal. The styloid process is in a position to resist forward sliding of the metacarpal base.

The pisometacarpal ligament to the third metacarpal also is in a position to stabilize the pisiform on the triquetrum when flexor carpi ulnaris contracts, for example during clubbing or throwing. The muscle runs proximally from the pisiform to the humerus, and the ligament runs in the opposite direction from the pisiform to the third metacarpal.

Evolution of hominid hands

These analyses of gripping postures should help us to trace in fossil hands the early stages of tool-using behavior prior to the appearance of stone tools in the archeological record. Some of the unique configurations of the modern human hand occur in the hands of *Australopithecus afarensis*. All features of the joints at the base of the second metacarpal are present in these hominids and therefore should

Fig. 2. Right hand of *Homo sapiens*. A: Dots and lines represent the attachments and orientation of the pisometacarpal (left) and trapeziometacarpal (right) ligaments to the third metacarpal. B: Styloid process of the third metacarpal.

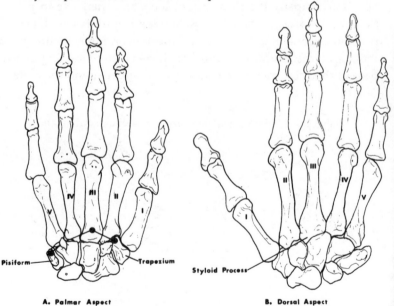

A. Palmar Aspect   B. Dorsal Aspect

have contributed to the potential for forceful pad-to-side pinch of objects (Marzke, 1983). A relatively long beak on the base of the first metacarpal, in the position of the anterior oblique ligament, may have served the same stabilizing function as the ligament in modern human hands. Although the thumb was shorter relative to the fingers than it is in modern humans, it was proportionately longer than it is in the pongids and would have been able to manipulate objects with the phalangeal portions of the index finger. These features also should have facilitated controlled manipulation and throwing of stones using a three-jaw chuck grip.

A groove across the distal aspect of the hamate hook in *A. afarensis* strongly suggests the presence of a pisometacarpal ligament to the third metacarpal, since this extension of the ligament occupies a similar groove in the modern human hand. Possibly, then, the hand was being used in activities such as hammering and clubbing which focused blows on the third metacarpal head, tending to hyperextend it and to require stabilization of the base. Perhaps, also, pounding with cylindrical objects such as small branches, or throwing of stones at predators or prey, involved strong adduction and flexion by flexor carpi ulnaris, requiring stabilization of the pisiform by the ligament. It is interesting to note, however, that the styloid process is absent on all three third metacarpals from Hadar (Bush *et al.*, 1982). If the functional interpretation of this structure in modern humans proposed here is correct, its absence in these early hominids may imply that the hand was only in the initial stages of adjustment to forces imposed by habitual and forceful tool use.

All tool using activities inferred from the Hadar hands are performed by chimpanzees. These primates pound nuts with stone and wood hammers (Sugiyama & Koman, 1979; Boesch & Boesch, 1983). They use a pad-to-side grip to hold twigs when they probe for insects (Van Lawick-Goodall, 1968; Nishida, 1973; McGrew, 1974). They also throw stones, branches, and other objects (Van Lawick-Goodall, 1970). The morphological features which distinguish the hand joints of the Hadar australopithecines from those of other primates should have (1) improved the strength of the pad-to-side grip, (2) improved the control of stones by the three-jaw chuck grip, and (3) stabilized the joints between the capitate and third metacarpal and the pisiform and triquetrum. This would have been an advantage as tool-using activities (involving pounding, hammering, clubbing, digging, and throwing) increased stresses on this region which might have led to sliding of the bones on one another and to deterioration of the joints.

The effect of these changes in hand morphology should have been to broaden the range of foods accessible to early hominids. They would have facilitated more firm and controlled grips of stones and sticks for pounding hard-shelled fruits and nuts and for digging for underground food and water sources. The ability to grip firmly and control the position of a small stone by the thumb, index and middle fingers may have allowed them to throw the stone with sufficient aim and velocity to stun or kill small animals.

Another important factor in the evolution of hominid hands was illustrated in the films of the archeologist. During digging and throwing, the trunk was contributing leverage to the activity. What is required in using tools for foraging is the ability to stand steadily on the hindlimbs to aim, and the ability to check forward momentum and rotation of the trunk as it lends force, speed and direction to a throw or to a blow with a stick or stone. The advantages of using these objects forcefully and accurately in pounding, digging and throwing may have been a factor in the initial hominid trend toward body proportions favoring balance of the trunk on the hindlimbs and toward changes in the relative size, orientation and attachments of the gluteus maximus, enhancing control of the trunk's position over the hindlimb during movements of the forelimbs. There is evidence that advances had been made toward improved balance in upright posture by the time of *Australopithecus afarensis* (Jungers & Stern, 1983).

It seems likely that the focus of selection early in hominid evolution was on structural features of both the hand and the trunk which facilitated accurate and forceful wielding of tools, and that modifications described above in both regions would have been mutually reinforcing.

Acknowledgements

The subject of the films and a source of valuable information on tool use was Mr S. Shackley. Dr R. Marzke (Department of Physics, Arizona State University) collaborated in the development of the model to explain the third metacarpal styloid process. I thank R. L. Wilson, MD, R. H. Gelberman, MD and Mr J. Sykes for providing the human hands and laboratory facilities for dissection. The examination of hand skeletons was made possible by Mr P. D. Bottjer, Museum of Comparative Zoology at Harvard University, Dr D. Johanson, Cleveland Museum of Natural History (hominoid skeletons and *Australopithecus afarensis*) and Dr A. Zihlman, University of California at Santa Cruz. The magnetic resonance images were acquired with the kind assistance of T. Brady, MD of Massachusetts General Hospital and J. Levy, MD of Scottsdale Memorial Hospital. The technical assistance of Mr R. Barnes, Ms M. Sauther, and Mr M. McCarthy (who drew the figures) is gratefully acknowledged. The study was supported by funds from the L. S. B. Leakey Foundation and Arizona State University.

References

Boesch, C. & Boesch, H. (1983) Optimisation of nut-cracking with natural hammers by wild chimpanzees. *Behaviour*, **83**, 265–85

Bush, M. E., Lovejoy, C. O., Johanson, D. C. & Coppens, Y. (1982) Hominid carpal, metacarpal, and phalangeal bones recovered from the Hadar Formation: 1974–1977 collections. *Am. J. Phys. Anthropol.*, **57**, 651–77

Darwin, C. (1874) *The Descent of Man and Selection in Relation to Sex*, 2nd ed. New York: Wheeler

Eaton, R. G. & Dray, G. J. (1982) Dislocations and ligament injuries in the digits. In *Operative Hand Surgery*, Vol. 1, ed. D. P. Green. New York: Churchill.

Jungers, W. L. & Stern, J. T., Jr (1983) Body proportions, skeletal allometry and locomotion in the Hadar hominids: a reply to Wolpoff. *J. Hum. Evol.*, **12**, 673–84

Koebke, J. (1983) A biomechanical and morphological analysis of human hand joints. *Adv. Anat. Embryol. Cell Biol.*, **80**, 1–85

Lawick-Goodall, J. Van (1968) The behaviour of free-living chimpanzees in the Gombe Stream Reserve. *Anim. Behav. Monogr.*, **1**, 161–311

Lawick-Goodall, J. Van (1970) Tool-using in primates and other vertebrates. *Adv. Study Beh.*, **3**, 195–249

Lewis, O. J. (1977) Joint remodelling and the evolution of the human hand. *J. Anat.*, **123**, 157–201

Long, C. II (1981) Electromyographic studies of hand function. In *The Hand*, vol. 1, ed. R. Tubiana. Philadelphia: W. B. Saunders

Marzke, M. W. (1983) Joint functions and grips of the *Australopithecus afarensis* hand, with special reference to the region of the capitate. *J. Hum. Evol.*, **12**, 197–211

Marzke, M. W. (1984) The morphological basis of hominid manipulatory behavior. *Am. J. Phys. Anthropol.*, **63**, 192

McGrew, W. C. (1974) Tool use by wild chimpanzees in feeding upon driver ants. *J. Hum. Evol.*, **3**, 501–8

Napier, J. (1962) Fossil hand bones from Olduvai Gorge. *Nature*, **196**, 409–11

Nishida, T. (1973) The ant-gathering behaviour by the use of tools among wild chimpanzees of the Mahali Mountains. *J. Hum. Evol.*, **2**, 357–70

Sugiyama, Y. & Koman, J. (1979) Tool-using and -making behavior in wild chimpanzees at Bossou, Guinea. *Primates*, **20**, 513–24

Washburn, S. L. (1959) Speculations on the interrelations of the history of tools and biological evolution. In *The Evolution of Man's Capacity for Culture*, ed. J. N. Spuhler. Detroit: Wayne State University Press

II.9

Three-dimensional computer imaging: some anthropological applications

G. C. CONROY AND M. W. VANNIER

Introduction

A major theme in biological research is the analysis of size and shape (Thompson, 1917; Huxley, 1932; Gould, 1971; Oxnard, 1973). An extension of this line of inquiry in many anthropological investigations is the desirability of visualizing intracranial size and shape in more than two dimensions without having physically to invade the specimen under study. Conventional imaging techniques, such as X-ray and computed tomography (CT), create two-dimensional images and thus are not ideally suited to this task. Even if a contiguous sequence of CT scans were available, the investigator would have to be a spatial genius in order to extract visually three-dimensional information from the CT data. Traditionally, anthropologists have had to rely upon osteology collections, primate cadavers and/or, unfortunately, terminal animal experimentation in order to collect three-dimensional data on cranial and intracranial size and shape.

What has been lacking up to now is a computer algorithm that would: (1) extract only the particular region of interest (e.g. osseous contours) from each sequential two-dimensional CT scan; (2) then 'create' the missing third dimension by displaying the sequential regions of interest simultaneously; and (3) present the result in a recognizable form. Such a set of computer programs has recently been developed at Washington University specifically for the purpose of three-dimensional surface reconstruction from sequential series of high-resolution CT scans (Vannier et al., 1983a,b,c,d; Marsh & Vannier, 1983; Vannier et al., 1984). These programs have been written in the Fortran IV and Macro-11 languages to operate on a minicomputer (DEC, Model PDP-11) incorporated in the CT viewing console used at the Mallinckrodt Institute of Radiology (Siemens Evaluscope RC).

Methods

The surface reconstruction computer program for skull imaging processes the original high-resolution CT scan sequence from a cartridge disk (DEC RK07) and loads the image into the 256 × 256 display memory of the evaluation console. Each column of the CT image is examined in left to right order. The osseous surface contour is extracted by comparing each value of CT density in the column from top to bottom of the image with a preset threshold. This threshold represents the CT attenuation that distinguishes bone from soft tissue and air (in a living subject), bone from air (in an osteological specimen), or stone matrix from mineralized bone (in a fossil specimen) (Vannier *et al.*, 1983*a,b,c,d*; Conroy & Vannier, 1984). The index of the element in each column where this transition takes place is entered into a storage vector. This is emitted to the display after all of the columns have been inspected to form the osseous contour for the CT scan slice being processed. This contour vector is scaled and output to the cartridge disk as a line in the reconstructed osseous three-dimensional surface image. To complete the surface reconstruction, each succeeding CT scan is loaded into display memory, the osseous contour is extracted, and the result is written on the cartridge disk.

To illustrate three-dimensional surface imaging by CT reconstruction, sequential high-resolution, narrowly collimated (2 mm) CT scans of a pongid skull (*Gorilla*) and a 30 million year old matrix-filled fossil artiodactyl skull (*Merycoidodon*) were produced using the Siemens Somatom 2 and DR 3 CT scanners available in the Mallinckrodt Institute of Radiology (Washington University School of Medicine). The scans were automatically stored on 8″ floppy disks and magnetic tape for off-line storage. Disks containing the original scan data were then copied into a CT scan evaluation console (Siemens Evaluscope RC) for three-dimensional surface reconstruction. These reconstructions were made by using the programs developed for this purpose (Vannier *et al.*, 1983*a,b,c,d*, 1984). More than 50 three-dimensional views were created for each skull from the set of original CT scans. The number of CT scans in a set ranged from 35 for the fossil skull to 75 for the skull of the male gorilla. The three-dimensional views were then stored in the CT scanner evaluation console disk memory in the same format as the ordinary CT scans. The three-dimensional images were archived to blank floppy disks, subsequently reviewed and manipulated using display window level and width controls, and then photographed like any ordinary CT scan.

Three-dimensional views produced for each specimen consisted of frontal, rear, 45-degree oblique (anterior and posterior), top, bottom, and both lateral projections. Select portions of the skull were then made 'transparent' to view intracranial size and shape (e.g. sagittal views).

Results

Our present research is designed to develop (and adapt) new techniques in three-dimensional image analysis (and display) that can be directly applied to anthropological problems. We have focused our efforts in this paper on several problem areas of current paleoanthropological interest. These include the non-invasive determination of endocranial volume and shape, and the non-invasive 'removal' of matrix from fossil skulls.

The computer algorithms produce high-resolution images made up of pixels less than 1 mm^2 in area. The following parameters can be generated accurately (and instantaneously) on the computer screen:

1. Euclidean distance between any two points
2. Euler angle between any two structures
3. Area of any region of interest
4. Volume of any region of interest
5. Densitometric profiles of any skull section
6. Selected portions of the calvaria can be made 'transparent' so that underlying structures can be visualized and measured
7. Any bilaterally symmetrical structure (e.g. the face) can be 'rotated' about an arbitrary axis and superimposed on the contralateral side to demonstrate graphically and quantify asymmetry (or symmetry)

Illustration of computer imaging techniques for (non-invasive) determination of endocranial volume and shape in osteological specimens

We are investigating the application of CT scanning procedures to measure, accurately and non-invasively, endocranial volume and to display three-dimensional endocranial shape. Our motivation for creating such three-dimensional images is based on the observation that endocranial shape is an accurate reflection of overall brain shape in primates and is, of course, the only direct evidence of brain size and shape in fossil primates (Radinsky, 1979).

In addition, the analysis of brain shape in human and non-human primates has taken on added significance in recent years due to the fact that cortical asymmetries have recently been associated with handedness, certain learning disabilities, autoimmune diseases, and hemispheric asymmetry in processing of auditory-dependent activities (McRae, Branch & Milner, 1968; LeMay, 1976, 1977; Galaburda *et al.*, 1978; Petersen *et al.* , 1978; Geschwind & Behan, 1982; Marx, 1982, 1983). Importantly, some of these asymmetries have already been identified in endocasts of Old World monkeys (Falk, 1978*a,b*; LeMay, Billig & Geschwind, 1982).

Precise determination of many intracranial parameters is difficult to obtain using conventional two-dimensional imaging techniques such as X-ray. In such pictures, all the three-dimensional information is superimposed onto a two-dimensional plane which obscures important anatomical detail. Fig. 1 is a standard X-ray of a gorilla skull. Fig. 2 is an illustration of a three-dimensional computer-generated image of that same skull, reconstructed from 2 mm CT slices. In this case the computer has generated a sagittal view of the skull in order to view intracranial structures such as paranasal and sphenoidal sinuses. From this view, precise intracranial linear and angular measurements

Fig. 1. Lateral X-ray of a gorilla skull.

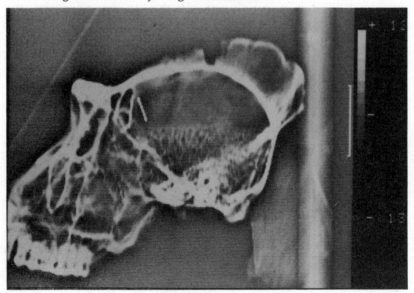

can be produced instantaneously (e.g. maximum length and height of the endocranial cavity). In addition, the angle that each diameter makes with the horizontal plane is also recorded.

Another parameter that can be generated easily from this view is the mid-sagittal cross-sectional area of the endocranial cavity (Fig. 3). In this gorilla skull this dimension is 2829 mm^2. Of course, the cross-sectional area of any anatomical region can be generated just as easily.

Another major goal of many paleoanthropological studies is the accurate assessment of endocranial (brain) volume (see Holloway, 1975; Radinsky, 1982; Jerison, 1973; Tobias, 1971; and references therein). The methods and problems associated with current procedures for cranial capacity estimates are reviewed by Hambly (1947), Tildesley (1956), Jerison (1973), Holloway (1976) and Radinsky (1979). Various procedures have been devised to calculate cranial capacity in fossil and living primate (including hominoid) skulls (Holloway, 1973; Jerison, 1973, 1979; Radinsky, 1979; Gurche, 1982). For example, Holloway (1973) found it necessary to employ at least four different methods for reconstructing endocranial capacity in early hominoids: (1) direct water displacement of either a full or hemiendocast with minimal plasticine reconstruction; (2) the partial endocast methods

Fig. 2. Three-dimensional sagittal view of the same gorilla skull as in Fig. 1.

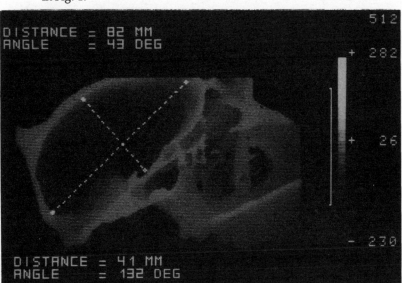

described by Tobias (1967, 1971); (3) extensive plasticine reconstruction (involving close to half of the total endocast); and (4) the formula $V = f[1/2(LWB + LWH)]$ devised by Mackinnon, Kennedy & Davies (1956). As Holloway (1972) admits, however, some of these methods rely on a certain subjective 'feel', based on familiarity with other fossil endocasts.

Analyses of cranial volume and shape have also been an important component of studies on the evolutionary history of other mammalian groups (e.g. Jerison, 1973; Radinsky, 1973, 1975, 1977). For example, Radinsky (1981a,b) used 15 variables of the neurocranium (including brain volume, orbit area, and auditory bulla volume) and splanchnocranium to analyze the evolution of skull shape in carnivores. Our new methods of three-dimensional reconstruction from CT scans should allow us to measure accurately these parameters of volume and area without having to 'invade' the skull in any manner. This is due to the fact that the geometrical space of the endocranium is accurately reproduced by three-dimensional reconstruction of the serial CT scans and thus its volume should be amenable to precise determination by the computer program.

Fig. 3. Three-dimensional sagittal view of the same gorilla skull as in Figs 1 and 2, with computed cross-sectional area of endocranial cavity.

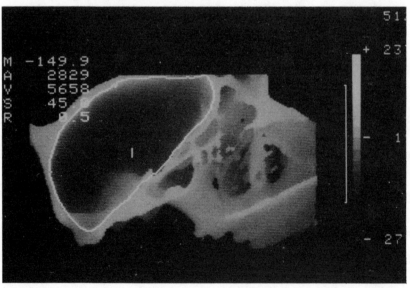

We have undertaken several experiments to test this prediction. In these experiments, several primate skulls (two *Homo sapiens*, one *Gorilla*, one *Papio*) were CT scanned at 2 mm intervals. As each 2 mm skull section was brought up on the computer screen for each animal, the outline of the endocranial cavity was traced with a marker stylus on the resistor pad built into the CT viewing console. The computer then automatically computed the volume of that section of the endocranial cavity outlined by the operator (Fig. 4). By summing all volumes generated at each CT slice, the total endocranial volume for each specimen was determined.

The accuracy of the CT computed volumes was assessed by measuring endocranial volume directly in each of the skulls by filling them with seed and measuring the volume of seed in a graduated cylinder. In all cases, the CT-derived volumes were within 1–3% of the directly measured endocranial volumes. We have now extended these experiments to include matrix-filled fossil skulls (Conroy & Vannier, unpublished). We are thus confident that our methods provide a highly reliable, non-invasively derived, estimate of intracranial volume in living subjects, osteological specimens, and fossil specimens.

Fig. 4. Endocranial volume determination of a 2 mm CT slice of a gorilla skull.

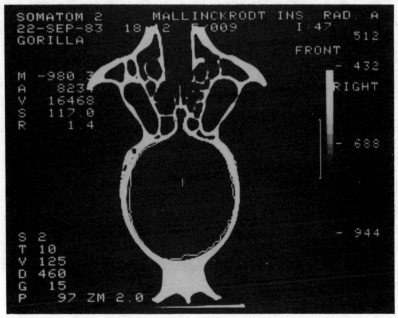

Fig. 5. (a) Lateral view of *Merycoidodon*. (b) Three-dimensional
reconstruction of sagittal view of *Merycoidodon*.

(a)

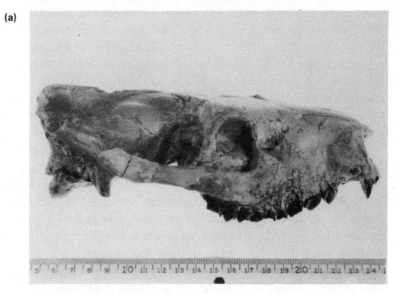

(b)

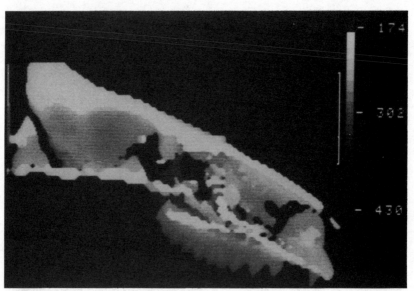

Fig. 6. (a) Top view of *Merycoidodon*. (b)'Bird's eye' view of
Merycoidodon with top of calvaria and intracranial matrix 'removed'.

(a)

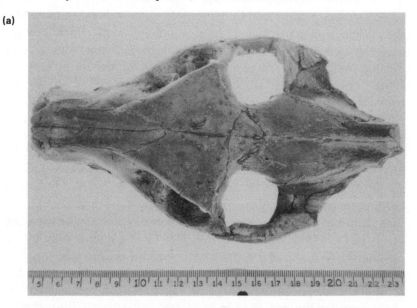

(b)

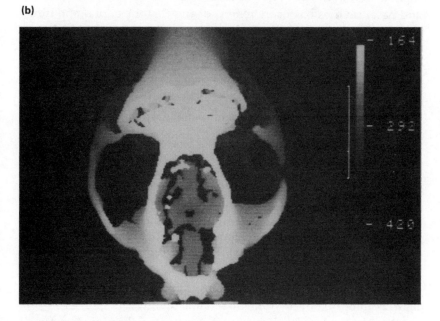

*Computer imaging techniques for (non-invasive) 'removal' of
matrix from the endocranium of fossil skulls*

A major problem in paleontology in general, and paleoanthropology in particular, is how to remove hardened matrix ju-
diciously from fossil skulls (particularly from the brain case) without
causing irreparable damage to the original fossil (Conroy & Vannier,
1984). Even a quick perusal through large paleontology collections will
reveal that such matrix removal cannot often be done safely without
adversely affecting the original specimen. The new computer imaging
techniques described here can deal with this problem in a novel way.

The specimen we have chosen to illustrate is a fossil ungulate,
Merycoidodon culbertsonii (AMNH 39460), from the Oligocene of North
America (approximately 30 million years old); its cranial and nasal
cavities are completely filled with a hard, sandstone matrix. Details of
the scanning procedure and three-dimensional reconstruction are
given in Conroy & Vannier (1984). Fig. 5a is a lateral view of the
original fossil. After the specimen has been scanned and reconstructed
in three dimensions by the computer, it can be 'sectioned' on the
computer screen in any desired plane. Fig. 5b is a computer-generated
sagittal view of the same specimen. Note that the matrix filling cranial
and nasal cavities has been 'removed' and that the supra- and infra-
tentorial portions of the cranial cavity are now clearly distinguishable.
Fig. 6a is a top view of the original specimen and Fig. 6b is a
computer-generated image of the same view; however, in the latter
case the computer has 'removed' the top of the calvaria and the
intracranial matrix so that the investigator can look inside the skull in
a 'bird's eye' view. Such intracranial views would be impossible to
obtain by any other method.

Conclusions

New, non-invasive, three-dimensional computer imaging
techniques can have important applications for anthropological
research of the future. We have demonstrated the power and versatility
of some of these techniques which allow anthropologists to view and
analyze material in ways never before possible. Skulls (of living
subjects, osteological specimens, or fossil specimens) can be reconstructed in three dimensions to sub-millimeter accuracy, hardened
matrix can be 'removed' from intracranial cavities, and portions of the
skull can be made 'transparent' so that intracranial parameters can be
accurately measured and evaluated. Most importantly, this is all
accomplished in a safe, non-destructive manner, preserving the original specimen.

Acknowledgements
We gratefully acknowledge the technical support of R. Knapp in all phases of this project and financial support from the National Science Foundation. Dr M. Novacek provided the loan of fossil specimens used in this study.

References

Conroy, G. & Vannier, M. W. (1984) Noninvasive three dimensional computer imaging of matrix filled fossil skulls by high resolution computed tomography. *Science*, **226**, 457–8

Falk, D. (1978*a*) External neuroanatomy of Old World monkeys. *Contrib. Primatol.*, **15**, 1–95

Falk, D (1978*b*) Cerebral asymmetry in Old World monkeys. *Acta Anat.*, **101**, 334–9

Galaburda, A., LeMay, M., Kemper, T. & Geschwind, N. (1978) Right–left asymmetries in the brain. *Science*, **199**, 852–6

Geschwind, N. & Behan, P. (1982) Left-handedness association with immune disease, migraine, and developmental learning disorder. *Proc. Natl Acad. Sci.*, **79**, 5097–100

Gould, S. J. (1971) Geometric similarity in allometric growth: a contribution to the problem of scaling in the evolution of size. *Am. Naturalist*, **105**, 113–36

Gurche, J. (1982) Early primate brain evolution. In *Primate Brain Evolution*, ed. E. Armstrong & D. Falk, pp. 227–46. New York: Plenum Press

Hambly, W. (1947) Cranial capacities; a study in methods. *Fieldiana; Anthropol.* **36**, 25–75

Holloway, R. (1972) Australopithecine endocasts, brain evolution in the Hominoidea, and a model of hominoid evolution. In *Functional and Evolutionary Biology of the Primates*, ed. R. Tuttle, pp. 185–204. Chicago: Aldine

Holloway, R. (1973) Endocranial volumes of early African hominids, and the role of the brain in human mosaic evolution. *J. Hum. Evol.* **2**, 449–59

Holloway, R. (1975) *43rd James Arthur Lecture on the Evolution of the Human Brain: The Role of Human Social Behavior in the Evolution of the Brain*. New York: American Museum of Natural History

Holloway, R. (1976) Some problems of hominid brain endocast reconstruction, allometry, and neural reorganization. In *Colloquium VI of the IX Congress of the UISPP, Nice, 1976*, pp. 69–119. Pretirage

Huxley, J. (1932) *Problems of Relative Growth*. London: Methuen

Jerison, H. (1973) *Evolution of the Brain and Intelligence*. New York: Academic Press

Jerison, H. (1979) Brain, body and encephalization in early primates. *J. Hum. Evol.*, **8**, 615–35

LeMay, M. (1976) Morphological cerebral asymmetries of modern man, fossil man, and non-human primate. *Ann. NY Acad. Sci.*, **280**, 349–60

LeMay, M. (1977) Asymmetries of the skull and handedness. *J. Neurol. Sci.*, **32**, 243–53

LeMay, M., Billig, M. & Geschwind, N. (1982) Asymmetries of the brains and skulls of nonhuman primates. In *Primate Brain Evolution*, ed. E. Armstrong & D. Falk, pp. 263–78. New York: Plenum Press

Marsh, J. & Vannier, M. (1983) The 'third' dimension in craniofacial surgery. *Plast. Reconstr. Surg.*, **71**, 759–67

Marx, J. (1982) Autoimmunity in left-handers. *Science*, **217**, 141–7

Marx, J. (1983) The two sides of the brain. *Science*, **220**, 488–90

Mackinnon, I., Kennedy, J. & Davies, T. (1956) The estimation of skull capacity from roentgenologic measurements. *Am. J. Roent. Rad. Ther. Nucl. Med.*, 76, 303–10

McCrae, D., Branch, C. & Milner, B. (1968) The occipital horns and cerebral dominance. *Neurology*, 18, 95–8

Oxnard, C. (1973) *Form and Pattern in Human Evolution.* Chicago: University of Chicago Press

Petersen, M., Beecher, M., Zoloth, S., Moody, D. & Stebbins, W. (1978) Neural lateralization of species-specific vocalizations by Japanese macaques. *Science*, 202, 324–6

Radinsky, L. (1973) Evolution of the canid brain. *Brain, Beh. Evol.*, 7, 169–202

Radinsky, L. (1975) Evolution of the felid brain. *Brain, Beh. Evol.*, 11, 214–54

Radinsky, L. (1977) Brains of early carnivores. *Paleobiol.*, 3, 333–49

Radinsky, L. (1979) *The Fossil Record of Primate Brain Evolution. 49th James Arthur Lecture on the Evolution of the Human Brain.* New York: American Museum of Natural History

Radinsky, L. (1981a) Evolution of skull shape in carnivores. 1. Representative modern carnivores. *Biol. J. Linn. Soc.*, 15, 369–88

Radinsky, L. (1981b) Evolution of skull shape in carnivores. 2. Additional modern carnivores. *Biol. J. Linn. Soc.*, 16, 337–55

Radinsky, L. (1982) Some cautionary notes on making references about relative brain size. In *Primate Brain Evolution*, ed. E. Armstrong & D. Falk, pp. 29–38. New York: Plenum Press

Thompson, D'Arcy (1917) *On Growth and Form.* Cambridge: Cambridge University Press

Tildesley, M. (1956) A critical survey of techniques for the measurements of cranial capacity. *J. R. Anthropol. Inst., London*, 83, 182–93

Tobias, P. (1967) *Olduvai Gorge*, vol. 2. Cambridge: Cambridge University Press

Tobias, P. (1971) *The Brain in Hominid Evolution.* New York: Columbia University Press

Vannier, M., Gado, M. & Marsh, J. (1983a) Three dimensional display of intracranial soft tissue structures. *Am. J. Neuroradiol.*, 4, 520–1

Vannier, M., Marsh, J. & Warren, J. (1983b) Three dimensional computer graphics for craniofacial surgical planning and evaluation. *Comput. Graph.*, 17, 263–73

Vannier, M., Marsh, J. & Warren, J. (1984) Three dimensional CT reconstruction images for craniofacial surgical planning and evaluation. *Radiol.*, 150, 179–84

Vannier, M., Marsh, J., Warren, J. & Barbier, J. (1983c) Three dimensional CAD for craniofacial surgery. *Electron. Imaging*, 2, 48–54

Vannier, M., Marsh, J. Warren, J. & Barbier, J. (1983d) Three dimensional computer aided design of craniofacial surgical procedures. *Diagn. Imaging*, 5, 36–43

Part III

Functional anatomy and evolution

Introduction *H. Preuschoft*

All past IPS meetings have devoted time to macroscopic morphology, but compared to the state before the foundation of the society (before the early 1960's), the share of morphology is restricted, and its subjects have undergone changes. We may, and should, ask why this is so. A simple explanation would be the advent of new disciplines like social behaviour, ecology, sociobiology, karyology, or biochemistry. A better proposal is that the descriptive morphology of the primates was of a high standard long before the other fields came into being. This is largely due to its methodological simplicity and led to a feeling that everything is done, that the morphology and anatomy of primates is sufficiently known and needs no further efforts. This may be to a large extent true. The wealth of descriptive information so far compiled is impressive; in fact too much is known to be understood or used to an extent desirable and theoretically possible. From this viewpoint, descriptive morphology might not be a necessary subject of new studies or of conference papers!

Despite this, a continuous interest in the problems of morphology persists. It is promoted by a number of sources, two of which are dealt with specifically in this section: the desire to comprehend why nature has produced the observed forms; and the interpretation of fossils which represent evolutionary stages. Both aspects are closely related. If we can understand forms specific to living animals, we should be able to 'understand' the forms of fossils as well, i.e. to know how they come about and what makes them advantageous for an animal.

The great and permanently increasing number of fossils, such as those discovered in Kenya through the efforts of the Congress host, urgently demands an interpretation. It also offers us possibilities to learn much about the sequence of forms leading to the present variance, and about pathways and the causes of evolution.

The most numerous and valuable information about the taxonomic position of an animal is commonly considered to be contained in the skull. No doubt it also provides worthwhile information about the way of life. But our ability to get this latter sort of information from the skull is less developed than in the case of the post-cranial skeleton. Determining the sequence of forms and their relations to each other, culminating in taxonomic assignments, is not the aim of this section. This was the focus of attention in other sessions of the Congress. Here, the major emphasis is placed on spotting potential causes of morphological change during evolution. Similar attempts have been made successfully with regard to the locomotor apparatus, but for the skull, few of the reasons for the diversification of forms are understood. We are just now making our first steps towards understanding the mechanical factors influencing skull shape.

Interpretations of fossils may be based on similarities with other, mostly living, forms which are better known. Even the bulk of descriptive data compiled to date is inadequate for making these comparisons, and often it is easier to obtain the necessary facts by undertaking new investigations than from digging them out of the literature. Since we assume that body shape is 'adapted' to a way of life, we may infer that a fossil was similar in behaviour and in the use it makes of its environment to certain living forms. We should never lose sight of the essential simplicity of this approach (see also Preuschoft, 1978), although the morphological comparisons made today use highly sophisticated methods. This comparative approach also implies a radical reduction of behaviour to more or less linear categories, such as the often-used locomotor categories.

In an important paper, Bock & von Wahlert (1965) introduced a principle distinction between the 'biological role' played by features and their (mechanical) 'function'. The relation between morphological feature and function is a very close one (Pauwels, 1960; Kummer, 1972; Amtmann, 1979; see below). However, it cannot be described in familiar terms such as arboreality, brachiation, food intake and climbing propensities. Instead we have to use categories unfamiliar to biologists such as direction of force, point of application, frequency, torsion, and moment of resistance. These engineering terms are indeed suited to describe at least part of our physical reality. As biologists have accepted the findings of chemistry, so are they learning to deal with aspects of physics.

On this basis, we may infer from variants in shape details about magnitudes and directions of external forces that were applied to fossil skeletal elements. These applications of external forces constitute the complex we call 'behaviour', but in most cases only that behaviour associated with considerable expenditure of force – such as locomotor or masticatory behaviour – exert influence on shape (see Preuschoft, 1979). Within these limits, very reliable conclusions can be drawn. From 'functions' in this strict sense, we may proceed to conclusions concerning the 'biological roles' of characters. These roles are much less tightly bound to morphology. There is a gap between what an animal can cope with mechanically, and what is realised under normal conditions. This gap is often wide, especially since species do not always exhaust their possibilities nor realise all their potentials. The very capacity to adapt to changing environments stems from the loose relation between structure and biological role (see Chivers *et al.*, 1984, for further details). Unfortunately, the foregoing step, namely the definition of function, is too often neglected, so the final conclusions about biological roles are weakly founded.

When asking about the 'causes' leading to species-specific forms, we may distinguish between ultimate and proximate causes. No one doubts that, ultimately, all morphological features are designed to allow the animal to make use of the resources in its environment, that is to play its biological role with a minimum input of energy. Generations of biologists have contented themselves with repeating this fundamental principle of evolutionary theory. Most have not, however, given much attention to the problem of how this is accomplished; in other words, the proximate reasons are often forgotten, or in other cases not valid.

The paper by Lucas *et al.* in the previous section (Chapter II.7)* begins with this rather general level. In a series of papers, these authors have undertaken to clarify the relation between total grinding surface of molars and premolars and the efficiency of triturating the amount of food necessary for an animal. They take into account the highly variable and little known properties of the food substance itself. Such considerations are here applied to the situation in early hominids. In this section, Demes *et al.* (Chapter III.1) use a similar approach to show how increases in body size require morphological differences in hominoid skulls, in order to keep the chewing forces

---

* This paper was originally designed as part of an integrated presentation with the papers that follow.

constant. Their paper combines information obtained from deliberate, morphometric studies with new ideas in biomechanics.

This detailed type of information is also illustrated by Schmid and Stratil (Chapter III.2), who found that the rates of growth and the degree of sexual dimorphism were dissimilar in different parts of the skull of one species. In contrast, Demes *et al.* compared size differences between species. Both teams arrived independently at convergent results. This parallelism gives confidence that size-dependent shape differences are correctly identified.

A new biomechanical approach is detailed in Preuschoft *et al.* (Chapter III.3), a paper upon which the Demes *et al.* study is based. A theoretical model is proposed to show the external forces acting on the upper jaw and the internal forces or stresses evoked by them. The latter are related to the resistance offered by the shape of the upper jaw. This approach is designed to investigate, in the precise terminology of physics, a more proximate cause: the necessity to sustain stresses created during normal 'function' (in the sense defined by Bock & von Wahlert, 1965). A theory exists to explain a yet more proximate reason, namely how bony structures assume their shape as a consequence of mechanical stressing during life (Pauwels, 1960; see above). Although the influence of stresses on shape is proven by experimental evidence and by clinical experience, the extent to which the process of intra-vital 'functional adaptation' is the decisive factor is debated.

A rival approach to the most proximate cause, that asking why bony structures assume their definite forms, uses embryological evidence. This approach is taken by Schneck (Chapter III.4) who aims at principal evolutionary tendencies among the higher primates. The reduced olfactory system in higher primates leads to reorganisation in the interorbital region, incorporating changes in neighbouring organ systems. His work on the ontogenetic development of hominoids, in particular on hylobatid skulls, indicates the importance of growth processes as factors defining shape.

This starting point of the ontogenesis of the skull is also used by Zeller (Chapter III.5). His contribution to this section, based on a comprehensive study of the still little known early stages of skull development in the Tupaiidae, emphasises yet again the taxonomic aspect: the characteristics are used to establish phylogenetic relationships of the tree shrews and to distinguish them from primates.

Only reliably proven facts are worthy of being subjected to a causal analysis. Jacobshagen (Chapter III.6) quantified orbital contours – one of the obvious features that are so difficult to identify clearly – by using stereometric techniques. Through investigation of morphometric similarities and sexual dimorphism, he proceeds towards defining the determining factors of this morphological trait: allometric influences at least can be shown to be limited.

Some of these papers were derived from presentations originally planned as an integrated symposium. Due to lack of funds, the symposium could not take place and several independent contributions were ultimately combined. Despite this, and in conjunction with the paper by Lucas *et al.* (Chapter II.7), the papers here fit together and form a multi-dimensional network to illuminate many aspects of skull morphology. Major objectives of future research can be derived from the approaches presented here.

References

Amtmann, E. (1969) Biomechanical Interpretation of Form and Structure of Bones: Role of Genetics and Function in Growth and Remodeling. In *Environment, Behavior and Morphology: Dynamic Interactions in Primates*, ed. M. E. Morbeck, H. Preuschoft & N. Gomberg, pp. 347–66. Stuttgart: Gustav Fischer Verlag

Bock, W. J. & Wahlert, G. von (1965) Adaptation and the form–function complex. *Evolution*, **19**(3), 269–99

Chivers, D. J., Andrews, P., Preuschoft, H., Bilsborough, A. & Wood, B. A. (1984) Food acquisition and processing in primates: Concluding discussion. In *Food Acquisition and Processing in Primates*, ed. D. Chivers, B. Wood & A. Bilsborough, pp. 545–56. New York: Plenum Press

Kummer, B. (1972) Biomechanics of bone: Mechanical properties, functional structure, functional adaptation. In *Biomechanics*, ed. Y. C. Fung, N. N. Perrone & M. Anlicker, pp. 237–71. Englewood Cliffs, N.J.: Prentice-Hall

Pauwels, F. (1960) Eine neue Theorie über den Einfluß mechanischer Reize auf die Differenzierung der Stützgewebe. *Z. Anat. Entwickl. Gesch.*, **121**, 478–515

Preuschoft, H. (1978) Recent results concerning the biomechanics of man's acquisition of bipedality. In *Proc. 5th Congr. Int. Primat. Soc.*, ed. D. Chivers, pp. 435–458. London: Academic Press

Preuschoft, H. (1979) Motor behavior and shape of the locomotor apparatus. In *Environment, Behavior and Morphology: Dynamic Interactions in Primates*, ed. M. E. Morbeck, H. Preuschoft and N. Gomberg, pp. 263–275. Stuttgart: Gustav Fischer Verlag

III.1

Functional significance of allometric trends in the hominoid masticatory apparatus

B. DEMES, N. CREEL AND H. PREUSCHOFT

Introduction

Interspecific allometric analyses of the skulls of four great ape species and five gibbon species revealed that shape changes associated with increasing body size are similar in the two groups (Creel, unpublished). Agreement between allometric trends in independently evolving phyla suggests that biomechanical constraints associated with increasing size are evoking similar functional solutions. If this is the case, shared allometric trends should be functionally interpretable, i.e. they should be explicable in biomechanical terms. Analysis of a number of size-related shape changes occurring in the masticatory apparatus of both great apes and gibbons indicates that parallel trends in the two groups are indeed amenable to biomechanical interpretation. Maintaining or increasing maximum bite force in larger animals seems to be a primary factor in the allometric adaptations of both groups.

Methods

The work reported here was based on tri-axial coordinates of 32 anatomical points on the skull, plus measurements of 14 linear dimensions, primarily of the teeth and palate (see Creel & Preuschoft, 1976, for definitions of points and measurements). Separate male and female samples were employed; sample sizes ranged from 8 to more than 50; most samples contained at least 25 specimens.

A measure of overall size was calculated for each skull as the square root of the sum of the squares of the distances between each anatomical point and the centroid of all points, divided by the number of points (Sneath, 1967). The resulting linear measure will be called the Sneath variable. Correlations between species means for the Sneath variable and body weight are high (0.92 to 0.98) for both great apes and gibbons, although cranial size increases less rapidly than body weight. All interspecific regressions were computed twice, once with the Sneath variable and once with body weight as the independent variable. As cranial size is more directly related to the biomechanical functioning of the skull, slopes derived with the Sneath variable are emphasized in the following; however, the reported trends are apparent regardless of the size variable employed.

Interspecific regressions were computed for the three orthogonal coordinates of each point, conventional measurements of the palate and maxillary teeth, and surface crown areas of maxillary molar teeth (as approximated by the product of their buccolingual and mesiodistal diameters). Separate regression slopes were calculated for male and female samples. Allometric trends suggested by these slopes were explored further by regressing distances between selected points on the Sneath size variable. The cube root of body weight and the square root of areas were employed in all regressions; the exponent indicating isometry is thus always 1.0

Results: allometric trends and biomechanical compensations

Total molar crown area, the sum of the areas of the individual teeth, is positively allometric in great apes and in gibbons with respect to both the Sneath measure of overall cranial size and body weight (Table 1). The mean exponent for the Sneath size variable is about 1.7.

Table 1. *Coefficients of allometric slopes of biomechanically relevant variables regressed on the Sneath measure of overall cranial size. See text for definitions of variables. A coefficient of 1.0 indicates isometry*

	Great apes		Gibbons	
	females	males	females	males
Total molar crown area	1.88	1.27	1.77	1.64
Sum of molar lengths	1.98	1.30	2.02	1.85
Sum of molar breadths	1.62	1.15	1.56	1.46
Palate length to 2nd molar	1.58	1.19	1.70	1.67
Palate breadth at 2nd molar	0.94	0.81	1.62	1.43
Load arm of bite force	1.69	1.53	1.55	1.60
Power arm of temporal m.	1.45	1.16	1.62	1.57
Power arm of masseter and med. pterygoid muscles	1.59	1.54	1.63	1.64
Temporal muscle force	1.94	1.41	1.47	1.88

For body weight it is about 1.3. Male great apes exhibit the smallest exponents, i.e. their crown areas increase least rapidly with cranial and body size. Their values are nonetheless clearly positively allometric. Thus, in great apes and gibbons total molar crown area increases more rapidly among species than does overall cranial size or body weight. As a result, bite force per unit area in larger species will be diminished in the absence of compensations to increase it, i.e. if the components of the musculoskeletal system are linked to feeding scale isometrically.

Pilbeam & Gould (1974) and Shea (1983) have also reported positive interspecific allometry of tooth area to cranial size measures in various groupings of hominoid primates, while Susman & Jungers (1981) found the same relative to body weight in African apes. On the other hand, Kay (1975 *a,b*) and Gingerich, Smith & Rosenberg (1982) reported roughly geometric interspecific scaling in respect to body weight for non-insectivorous primates as a whole. If Kay's conclusion that folivorous species tend to have larger teeth for their weight than frugivorous species is correct, the large crown area exponents for great apes and gibbons may be explained in part by the greater amount of leaves in the diets of the larger species of these groups. However, this does not affect the validity of the arguments that follow nor their extension to other primates, because the head and skull furnish the mechanical components of the masticatory apparatus. It is their size relative to tooth area that is crucial, not the mass of the body. As the head is negatively allometric to body mass, geometric scaling of tooth area to body weight implies positive allometric scaling of tooth area to head and skull size in primates as a whole.

The positive allometry of crown areas in great apes and gibbons is attributable primarily to an overproportional increase in molar length. Although widths are also positively allometric, their rates of increase are considerably exceeded by those for lengths. Trends in the palate reflect those in the teeth; the length of the palate (distance from prosthion to line connecting rear margins of maxillary second molars in plane parallel to Frankfurt plane) also increases more rapidly with size than does its width (Table 1). This is consistent with the conclusions of Hylander (1975) and Wolff (1982, 1984) that in animals with fused mandibular symphyses, bite force per unit of muscle force is greater for relatively narrow dental arcades. The observed allometric trend of snout elongation relative to width thus allows larger animals to achieve a greater bite force relative to muscle mass. The elongation of the cheek teeth presumably plays a role in decreasing relative snout width; however, the shape of teeth also may be influenced by factors more directly related to their crushing, grinding, and shearing functions (Kay, 1975b). Whether and how these are related to dental size remains unclear.

In mechanical terms, the jaws can be regarded as levers loaded by the bite force (Fig. 1a). As the snout is elongated, the load arm of the bite force becomes longer. The load arm, the distance between the temporomandibular joint and the occlusal surfaces measured in the plane of the tooth row, can be approximated in our data by the horizontal distance between the external acoustic meatus (EAM) and the middle of the second molar. This distance scales positively with a mean exponent of about 1.6 for the four samples (Table 1). As the length of the load arm increases, equivalent bite force can be maintained by lengthening the power arms of the masticatory muscles and/or by increasing their cross-section and thus the moments and force which they can exert.

Fig. 1. Biomechanical parameters of the masticatory apparatus and their estimates: (a) load arm of bite force; (b) power arm of the temporal muscle; (c) power arm of masseter and pterygoid muscles; (d) cross-sectional area of the temporal muscle. See text for descriptions and discussion.

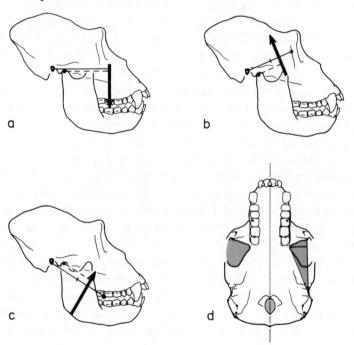

The power arm of the temporal muscle is the shortest distance between the temporomandibular joint and the line of action of the muscle (Fig. 1b). The best approximation in our data is the distance between the EAM and the point frontomalare temporale. This distance scales positively allometrically, with exponents between 1.16 and 1.62 (Table 1). The lower value is for male great apes, in accordance with their smaller exponent for molar crown area. The power arms of the masseter and medial pterygoid muscles are strongly dependent on the vertical dimensions of the face. This may be related to positively allometric upper facial heights in both groups of hominoid primates (Creel, unpublished). The power arms of these two muscles have been approximated as one half the distance between the EAM and the rear margin of the maxillary second molar (Fig. 1c). This measure too is positively allometric in all samples, with a mean exponent of about 1.6 (Table 1).

The maximum force of a muscle is proportional to its cross-sectional area perpendicular to the direction of its fibers. Weijs & Hillen (1984) have shown that in humans the physiological cross-section of the temporal muscle is proportional to the area of a plane enclosed by the temporal fossa and the zygomatic arch. To gain some idea of the change in force of the temporal muscle with size in great apes and gibbons, we have assumed that the same proportionality holds for other hominoid species and that this area can be very roughly estimated as a triangle with corners at the EAM, frontomalare temporale and the deepest point of the postorbital constriction (Fig. 1d). This measure is also positively allometric, with exponents of about 1.4–1.9 for its square root. This is in agreement with the results of Corruccini (1980), who made direct measurements of the length and breadth of the infratemporal fossa in many groups of primates and computed interspecific regressions on a composite measure of cranial size.

We have no measurements suitable for estimating masseter and medial pterygoid cross-sections. In the calculations which follow, we have assumed that these scale with the same exponents as the temporal muscle. This may be an underestimation. According to Schumacher (1961) and DuBrul (1977), the masseter–pterygoid complex is normally more pronounced in folivorous animals than in those with other diets. As the largest species among both great apes and gibbons have a larger proportion of leaves in their diet than smaller species (Kay, 1975a), it is likely that masseter and medial pterygoid cross-sections increase at a more rapid rate than our estimate.

The observations reported above indicate that the loss of bite force

Fig. 2. Regression slopes of total molar crown area and bite force on the Sneath size variable for male and female great apes and gibbons. The solid circle indicates the bite force developed by a mean female *Pan paniscus* skull enlarged isometrically to the size of a mean female *Gorilla gorilla* skull, the open circle the same for a mean female *Hylobates klossii* skull enlarged to female *Hylobates syndactylus* size.

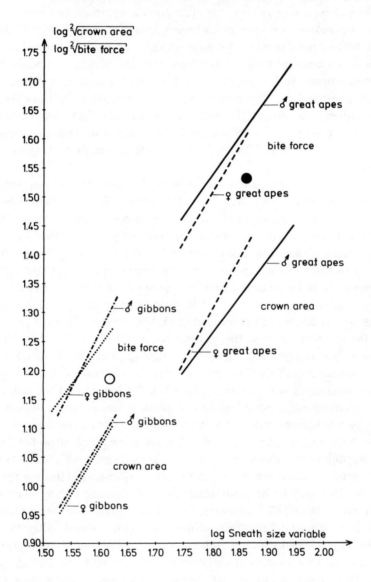

resulting from the positively allometric lengthening of the lever arm in larger species is compensated by more than isometrically increasing muscle forces and muscle power arms. As all forces must be in equilibrium at the temporomandibular joint, this can be examined quantitatively by solving the equation

$$\text{bite force} = \frac{\text{muscle force} \times \text{power arm}}{\text{load arm}}$$

Bite force has been estimated for the males and females of each species with values calculated for the 'mean' skull of the appropriate sample. The slopes of the interspecific regressions of these forces on the Sneath size variable are shown in Fig. 2, together with the slopes for molar crown area. The exponents for bite force are positively allometric for both great apes and gibbons and collinear for the two groups, indicating that larger species tend to possess more bite force for their size than do smaller ones. The slopes for bite force and crown area are roughly parallel.

It follows from the above that smaller species enlarged isometrically to the size of larger ones would be able to generate less bite force than if their shapes had been modified in accordance with the observed allometric trends. In Fig. 2, the bite forces of a 'mean' female *H. klossii* cranium enlarged isometrically to the size as a 'mean' *H. syndactylus* skull and a female pygmy chimpanzee skull enlarged to female gorilla size are shown. In both cases the calculated bite forces clearly lie below the empirically determined regression line, demonstrating that size-related shape changes among great ape and gibbon species serve to magnify bite force.

Dividing bite force by crown area yields a measure of bite pressure, i.e. bite force per unit of occlusal surface. Bite pressure is an important indicator of grinding efficiency. Enlarging the grinding surfaces of molar teeth yields a corresponding increase in amount of food processed only if bite force increases at the same rate as surface area, thus maintaining bite pressure. As Fig. 2 shows, the regression slopes of both variables on overall cranial size are roughly parallel. In hominoid primates as a whole, crown area and bite force increase at about the same rate as species become larger.

Estimated bite pressure varies greatly among species (Fig. 3). However, it shows no readily discernible relation to size, nor to diet or methods of food processing. Most great ape species seem to develop higher pressures than gibbon species; orangutans are an exception. In nearly all species, males can generate considerably greater bite pressure than can females. This difference, which is particularly pronounced in great apes, may reflect differences in feeding behavior or other uses of the dentition between sexes.

The allometric trends described for the masticatory apparatus also influence the equilibrium of forces at the atlanto-occipital joint and evoke correlated morphological changes. These are described elsewhere (Demes, 1984, 1985).

The assumption that mechanical requirements are ultimately responsible for many of the morphological differences in the skulls of hominoid primates of varying size seems well supported by the analyses described above. It is also in line with the results of biomechanical analyses of the hominoid mandible (Demes, Preuschoft & Wolff, 1984) and maxilla (Preuschoft *et al.*: Chapter III.3). The skulls of primates and other vertebrates display a multitude of major and minor differences whose functional significance is more often than

Fig. 3. Estimated occlusal pressure developed by 'mean' male and female skulls of nine species of great apes and gibbons plotted against the mean Sneath size variable for the species.

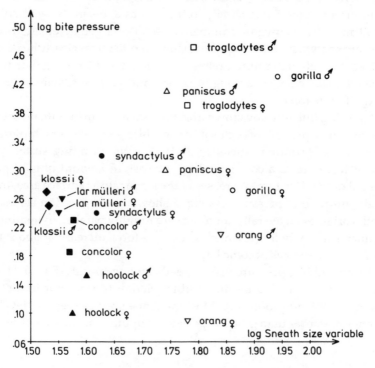

not surprisingly poorly understood. A melding of allometric and biomechanical methodologies offers a promising avenue for improving our understanding of cranial variation within and among vertebrate species.

References

Corruccini, R. S. (1980) Size and positioning of the teeth and infratemporal fossa relative to taxonomic and dietary variation in primates. *Acta Anat.*, **107**, 231–5

Creel, N. & Preuschoft, H. (1976) Cranial Morphology of the Lesser Apes. A multivariate statistical study. In *Gibbon and Siamang*, ed. D. Rumbaugh, pp. 219–303. Basel: Karger

Demes, B. (1984) Biomechanik der Atlantoociptalgelenks von Primaten. *Acta Anat.*, **128**, 19 (abstract)

Demes, B. (1985) Biomechanics of the primate skull base. *Adv. Anat., Embryol. Cell Biol.*, **94**

Demes, B., Preuschoft, H. & Wolff, J. E. A. (1984) Stress–strength relationships in the mandibles of hominoids. In *Food Acquisition and Processing in Primates*, ed. D. J. Chivers, B. A. Wood & A. Bilborough, pp. 369–90. London: Plenum Press

DuBrul, E. L. (1977) Early hominoid feeding mechanisms. *Am. J. Phys. Anthropol.*, **47**, 305–20

Gingerich, P. D., Smith, B. H. & Rosenberg, K. (1982) Allometric scaling in the dentition of primates and prediction of body weight from tooth size in fossils. *Am. J. Phys. Anthropol.*, **58**, 81–100

Hylander, W. L. (1975) The human mandible, lever or link? *Am. J. Phys. Anthropol.*, **43**, 227–42

Kay, R. F. (1975a) Allometry and early hominids. *Science*, **189**, 63

Kay, R. F. (1975b) The functional adaptations of primate molar teeth. *Am. J. Phys. Anthropol.*, **43**, 195–216

Pilbeam, D. & Gould, S. J. (1974) Size and scaling in human evolution. *Science*, **186**, 892–901

Preuschoft, H., Demes, B., Meyer, M. & Bär, H. F. (1985) Die biomechanischen Prinzipien im Oberkiefer von langschnauzigen Wirbeltieren. *Z. Morphol. Anthropol.*, **76**, 1–24

Schumacher, G. H. (1961) *Funtionelle Morphologie der Kaumuskulatur*. Jena: VEB Gustav Fischer

Shea, B. T. (1983) Size and diet in the evolution of African ape craniodental form. *Folia Primatol.*, **40**, 32–68

Sneath, P. H. A. (1967) Trend-surface analysis of transformation grids. *J. Zool. Lond.*, **151**, 65–122

Susman, R. L. & Jungers W. L. (1981) Comment to paper by S. C. Johnson: Bonobos: generalized hominid prototypes of specialized insular dwarfs? *Curr. Anthropol.*, **22**, 369–71

Weijs, W. A. & Hillen, B. (1984) Relationship between the physiological cross-section of the human jaw muscles and their cross-sectional area in computer tomograms. *Acta Anat.*, **118**, 129–38

Wolff, J. E. A. (1982) Die funktionelle Gestalt der menschlichen Unterkiefersymphyse. München: Minerva Publikation, Saur GmbH

Wolff J. E. A. (1984) A theoretical approach to solve the chin problem. In *Food Acquisition and Processing in Primates*, ed. D. J. Chivers, B. A. Wood & A. Bilsborough, pp. 391–405. London: Plenum Press

III.2

Growth changes, variations and sexual dimorphism of the gorilla skull

P. SCHMID AND Z. STRATIL

Introduction

The Hominoidea are largely uniform at birth (Schultz, 1926, 1962; Schuchardt, 1953; Hofer, 1954; Biegert, 1957). At this stage the cranial topography is mostly the result of space demands of the brain and the sense organs. Later, the mechanical requirements of the developing masticatory apparatus become predominant (Biegert, 1957). When the permanent dentition appears the growth patterns of the different skull regions change in comparison to the fetal conditions (Schuchardt, 1953). The marked differences in growth rates lead to size and form changes. At the end of postnatal development, sexual dimorphism becomes evident (Randall, 1943/44; Schultz, 1962, 1969).

The purpose of this study was an analysis of growth, variability, and sexual dimorphism of the gorilla skull, based on a large sample (n = 131); a series of 85 measurements was taken. As the conventional reference points on the skull were defined for humans (Oppenheim, 1911, 1927; Martin, 1914; Mollison, 1938), new measurements were added and some classical distances were divided into smaller units (Stratil, 1983). The skulls were grouped into four dental age classes (Schultz, 1941; see also Table 1).

Table 1. *Sample size per age group*

Age class	Definition	*n*	Sex male	female	indet.
			Sex		
Infant	Deciduous dentition	15	7	5	3
Juvenile I	M1 in occlusal position	16	6	6	4
Juvenile II	Permanent dentition without functional M3	17	8	9	
Adult	Permanent dentition completed	83	47	36	

Results

Cranial growth

Without considering sex, the relative growth rates are expressed as percentage increase of a given dimension in respect to the youngest age class (infant).

The intensities of growth are different for the various skull parts (Table 2, Fig. 1). The growth rate of the brain case is four times lower than for other skull regions. The skull base grows three times faster than the brain section, but still somewhat slower than the face and the jaw regions.

The orbital part of the face shows a frontally directed growth. The increase in height of the upper face is small. The middle face (lower border of the orbitae to rhinion) displays a remarkable change in its proportions. The midface rotates upward and the increase of height is considerable. Subsequently, the lower part of the face shows a strong tendency to grow forwards and downwards. The mandible mesial to the M1 does not become much bigger, with the exception of the symphysis, but there is a substantial increment in height of the ascending ramus.

Table 2. *Mean growth rates of the different skull regions*

Brain case		**20**
	Sagittal measurements	26
	Transversal measurements	17
	Frontal measurements	18
Skull base		**60**
	Sagittal measurements	83
	Transversal measurements	37
Facial region		**80**
	Sagittal measurements	71
	Transversal measurements	74
	Frontal measurements	97
Upper face	Sagittal measurements	55
	Transversal measurements	77
	Frontal measurements	80
Lower face	Sagittal measurements	84
	Transversal measurements	73
	Frontal measurements	107
Mandibula		**90**
	Sagittal measurements	89
	Transversal measurements	59
	Frontal measurements	126

In most skull regions the increase of the sagittal measurements exceeds that of the transversal ones. The frontal-directed dimensions show low growth intensities in the brain part, whereas in the jaw region, the frontal dimension dominates the transverse measurements.

Ontogenetic development reveals that 80% of the dimensions undergo their greatest expansion during the eruption of the permanent dentition (juvenile I/II). Dimensions of the brain case which do not include cranial superstructures increase at a minimal rate. The formation of the supraorbital region and of the crests only takes place in the final stage of ontogeny.

Variability

In the different skull parts, the coefficient of variation displays values from 11% to 13%. Here again, the brain case is an exception in clearly showing a lower variability. In the skull base only the basion–nuchal crest distance is highly variable. The area of attachment of the nuchal musculature mirrors the relations of the jaw apparatus.

In the face, the supraorbital torus (V = 26%) and the interorbital region (V = 21%) show a rather striking variability.

If the coefficients of variation are calculated separately for each sex, the variability of the male skull appears to be more pronounced.

Fig. 1. Dimensions with a growth rate of more than 100%.

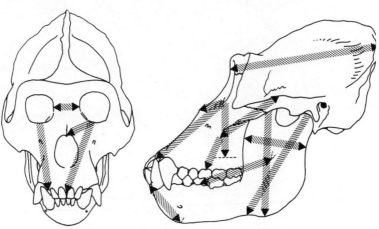

Sexual dimorphism

The sexual dimorphism is defined as the difference in skull dimensions between the sexes, with measurements of the females being taken as 100%. The dimorphism remains insignificant until the last stage of ontogeny. The intensive growth in the males during the final stage leads to an extensive sexual dimorphism in adult gorilla skulls. On the average, dimorphism is more pronounced in the sagittal than in the transversal dimensions.

The various skull regions are equally dimorphic (18%), with the exception of the brain case (10%, see also Table 4). The most dimorphic measurements of the brain case include cranial superstructures. In the skull base, the variations observed in the longitudinal dimensions are twice as important as those in the latitude. For instance, the basion–nuchal crest distance shows a very marked difference between the sexes (37%).

The face displays the most remarkable sexual dimorphism of dimensions starting at the lower orbit margins with a downward orientation. The dimensions of the lateral midface are far less dimorphic. The strongest sex differences are in the interorbital breadth. The thickness of the mandibular corpus and symphysis are only slightly sex dimorphic, whereas dimorphism in dimensions of their heights is much more pronounced.

Fig. 2. Dimensions with a variabilitty of more than 13%.

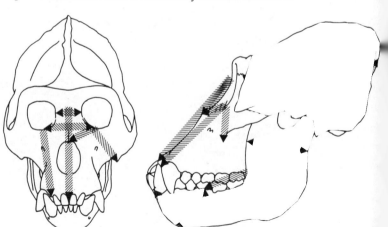

Table 3. *Mean coefficient of variation of different skull regions*

Skull region	Coefficient of variation
Brain case	7.2
Skull base	11.4
Face	12.8
Upper jaw	11.8
Lower jaw	10.6

Table 4. *Sexual dimorphism of measurements in different skull regions*

Brain case		**10**
	Sagittal measurements	15
	Transversal measurements	8
	Frontal measurements	7
Skull base		**20**
	Sagittal measurements	26
	Transversal measurements	13
Facial region		**21**
	Sagittal measurements	21
	Transversal measurements	19
	Frontal measurements	24
Mandibula		**17**
	Sagittal measurements	19
	Transversal measurements	15
	Frontal measurements	18

Discussion

The intensities of growth are dissimilar in the different skull regions. The brain part and the cranial base display lower growth rates than the remaining skull. Even extensively increasing brain case dimensions never reach the average growth rates of the face. The small increase of the brain case is due to the negative allometric growth of the brain, which very early in ontogeny arrives at about 90% of its final size (Schultz, 1965; Gould, 1971, 1975; Pilbeam & Gould, 1974; Shea, 1983).

The intermediate growth intensity of the skull base has been less noted in the literature. This intermediate intensity is the result on the one hand of the low breadth increase caused by brain case growth and, on the other, of an extensive growth of the sagittal dimensions, connected with the development of the jaws.

The ontogeny of the lower face is dominated by the development of the jaws which, contrary to the brain, grow in a positive allometric fashion (Biegert, 1957, 1963; Freedman, 1962; Vogel, 1966; Pilbeam & Gould, 1974). Consequently, this study shows how crucial for any ontogenetical study is a distinction of the different skull regions. This fact has been frequently neglected in previous investigations (Schultz, 1962; 1969).

In the different skull regions, the sagittal dimensions always grow more rapidly than the transversal ones. The sagittal structures of the skull interact functionally with the developing jaw apparatus. It is in the light of mandibular leverage that this becomes evident. The main

Fig. 3. Dimensions with a sexual dimorphism of more than 26%.

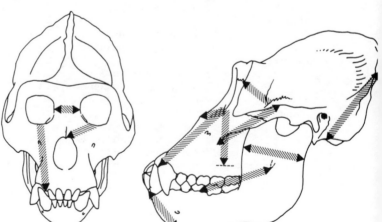

masticatory forces act in the sagittal plane to move sagittal-oriented lever arms around the mandibular joint. The result is a massive growth of the sagittal dimensions to enhance the moments of the acting forces. The effectiveness of the masticatory complex is related to the increase in body size. Meanwhile, the growth of the breadth dimensions is correlated with development of the brain which reaches its final size early.

Our investigation shows that the superstructures of the brain case are not formed until the last stage of ontogeny. Immediately before this phase there is a considerable increase in body weight (Grether & Yerkes, 1940, Dixon, 1981). This gives us the impression that in the previous stages the surface of the brain case without superstructures is large enough for the attachment of musculature (Ashton & Zuckerman, 1956). The weight increase parallels the eruption of the permanent dentition and the formation of cranial superstructures.

The interorbital breadth exhibits the highest growth rate of all measurements. This may be related to the pneumatization of the fronto-ethmoidal paranasal complex (Cave, 1961; Schultz, 1969). It reflects the better attachment of the growing jaws to the brain case.

Sexual dimorphism remains insignificant until the last stage of ontogeny (Randall, 1943–44; Ashton, 1957, Schultz, 1962, 1969). Body weight dimorphism in the gorilla develops only after 6 years of age

Fig. 4. Three postnatal stages of the gorilla skull. Orientation on mandibular joint and lower orbital border.

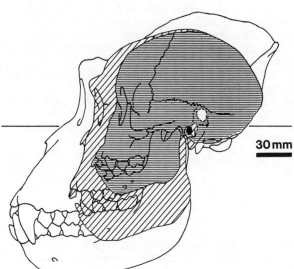

30 mm

(Brandes, 1930; Schaller, 1963; Groves, 1970; Dixon, 1981). Our results illustrate the correlation of body weight increase, eruption of permanent dentition, development of cranial superstructures, and sexual dimorphism. Sexual dimorphism becomes socially important with the beginning of puberty. In our study 13 of 17 intensively growing dimensions are at the same time highly dimorphic. It seems that a distinct sexual dimorphism is an effect of intensive growth. Such strong dimorphic measurements also cause a high coefficient of variation. The maintenance of functionality in an adult animal requires intensive growth of specific skull dimensions, which are related to the jaw apparatus, and the factor of body size has considerable influence. The result is a significant variability of intensively growing dimensions due to the huge differences in body weight between males and females. Moreover this study shows that most dimensions with little increase display only a slight sexual dimorphism in the gorilla skull.

Acknowledgement

Our thanks go to Professor Dr med. J. Biegert for his helpful comments and his kindness to let us study the material.

References

Ashton, E. H. (1957) Age changes in dimensional differences between the skulls of male and female apes. *Proc. Zool. Soc. Lond.*, **128**, 259–65

Ashton, E. H. & Zuckerman, S. (1956) Cranial crests in the Anthropoidea. *Proc. Zool. Soc. Lond.*, **126**, 581–634

Biegert, J. (1957) Der Formwandel des Primatenschädels und seine Beziehungen zur ontogenetischen Entwicklung und den phylogenetischen Spezialisationen der Kopforgane. *Gegenbauers Morphol. Jb.*, **98**, 77–199

Biegert, J. (1963) The evaluation of characteristics of the skull, hands and feet for primate taxonomy. In *Classification and Human Evolution*, ed. S. L. Washburn, pp. 116–45. Chicago: Aldine

Brandes, G. (1930) Wichtige Daten über das Heranwachsen des Gorilla. *Zool. Garten*, **3**, 104–16

Cave, A. J. E. (1961) The frontal sinus of the gorilla. *Proc. Zool. Soc. Lond.*, **136**, 359–73

Dixon, A. F. (1981) *The Natural History of the Gorilla*. London: Weidenfeld & Nicolson

Freedman, L. (1962) Growth of muzzle length relative to calvaria length in *Papio*. *Growth*, **26**, 117–28

Gould, S. J. (1971) Geometric similarity in allometric growth: a contribution to the problem of scaling in the evolution of size. *Am. Naturalist*, **105**, 113–36

Gould, S. J. (1975) Allometry in primates, with emphasis on scaling and the evolution of the brain. In *Contrib. Primatol.*, **5**, 244–92

Grether, W. F. & Yerkes, R. M. (1940) Weight norms and relations for chimpanzee. *Am. J. Phys. Anthropol.*, **27**, 181–97

Groves, C. P. (1970) *Gorillas*. London: Arthur Barker

Hofer, H. (1954) Die cranio-cerebrale Topographie bei den Affen und ihre Bedeutung für die menschliche Schädelform. *Homo*, 5, 52–72

Martin, R. (1914) *Lehrbuch der Anthropologie.* Jena: Fischer

Mollison, T. (1938) Spezielle Methoden anthropologischer Messung. In *Handbuch der Biologischen Arbeitsmethoden, Abt. VII, Teil. 2*, ed. E. Abderhalden, 523–682. Berlin & Wien: Urban & Schwarzenberg

Oppenheim, S. (1911) Zur Typologie des Primatencraniums. *Z. Morphol. Anthropol.*, 14, 1–203

Oppenheim, S. (1927) Methoden zur Untersuchung der Morphologie der Primaten, Kraniologie. In *Handbuch der Biologischen Arbeitsmethoden, Abt. VII, Teil. 2*, ed. E. Abderhalden 531–608. Berlin & Wien: Urban & Schwarzenberg

Pilbeam, D. P. & Gould, S. J. (1974) Size and scaling in human evolution. *Science*, 186, 892–901

Randall, F. E. (1943–1944) The skeletal and dental development and variability of the gorilla. *Human Biol.*, 15, 236–54, 307–37; 16, 23–76

Schaller, G. B. (1963) *The Mountain Gorilla: Ecology and Behavior.* Chicago: University of Chicago Press

Schuchardt, E. (1953) Ueber Wachstumsrelationen am Schädel und Gehirn von Säugetieren in Ontogenese und Phylogenese. *Z. Morphol. Anthropol.*, 45, 73–134

Schultz, A. H. (1926) Fetal growth of man and other primates. *Q. Rev. Biol.* 1, 465–521

Schultz, A. H. (1941) Growth and development of the orang-utan. *Contrib. Embryol.*, 29, 57–110

Schultz, A. H. (1962) Metric age changes and sex differences in primate skulls. *Z. Morphol. Anthropol*, 52, 239–55

Schultz, A. H. (1965) The cranial capacity and the orbital volume of hominoids according to age and sex. *Homenaje a Juan Comas II, Mexico*, 337–57

Schultz, A. H. (1969). The skeleton of the chimpanzee. In *The Chimpanzee*, vol. 1, ed. G. H. Bourne, pp. 50–103. Basel: Karger

Shea, B. T. (1983) Size and diet in the evolution of African ape craniodental form. *Folia Primatol.*, 40, 32–68

Stratil, Z. (1983) Alters- und geschlechtsbedingte Veränderungen am Gorillaschädel. Diplomarbeit, Zürich, Anthropologisches Institut und Museum

Vogel, C. (1966) *Morphologische Studien am Gesichtsschädel catarrhiner Primaten. (Bibl. primatol.*, Fasc. 4.) Basel: Karger

III.3

The biomechanical principles realised in the upper jaw of long-snouted primates

H. PREUSCHOFT, B. DEMES, M. MEYER AND
H. F. BÄR

Introduction

One of the major unresolved problems in functional morphology is the understanding of the biomechanical function (not
biological role, both terms in the sense of Bock & von Wahlert, 1965) of
the cranium. Skulls are commonly considered the most informative
documents of human evolutionary history. Our inability, however, to
answer questions about the functional meaning of traits is a serious
obstacle to understanding human evolution. This is true in spite of the
many approaches made to the biological role of skull morphology.
Because of its three-dimensional shape as well as the widespread
application of forces, that is insertion of muscles, the cranium has
resisted most attempts to unveil the mechanical principles of its
construction. A recent attempt to interpret the neurocranium as a shell
has been made by Demes (1985), who also reviewed the literature.
Other approaches to skull function have started from the mandible
(Wolff, 1982, 1984, 1985; Demes, Preuschoft & Wolff, 1984). Here we
propose a theoretical model of the upper jaw as a testable hypothesis.
Subsequently, it will be tested by an empirical analysis of the strength
properties of the upper jaw. The basis of this procedure is Pauwels'
theory of causal morphogenesis (Pauwels, 1960).

The upper jaw as a whole is a projecting bony structure, covered by
little more than skin. Muscle insertions are confined to the most
occipital section. The forces resulting from biting and chewing are the
major external loads it must be able to resist. A failure and subsequent
fracture from overloading of the jaw will reduce considerably the
animal's chances to survive. Resistance to these loads is provided by
nothing else than the bone substance itself; there are no soft tissues to

reduce the stresses as is the case in extremity bones (Pauwels, 1950*a,b*, 1980; Kummer, 1959*a,b*, 1961, 1972; Preuschoft, 1969, 1970, 1971).

Methods

For the construction of the mechanical model, we have used the methods of theoretical statics. In order to check the correctness of the hypothesis, we consider bone as a homogeneous material. If the 'material-dictated' strength properties are given, the actual net strength of a lengthy element like a snout is proportional to its profile. To obtain these profiles, the skulls of a subadult male gorilla, an adult male savannah baboon and a young Sunda gavial (*Tomistoma schlegeli*, length of tooth row 27 cm) were 'sectioned' with the aid of computer tomography.

Photographs of the sections have been enlarged and used for measuring the area of the bony cross-section and the axial as well as the polar moments of resistance. All calculations have been made twice; with and without the alveolar process, because this structure seems to vary independently from the strength requirements against shearing, bending, and torsion (Preuschoft *et al.*, 1985; see below).

A complete analysis requires viewing of a three-dimensional system from the side, from above, and from in front; more precisely, a projection into three planes.

Biomechanical model: lateral aspect

The most illustrative approach seems to be offered by a side view of the long, slender snout of a crocodile (Fig. 1a). The object seized between the tooth rows is pressed by the lower jaw against the upper, thus exerting bite forces in both directions. If we observe the upper jaw turned upside down (Fig. 1b), we have the well-known situation of a simple balancing scale or a two-armed lever. It is hung up by the muscles; on one side the joint force is applied, on the other the bite force. Whereas the lever arm of the joint force is constant, and the force itself cannot exceed a certain value without inflicting damage to the joint, the lever arm of the bite force may change, as well as its magnitude: the more occipital the bite point, the greater the bite force.

Possible bite forces can increase according to an exponential function. They are easiest to determine by the equilibrium of forces about the mandibular joint, under the assumption of constant muscle forces. In reality, however, the muscle forces may not assume their maximal values if the bite point is near the tip of the snout. If the bite point is moved rearward, the bite forces can assume higher values because the joint force necessary to balance the system remains lower (Wolff, 1982). This does not alter the exponential increase of the bite forces (Fig. 2).

The bite forces are directed more or less perpendicular to the long axis of the skeletal element under consideration, thus creating shearing stresses. Shearing strength is determined by the cross-sectional area of the bone, because shearing forces are spread more or less evenly over the entire cross-sectional area.

On the basis of Pauwels' theory, we may expect the cross-sectional areas to become greater occipitally, following the same curve as do the maximal bite forces.

Fig. 2 shows the cross-sectional areas plotted against the length of the snout. Since canine biting is usually done on one side only, and the nasal opening does not allow for transmitting forces from one side to the other, this region of the jaw should be strong enough to sustain the entire possible bite force by one half of its cross-section. Taking this into account, the increase of the cross-sectional areas is proportional to the increase of the shearing forces. As can be seen from Table 1, the shearing stresses in all animals investigated remained about the same over the length of the snout.

Biting also tends to bend the upper jaw. This bending causes a forward shift of the nasal roof in relation to the palate. This shift can be

Fig. 1. (a) Crocodile skull in side view with an object between the teeth. The adduction of the mandible exerts pressure against the object, and against the upper jaw. (b) If the upper jaw is viewed upside down, it is very similar to the well-known model of a two-armed lever, hung up by the muscles.

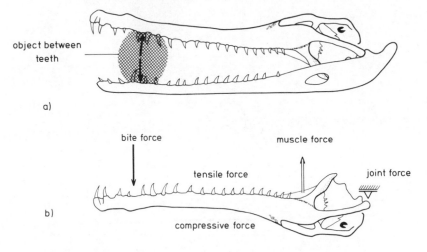

Fig. 2. Abscissa: Length of the snout, i.e. distance between most rostral teeth and occipital margin of the palatal plate (crocodile), or root of zygomatic arch (primates). Ordinate: Areas of cross-sections through the upper jaws. Values with and without the alveolar process are shown. For the sections through the nasal opening, one half of the actual values is also indicated. The intervals between the areas with and without alveolar process in the primates are hatched.

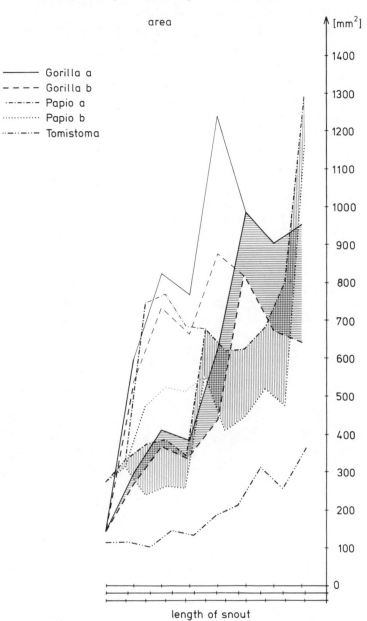

excluded by a prop between the parts. This prop exists in the form of the bony nasal septum (Fig. 3).

Biting on the incisors means, in terms of mechanics, the application of a load concentrated on the far end of a plate. Bending moments increase linearly from the point of force application. The optimal shape of a plate loaded this way, a 'body of equal strength', which combines a maximum of strength with a minimum of material, is shown in Fig. 4. It resembles the form of a typical primate premaxilla.

Biting on the canines means the application of a load distributed over the length of the canines. The palatal 'plate' in this section is supported by two 'braces' in the form of the lateral walls of the nasal opening. If their width is constant, their height must increase linearly to offer equal strength against bending by a force distributed over the length of the canine (Fig. 4 b). This again is a very common morphological trait.

Behind the canine, and occipital of the nasal opening, the upper jaw can best be described as a short, wide tube (Fig. 4c). The bite force or chewing force can be either concentrated on one premolar or molar, or distributed over several cheek teeth. The greatest bending moments,

Table 1. *Shearing stresses*

Shearing stress (t_q) evoked by maximal shearing force (bite force, B)
Bite moment $(M_b) = 50$ kpcm
Load arm (l)
Bite force at cross section (B)
Cross-sectional area (A)

Relative change of shearing stress $(t_{qrel}) = \dfrac{t_{max} - t_{min}}{t_{max}} \times 100$

Abbreviations: (r)   First cut through the most rostral part of the snout
(m) Halfway between (r) and (o)
(o) Root of zygomatic arch or (in the crocodile) of palatal plate

		l (cm)	B (kp)	A (cm$_2$)	t_q (kp/cm$_2$)	t_{qrel} (%)
Gorilla	r	13.2	3.8	5.96	0.64	
	m	11.6	4.2	7.58	0.55	14
	o	9.2	5.4	9.06	0.60	
Papio	r	13.4	3.7	3.36	1.10	
	m	10.2	4.9	6.80	0.72	35
	o	7.0	7.1	8.02	0.88	
Tomistoma	r	25.3	2.0	1.18	1.70	
	m	18.9	2.7	1.40	1.93	21
	o	12.5	4.0	2.61	1.53	

however, occur in this region as well as in the more rostral, if biting is done on the front teeth. The strength of the tube against bending grows by the second power of its height. Therefore, a parabolically curved contour will provide equal strength without superfluous weight. In fact, the profile of the upper jaw in Fig. 4c is described best by a square-root function which has its zero point at the tips of the incisors.

If we now combine the sections, we arrive at the shape characteristic of our example, namely the baboon skull (Fig. 4d).

However, what provides strength is not the outline, but the 'moment of resistance' of a profile. We have calculated the moments of resistance, or shape-dependent strength properties, in several primate skulls, with and without the alveolar process. These empirically observed strength properties of two primate skulls are shown in Fig. 5. In all cases the values increase rearward much faster than linearly. Table 2 shows the bending stresses which occur under a high load on the incisors in the rostral, middle and occipital section of the jaw.

The hyperbolic increase of bending strength does not correspond to the linear growth of the bending moments in the upper jaw. The stresses become smaller towards the zygomatic arch.

Fig. 3. Side view of a baboon skull, with roof of nose and palatal plate drawn as beams. If a bite force is applied, the upper jaw tends to be bent dorsally concave. A prop in the form of the bony nasal septum would be shortened markedly, and therefore can be a means to exclude bending of the system.

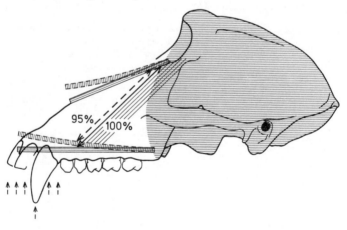

Fig. 4. (a) Short plate, loaded by a force, **P**, concentrated on its far edge, and shaped as a body of equal strength. (b) Plate, loaded by a force distributed over its right margin, and supported by two props shaped as bodies of equal strength. (c) Rectangular tube, shaped as a body of equal strength against loads which are concentrated to a point distal to its free edge. (d) Combination of the elements shown in (a)–(c) to give something similar to a baboon skull.

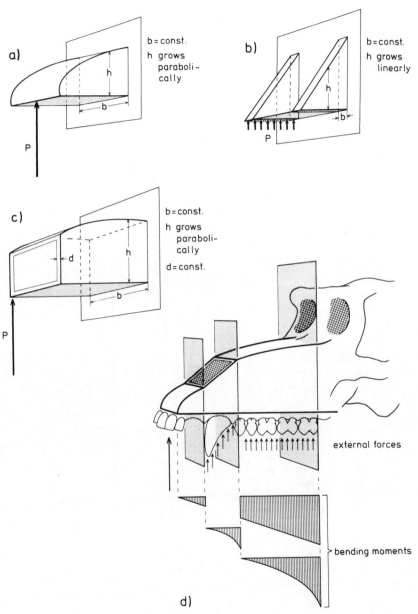

Fig. 5. Abscissa: Length of the snout as in Fig. 2. Ordinate: Axial moments of inertia of cross-sections through upper jaws as a measure of bending strength.

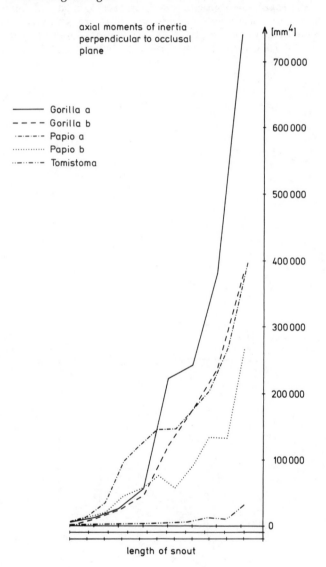

Biomechanical model: top view

As soon as an animal has seized prey with its teeth – as in the crocodile or baboons – or tries to rip off twigs or bark from a stem – as baboons or gorillas may do – the jaws, and in fact the entire skull, are exposed to forces in the occlusal plane of the tooth row. The sideways movement is controlled by the neck muscles and, because of the limited torque these can provide, the greatest possible forces can again be much greater if applied to the occipital than to the rostral part of the jaws. As a result of previous work (Hiiemae, 1967, 1978, 1984; Kay & Hiiemae, 1974; Hylander, 1975, 1979; Maier & Schneck, 1981; Maier, 1984), we know that the bite forces in the chewing process also exert strong components in the occlusal plane. A calculation of the numerical values of these force components and bending moments is not possible, because the muscle forces are neither known, nor can they be derived from other values.

The shearing components of the external forces and the bite forces in this plane seem to be proportional to the sagittal force components, and thus to the shearing strength of the upper jaw.

Table 2. *Bending stresses*

Normal stresses ($s_{d,z}$) evoked by bending in the sagittal plane in the case of biting on the most rostral teeth
Bite moment (M_b) = 50 kpcm
Axial moment of inertia (J) vertical to the occlusal plane
Moment of resistance on the side of the nasal roof (W_o)
Moment of resistance on the palate (W_u)
Bending moment evoked by bite force applied to the incisors (M_B)
Relative change of normal stress (s_{rel}) = $\dfrac{s_{max} - s_{min}}{s_{max}} \times 100$

		J (cm^4)	W_o (cm^3)	W_u (cm^3)	s_d (kp/cm^2)	s_z (kp/cm^2)	M_B (kpcm)	s_{drel} (%)	s_{zrel} (%)
Gorilla	r	1.23	1.26	1.41	6.89	6.16	8.68		
	m	5.65	3.28	3.36	4.20	4.10	13.77	67	76
	o	38.31	9.27	14.81	2.30	1.44	21.28		
Papio	r	1.33	0.99	1.22	6.85	5.56	6.78		
	m	14.55	6.53	5.80	2.62	2.95	17.12	62	55
	o	26.64	6.78	11.04	4.05	2.49	27.46		
Tomistoma	r	0.23	0.30	0.34	30.59	27.00	9.18		
	m	0.47	0.42	0.50	46.10	38.72	11.76	58	42
	o	1.74	1.53	1.32	19.47	22.57	14.33		

A long snout will also be bent in the occlusal plane. The increase of moments of resistance against bending in the plane of the tooth row is again faster than the linear increase of the bending moments.

Biomechanical model: anterior view

To complete the analysis, we shall examine the system from the front. Cross-sections are often more informative than the frontal aspect of the entire skull.

Since chewing is regularly and biting often done on one side alone, the bite forces evoke a torsional moment in the upper jaw. This can be seen best on a cross-section (Fig. 6). The torsional moments are kept low by a short distance between the biting tooth and the center of gravity of the cross-section. A medial inclination of the chewing forces, which also causes the usual inclined implantation of the cheek teeth, leads to a reduction of the torsional moments.

Here we have a very good reason why selection favors, in many animals (crocodiles, prosimians, gibbons), a narrow dental arcade rostral to the insertion of the jaw muscles (Fig. 7). Since the lever arms

Fig. 6. Cross-section through the upper jaw of a baboon with center of gravity. Possible bite forces applied to the teeth evoke torsional moments (bite force × distance from center of gravity).

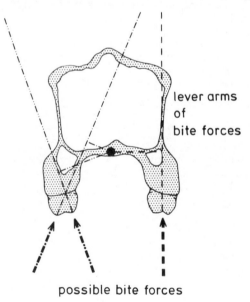

lever arms
of
bite forces

possible bite forces

of the bite forces increase occipitally with the bite forces themselves (see above), the torsional moments grow faster than linearly.

Torsional strength depends on the 'polar moment of resistance' (Preuschoft *et al.*, 1985). The plot of torsional strength (Fig. 8) does not coincide straightforwardly with the increase of torsional moments. This depends largely on local reinforcements of the alveolar arch, or on the varying thickness of the walls, a trait which is highly influenced by local stress concentrations.

According to Table 3 the torsional stresses decrease from the tip of the snout towards its base.

Discussion and conclusion

If the upper jaw, from the tip of the snout to the root of the zygomatic arch, is interpreted as a beam loaded by bite forces and balanced by the masticatory muscles, we find a fair coincidence between the pattern of shearing forces and the arrangement of bone material, or shape-dictated strength properties of the upper jaw.

The bending and rotating moments increase occipitally less than bending and rotational strength. This means that the bending and, to a lesser degree, rotational stresses decrease towards the base of the snout.

Fig. 7. The dental arcade of many primates is wide occipital to the zygoma, but narrow in front of it – a trait which keeps down the torsional moments in the snout.

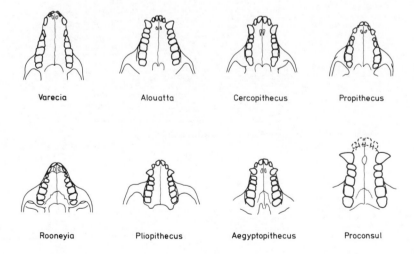

Varecia   Alouatta   Cercopithecus   Propithecus

Rooneyia   Pliopithecus   Aegyptopithecus   Proconsul

Fig. 8. Abscissa: Length of the snout as in Fig. 2. Ordinate: Polar moments of inertia of cross-sections through the upper jaws as a measure of torsional strength.

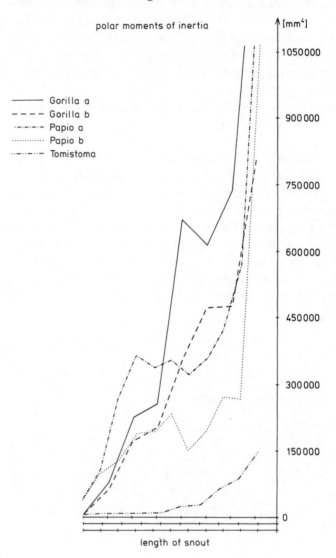

polar moments of inertia

[mm⁴]

——— Gorilla a
– – – Gorilla b
·–·–·– Papio a
·············· Papio b
··–··–·· Tomistoma

length of snout

The safety of a construction is estimated by a combination of normal stresses and shearing stresses which act in the plane of a cross-section. As bone is less resistant to shearing than to compression or tension (Yamaha, 1973), shearing and torsional stresses are given more weight.

In Table 4, the combination of stresses is calculated for rostral, middle, and occipital cross-sections. As can be seen, the net stresses decrease from tip towards the base of the snout, although the differences are not great. The possible reasons for this lack of precise coincidence are discussed elsewhere (Preuschoft *et al.*, 1985).

This result falls in line with what has been found in the case of extremity bones (Kummer, 1959*b*, 1972; Pauwels, 1965) and in the case of the mandible (Hylander, 1975; Wolff, 1982, 1984, 1985; Demes *et al.*, 1984). Whereas the extremity bones are stressed primarily by bending and compression, in the jaws the dominating stress quality seems to be shear.

We are inclined to draw the general conclusion that our results show the existence of a causal relation between shape and mechanical function for the skull not less than for extremity bones.

Table 3. *Torsional stresses*

Torsional stress (t_t) vertical to occlusal plane
Bite moment (M_b) = 50 kpcm
Lever arm of the bite force in the transversal plane (h)
Torsional moment (M_t) = $B \times h$
Polar moment of inertia (J_p)
Polar moment of resistance (W_p)

Relative change of torsional stress $t_{trel} = \dfrac{t_{t\,max} - t_{t\,min}}{t_{t\,max}} \times 100$

		h (cm)	M_t (kpcm)	J_p (cm⁴)	W_p (cm³)	t_t (kp/cm²)	t_{trel} (%)
Gorilla	r	2.3	8.74	8.01	3.74	2.34	
	m	2.7	11.34	25.74	8.00	1.42	65
	o	2.7	14.58	73.89	17.87	0.82	
Papio	r	2.5	9.25	10.31	4.08	2.27	
	m	2.3	11.27	35.76	10.08	1.12	55
	o	2.1	14.91	57.54	14.65	1.02	
Tomistoma	r	0.9	1.80	0.65	0.60	3.00	
	m	1.2	3.24	1.14	0.92	3.52	48
	o	1.5	6.00	8.80	3.28	1.83	

Table 4. *Combined stresses*

Combined stress ($sv_{d,z}$) under a load concentrated on the most rostral teeth

$$sv_{d,z} = \sqrt{(s_{d,z})^2 + 4(t_{ges})^2}$$

Shearing stress (t_q)
Torsional stress (t_t)
Combination of t_q and $t_t = t_{ges}$
Normal stresses ($s_{d,z}$) as in Table 2

Relative change of combined stress ($sv_{d,zrel}) = \dfrac{sv_{d,zmax} - sv_{d,zmin}}{sv_{d,zmax}} \times 100$

		t_q	t_t	t_{ges}	s_d (kp/cm²)	s_z	sv_d	sv_z	sv_{drel} (%)	sv_{zrel} (%)
Gorilla	r	0.64	2.34	2.98	6.89	6.16	9.11	8.57		
	m	0.55	1.42	1.97	4.20	4.10	5.73	5.69	60	63
	o	0.60	0.82	1.42	2.30	1.44	3.64	3.18		
Papio	r	1.10	2.27	3.37	6.85	5.56	9.61	8.74		
	m	0.72	1.12	1.84	2.62	2.95	4.52	4.72	53	48
	o	0.88	1.02	1.90	4.05	2.49	5.55	4.54		
Tomistoma	r	1.70	3.00	4.70	30.59	27.00	32.00	28.59		
	m	1.93	3.52	5.45	46.10	38.72	47.37	40.22	57	42
	o	1.53	1.83	3.36	19.47	22.57	20.60	23.55		

Acknowledgements

The opportunity to investigate the primate skulls was kindly offered through the courtesy of Dr M. Sakka, Paris, and Drs Autissier and Binnert, Dijon. The work was done on the CT of the Hôpital Générale in Dijon. The crocodile was investigated on the CT of Dr Ting, Bochum.

References

Bock, W. J. & Wahlert, G. von (1965) Adaptation and the form–function complex. *Evolution*, **19**(3), 269–99

Demes, B. (1985) Biomechanics of the primate skull base. *Adv. Anat., Embryol. Cell Biol.*, **94**, Berlin: Springer Verlag

Demes, B., Preuschoft, H. & Wolff, J. E. A. (1984) Stress–strength relationship in the mandible of hominoids. In *Food Acquisition and Processing in Primates*, ed. D. J. Chivers, B. A. Wood & A. Bilborough, pp. 369–90. New York: Plenum Press

Hiiemae, K. (1967) Masticatory function in the mammals. *J. Dent. Res.*, **46**, 883–93

Hiiemae, K. (1978) Mammalian mastication: a review of the activity of the jaw muscles and the movements they produce in chewing. In *Development, Function and Evolution of Teeth*, ed. P. M. Butler & K. A. Joysey, pp. 359–98. London: Academic Press

Hiiemae, K. (1984) Functional aspects of primate jaw morphology. In *Food Acquisition and Processing in Primates*, ed. D. J. Chivers, B. A. Wood & A. Bilsborough, pp. 257–81. New York: Plenum Press

Hylander, W. L. (1975) The human mandible, lever or link? *Am. J. Phys. Anthropol.*, **4**, 227–42

Hylander, W. L. (1979) An experimental analysis of temporo mandibular joint reaction force in macaques. *Am. J. Phys. Anthropol.*, **51**, 443–56

Kay, R. F. & Hiiemae, K. (1974) Jaw movement and tooth use in recent and fossil primates. *Am. J. Phys. Anthropol.*, **40**, 227–56

Kummer, B. (1959a) *Bauprinzipien des Säugerskeletes. Stuttgart: Thieme*

Kummer, B. (1959b) Biomechanik des Säugerskelettes. *Handb. Zool.* 8, part 24

Kummer, B. (1961) Statik und dynamik des menschlichen Körpers. *Handb. gesamt. Arbeitsmed.*, **1**, 9–63

Kummer, B. (1972) Biomechanics of bone: mechanical properties, functional structure, functional adaptation. In *Biomechanics, its Foundation and Objectives*, ed. Y. C. Fung, N. N. Perrone & M. Anlicker, pp. 237–71. Englewood Cliffs, NJ: Prentice Hall

Maier, W. (1984) Tooth morphology and dietary specialization. In *Food Acquisition and Processing in Primates*, ed. D. J. C. Chivers, B. Wood & A. Bilsborough, pp. 303–30. New York: Plenum Press

Maier, W. & Schneck, G. (1981) Konstruktionsmorphologische Untersuchungen am Gebiss der hominoiden Priaten. *Z. Morphol. Anthropol.*, **72**, 127–69

Pauwels, F. (1950a) Die Bedeutung der Bauprinzipien der unteren Extremität für die Beanspruchung des Beinskelettes. *Z. Anat. Entwickl.-Gesch.*, **114**, 525–38

Pauwels, F. (1950b) Die Bedeutung der Muskelkräfte für die Regelung der Beanspruchung des Röhrenknochens während der Bewegung der Glieder. *Z. Anat. Entwickl.-Gesch.*, **115**, 327–51

Pauwels, F. (1960) Eine neue Theorie über den Einfluss mechanischer Reize auf die Differenzierung der Stützgewebe. *Z. Anat. Entwickl.-Gesch.*, **121**, 478–515

Pauwels, F. (1965) *Gesammelte Abhandlungen zur funktionellen Anatomie des Bewegungsapparates.* Berlin: Springer Verlag

Pauwels, F. (1980) *Biomechanics of the Locomotor Apparatus: Contributions on the Functional Anatomy of the Locomotor Apparatus.* Berlin & New York: Springer

Preuschoft, H. (1969) Statische Untersuchungen am Fuß der Primaten. I. Phalangen und Metatarsalia. *Z. Anat. Entwickl.-Gesch.*, **129**, 285–345

Preuschoft, H. (1970) Functional anatomy of the lower extremity. In *The Chimpanzee*, ed. G. Bourne, vol. 3, pp. 221–94. Basel: Karger

Preuschoft, H. (1971) Body posture and mode of locomotion in early Pleistocene hominids. *Folia Primatol.*, **14**, 209–40

Preuschoft, H., Demes, B., Meier, M. & Bär, H. F. (1985) Die biomechanischen Prinzipien im Oberkiefer von langschnauzigen Wirbeltieren. *Z. Morphol. Anthropol.*, **76**, 1–24

Szabo, I. (1975) *Einführung in die Technische Mechanik. Berlin: Springer*

Wolff, J. E. A. (1982) *Die Funktionelle Gestalt der Menschlichen Unterkiefersymphyse.* München: Minerva-Press

Wolff, J. E. A. (1984) A theoretical approach to solve the chin problem. In *Food Acquisition and Processing in Primates*, ed. D. J. Chivers, B. A. Wood & A. Bilsborough, pp. 391–405. New York: Plenum Press

Wolff, J. E. A. (1985) Mechanik des Unterkiefers mit beweglicher Symphyse. *Z. Morphol. Anthropol.*, **76**, 25–35

Yamaha, H. (1973) *Strength of Biological Materials.* Huntington, NY: R. E. Krieger Publishing Co.

III.4

Some aspects of the development of the orbitotemporal region in hominoid primates

G. H. SCHNECK

Introduction

Our present knowledge of skull morphology is based on the studies of cleaned skulls of postnatal stages and microscopic slide series of prenatal (embryonic and fetal) stages. Because a profound understanding of any structural complex can only be achieved if the corresponding morphogenetic process is considered, it is ideal to have a close series of different stages of development from each species under investigation. This has been possible, for example, in the Tachyglossidae (*Tachyglossus aculeatus*: Gaupp, 1908; Kuhn, 1971) and the Tupaiidae (*Tupaia belangeri*; Zeller, 1983).

Within the primates, only *Homo* shows a relatively comprehensive series of known fetal developmental stages (up to 93 mm crown–rump length (CRL). While nearly 30 different species of monkeys with up to six stages are described, comprising all subfamilies including *Daubentonia* (Maier, unpublished), only one pongid stage has been published until now (*Pan troglodytes*; Starck, 1960). Due to the existence of two microscopic slide series at our Institute, one of *Hylobates moloch* of 51 mm HL and one of a *Gorilla* of about 48 mm HL, we are able to elucidate some aspects of late fetal development among hominoid primates.

In this paper, our interest concentrates on the orbitotemporal region which seems to be a highly variable structural complex, especially in its interorbital part. This is due to its central position between the rear of the nasal capsule, the orbitae (concerning size and direction of the eyes as a whole), the forebrain and the ear capsule. The anterior orbitotemporal part may also be affected by the bending of the central stem.

Morphology

The *Hylobates* of 51 mm HL (Fig. 1) is the most advanced fetal stage of all hominoids ever examined. The small orbitosphenoid and the central stem (basipresphenoid) have already fused to build the bony presphenoid. The latter is separated by a triangular intersphenoidal synchondrosis from the basisphenoid, which itself is still separated from the large alisphenoid by a small synchondrosis.

Fig. 1. Dorsal view of the ethmoidal and orbitotemporal region of the plate – reconstruction of the fetal skull of *Hylobates moloch* (C 12, 51 mm HL). Abbreviations: anc = anterior nasal cupula; asph = alisphenoid; cd = craniopharyngeal duct; cpl = cribrosal plate; ethm = ethmoidal bone; ethmp = ethmoidal processus of the presphenoid; fe = epiphanial foramen; fr = frontal bone; hypf = hypophyseal fossa; 'is' = interorbital septum' (not in the strict sense); lacr = lacrimal bone; max = maxillary bone; mec = Meckel's cartilage; of = optic foramen; ovf = oval foramen; pmax = premaxillary bone; pnc = posterior nasal cupula; psph = presphenoid bone; sp = sphenoidal plane; tn = nasal roof and supraseptal sulcus.

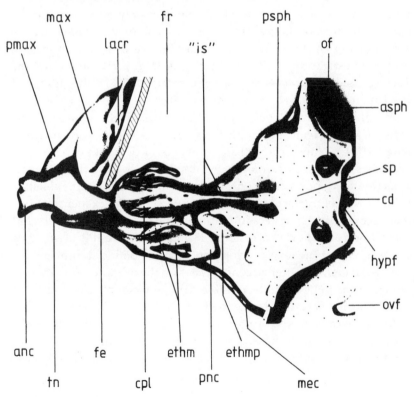

The rear of the nasal capsule, i.e. the cartilaginous posterior nasal cupula, is attached to the nasal septum by connective tissues only; it contains the small ethmoturbinal recessus and extends backwards until half-way between the posterior border of the cribrosal plate and the anterior border of the optic foramina. The floor of this cupula, the posterior transversal lamina, which separates the nasopharyngeal duct from the ethmoturbinal recessus, continues anteriorly into a short posterior cartilago paraseptalis, which is linked with its anterior-most part continuously to the nasal septum in a frontal plane somewhat behind the cribrosal plate.

The ventral border of the nasal septum is embraced by the central and lateral parts of the V-shaped vomer, whereas the posterior paraseptal cartilagines and the floor of the posterior nasal cupulae are supported by the two dorsal ends of the vomer, which is detached in this function posteriorly by the lateral (perpendicular) laminae of the palatine bones. Behind the posterior cupulae these upper rims of the palatine bones support the bony ethmoidal processes of the pre-sphenoid; these continue rostrally until about the rear of the cribrosal plate, covering the posterior cupulae from lateral and being supported in its rostral parts by the dorsal aspects of the antorbital planum. Such an ethmoidal processus normally arises from an antorbital processus of the orbitosphenoid (pila preoptica; Heckmann, 1955; Maier, 1983); the exact manner of origin is still controversial (see Reinbach, 1952; Spatz, 1964). But, since the orbital processus of the frontal bone covers the anterior dorsal rim of the ethmoidal processus, the 'central stem' does not build a part of the medial orbital wall in this stage of development and therefore no interorbital septum in the strict sense is present, although there obviously exists a broad interorbital lamina.

Maier recently (1983, unpublished) discussed the probable mechanical meaning of the interorbital and posterior septal construction in different primate species as well as in different fetal stages, and there seems to be little doubt that the obvious stoutness of these structures can be well explained as adaptations to fetal habits like swallowing and chewing-like actions of the mastication apparatus as a whole. This would well fit into the observations on fetal movements made by Hooker (1952) and Humphrey (1971).

In the much younger *Pan* fetus, Starck (1960) described a small but distinct interorbital septum; the posterior cupula and the small ethmoturbinal recessus reach back to just before the optic foramina. A similar condition has been observed by Reinbach (1963) and by Grube

& Reinbach (1976) for two *Homo* stages (93 mm and 80 mm CRL) which are close to the *Pan* ones.

In the *Gorilla* fetus, which is close to the *Hylobates* stage, the distance between the cribrosal plate and the optic foramina is extremely short. Thus the tiny ethmoturbinal rescesses come into a position below the optic foramina and the posterior cupula extends even further back and is in continuous chondral linkage with the cartilaginous alisphenoid–basisphenoid connection. Therefore no interorbital septum is present! Basisphenoid and presphenoid are already fused, and no ethmoidal processes exist.

The dorsal aspects of the orbitotemporal area differ significantly among hominoids. In *Pan* (Starck, 1960) as well as in *Homo* (Macklin, 1921; Reinbach, 1963; Bersch & Reinbach, 1970; Grube & Reinbach, 1976), a distinct supraseptal plane combined with an orbitonasal commissure exists, although the latter is of a different shape in each species. Only the lateral rims of the commissures and the orbital wings are underlaid by the orbital processes of the frontal bones. In *Hylobates*, the narrow central stem between the cribrosal plate and the preoptic pillar shows a free dorsal margin which projects partly beyond the level of both the cribrosal plate and the short sphenoidal plane. No supraseptal plane exists; the frontal bones reach the dorsal aspects of the nasal capsule and parts of the central stem and underlie the pre- and orbitosphenoid. In the slightly younger *Gorilla*, again, a unique supraseptal structure (Fig. 2) marks the extremely short distance between the cribrosal lamina and the optic foramina: the anterior roots of the tiny orbital wings are covered by a second cartilaginous plane which extends laterally as far as the lateral border of the optic foramina and which is linked to the central stem only in its medial anterior and posterior parts, in its main part being attached to the preoptic roots by connective tissue only. No orbitonasal commissure is present, the orbital processes of the frontal bones being supported on a dorsolateral sulcus of the sidewall of the nasal capsules far back into the field of the optic foramina.

Conclusions

We are still too far away from having a consistent model of the orbitotemporal region in terms of genetic, developmental and functional conceptions, although Maier (1983; and unpublished) recently discussed the probable mechanical meaning of this structural complex in different primates. Among the hominoids there exist different

Fig. 2. Cross-section through the anterior orbitotemporal part of an advanced fetus of *Gorilla gorilla* (about 48 mm HL, section 211). Abbreviations: fr = frontal bone; max = maxillary bone; ns = nasal septum; pal = palatine bone; pnc = posterior nasal cupula; ppc = posterior paraseptal cartilage; prr = preoptic root of the orbital wing; psph = presphenoid ossification; rethm = ethmoturbinal recessus; usc = upper supraseptal cartilage (not identical with the supraseptal plane according to Reinbach (1952) and others); vo = vomer.

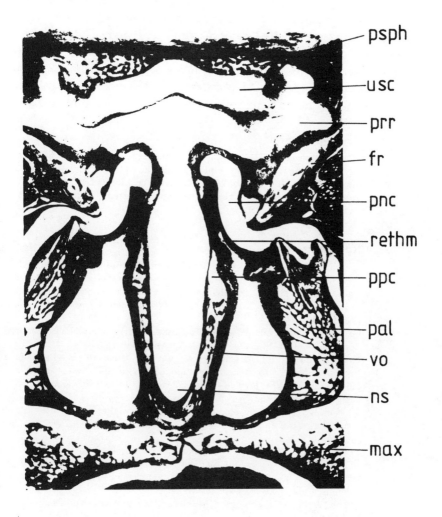

types of orbitotemporal structures reflecting not only different transitional stages of development but also representing species-specific differences of taxonomic significance. Considering the presence and size of the ethmoturbinal recessus and of the interorbital construction of the septum, the hominoid primates exhibit a more plesiomorphic character than do the cercopithecoids in terms of a possible hypothetical early anthropoid stage, with *Hylobates* being more advanced. As far as the supraseptal structures are concerned, *Hylobates* in some ways resembles the younger stages of *Ateles, Alouatta* (Maier, unpublished) and *Callithrix* (Simon, 1981) which show a completely free dorsal interorbital part of the central stem, whereas in *Saguinus* (Müller, 1981) a more modified stage is observed. In this respect *Hylobates* shows the most primitive structure among all known hominoid stages.

Acknowledgements

The *Hylobates* material was available through the courtesy of Dr E. Boterenbrood from the Hubrecht Laboratory in Utrecht, Netherlands; it was prepared by Mrs Bocktenk. Professor W. Maier gave access to the *Gorilla* material and read the manuscript. Mr H. Schneeberger prepared the drawing, Mrs U. Trautmann and Mr. J. Herforth produced the photos.

References

Bersch, W. & Reinbach, W. (1970) Das Primordialcranium eines menschlichen Embryo von 52 mm Sch.–St.–Länge. *Z. Anat. Entwickl.-Gesch.*, **132**, 240–59

Gaupp, E. (1908) Zur Entwicklungsgeschichte und vergleichenden Morphologie des Schädels von *Echidna aculeata* var. *typica. Semon. Zool. Forsch. Austr.*, **6**, 539–788

Grube, D. & Reinbach, W. (1976) Das Cranium eines menschlichen Embryo von 80 mm Sch.–St.–Länge. *Z. Anat. Embryol.*, **149**, 183–208

Heckmann, U. (1955) Das Chondrocranium und Osteocranium eines nahezu geburtsreifen Kaninchen. Dissertation, University of Frankfurt am Main

Hooker, D. (1952) *The Prenatal Origin of Behaviour.* Lawrence, Kansas: University of Kansas Press

Humphrey, T. (1971) Development of oral and facial motor mechanisms in human fetuses and their relation to craniofacial growth. *J. Dent. Res.*, **50**, 1428–41

Kuhn, H.–J. (1971) Die Entwicklung und Morphologie des Schädels von *Tachyglossus aculeatus. Abh. Senckbg. Naturf. Ges.*, **528**, 192 pp

Macklin, C. H. C. (1921) The skull of a human fetus of 43 millimeters greatest length. *Contrib. Embryol.*, **48**, 57–103

Maier, W. (1983) Morphology of the interorbital region of *Saimiri sciureus. Folia Primatol.*, **41**, 277–303

Müller, D. (1981) Beitrag zur Craniogenese von *Saguinus tamarin* Link, 1795 (Platyrrhini, Primates). *Cour. Forsch.-Inst. Senckenberg*, **46**, 1–100

Reinbach, W. (1952) Zur Entwicklung des Primordialcraniums von *Dasypus novemcinctus* Linne (Tatusia novemcincta Lesson). I. *Z. Morphol. Anthropol.*, **44**, 375–444

Reinbach, W. (1963) Das Cranium eines menschlichen Feten von 93 mm Sch.-St.-Länge. *Z. Anat. Entwickl.-Gesch.*, **124**, 1–50

Reinhard, W. (1958) Das Cranium eines 33 mm langen Embryos des Mantelpavians *Papio hamadryas* L. *Z. Anat. Entwickl.-Gesch.*, **120**, 427–55

Simon, K.-H. (1981) Beitrag zur Craniogenese von *Callithrix jacchus* L. (Platyrrhini, Primates). *Cour. Forsch.-Inst. Senckenberg*, **45**, 1–106

Spatz, W. B. (1964) Beitrag zur Kenntnis der Ontogenese des Cranium von *Tupaia glis* (Diard 1820) *Geg. Morphol. Jb.*, **106**, 321–416

Starck, D. (1960) Das Cranium eines Schimpansenfetus (*Pan troglodytes* (Blumenbach 1799)) von 71 mm SchStlg., nebst Bemerkungen über die Körperform von Schimpansenfeten. *Geg. Morphol. Jb*, **100**, 559–647

Zeller, U. (1983) Zur Ontogenese und Morphologie des Craniums von *Tupaia belangeri* (Tupaiidae, Scandentia, Mammalia) Dissertation, University of Göttingen

III.5

The systematic relations of tree shrews: evidence from skull morphogenesis

U. A. ZELLER

Introduction

The systematic position of the Tupaiidae within the Eutheria has been controversial for a long time and is still being discussed. Haeckel (1866), Lyon (1913) and Weber (1928) united them with the Macroscelididae into the suborder Menotyphla of the Insectivora. On the other hand, Gregory (1910), Carlsson (1922), LeGros Clark (1971) and others have emphasized their close relationships to the Primates, and Simpson (1945) classified the tree shrews as a superfamily Tupaioidea of the infraorder Lemuriformes. Recently, it has been pointed out by van Valen (1965), Martin (1968), Campbell (1974), Luckett (1980) and others that in the past the comparison between the Tupaiidae and other eutherians was often imprecise because the polarity of the characters used in the comparative analysis was not clearly determined. According to Hennig (1950), only shared apomorphous features are relevant for the ascertainment of phylogenetic relationships. Both tupaiids and primates stand close to the basal *'Bauplan'* of the Eutheria and therefore share many plesiomorphous eutherian characters (Starck, 1975; Zeller, 1983; Kuhn, in press). The main question remains: Can shared apomorphous features in Tupaiidae, Primates and/or other mammals be proved? Features mentioned in this respect are often symplesiomorphies or results of convergent evolution. Butler (1972), therefore, classified the Tupaiidae as Scandentia, a separate order of the Eutheria, and others, such as Starck (1978), Luckett (1980) and Novacek (1980) accepted this classification.

The Tupaiidae are divided into two subfamilies, the Tupaiinae and the Ptilocercinae (Lyon, 1913). In the discussion on the systematic relations of tree shrews the comparison between the subfamilies has been neglected. However, only apomorphous features present in both the Tupaiinae and the Ptilocercinae are characteristic of the family Tupaiidae and only these features are relevant for the evaluation of the systematic position of tree shrews.

The morphogenesis of the skull of *Tupaia belangeri* Wagner, 1841 was investigated in a series of 29 dated embryos (Zeller, 1983). A fetus of *Ptilocercus lowii* of 30 mm crown–rump length (CRL) was available for comparison.

Results

The following evidence is relevant for the evaluation of the systematic relationships of tree shrews. Special attention is given to the in-group comparison between *Tupaia* and *Ptilocercus*. Both share a number of synapomorphous characters compared to basal eutherians:

1. The tympanic bulla is composed of the entotympanic and the caudal tympanic process of the petrosal. In both groups the entotympanic is rostrally fused with the tubal cartilage.
2. The Musculus tensor tympani is absent.
3. The Jugal is pierced by the Fenestra malaris.
4. The Nervus saccularis maior, a branch of cranial nerve VIII, traverses the medial wall of the otic capsule through a separate Foramen acusticum medium.
5. Both have lost the third upper incisor and the first premolar of both jaws (Gregory, 1910; Butler, 1980).

These features are synapomorphous for the Tupaiinae and the Ptilocercinae. They are autapomorphous for the Tupaiidae and were already present in the common ancestor of the Tupaiinae and the Ptilocercinae. The Tupaiidae, therefore, is a monophyletic group.

The reduction of the Cartilago paraseptalis and the formation of the postorbital bar are two other shared derived traits of Tupaiinae and Ptilocercinae, but as they occur widely scattered among many other eutherian groups they are, therefore, of only little morphological interest here.

Besides these apomorphies, Tupaiinae and Ptilocercinae share many plesiomorphous eutherian characters (Fig. 1). The nasal region exhibits all characters typical for the chondrocranium of macrosmatic Eutheria. A broad Cupula nasi anterior supports the Rhinarium. The elements of the floor of the nasal capsule are well developed. The Lamina transversalis anterior is a broad cartilaginous plate and is connected with the Cartilago paraseptalis, which lodges a well-developed organ of Jacobson. The Lamina transversalis posterior forms the floor of the caudal two-thirds of the Recessus ethmoturbinalis and is medially not joined to the nasal septum. Like many other moderately macrosmatic eutherians, the interior of the nasal capsule of the Tupaiidae contains two fronto- and three ethmoturbinals.

The elements of the primary side wall of the cranial cavity are well developed and in an upright position. In 28-day-old embryos of *Tupaia* a Commissura orbitoparietalis is present and connects the Ala orbitalis with the Lamina parietalis of the otic region. In the 30 mm stage of *Ptilocercus* this commissure is lacking, but it may have been present in earlier stages.

The canalicular parts of the otic capsules are upright in a nearly vertical position forming parts of the side wall of the braincase in the otic region. The occipital arches are set upright and the Foramen occipitale magnum faces caudally. The lacrimal bone has a large facial extension. In *Ptilocercus* it is partially hidden by the facial extension of the maxilla. The ectotympanic bone is ringshaped. All these features are plesiomorphous eutherian characters and therefore provide no evidence for tupaiid relationships to other mammalian groups.

Aside from the synapomorphous and symplesiomorphous features of Tupaiinae and Ptilocercinae there are also remarkable differences between *Tupaia* and *Ptilocercus*. In *Tupaia* the orbits are laterally orientated; in *Ptilocercus* they are shifted frontally. Both *Tupaia* and

Fig. 1. *Tupaia belangeri* embryo, day 34 of ontogeny. Model of the cranium in the right lateral view. Membrane bones reconstructed on the left side only. Meckel's cartilage and Reichert's cartilage removed in most parts.

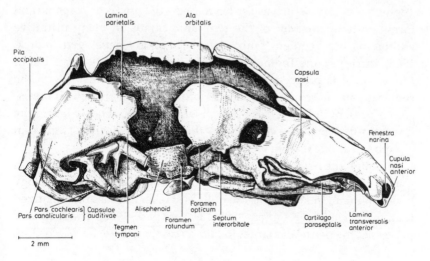

Ptilocercus possess two fronto- and three ethmoturbinals, which is the plesiomorphous condition for eutherian mammals. Additionally, in *Ptilocercus* a septoturbinal is present in the anterior region of the nasal capsule. Septoturbinals supported by cartilage are very rare among recent mammals and are otherwise found only in *Dasypus* (Reinbach, 1952), *Zaedyus* (Reinbach, 1955), *Tarsius* (Wünsch, 1975) and *Papio* (Reinhard, 1958). The presence of the septoturbinal in *Ptilocercus* is an autapomorphous feature.

In moderately macrosmatic eutherians, an interorbital part of the trabecular plate is present between the anterior root of the Ala orbitalis and the Cupula nasi posterior. In *Ptilocercus* this part of the trabecular plate is short and flat, and the Recessus ethmoturbinalis extends far backwards towards the anterior root of the Ala orbitalis. In *Tupaia*, however, the interorbital part of the trabecular plate is long and forms a high interorbital septum, which is present in all developmental stages and also in the adult skull of *Tupaia*. The interorbital septum of *Tupaia* is regarded here as an autapomorphous feature.

The Ala temporalis is a progressive part of the mammalian skull and forms the secondary side wall of the braincase in the orbitotemporal region (Gaupp, 1900; Kuhn, 1971). Primitively, in eutherians, the Ala temporalis lies behind the maxillary nerve. In *Ptilocercus*, the Ala temporalis lies behind and lateral to the maxillary nerve, which leaves the cranial cavity through the orbitotemporal fissure. In *Tupaia*, the Ala temporalis surrounds the maxillary nerve, which leaves the cranial cavity through a Foramen rotundum. This is an autapomorphous feature of *Tupaia*.

Another progressive element of the skull of the Eutheria is the Tegmen tympani, which arises from the cartilaginous ear capsule and forms parts of the roof of the tympanic cavity. In many primitive eutherians the Tegmen tympani is only poorly developed (Starck, 1967). In *Tupaia*, the Tegmen tympani remains relatively small, but in *Ptilocercus* it is progressively enlarged and medially fused with the cochlear part of the otic capsule. Therefore, a lateral prefacial commissure is present in *Ptilocercus* through which the facial nerve leaves the Cavum supracochleare and enters the tympanic cavity. This is an autapomorphous feature of *Ptilocercus*.

Although the basic composition of the tympanic bulla is the same in *Tupaia* and *Ptilocercus*, there are also differences in bulla morphology between them. In *Ptilocercus* the bulla is smaller and less pneumatized than in *Tupaia* (van Kampen, 1905; LeGros Clark, 1926). The tympanic process of the petrosal is larger in *Ptilocercus* than in *Tupaia*. According to Gregory (1910), Cartmill & MacPhee (1980) and MacPhee (1981), the alisphenoid contributes to the formation of the rostral part of the tympanic bulla floor in *Ptilocercus*. However, in the 30 mm fetus of *Ptilocercus*, the precartilaginous anlage of the entotympanic lies ventral to the alisphenoid. In *Ptilocercus*, as in *Tupaia*, the latter contributes only to the formation of the roof of the tympanic cavity. In the adult osteocranium the rostral part of the tympanic bulla, which is pierced by the opening for the auditory tube, is clearly separated by a suture from the alisphenoid in *Ptilocercus*. But there is still a difference in the shape of the rostral part of the tympanic bulla between *Tupaia* and *Ptilocercus*. The opening for the auditory tube is larger in *Ptilocercus* and the rostral part of the bulla surrounding this opening is only medially in direct continuation with the remaining part of the entotympanic.

Discussion and conclusions
The main differences between *Tupaia* and *Ptilocercus* concern the caudal Recessus ethmoturbinalis, the alisphenoid, the Tegmen tympani and the Bulla tympanica. They are autapomorphous for the Tupaiinae and for the Ptilocercinae, respectively. These features are known to have evolved independently also within several other mammalian orders. They are, therefore, not valid for assessment of relationships of the tree shrews to other eutherian taxa. Because of the numerous differences in skull morphology as well as the known differences in ecological adaptation, an early separation of the Tupaiinae and the Ptilocercinae is likely. This took place probably earlier than the Miocene, because there was already a great similarity between the Sivalik fossil tree shrews and the Tupaiinae (Chopra, Kaul & Vasihat, 1979).

The skull of the Tupaiidae is characterized by a number of autapomorphies, a large number of plesiomorphies and characters, which are autapomorphous for the Tupaiinae and for the Ptilocercinae, respectively.

According to Saban (1956), Spatz (1964) and Starck (1975), the Tupaiidae are close to the Primates in the following features:

1. The reduction of the nasal capsule
2. The presence of an interorbital septum
3. The progressive enlargement of the Tegmen tympani
4. The reduction of the primary side wall of the braincase
5. Rostrally shifted orbits.

Testing the validity of these features regarding the assessment of tupaiid–primate relationships on the basis of the results of the in-group comparison between *Tupaia* and *Ptilocercus*, the following comments should be made.

1. The nasal region of tupaiids resembles that of primitive eutherians. It appears to be reduced only in comparison to secondarily extremely macrosmatic mammals, e.g. Dasypodidae, Pholidota and Tubulidentata.
2. The interorbital septum occurs only in Tupaiinae. It is lacking in *Ptilocercus* and is therefore not characteristic for tupaiids.
3. A progressive enlargement of the Tegmen tympani comparable to that of Primates occurs only in *Ptilocercus*. In *Tupaia*, it remains relatively small.
4. The primary side wall of the braincase of the Tupaiidae is well developed. A Commissura orbitoparietalis is present in the ontogeny of *Tupaia*.
5. Rostrally shifted orbits are only present in *Ptilocercus*.

Only synapomorphous features present in the Tupaiinae and in the Ptilocercinae are relevant for the evaluation of tupaiid relationships with other mammalian groups. Apomorphous features present only in *Tupaia* or in *Ptilocercus*, like the interorbital septum of Tupaiinae, the enlarged Tegmen tympani and the rostrally shifted orbits of Ptilocercinae, are autapomorphous for the Tupaiinae and for the Ptilocercinae, respectively. These features, therefore, are not valid for the assessment of tupaiid relationships.

These results lead to the conclusion that skull morphogenesis does not provide any evidence for tupaiid–primate relationships and strongly support the classification of the Tupaiidae as a separate order, Scandentia.

Acknowledgements

I thank Professor Dr H.-J. Kuhn for providing the *Tupaia* material from his collection. The *Ptilocercus* fetus was loaned by the Hubrecht Laboratory (Utrecht, Netherlands) and I am greatly obliged to Dr E. C. Boterenbrood for providing the specimen. The adult osteocranium of *Ptilocercus* was studied in the collection of the United States National Museum (Washington, D.C.) during a 10-week graduate research appointment.

References

Butler, P. M. (1972) The problem of insectivore classification. In *Studies in Vertebrate Evolution*, ed. K. A. Joysey & T. S. Kemp, pp. 253–65. Edinburgh: Oliver & Boyd

Butler, P. M. (1980) The tupaiid dentition. In *Comparative Biology and Evolutionary Relationships of Tree Shrews*, ed. W. P. Luckett, pp. 171–204. New York & London: Plenum Press

Campbell, C. B. G. (1974) On the phyletic relationships of the tree shrews. *Mammal Rev.* **4**, 125–43

Carlsson, A. (1922) Uber die Tupaiidae und ihre Beziehungen zu den Insectivora und den Prosimiae. *Acta Zool.*, **3**, 227–70

Cartmill, M. & MacPhee, R. D. E. (1980) Tupaiid affinities: the evidence of the carotid arteries and cranial skeleton. In *Comparative Biology and Evolutionary Relationships of Tree Shrews*, ed. W. P. Luckett, pp. 95–132. New York & London: Plenum Press

Chopra, S. R. K., Kaul, S. & Vasihat, R. N. (1979) Miocene tree shrews from the Indian Śivaliks. *Nature*, **281**, 213–14

Chopra, S R. K. & Vasihat, R. N. (1979) Śivalik fossil tree shrews from Haritalyangar, India. *Nature*, **281**, 214–15

Gaupp, E. (1900) Das Chondrocranium von *Lacerta agilis*. Ein Beitrag zum Verständnis des Amniotenschädels. *Anat. Hefte, 1. Abt.*, **15**, 433–595

Gregory, W. K. (1910) The orders of mammals. *Bull. Am. Mus. Nat. Hist.*, **27**, 1–524

Haeckel, E. (1866) *Generelle Morphologie der Organismen*. Berlin: G. Reimer

Hennig, W. (1950) *Grundzüge einer Theorie der Phylogenetischen Systematik*. Berlin: Deutscher Zentralverlag

Kampen, P. N. van (1905) Die Tympanalgegend des Säugetierschädels. *Morphol. Jb.*, **34**, 321–722

Kuhn, H.-J. (1971) Die Entwicklung and Morphologie des Schädels von *Tachyglossus aculeatus*. *Abh. Senckenb. Naturforsch. Ges.*, **528**, 1–192

Kuhn, H.-J. (in press) Vergleichende Untersuchungen zur Ontogenese der Primaten. *Verh. Zool. Ges.*

LeGros Clark, W. E. (1926) On the anatomy of the pen-tailed tree-shrew (*Ptilocercus lowii*). *Proc. Zool. Soc. Lond.*, 1179–309

LeGros Clark, W. E. (1971) *The Antecedents of Man. An Introduction to the Evolution of the Primates*, 3rd ed. Chicago: Quadrangle Books

Luckett, W. P. (1980) The suggested evolutionary relationships and classification of tree shrews. In *Comparative Biology and Evolutionary Relationships of Tree Shrews*, ed. W. P. Luckett, pp. 3–31. New York & London: Plenum Press

Lyon, M. W. (1913) Tree shrews: an account of the mammalian family Tupaiidae. *Proc. U.S. Natl Mus.*, **45**, 1–188

MacPhee, R. D. E. (1981) Auditory regions of primates and eutherian insectivores. Morphology, ontogeny, and character analysis. *Contrib. Primatol.*, **18**, 1–282

Martin, R. D. (1968) Reproduction and ontogeny in tree-shrews (*Tupaia belangeri*), with reference to their general behaviour and taxonomic relationships. *Z. Tierpsychol.*, **25**, 409–532

Novacek, M. J. (1980) Cranioskeletal features in tupaiids and selected eutheria as phylogenetic evidence. In *Comparative Biology and Evolutionary Relationships of Tree Shrews*, ed. W. P. Luckett, pp. 35–93. New York & London: Plenum Press

Reinbach, W. (1952) Zur Entwicklung des Primordialcraniums von *Dasypus novemcinctus* Linné (*Tatusia novemcincta* Lesson). I. *Z. Morphol. Anthropol.*, **44**, 375–444; II. *Z. Morphol. Anthropol.*, **45**, 1–72

Reinbach, W. (1955) Das Cranium eines Embryos des Gürteltieres *Zaedyus minutus* (65 mm Sch.-St.). *Morphol. Jb.*, **95**, 79–141

Reinhard, W. (1958) Das Cranium eines 33 mm langen Embryos des Mantel-pavians, *Papio hamadryas* L. *Z. Anat. Entwickl.-Gesch.*, **120**, 427–55

Saban, R. (1956) Les affinités du genre *Tupaia* Raffles 1821, d'après les caractères morphologiques de la tête osseuse. *Ann. Paléont.*, **42**, 169–224; **43**, 1–44

Simpson, G. G. (1945) The principles of classification and a classification of mammals. *Bull. Am. Mus. Nat. Hist.*, **85**, 1–350

Spatz, W. B. (1964) Beitrag zur Kenntnis der Ontogenese des Craniums von *Tupaia glis* (Diard 1820). *Morphol. Jb.*, **106**, 321–416

Starck, D. (1967) Le crâne des Mammifères. In *Traité de Zoologie*, ed. P. Grassé, vol. 16, Part 1, pp. 405–549. Paris: Masson

Starck, D. (1975) The development of the chondrocranium in Primates. In *Phylogeny of the Primates. A multidisciplinary Approach*, ed. W. P. Luckett & F. S. Szalay, 127–55. New York & London: Plenum Press

Starck, D. (1978) *Vergleichende Anatomie der Wirbeltiere auf Evolutionsbiologischer Grundlage*, vol. 1. Berlin, Heidelberg & New York: Springer Verlag

Valen, L. van (1965) Treeshrews, primates, and fossils. *Evolution*, **19**, 137–51

Weber, M. (1928) *Die Säugetiere*, vol. 2, 2nd edn. Jena: Gustav Fischer

Wünsch, D. (1975) *Zur Kenntnis der Entwicklung des Craniums des Koboldmaki, Tarsius bancanus, Horsfield, 1821.* (*Beiträge zur Kenntnis des Primaten – Craniums IV.*) Frankfurt am Main: Selbstverlag des Zentrums der Morphologie

Zeller, U. (1983) Zur Ontogenese und Morphologie des Craniums von *Tupaia belangeri* (Tupaiidae, Scandentia, Mammalia). Dissertation, University of Göttingen

III.6

Size and shape of the orbital outline: a multivariate comparison and analysis of intraspecific variation in four hominoid species

B. JACOBSHAGEN

Introduction

The orbital opening has a complex form with a high degree of individual, as well as interspecific, variation (Jacobshagen, 1982). However, it is difficult to determine this variation by traditional means, descriptively or in terms of typological assignment. Therefore, an adequate morphometric characterization must be performed. Conventional measures of orbital traits are height and breadth numbers which account for only a small part of the total variation. A considerable component of morphological information is lost in this way.

An adequate biomathematical approach has to be found to come closer to an analysis of the biological causes of orbital size and shape variation. One possible way of quantifying the curvature of the inner orbital margin is to define the positions of a sufficient number of landmarks in terms of coordinates. These landmarks need not be defined by conventions as are most of the familiar anatomical landmarks. The single measurement point does not contribute much information to the whole, nor does it give any special information. The fundamental step is the accumulation of morphological information when a number of landmarks are used.

Two methodological problems present themselves: (1) coordinates must be collected, and (2) a transformation of the inherent information must be performed. There is no exclusive method for coordinate measurements. Depending upon the purpose, for specialized or nonspecialized investigations, different methods may be appropriate. For looking only at the oribital contour photography is best, using an arrangement that allows a rectangular view to the plane of the orbital opening. For all-round craniometric data collection, any kind of stereometric device is to be preferred.

Methods

For this study, stereophotogrammetry after Kellner was applied for the measurement of some 300 landmarks per skull (see Jacobshagen, 1980, 1981a, 1981b). A series of 40 3-D coordinates was used for the description of the orbital size and shape. The total data collection, as well as the orbital data, were focused on five samples of adult hominoid primates (excluding Hylobatidae): *Pan* (males, $n = 25$, *Gorilla* (males and females, $n = 30/29$), *Pongo* (males, $n = 30$) and *Homo* (males and females, total $n = 25$).

As the original data were three-dimensional and the orbital data analysis was designed within the limits of two dimensions, some transformation of the orbital coordinates was necessary. The reduction from three to two dimensions equals a projection. To avoid as much distortion as possible, this projection had to be carried out rectangular to the plane of the orbital margin, defined by the middle portions of the orbital upper and lower margin. Additionally, the new coordinate system need no longer be related to the skull as a whole, but only to the orbital outline itself.

The center of a rectangle constructed around the orbit proved appropriate. Furthermore, instead of Cartesian coordinates, which were used previously, polar coordinates were subsequently used.

On this level there are still two fundamental disadvantages. First, the coordinates have a random relation to the bony structure, because most of them are undefinable; they were merely dotted along the orbital curvature. Secondly, the information given by single points, especially neighbouring ones, is highly correlated; there is a considerable redundancy. A solution to both problems is another data transformation. Here, the Fourier transformation was applied (Lestrel, 1974, 1975). The mathematical expression is

$$f(\theta) = a_\bigcirc + \sum_{i=1}^{n} a_i \cos i\theta + \sum_{i=1}^{n} b_i \sin i\theta$$

where $a_\bigcirc$ = constant term, equals the mean of the vectors
   i = order
   θ = angle (within the interval $-\pi, \pi$)

In this way the information of the orbital contour is expressed in a series of components representing size and shape. The constant term

$a_\bigcirc$ is a measure of size – it is equal to the radius of a circle of the same area (the mean of the individual vectors in the polar coordinate system). The shape is given by the linear combination of sine and cosine subfunctions related to finer details with increasing order. Mathematically, these components are orthogonal to each other. If irregular coordinates are given, a suitable interpolation is necessary to feed equidistant angular samples into the Fourier transformation algorithm. For storage, the Fourier series was truncated after fourteenth-order coefficients, which was sufficient for fine accuracy (0.6 mm maximum deviation from the raw data). Thus, 29 parameters were necessary for each individual orbital contour.

Results

The orbital data allow a variety of procedures to be used to visualize both intraspecific and interspecific variation. A special merit of this kind of data is their graphical quality because of the ease of revisualization: individual contours can be plotted either separately or with superimposition (Jacobshagen, 1982). In the latter case it is useful that the size scale can be adjusted to a common value to enable a display of shape variation (Fig. 1a). The typical shape within each group is found by averaging the orbital contour parameters before plotting (Fig. 1b). In terms of Fourier coefficients (a_i resp. b_i; see eqn above), the average outlines show marked differences (Fig. 1c). In addition to this display of 'graphical statistics' the data can be used for numerical evaluation.

To determine shape similarities, simple Penrose distances and multiple discriminant analysis were applied. The latter gave good separation with very little overlap, using 22 parameters (Fig. 2). The first two discriminant functions represent more than 86% of the total variation. The essential components of the first function are cosine-coefficients of the second, third and fourth order, which are of great influence on the gross orbital form. The second function is primarily a result of size variation; shape parameters add only very little information to this function. The third function contributes mainly to the separation of the human group; the fourth function has its main effect on sex discrimination in the gorilla. If the size variable $a_\bigcirc$ is excluded from the analysis, the separation within the African apes is less marked. The stereodendrogram of Fig. 2 also shows, by its hierarchical part, that the greatest similarity encountered in this material was found between the male and female gorillas. The difference between

Fig. 1. Orbital contours in five hominoid samples (left orbits). (a) Superimpositions of size-normalized orbital outlines. (b) Mean orbital outlines. (c) Diagrams showing first to tenth order of Fourier coefficients (mm), cosine-coefficients in black, sine-coefficients in white (first order closest to the bottom line).

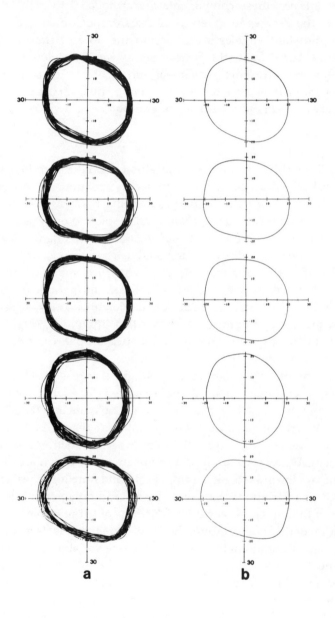

a   b

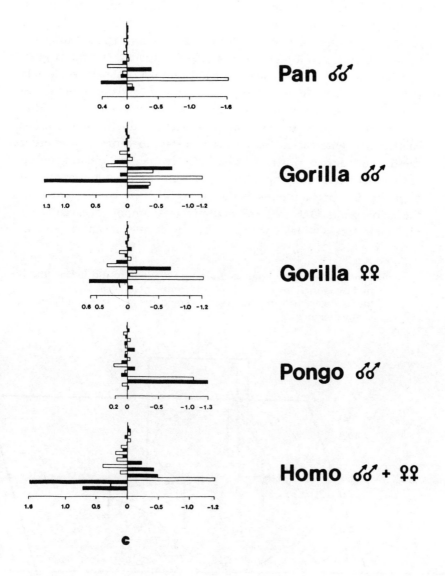

Pan ♂♂

Gorilla ♂♂

Gorilla ♀♀

Pongo ♂♂

Homo ♂♂ + ♀♀

c

orangutan and chimpanzee as well as between chimpanzee and female gorillas is only slightly greater, whereas a considerable average distance was found in the comparison of man with the Great Apes.

For the analysis of intraspecific variation, a factor analysis was applied for each sample. Although Fourier-coefficients are orthogonal to each other as mathematical descriptors, this is not necessarily true in the biological sense, because structures of different period, that is, rough and fine details of the curvature, may correlate more or less due to developmental mechanisms. Thus, 10–12 factors account for some 85% of the total variation in each sample. Compared with the original Fourier series (a_0 and 28 coefficients), this means a considerable data reduction. Despite an overall similarity in the factor patterns of the five samples, each group showed characteristic differences (Table 1). In the chimpanzee sample, the maximum variation is due to higher-order coefficients, whereas in the gorilla there are loadings of low-order coefficients contributing to the first factor. In man, a correlating group of five coefficients ranging from low to high order is dominant in the variation. Of special interest is the place of the size component a_0 in the factor results. Only in the orangutan is this component essential for the first factor; in females and in the human sample, it can be found in

Fig. 2. Stereodendrogram combining a diagram resulting from the first two functions of a multiple discriminant analysis with a hierarchical clustering (pairwise average linkage) based on Penrose shape distances.

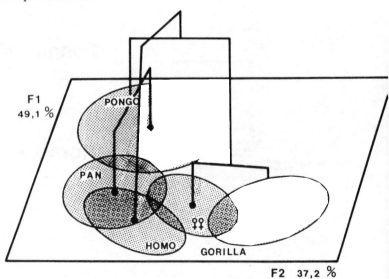

the third factor. In the chimpanzee, the size is of even lower importance (fourth factor) with regard to the correlation structure. Typical values of relatively high correlations are approximately $r = 0.4$ between size ($a_\bigcirc$) and shape data. Therefore, no strong dependence between size and isolated shape variables need be stated.

Conclusions

The complete quantification of the orbital form proved adequate for the numerical evaluation and graphical display. Hitherto, conventional morphometrics have not allowed this kind of characterization, and descriptive methodology had to be added. The results were two different sets of descriptors, both insufficient and incompatible to each other.

The interspecific similarity pattern (given by the F1–F2 plane in Fig. 2) shows three major 'types' of orbital contours represented by the triangle *Pongo–Homo–Gorilla* (males). Although a visual comparison of the orbital contours in male and female gorillas shows only small differences, these are remarkably clear after Fourier transformation.

Many factors of different origin, e.g. *'Bauplan'* characters and functional stress, influence the orbital outline (compare Vogel, 1966). Among these, the eye is not of any significance (Schultz, 1940).

Concerning intraspecific variation, female gorillas display the greatest amount of shape homogeneity, whereas in *Pongo* we find more intragroup variation than in the other samples. The reason might be due to the intraspecific distribution of geographical origins. The orangutan sample contains specimens of both subspecies (for morphometric differences see Jacobshagen, 1979). Allometric trends seem to be of small influence within these samples of adult specimens.

Table 1. *Factor analyses of orbital contour data. The first four factors are listed, accounting for about half of the total variation. Variables (=coefficient numbers) are listed if factor loadings are ≥ 0.50*

Factor	Pan	Gorilla (δ)	Gorilla ($\female$)	Pongo	Homo
1	17, 20, 22 23, 26, 27	1, 5, 9	1, 5	$a_\bigcirc$, 3	2, 6, 12, 15, 20
2	9, 14	$a_\bigcirc$, 7, 17	9, 17, 22	1, 4, 5	1, 3, 5, 22
3	1, 5	4, 20, 22, 26, 28	$a_\bigcirc$	6, 10	$a_\bigcirc$, 8
4	$a_\bigcirc$, 4	8, 14, 16, 18	10, 12, 18	11, 15, 26	9, 10, 21

References

Jacobshagen, B. (1979) Morphometric studies in the taxonomy of the orangutan (*Pongo pygmaeus* L.1760). *Folia Primatol.*, **32**, 29–34

Jacobshagen, B. (1980) Grenzen konventioneller Techniken und Möglichkeiten alternativer Ansätze in der Anthropometrie. Mit einem Beispiel für den Einsatz der Biophotogrammetrie in der Schädelmesstechnik. *Z. Morphol. Anthropol.*, **71**(3), 306–21

Jacobshagen, B. (1981*a*) Die Variabilität des Schädels pongider und hominider Primaten. Vergleichende funktionell-morphologische Untersuchungen unter besonderer Berücksichtigung der vom Kauapparat belasteten Strukturen. Dissertation, University of Hamburg

Jacobshagen, B. (1981*b*) The limits of conventional techniques in anthropometry and the potential of alternative approaches. *J. Hum. Evol.*, **10**, 633–7

Jacobshagen, B. (1982) Variations in size and shape of the orbital contour. A comparison between man and the great apes using Fourier analysis. *Anthropos (Brno)*, **21**, 113–30

Lestrel, P. E. (1974) Some problems in the assessment of morphological size and shape differences. *Yearb. Phys. Anthropol.*, **18**, 140–62

Lestrel, P. E. (1975) Fourier analysis of size and shape of the human cranium: a longitudinal study from four to eighteen years of age. Ph.D. dissertation, UCLA.

Schultz, A. H. (1940) The size of the orbit and of the eye in primates. *Am. J. Phys. Anthropol.*, **26**, 389–408

Vogel, C. (1966) Morphologische Studiem am Gesichtsschädel Catarrhiner Primaten. *Bibl. Primatol.*, Fasc. 4. Basel: S. Karger

Part IV

Evolutionary genetics

Editors' introduction

While paleontologists deal with the time dimension of evolution and comparative morphologists study the similarities of form and function between living and past species, the evolutionary geneticist examines the processes of evolution. With the discovery of DNA as the basis for heredity and with the recent development of techniques for examining and even creating these biochemical processes, our understanding of how evolution proceeds has been greatly enhanced. Most evolutionary biologists accept that there is a genetic basis to changes in the physiology, morphology and behaviour of animals, and that organic evolution occurs when the underlying genetic changes are transmitted to subsequent generations.

For paleontologists working with fossilised fragments of what may be only a single individual, neither the protein sequences nor the population processes of divergence and speciation can be identified. However, studies of modern primate populations and their genetic diversity provide clues about the mode and rates of evolution – essential elements for understanding past processes of diversification and alteration.

The papers in this section approach questions about how the genetic basis of evolution can be measured and how it has acted on modern primates to create diversity. They deal primarily with mechanisms of genetic change in different species of primates.

Seth and Seth (Chapter IV.1) discuss the evolution of primates by reviewing recent work on the different blood proteins, enzyme systems, and immune responses of many different species. They have applied these data to deriving dates of differentiation. While the attempt to make use of 'molecular clocks' is controversial and is based on assumptions that rates of genetic change are similar for the different systems, they use many different microgenetic techniques in combination with paleontological evidence to establish evolutionary relationships between species. While such a review is still speculative and contains assumptions that may not be valid in the light of further research, it provides an intriguing body of evidence for episodes of differentiation.

Turner *et al.* (Chapter IV.2) provide data on the degree of morphological and genetic similarity between different populations of a single primate species and compare this with the degree of similarity between different, closely related, species. They conclude that morphological differences may reflect local adaptations at both the population and species levels, while the electrophoretic data on blood proteins were not as reliable indicators of population differentiation. The authors suggest that the available techniques for genetic study do not yet reflect the processes of adaptation and diversification found in wild populations.

VandeBerg and Cheng (Chapter IV.3) describe a long-term effort to characterise biochemical genetic markers in five sub-species of baboons (*Papio*). They discuss the different markers and their specificity among the different sub-species, and relate their work primarily to its biomedical applications. While the applications of their research are directed towards managing captive populations and understanding the genetic basis of diseases, the diversity of different markers described contributes to our ability to refine and focus questions on the processes of evolution in different populations.

In terms of our understanding of the rates and types of evolution, genetic studies have a great deal to contribute. We have yet to approach such questions as how the degree of genetic similarity between species or populations is related to rates of genetic change (rates of mutation, drift, or 'molecular drive'), to important events in the past affecting geographic distribution (sea level changes) or population sizes (major epidemics, episodes of extreme predation, or explosions), and to behaviour such as mating patterns (e.g. preferential matings with kin). Studies of genetics may not answer the question of *why* evolution has taken place, but they can tell us more about *when* it is likely and *how* it occurs.

IV.1

A review of evolutionary and genetic differentiation in primates

S. SETH AND P. K. SETH

Introduction

The physical and biotic uniqueness of primate environments provides an evolutionary arena where the different species of primates show convergent adaptation on a variety of levels of organisation: genetic, biochemical, physiological, anatomical, behavioural, population biology, life history, and speciational. The remarkable similarity in the biology and behaviour of man and non-human primates has long intrigued members of our own species and may be better understood by evolutionary systematics involving proteins and enzymes. It is only during the last few years that evolutionary processes and their long-term results have been considered at the basic level of genes.

To gain insight into the genetic structure and to monitor the dynamics of the gene pool of primate species, both in time and space, population genetics of the non-human primates provides a useful diagnostic tool for delineating the underlying evolutionary systematics. Molecular biology provides an entirely different kind of evidence that overcomes the traditional difficulties and settles evolutionary problems in ways that are independent of any particular scientist or laboratory. The aim of this paper is to compare and contrast evolutionary patterns, adaptive strategies and genetic differentiation in primates in an attempt to elucidate the microevolutionary processes involved.

The evidence from seroprimatology

Distribution of the various blood groups in the non-human primates reveals striking differences and similarities among species which cannot be explained by chance or genetic drift. The human type ABO blood groups, or their homologues, are found not only in man and anthropoid apes, but also in the Cercopithecoidea, Ceboidea, numerous mammalian species, birds, bacteria and plants, together with the occurrence of natural antibodies and other substances (lectins, snail extracts) with anti-A, anti-B or anti-H specificity. Among the great apes, blood groups O and A occur together only in chimpanzees (Table 1). In gibbons and orangutans, as in man and chimpanzees, isoagglutination is a normal and regular phenomenon but in the gibbon and orangutan, only groups A, B and AB have been found. It is noteworthy that group B red cells of gibbons are strongly and regularly agglutinated by anti-H lectin, and to the same titer as human group O red cells. Of all the gorillas, chimpanzees, gibbons and orangutans tested, only one orangutan was not a secretor. The red cells of gorillas do not give a clear-cut reaction in agglutination tests. In this respect, these reactions resemble those of monkeys rather than those of other apes and man (Wiener, Moor-Jankowski & Gordon, 1963, 1966; Moor-Jankowski & Wiener, 1972). A similar evolutionary pathway of red cell antigens of nonhuman primates, i.e. sharing of common antigens, is observed between the human Rh blood group system and the chimpanzee RCEF blood group system (Socha & Moor-Jankowski, 1980) and between the human MNSs blood groups and the VABD system in chimpanzees (Socha & Moor-Jankowski, 1979). Such an attempt at genetic differentiation between the mountain and lowland gorillas, using both human-type and simian-type blood systems, failed to differentiate between the two (Socha et al., 1973). On the contrary, this

Table 1. Distribution of ABO blood groups

	Number of observations	Blood groups			
		A	B	AB	O
Chimpanzee	1132	967	–	–	165
Gorilla	48	2	46	–	–
Orangutan	131	75	26	30	–
Gibbon	57	11	24	22	–
Siamang	2	–	2	–	–
Rhesus	189	40	77	23	49
Baboon	1217	578	425	3	211
Vervet	116	25	15	–	76
Cynomolgus	540	205	190	137	8
Cercopithecus	8	1	–	–	7
Spider monkey	15	10	4	–	1

attempt at comparison for the homologues, using reagents prepared in chimpanzees by iso- or cross-immunization, demonstrated that the gorillas were polymorphic for the chimpanzee VAB and CEF systems (Wiener *et al.*, 1976). The very fact that isoantisera raised in chimpanzees could be used for blood typing gorilla red cells as well, without interference from nonspecific heteroagglutinins, confirms the serological closeness between the two species.

The isoimmune chimpanzee serum (anti-L) not only detects polymorphism in chimpanzee red cells, but also reacts selectively with human red cells of Rh_o type (Moor-Jankowski & Socha, 1978). It is, however, significant to observe that this chimpanzee isoimmune serum failed to detect a distinct polymorphism in the other anthropoid apes. In contrast, the human anti-Rh_o antiserum reveals polymorphism not only in man but also in the red cells of the chimpanzee and the gorilla but did not detect any polymorphism in the red cells of other anthropoid apes. Thus, it could be inferred that the human Rh-Hr blood group system is a typical kind of simian-blood group that reflects taxonomic proximities amongst the higher primates, including man. Likewise, studies on serum globulins revealed analogous cross-specificities between related species of primates; for instance, reagents prepared in apes and monkeys have helped to detect Gm types of human blood (Wiener *et al.*, 1972; Moor-Jankowski *et al.*, 1977). This clearly emphasizes the importance of seroprimatology as a diagnostic tool within evolutionary genetic systematics; its significance lies in the recognition of the presence in monkeys of blood groups homologous, i.e. the human-type, and analogous, i.e. simian-type, to the human blood groups.

It is of interest to note that statistically significant differences exist between *Hylobates lar pileatus* and *H. lar lar* in the distribution of the human-type ABO and MN blood group systems. Of all the primate species examined, only man and gibbon share the sex-linked blood group antigen X_g^a (Gavin *et al.*, 1964; Moor-Jankowski & Wiener, 1972); there are, however, similar differences between the two subspecies of gibbon, as for human ABO and MN systems. While the simian-type blood systems show marked differences between *Pan paniscus* and *Pan troglodytes*, supported by much other biochemical evidence, the anti-globulin inhibition test supports the contention of Schmitt, Spielmann & Weber (1961) of a close relationship between the two species (Wiener *et al.*, 1970). This further confirms that both these species of genus *Pan* are more closely related to man than are the other apes (Moor-Jankowski *et al.*, 1972).

The rhesus graded D^{rh} serum is comparable to the A_1A_2 human subgroups. Similar systems have not been observed in the other primate species examined for their simian-type blood systems, namely chimpanzees, gibbons and baboons. Such a serological characteristic parallels that of the MNSs system in man and the VAB system in chimpanzees (Socha et al., 1976).

The baboon anti-B^P serum gives type-specific reactions with red cells of geladas, rhesus monkeys, pig-tailed macaques and cynomolgus monkeys. Thus it clearly indicates that this immunogenic factor, the B^P antigen, is not only found in the baboons but is also commonly found in the red cells of many simians other than baboons. Of importance is the fact that B^P specificity is identical with a subspecificity of an analogous blood group system of macaques, namely the D^{rh} blood group system. Such a serological relationship among primates suggests that the processes of speciation at the molecular level probably were directed differently for different structures defined by these methods. For instance, the human-type blood groups and the simian-type blood groups not only have different biological interpretations but give rise to varying conclusions based on comparative blood typing.

An understanding of the evolutionary processes, therefore, necessitates comparison of protein structures, especially useful for the study of polymorphism, differential mobility of red cell enzymes and serum proteins. Some proteins are typically polymorphic in man, e.g. haptoglobins, but monomorphic in anthropoid apes and monkeys (S. Seth et al., 1983). Compared with human proteins, some components in these nonhuman primates are slow moving, some have almost uniform and similar electrophoretic mobilities and still others show differential mobilities and also differential staining (Seth, Seth & Saxena, 1975b).

There is a considerable degree of heterogeneity in the blood loci of langurs (Hrdy, Barnicot & Alper, 1975) contrary to the reports for some other species of leaf monkeys. For example, Presbytis entellus displays polymorphisms for C'3, Gc, glycine-rich β-glycoprotein, $α_1$-antitrypsin, PGM, 6-PGD, AK, superoxide dismutase, malate dehydrogenase and PHI; the species, however, is monomorphic for transferrin, hemoglobin, PGM1, G-6-PD, albumin, thyroxine-binding prealbumin and ceruloplasmin. In addition, acid phosphatase and lactate dehydrogenase show variable band strengths in P. entellus that might suggest polymorphism (S. Seth et al., 1983). In contrast, Presbytis cristatus is monomorphic for these systems (Hrdy et al., 1975).

Unlike the restricted polymorphic blood systems in primates, transferrin (Tf) polymorphism, involving two or more codominant autosomal alleles, is common to most primates. The marked similarities in the Tf gene frequencies among rhesus monkey populations in northern India, Nepal, Bangladesh and China suggest considerable gene flow across these countries in this northern range (Devor, 1978). Likewise, Prychodko and his group (1969) suggest admixture amongst the macaque species in Thailand based on the geographical comparisons of their gene frequencies. Tf, albumin, prealbumin, CA II and the PHI loci provide useful genetic markers in the rhesus monkeys, for phenotypes of all these five loci are detectable as electrophoretic variants representing mutually codominant alleles.

All the nonhuman primates thus far studied, have a serum protein which reacts specifically with rabbit anti-human Gc anti serum. No phenotypic variation was noted except in the case of the orangutan. Such evidence suggests that the Gc system represents serum proteins of considerable antiquity and relative immunological stability.

Based on the genetic differentiation between primate species in terms of immunological cross-reaction of serum albumins, Sarich & Wilson (1967a,b) suggested that man, chimpanzee and gorilla diverged only about 5 million years ago, provided albumin evolves at a constant rate.

Hemoglobins of the African apes are much more closely related to human hemoglobin, based on the cross-reaction data, than to that of the Asiatic apes (Garver & Talmage, 1975). Similar results have been obtained for transferrins, thyroglobulins, serum albumins, lens proteins and immunoglobulins. These data reflect a more recent divergence of the African apes from the evolutionary lineage leading to man than the estimates generally arrived at from the fragmentary palaeontological records (Sarich & Wilson, 1967a).

The amino acid sequences of the chimpanzee hemoglobin have an identical primary structure to that of man, while gorilla hemoglobin has two amino acid replacements (α, $23^{Glu-Asp}$, β, $104^{Arg-Lys}$). Only three substitutions were identified in the β-chain of the hemoglobin A in *Hylobates* ($80^{Asu-Asp}$, $87^{Thr-Sys}$, $125^{Pro-Glu}$) compared to the human β-chain (Boyer *et al.*, 1971). The α-chain of the hemoglobin of the African green monkey has five substitutions, whereas the rhesus monkey hemoglobin α-chain has four. Significantly, all the four replacements in the rhesus α-chain are exactly duplicated in the African green monkey polypeptide. This suggests that the additional substitution in the α-chain of the hemoglobin in the African green monkey, namely histidine at position 78, probably occurs in an antigenically unreactive area of the human hemoglobin. It is of interest to note that the substitutions at positions 87 and 125 are also found in the human δ-chain and also in the capuchin and squirrel monkey β-chains, all of which are immunologically distinguishable from human hemoglobin A. α- and β-hemoglobin chains of most primate species are similar to those in man, differing only in a few amino acid sites (Matsuda *et al.*, 1968; Wade *et al.*, 1970). Interspecies differentiation of the hemoglobin molecule among primates also indicates variations in their functional properties, thereby suggesting the importance of natural selection as a cause of such variations (Sullivan, 1972). Though electrophoretic studies of hemoglobin yielded no evidence for intraspecies polymorphic variation in hemoglobin, isoelectric focussing has recently yielded conflicting results (Basch, 1972; Wu *et al.*, 1977; Smith & Ferrell, 1980). Rhesus monkey hemoglobin exhibits identical electrophoretic mobility with that of human hemoglobin A, a component also shared by almost every member of the genus *Macaca*.

Rhesus monkey hemoglobin differs from human hemoglobin at 12 positions, whereas African green monkey hemoglobin has 11 substitutions (Matsuda *et al.*, 1968, 1973). The hemoglobin in baboons is more antigenically deficient than that of the other Old World monkeys and produces only 25% inhibition. Studies on peptide mapping suggest that the baboon hemoglobin appears to have more variability than other vertebrate hemoglobins (Buettner-Janusch & Hill, 1965*b*). Immunochemical studies support this observation and reveal that the hemoglobin in baboons has been evolving at a more rapid rate than the hemoglobin in other Old World monkeys. Among the anthropoid apes, only the orangutan exhibits a considerable degree of hemoglobin polymorphism (de Boer & Meera Khan, 1982).

Of the 133 homologous residues of the erythrocyte enzyme carbonic anhydrase I (CA I), chimpanzee and man differ at only one site, whereas the orangutan differs from the chimpanzee at three sites and from man at four sites. These hominoids differ from the cercopithecoids at 4–6 sites. This clearly indicates the proximity of man and chimpanzee. In primates, and possibly in many other mammals, the concentration of CA I in erythrocytes is relatively high compared to that of CA II (the two carbonic anhydrases being products of alleles at two separate loci which are linked (De Simone, Magid & Tashion, 1973)). Comparison of a total of 23 residues located in the active sites of the homologous forms of both CA isozymes in several primates and mammalian species reveals that the three histidyl residues, forming ligands to the zinc, are the same for all the enzymes (Tashian *et al.*, 1976). About six species of macaques, baboons, patas monkeys, vervets and man exhibit CA II polymorphism. The loci specifying the CA I and CA II isozymes are closely linked in *Macaca nemestrina*, guineapigs and mice (Carter, 1972; Eicher *et al.*, 1976; Tashian & Carter, 1976). Variants of CA I are found in rhesus monkey populations from West Pakistan, Thailand and China but, interestingly, 164 rhesus monkeys from India were monomorphic for this isozyme (Tashian *et al.*, 1971, Nozawa *et al.*, 1975).

Serum aminopeptidases are monomorphic in the Kenyan vervets, *Cercopithecus aethiops* (McDermid, Vos & Downing, 1973; Dracopoli & Brett, 1982). Intraspecies polymorphism of cytoplasmic isocitrate dehydrogenase appears to be fairly common among primates (Schmitt & Ritter, 1973). Polymorphism of either form of lactate dehydrogenase, i.e. cytoplasmic and mitochondrial, in primate species is quite rare and occurs only at the subfamily level. Likewise, electrophoretic variants of cytoplasmic malate dehydrogenase are extremely rare: only one gorilla has so far been reported to possess the variant. Biochemical and genetic evidence indicates that only one gene is responsible for the production of G6PD in man, chimpanzee, gorilla, orangutan, rhesus monkey and the African green monkey (Wijnen *et al.*, 1982); the gene is X-linked.

Since the primary structure of a protein has a colinear correspondence of DNA, the amount of genetic change that has accumulated in a limited portion of a chromosome since divergence and speciation can be directly assessed. *Macaca* has the least DNA content (5.39 pg) of members of the subfamily Cercopithecinae; the DNA content in *Macaca* approaches that in man (6.0 pg) (Manfredi-Romani, 1971). These differences in DNA content may be due to the varying heterochromatic content in these species (Seth & Saxena, 1977).

Satellite DNA, with some exceptions, appears to be evolving rapidly and is among the most obvious, quantitative and qualitative, alterations in genomal DNA correlating with the evolution of species. Satellite A DNA of the chimpanzee shares many physical properties with human satellite III DNA. This and cross-hybridization studies indicate underlying base sequence homology (Seth *et al.*, 1976). There exist chromatin similarities between man and chimpanzee (Pearson *et al.*, 1973; Seth, 1975).

The excellent conservation of the α-globin gene cluster in primate evolution provides a unique opportunity to study the major interspecies sequence differences in any particular Alu family. In particular, the restriction maps of regions containing the $\alpha\psi$, α_2 and α_1 globin genes in man and chimpanzee are nearly identical (Sawada *et al.*, 1983). There is evidence that the $\alpha\psi$ gene was inactivated significantly further back in time than the divergence of man and chimpanzee (Proudfoot & Maniatis, 1980). The structure and position of the $\alpha\psi$ gene has not altered since the divergence of man and chimpanzee and it is at least as well conserved as its immediate flanking sequence.

Like all other aspects of the biological system, karyotypes change through time and do so at rates that may vary considerably among lineages. A remarkable feature of the karyotype evolution in primates is the apparent specialization of different taxa: pericentric inversions are characteristic of the Pongidae, Robertsonian fusions of the lemurs, and fission of the Cercopithecinae (Dutrillaux, 1979). *Papio* appears to have experienced relative chromosomal stability, although the species is well differentiated through gene mutations (Soulie & De Grouchy, 1981). Broadly speaking, comparison of the unbanded karyotypes finds the genera *Macaca*, *Papio*, *Mandrillus*, *Theropithecus* and *Cercocebus* indistinguishable (Chiarelli, Koen & Ardito, 1979). The Hylobatinae contrast with other primates by the difficulty encountered in restructuring their phylogeny through homoecology of banding patterns. This is true for inter- and intra-group comparisons between the Hylobatinae and other Pongidae.

Discussion

Like human populations, the nonhuman primates adapt readily to new ecological conditions and differentiate in directions that are predictable. Viewed in a wider perspective of microdifferentiation, the evolutionary and genetic differentiation in the nonhuman primate species represents a potential reservoir of variables delineating the underlying processes.

Thus, the simian-type blood group systems are found to be shared only by very closely related species of primates; the degree of cross-reactivity of the isoimmune reagents (as measured by the level of polymorphism they detect) possibly reflects the taxonomic proximity of the primate species tested with these reagents.

Immunological data based on antigenic cross-reactions of primate transferrins and immunoglobulins (Wang *et al.*, 1968), serum albumin (Hafleigh & Williams, 1966; Sarich & Wilson, 1967*a,b*; Kaur *et al.*, 1976), thyroglobulins (Goodman, 1967) and lens proteins (Maisel, 1965) agree, in general, with the systematics of primates established by morphology. An important and consistent conclusion of the immunological studies is the marked similarity of human proteins, blood types and satellite DNA to those of African apes, suggesting thereby a more recent time of divergence of lineages than indicated by paleontological estimates (Goodman, 1967; Wilson & Sarich, 1969). This clearly indicates that the rates of molecular evolution can be independent of the rates of morphological evolution. Using a multi-disciplinary approach such as immunological, DNA hybridization, and electrophoretic techniques together with geological and paleontological data, to establish evolutionary and genetic proximities in primates, reveals that the New World monkeys share with the Old World (particularly the higher) primates a long period of common ancestry subsequent to the divergence of any lineage leading to a modern prosimian (Cronin & Sarich, 1975). As a consequence thereof, the length of this common ancestral branch makes it highly probable that the morphological similarities seen in the two groups which give them 'monkey' status are not due to parallelisms or convergences but due to the fact that their ancestor already possessed them.

Data based on the fibrinopeptide amino acid sequences indicate that the African apes have a much closer genetic relationship to man than to the gibbon or the orangutan (Buettner-Janusch *et al.*, 1969; Mross, Doolittle & Roberts, 1970; Tashian & Stroup, 1970). Immuno-diffusion data support this genetic relationship. Studies based on hemoglobin suggest that the divergence of *Homo* from *Pan* and *Gorilla* might have been in the Pliocene, as recently as 5 million years ago. This close serological and molecular relationship between the African apes and man is not reflected in their taxonomic status because man is classified separately as the only living representative of Hominidae. Goodman (1967) proposes that these results merit the inclusion of *Pan* and *Gorilla* also within the Hominidae.

Morphological evidence indicates that the ancestors of the gibbon diverged earlier in primate evolution from the hominoid tree than the ancestors of modern apes, whose divergence is estimated at 20–30 million years ago. The lower values of inhibition produced by gibbon and orangutan hemoglobins demonstrate that these proteins are structurally more dissimilar to human and African ape hemoglobins and thereby support the view of an earlier branching of these species in hominoid evolution (Garver & Talmage, 1975). The genetic distances between the extant Hominoidea, based on an electrophoretic assay of 23 proteins, also exhibits a similar genetic variability between man, the great apes and the lesser apes (Ayala, 1975; King & Wilson, 1975; Bruce & Ayala, 1979).

The presence of common centromeric DNA sequences among higher primates and man signifies the existence of an evolutionary mechanism which has potentiated the comparative success of this group in evolution. Compared with other groups, e.g. rodents, primates have conserved certain DNA families within their constitutive heterochromatin. *In situ* DNA hybridization studies suggest that the evolutionary divergence of man and chimpanzee took place after the origin of the original satellite III sequence.

There is strong evidence that the Alu family sequences, interspersed throughout the genome by means of RNA intermediates, appear to be conserved throughout all lines of primate evolution (Deininger & Schmid, 1979). The conservation of this dimeric sequence as far back from humans as the prosimians suggests that the 300 bp organization is a common feature of all primates. Base sequences of African green monkey Alu family members are as closely related to the human consensus sequence as any randomly chosen human member (Schmid, personal communication). This finding agrees with the results of thermal stability studies on the divergence of short repetitive DNAs within primate species (Deininger & Schmid, 1976, 1979) that the repetitive human and chimpanzee DNA sequences are indistinguishable. The short interspersed repetitive sequences in bonnet monkey and human DNA exhibited only a 2% species-specific divergence, whereas in galago and human DNA it showed a more pronounced species-specific divergence (ca 10%).

Data show that the divergence of human and galago occurred about one-fourth of the way (7%/30%) from the initial formation of the dimer to the present. Therefore, the dimer formed just prior to, or roughly at, the beginning of the primate lineage and may have been an influence in this evolution.

Chromosomal evolution, an integral part of the evolution of organisms, displays great karyotypic diversity in the gibbons. Chromosomal evolution in the terrestrial Cercopithecidae, though diverse at the morphological level and comparable in intraclade genetic distance to the gibbons, displays an astonishing degree of karyotypic conservatism (Dene *et al.*, 1976); this variability between the gibbons and Old World monkeys is attributable to their socioecology (Marks, 1982).

Thus it can be concluded from the extensive comparative immunodiffusion, genetic, chromosomal and immunological studies on primates, that after the early divergence of gibbon and orangutan branches there was still a common ancestral line for man, chimpanzee and gorilla. In the descent of primate fibrinopeptides, where hominoids (chimpanzee and man) and cercopithecoids (macaques, vervet, drill) branch apart, the gibbons split off as a distinct lineage from the base of the cercopithecoids. No splitting occurs in the terminal descent of man and the chimpanzee: their fibrinopeptides are identical. The fibrinopeptides of the catarrhine primates are among the least rapidly evolving ones in mammals. This relationship supports a classification of the extant Hominoidea which places gorilla and chimpanzee with man in the family Hominidae. This agrees with the view that man originated from the same ancestral stock as that of chimpanzee and gorilla in Africa, a view that Darwin also held. On the other hand, data obtained with human DNA closely fits the pattern observed with the Asian apes, thereby suggesting that most of man's evolution since his divergence from the other apes occurred in Asia rather than in Africa (Todaro & Benveniste, 1977). The contention that animals with longer generation times accumulate fewer mutations per unit of chronological time as suggested by Kohne (1970), Lovejoy, Burstein & Heiple (1972) and others is subject to a direct test. If man had a common ancestor with the chimpanzee and gorilla as recently as 4 million years ago, then the effect of the recent prolonged generation time of the ancestral man would be even more difficult to detect. There is considerable paleontological evidence suggesting that the apes and the hominids had differentiated long before the time suggested by molecular systematics. There is no convincing evidence for animals whose locomotion resembled that of either humans or African apes prior to 5 million years ago (McHenry, 1975). The hard fossil evidence is, therefore, easily reconciled with a divergence time of 5 million years between the human and the African ape lineages. The molecular clock based on albumin and transferrin suggests that the divergence between the Anthropoidea and prosimians took place around 70 million years ago, i.e. very close to the beginning of the Tertiary period, that between the Old World and New World monkeys took place 35 million years ago, and that between the Cercopithecoidea and the Hominoidea took place around 20 million years ago (Cronin, 1977). Similar conclusions have been reached based on the morphological and fossil data (Hershkovitz, 1972; Hoffstetter, 1972, 1974; McKenna, 1969). There is sufficient evidence to suggest that the primate radiation began about 70 million years ago; e.g. the albumin immunological distance of 58 units along an average primate lineage from the beginning of the primate radiation to the present corresponds to a time of 58 × 60/50 or 70 million years (Sarich & Cronin, 1976).

References

Ayala, F. J. (1975) Genetic differentiation during the speciation process. *Evol. Biol.*, **8**, 1–78

Basch, R. S. (1972) Hemoglobin polymorphism in the rhesus macaque. *Nature*, **238**, 238–40

Boer, L. E. M. de & Meera Khan, P. (1982) Hemoglobin polymorphisms in Bornean and Sumatran orang utans. In *The Orangutan: Its Biology and Conservation*, ed. L. E. M. de Boer, pp. 125–34. The Hague: Junk

Boyer, S. H., Crosby, E. F., Noyes, A. N., Fuller, G. F., Leslie, S. E., Donaldson, L. J., Urablik, G. R., Schaefer, E. W. & Thummon, T. F. (1971) Primate hemoglobins: some sequences and some proposals concerning the character of evolution and mutation. *Biochem. Genet.*, **5**, 405–88

Bruce, E. J. & Ayala, F. J. (1979) Phylogenetic relationships between man and the apes: electrophoretic evidence. *Evolution*, **33**, 1040–56

Buettner-Janusch, J., Buettner-Janusch, V. & Mason, G. A. (1969) Amino acid composition and amino-terminal end groups of α and β chains from polymorphic hemoglobins of *Pongo pygmaeus*. *Arch. Biochem. Biophys.*, **133**, 164–70

Buettner-Janusch, J. & Hill, R. L. (1965*a*) Molecules and monkeys. *Science*, **147**, 836–42

Buettner-Janusch, J. & Hill, R. L. (1965*b*) Evolution of hemoglobins in primates. In *Evolving Genes and Proteins*, ed. V. Bryson & H. J. Vogel, pp. 167–00. New York: Academic Press

Carter, N. D. (1972) Carbonic anhydrase isozymes in *Cavia procellus*, *Cavia aperea* and their hybrids. *Comp. Biochem. Physiol.*, **438**, 743

Chiarelli, B., Koen, A. L. & Ardito, G. (1979) *Comparative Karyology of Primates*. The Hague: Mouton

Cronin, J. E. (1977) Anthropoid evolution: the molecular evidence. *Kroeber Anthropol. Soc. Papers*, **50**, 75–84

Cronin, J. E. & Sarich, V. M. (1975) Molecular systematics of the new world monkeys. *J. Hum. Evol.*, **4**, 357–75

Deininger, P. L. & Schmid, C. W. (1976) Thermal stability of human DNA and chimpanzee DNA heteroduplexes. *Science*, **194**, 846–8

Deininger, P. L. & Schmid, C. W. (1979) A study of the evolution of repeated DNA sequences in primates and the existence of a new class of repetitive sequences in primates. *J. Molec. Biol.*, **127**, 437–60

Dene, H., Goodman, M., Prychodko, W. & Moore, G. W. (1976) Immunodiffusion systematics of the primates. III. The strepsirrhini. *Folia Primatol.*, **25**, 35–61

Devor, E. J. (1978) Genetic variation in the transferrin alleles of rhesus macaques, *Macaca mulatta*. *Am. J. Phys. Anthropol.*, **48**, 165–9

Dracopoli, N. C. & Brett, F. L. (1982) Serum aminopeptidases in pregnant vervet monkeys (*Cercopithecus aethiops*). *Biochem. Genet.*, **20**, 825–31

Dutrillaux, B. (1979) Chromosomal evolution in primates: tentative phylogeny from *Microcebus murinus* (Prosimian) to man. *Hum. Genet.*, **48**, 251–314

Eicher, E. M., Stern, R. H., Womack, J. E., Davisson, M. T., Roderick, T. H. & Reynolds, S. C. (1976) Evolution of mammalian carbonic anhydrase loci by tandem duplication: Close linkage of Car–I and Car–2 to the centromere region of chromosome 3 of the mouse. *Biochem. Genet.*, **14**, 651–60

Garver, F. A. & Talmage, D. W. (1975) Comparative immunochemical studies of primate hemoglobins. *Biochem. Genet.*, **13**, 743–57

Gavin, J., Noades, J., Tippett, P., Sanger, R. & Race, R. R. (1964) Blood group antigen Xg^a in gibbons. *Nature, Lond.*, **204**, 1322–3

Goodman, M. (1967) Deciphering primate phylogeny from macromolecular specificities. *Am. J. Phys. Anthropol.*, **26**, 255–75

Hafleigh, A. S. & Williams, C. A. Jr (1966) Antigenic correspondence of serum albumins among the primates. *Science*, **151**, 1530–5

Hershkovitz, P. (1969) The recent mammals of the neotropical region: A zoogeographic and ecological review. *Q. Rev. Biol.*, **44**, 1–70

Hoffstetter, R. (1972) Relationship, origins and history of the ceboid monkeys and caviomorph rodents: a modern reinterpretation. In *Evolutionary Biology*, ed T. Dobzhansky, M. K. Hecht & W. C. Steere, pp. 323–47. New York: Appleton, Century Crofts

Hoffstetter, R. (1974) Phylogeny and geographical deployment of the primates. *J. Hum. Evol.*, **3**, 327–50

Hrdy, D. B., Barnicot, N. A. & Alper, C. A. (1975) Protein polymorphism in the hanuman langur (*Presbytis entellus*). *Folia Primatol.*, **24**, 173–84

Kaur, H., Seth, S., Seth, P. K. & Shrivastava, P. K. (1976) Alloalbuminaemia in *Macaca mulatta*. *Acta Anthropogenet.*, **1**, 49–51

King, M. C. & Wilson, A. C. (1975) Evolution at two levels. Molecular similarities and biological differences between humans and chimpanzees. *Science*, **188**, 107–16

Kohne, D. E. (1970) Evolution of higher organism DNA. *Q. Rev. Biophys.*, **3**, 327–76

Lovejoy, C. O., Burstein, A. H. & Heiple, K. H. (1972) Primate phylogeny and immunological distance. *Science*, **176**, 803–5

Maisel, H. (1965) Phylogenetic proteins of primate lens antigens. In *Protides of the Biological Fluids*, ed. H. Peeters, vol. 12, p. 146. Amsterdam: Elsevier

Manfredi-Romani, M. G. (1971) The variations in nuclear genetic material content of lymphocytes in cytotaxonomic picture of primates. *Proc. 3rd Int. Congr. Primat.*, Zurich 1970, **2**, 141–8

Marks, J. (1982) Evolutionary tempo and phylogenetic inference based on primate karyotypes. *Cytogenet. Cell Genet.*, **34**, 261–4

Matsuda, G., Maita, T., Ota, H., Araya, A., Nakashima, Y., Ishii, U. & Nakashima, M. (1973) The primary structures of α and β chains of adult hemoglobin of the Japanese monkey (*Macaca fuscata fuscata*). *Int. J. Peptide Protein Res.*, **5**, 405–18

Matsuda, G., Maita, T., Takei, H., Ota, H., Yamaguch, M., Miyauchi, T. & Migita, M. (1968) The primary structure of adult hemoglobin from *Macaca mulatta* monkey. *J. Biochem. (Tokyo)*, **64**, 279–82

McDermid, E. M., Vos, G. H. & Downing, H. J. (1973) Blood groups, red cell enzymes and serum proteins of baboons and vervets. *Folia primatol.*, **19**, 312–26

McHenry, H. M. (1975) Fossil and the mosaic nature of human evolution. *Science*, **190**, 425–31

McKenna, M. C. (1969) The origin and early differentiation of therian mammals. *Ann. N. Y. Acad. Sci.*, **167**, 217–40

Moor-Jankowski, J. & Socha, W. W. (1978) Blood groups of macaques: a comparative study. *J. Med. Primatol.*, **7**, 136–45

Moor-Jankowski, J. & Wiener, A. S. (1972) Red cell antigens of primates. In *Pathology of Simian Primates*, ed. R. N. T. W.-Fiennes, pp. 270–317. Basel: Karger

Moor-Jankowski, J., Wiener, A. S., Socha, W. W., Gordon, E. B. & Mortelmans, J. (1972) Blood groups of the dwarf chimpanzee (*Pan paniscus*). *J. med. Primatol.*, **1**, 90–101

Moor-Jankowski, J., Wiener, A. S., Socha, W. W. & Valerio, D. A. (1977) Blood groups of crab-eating macaques (*Macaca fascicularis*) demonstrated by isoimmune rhesus monkey (*Macaca mulatta*) sera. *J. Med. Primatol.*, **6**, 76–86

Mross, G. A., Doolittle, R. F. & Roberts, B. F. (1970) Gibbon fibrinopeptides: identification of a glycine-serine allelism at position B-3. *Science*, **170**, 468–70

Nozawa, K., Shotake, T., Ohkura, Y., Kitajima, M. & Tanabe, Y. (1975) Genetic variation within and between troops of *Macaca fuscata fuscata*. In *Contemporary Primatology*, ed. S. Kondo, M. Kawai & A. Ehara, pp. 75–89. Basel: Karger

Pearson, P. L., Geraedts, J. P. M. & Linden, A. G. J. M. van der (1973) Human chromosome polymorphism. *Symp. Medica Hoechst*, **6**, 201–13

Proudfoot, N. J. & Maniatis, T. (1980) The structure of a human α-globin pseudogene and its relationship to α-globin gene duplication. *Cell*, **21**, 537–44

Prychodko, W., Goodman, M., Poulik, E., Miki, R. & Tanaka, T. (1969) Geographic variations of transferrin allelic frequencies in continental and insular macaque populations. *Proc. Sec. Int. Congr. Primatol.*, **2**, 103–8

Sarich, V. M. & Cronin, J. E. (1976) Molecular systematics of the primates. In *Molecular Anthropology*, ed. M. Goodman, R. E. Tashian & J. H. Tashian, pp. 141–70. New York: Plenum

Sarich, V. M. & Wilson, A. C. (1967a) Immunological time scale for hominid evolution. *Science*, **158**, 1200–3

Sarich, V. M. & Wilson, A. C. (1967b) Rates of albumin evolution in primates. *Proc. Natl Acad. Sci.*, **58**, 142–8

Sawada, I., Beal, M. P., Shen, C. -K. J., Chapman, B., Wilson, A. C. & Schmid, C. (1983) Intergenic DNA sequences flanking the pseudo alpha globin genes of human and chimpanzee. *Nucleic Acids Res.*, **11**, 8087–101

Saxena, M. B. & Seth, P. K. (1979) A critical appraisal of chromosomal homology between Man and *Macaca mulatta*. *The Nucleus*, **22**, 116–24

Schmitt, J. & Ritter, H. (1973) Genetic polymorphism of isocitrate dehydrogenase in primates. *Humangenetik*, **19**, 327–9

Schmitt, J., Spielmann, W. & Weber, M. (1961) Serologische Untersuchungen zur Frage der verwandtschaftlichen Beziehungen von *Pan paniscus* Schwarz 1929 zu und Hominoiden. *Säugetierk, Z.*, **27**, 45–6

Seth, P. K. (1975) Evolutionary dynamics of chromosomal genetic material. *J. Cytol. Genet. Congr. Suppl.*, 165–72

Seth, P. K., Boer, L. E. M. de, Saxena, M. B. & Seth, S. (1976) Comparison of human and non-human primate chromosomes using the fluorescent benzimidazol and other banding techniques. *Chromosomes Today*, **5**, 315–22

Seth, P. K. & Saxena, M. B. (1977) Cytological mechanisms in the evolution of mammalian chromosomes. *The Nucleus*, **20**, 42–52

Seth, P. K., Seth, S. & Saxena, M. B. (1983) Chromosomal homology in *Macaca mulatta, Papio papio* and Man. In *Perspectives in Primate Biology*, ed. P. K. Seth, pp. 161–5. New Delhi: Today & Tomorrow's Printers and Publishers

Seth, S., Seth, P. K. & Berndt, H. (1975a) Group specific component in *Macaca*. *Humangenetik*, **28**, 329–30

Seth, S., Seth, P. K. & Dixit, V. P. (1983) Genetic variations in primates: red cell enzymes and serum proteins in rhesus, baboons and langurs. In *Perspectives in Primate Biology*, ed. P. K. Seth, pp. 161–5. New Delhi: Today & Tomorrow's Printers and Publishers

Seth, S., Seth, P. K. & Saxena, M. B. (1975b) Genetic variations in primates: red cell enzymes and serum proteins in *Macaca mulatta*. *Humangenetik*, **29**, 341–8

Simone, J. De, Magid, E. & Tashian, R. E. (1973) Genetic variation in the carbonic anhydrase isozymes of macaque monkeys. II Inheritance of red cell carbonic anhydrase levels in different carbonic anhydrase I genotypes of the pig-tailed macaque. *Macaca nemestrina. Biochem. Genet.*, **8**, 165–74

Smith, D. G. & Ferrell, R. E. (1980) A family study of the hemoglobin polymorphism in *Macaca fascicularis. J. Hum. Evol.*, **9**, 557–63

Socha, W. W. & Moor-Jankowski, J. (1979) Blood groups of anthropoid apes and their relationships to human blood groups. *J. Hum. Evol.*, **8**, 453–65

Socha, W. W. & Moor-Jankowski, J. (1980) Chimpanzee R–C–E–F. blood group system. A counterpart of the human Rh–Hr blood groups. *Folia Primatol.*, **33**, 172–88

Socha, W. W., Moor-Jankowski, J., Wiener, A. S., Risser, D. R. & Plonski, H. (1976) Blood groups of bonnet macaques (*Macaca radiata*) with a brief introduction to seroprimatology. *Am. J. Phys. Anthropol.*, **45**, 485–92

Socha, W. W., Wiener, A. S., Moor-Jankowski, J. & Mortelmans, J. (1973) Blood groups of mountain gorillas (*Gorilla gorilla beringei*). *J. Med. Primatol.*, **2**, 364–8

Socha, W. W., Wiener, A. S., Moor-Jankowski, J. & Valerio, D. (1976) The first isoimmune blood group system of rhesus monkeys (*Macaca mulata*): the graded D^{rh} system. *Int. Arch. Allergy Appl. Immunol.*, **52**, 355–63

Soulie, J. & De Grouchy, J. (1981) A cytogenetic survey of 110 baboons (*Papio cynocephalus*) *Am. J. Phys. Anthropol.*, **56**, 107–113

Sullivan, B. (1972) Variation in protein structure and functions: primate hemoglobins, *J. Mol. Evol.*, **1**, 295–304

Tashian, R. E. & Carter, N. D. (1976) Biochemical genetics of carbonic anhydrase. *Adv. Hum. Genet*, **7**, 1–56

Tashian, R. E., Goodman, M., Ferrell, R. E. & Tains, R. J. (1976) Evolution of carbonic anhydrase in primates and other mammals. In *Molecular Anthropology*, ed. M. Goodman, R. E. Tashian & J. H. Tashian, pp. 301–19. New York: Plenum

Tashian, R. E., Goodman, M., Headings, V. E., De Simone, J. & Ward, R. H. (1971) Genetic variation and evolution in the red cell carbonic anhydrase isozymes of macaque monkeys. *Biochem. Genet.*, **5**, 183–200

Tashian, R. E. & Stroup, S. R. (1970) Variation in the primary structure of carbonic anhydrase B in man, great apes, and old world monkeys. *Biochem. Biophys. Res. Commun.*, **41**, 1457–62

Todaro, E. J. & Benveniste, R. (1977) Reply: Sarich and Cronin (1977): Generation length and rates of hominoid molecular evolution. *Nature*, **269**, 354–5

Wade, P. T., Barnicot, N. A. & Huehns, E. R. (1970) Structural studies on the major and minor hemoglobin of the monkey *Macaca irus. Biochem. Biophys. Acta*, **221**, 450–66

Wang, A. C., Shuster, J., Epstein, A. & Fudenberg, H. H. (1968) Evolution of antigenic determinants of transferrin and other serum proteins in primates. *Biochem. Genet.*, **1**, 347–58

Wiener, A. S., Gordon, E. B., Socha, W. W. & Moor-Jankowski, J. (1970) Further observations on the immunological relationships among serum globulins of man and other primates, revealed by a serological inhibition test. *Int. Arch. Allergy*, **39**, 368–74

Wiener, A. S., Moor-Jankowski, J. & Gordon E. B. (1963) Blood groups of apes and monkeys, II the A–B–O blood groups, secretor and Lewis types in apes. *Am. J. Phys. Anthropol.*, **21**, 271–81

Wiener, A. S., Moor-Jankowski, J. & Gordon, E. B. (1966) The relationship of the H substance to the A–B–O blood groups. *Int. Arch. Allergy*, **29**, 82–100

Wiener, A. S., Socha, W. W., Arons, E. B., Mortelmans, J. & Moor-Jankowski,

J. (1976) Blood groups of gorillas: further observations. *J. Med. Primatol.*, **5**, 317–20

Wiener, A. S., Socha, W. W., Gordon, E. B. & Moor-Jankowski, J. (1972) The demonstration of human Gm-like serum α-globulin types using nonhuman primate reagents. I. Experiments with anti-gibbon globulin serum. *Int. Arch. Allergy Appl. Immunol.*, **43**, 16–24

Wijnen, J. Th., Rijken, H., Boer, L. E. M. de & Meera Khan, P. (1982) Glucose-6-phosphate dehydrogenase (G6PD) variation in the orang utan. In *The orangutan. Its Biology and Conservation*, ed. L. E. M. de Boer, pp. 109–18. The Hague: Junk

Wilson, A. C. & Sarich, V. M. (1969) A molecular time scale for human evolution. *Proc. Nat. Acad. Sci.*, **63**, 108–93

Wu, N., Sikkema, D. A., Zucker, R. M. & Altman, N. H. (1977) Studies of rhesus monkey (*Macaca mulatta*) hemoglobin. *Lab. Anim. Sci.*, **27**, 65–7

IV.2

Genetic and morphological studies on two species of Kenyan monkeys, *Cercopithecus aethiops* and *C. mitis*

T. R. TURNER, C. S. MOTT AND J. E. MAIERS

Introduction

Three populations of cercopithecine monkeys, specifically vervets and mitis, from Kenya and Ethiopia have been sampled and data collected for genetic analysis. In addition, morphological measurements were taken from the Kenyan vervet populations and the mitis populations. The two species represent very different adaptations. Vervets are semi-terrestrial and live along riverine forests in multi-male, multi-female groups. They are widely distributed throughout sub-Saharan Africa. Mitis monkeys, on the other hand, are arboreal animals living in rain forest environments in single male groups. They are found throughout the equatorial forest belt.

The first study of vervets was conducted in 1973 in Awash National Park, Ethiopia (Turner, 1981). A total of 125 animals, representing 93% of the vervets in the park, were trapped. The animals lived in seven contiguous groups along the Awash River and were members of the subspecies *Cercopithecus aethiops aethiops*.

The second trapping survey of vervets was conducted in Kenya in 1978–79 (Dracopoli *et. al.*, 1983). Animals at four sites were sampled. The sites were separated by between 90 and 300 km and varied in altitude and mean annual rainfall (Fig. 1). Sites A, B, and D were at 1000 m while site C was at 2000 m with a higher annual rainfall. Over 360 animals were trapped and this total represents between 64 and 88% of the animals at each site. All the animals were members of the subspecies *C. aethiops pygerythrus*.

The survey of the mitis monkeys was conducted in 1982 (Mott, Turner & Else, 1984). The 93 animals in the study were housed at the Institute of Primate Research in Kenya and were all originally obtained from either commercial trappers or during IPR trapping expeditions. Only adult animals were sampled. These animals represented three subspecies: 25 C. *mitis albotorquatus* from the island of Lamu at sea level; 14 C. *mitis stuhlmanni* which lived between 1200 and 3000 m; and 54 C. *mitis kolbi* which lived between 2500 and 3000 m above sea level. The mean annual rainfall of each of the sites increases with altitude.

Fig. 2 illustrates diagrammatically the vervet and mitis populations that are compared in this paper. We have two species of the genus *Cercopithecus*. In the mitis, three subspecies are compared, while in the vervets two subspecies are compared. Additionally, we have data on four populations of one of the vervet subspecies. Our study is one of the first among primates in which comparisons of genetic and

Fig. 1. Sites of *Cercopithecus mitis* and *C. aethiops* monkeys.

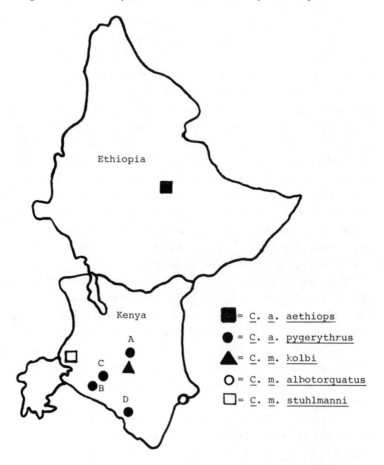

morphological data on different taxonomic groups are made. While the matrix we present gives us a good basis for a population, subspecies, and species comparison of genetic and morphological information, it is not complete since we have no local subdivided population data on the mitis. Despite this our data on genetic distance, F^{ST} values and morphological distance indicate potential problems in the use of protein polymorphism data in the determination of taxonomic categories.

Methods
Blood samples were collected from each animal and examined by electrophoresis. Morphometric measures were taken on all animals except for the Ethiopian vervet population.

Fig. 2. Subspecies of *Cercopithecus mitis* and *C. aethiops*.

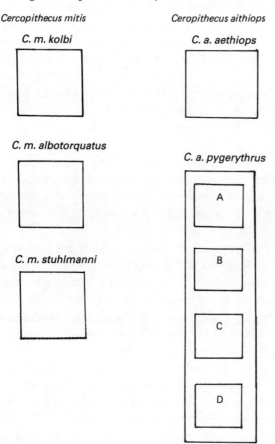

Cercopithecus mitis

C. m. kolbi

C. m. albotorquatus

C. m. stuhlmanni

Ceropithecus aithiops

C. a. aethiops

C. a. pygerythrus

A

B

C

D

Several standard statistics for the assessment of population differentiation were employed, including average heterozygosity ($\bar{H}$), F_{ST} and
genetic distance. All of these statistics were calculated from allele
frequencies.

F_{ST} (Wright, 1965) is the fixation index, or the ratio of the observed
variance in a subpopulation relative to the maximum theoretical
variance of the population, and goes from 0 to 1, with 0 indicating
identity.

Genetic distance is a measure that, in a single number, expresses
differences in gene frequency between a pair of populations and is the
average gene difference per locus. The same loci are used in the
comparison between different groups. There are several distance
measures; we employed Nei's (1975). In order to put morphological
comparisons between species into a form similar to genetic distance,
we used the M-statistic proposed by Cherry, Case & Wilson (1978).
Seven linear measures of body size were used: head, chest girth, lower
arm, upper arm, lower leg, upper leg, and body length. All measures
were normalized on total metric length so body size and sexual
dimorphism were factored out. Body weight was also ignored in this
measure. In this case the M-statistic was chosen rather than the
Mahalanobis D^2 because of the relatively small sample size (see
Atchley, 1980, and Kunkel et al., 1980).

Results

A summary of the genetic survey of the population is presented in Table 1. The number of animals surveyed, the number of loci
examined, the average heterozygosity, the number of polymorphic
loci, the proportions of polymorphic loci and the F_{ST} values are
presented.

The average heterozygosities of the populations are very similar,
4–5.6%. This is at the low end of the range for vertebrates in general
(Ayala, 1976). The proportion of polymorphic loci is also similar,
15–17%, somewhat lower than that found in humans (Harris, 1966).

The F_{ST} values have been calculated from the allele frequencies of the
polymorphic loci. These loci are also listed in Table 1. Since only the
adult mitis were sampled, we compared the gene frequencies of the
total vervet population and the adults-only vervet population to assess
the potential loss of variability in a population from the exclusion of
some of the members. Table 2 indicates that the frequencies for the
total population and the adults-only population are nearly identical. In
effect, both sets of frequencies represent samples of the total actual

population. Therefore, the adult mitis give a good indication of what is occurring in the population. However, a caution we are well aware of with the mitis is the small number of individuals in each sample cell. With these considerations in mind we can proceed with an analysis of the F_{ST} values. The lowest F_{ST} value, 0.062, is seen in the Awash population which is effectively a single population unit divided into small local social groups. The next lowest F_{ST} level, 0.112, is in the Kenya vervets who, while separated by geographic distance, are still members of a single subspecies, *C. aethiops pygerythrus*. The highest F_{ST} value, 0.168, is found in the mitis sample which represents three subspecies.

Genetic distances were then calculated for the various sets of populations (Table 3). The distances between the populations of *C. aethiops aethiops* in Ethiopia ranged between 0.0004 and 0.0162. The distances between *C. aethiops pygerythrus* at different sites in Kenya ranged between 0.0004 and 0.0159. These two ranges are nearly identical. The *C. mitis* populations showed genetic differences ranging between 0.0147 and 0.0372. Although this is higher than the vervet populations it is considerably lower than the values Ayala *et al.*(1974) suggest for subspecies differentiation, and lower than what is actually found in populations of *Drosophila wilhistoni* where subspecies differentiation is of the order of 0.20. No further population comparisons are possible for the genetic data. Populations of *C. aethiops aethiops* and *C. aethiops pygerythrus* share too few examined loci in common for comparison. We are as yet unaware of locus identity in *C. aethiops* and *C. mitis*.

Table 1. *Summary of genetic information*

	C. mitis	C. aethiops aethiops	C. aethiops pygerythrus
No. of animals	93	124	364
No. of loci	33	23	18
Average heterozygosity	4.6%	5.6%	4%
No. of polymorphic loci	5	4	3
Proportion of polymorphic loci	15%	17%	17%
Polymorphic loci	TF	TF	EST
	CA II	EST	GC
	DIA	PGM	ABO blood group
	PEP D	ADA	
	ES A		
F_{ST}	0.168	0.062	0.112

These samples need to be subjected to further electrophoretic analysis. A measure of morphological distance was obtained by the method described above (Table 4). The range of distance for the Kenya vervets is from 0.0160 to 0.0613 while the *mitis* range is between 0.0257 and 0.0588. We can say very little about structural morphological distinction in either the vervets or in the mitis. These ranges of differences may reflect local adaptations to differing environmental zones.

Table 2. *Allele frequencies*

Cercopithecus aethiops aethiops

		Adults only	Total population
TF	1	0.9627	0.9700
	2	0.0373	0.0300
EST	1	0.5227	0.4910
	2	0.4091	0.4490
	3	0.0682	0.0590
PGM	1	0.9265	0.9500
	2	0.0735	0.0500
ADA	1	0.6615	0.6710
	2	0.3308	0.3210
	3	0.0077	0.0080

Cercopithecus aethiops pygerythrus

		Adults only	Total population
GC	1	0.7632	0.8900
	2	0.2368	0.1100
EST	1	0.9230	0.9600
	2	0.0770	0.0400
ABO	1	0.7566	0.7400
	2	0.1974	0.2100
	3	0.0460	0.0500

Cercopithecus mitis

		C. m. kolbi	C. m. albotorquatus	C. m. stuhlmanni
TF	1	0.8611	0.0200	0.9286
	2	0.1111	0.9400	0.0000
	3	0.0185	0.0400	0.0000
	4	0.0093	0.0000	0.0714
CA II	1	0.3426	0.5600	1.0000
	2	0.4815	0.4000	0.0000
	3	0.1759	0.0400	0.0000
DIA	1	0.6389	0.6000	0.9643
	2	0.3611	0.4000	0.0357
PEP D	1	0.8056	0.8600	0.7857
	2	0.1204	0.1000	0.1429
	3	0.0740	0.0400	0.0714
ES A	1	0.8981	1.0000	1.0000
	2	0.0556	0.0000	0.0000
	3	0.0370	0.0000	0.0000
	4	0.0093	0.0000	0.0000

Table 3. *Nei's genetic distance*

Cercopithecus mitis

	1	2
1		
2	0.0372	
3	0.0147	0.0240

1 = *C. m. stuhlmanni*
2 = *C. m. albotorquatus*
3 = *C. m. kolbi*

Cercopithecus aethiops aethiops

Troop	1	2	3	4	5	6
1						
2	0.0057					
3	0.0042	0.0048				
4	0.0027	0.0054	0.0020			
5	0.0022	0.0062	0.0016	0.0007		
6	0.0021	0.0055	0.0021	0.0005	0.0004	
7	0.0048	0.0162	0.0066	0.0052	0.0034	0.0042

Cercopithecus aethiops pygerythrus

Sites	A	B	C
A			
B	0.0069		
C	0.0004	0.0043	
D	0.0034	0.0159	0.0055

Table 4. *Morphological distances*

Cercopithecus mitis

	1	2
1		
2	0.0542	
3	0.0257	0.0588

1 = *C. m. stuhlmanni*
2 = *C. m. albotorquatus*
3 = *C. m. kolbi*

Cercopithecus aethiops pygerythrus

Sites	A	B	C
A			
B	0.0160		
C	0.0489	0.0470	
D	0.0514	0.0613	0.0285

Discussion and conclusion

A comparison of the genetic and morphological distances between pairs of populations of *C. mitis* and *C. aethiops pygerythrus* is illustrated in Fig. 3. Taxonomically the *C.a. pygerythrus* groups represent local groups while the *mitis* populations represent different subspecies. There is some distinction between the genetic distances of local populations and subspecies, although there is considerable overlap between the higher values found in local populations and the lower values of the subspecies. This overlap and lack of real distinction allow us to pose two related questions. First, are electrophoretic data on the frequencies of alleles at protein and enzyme loci adequate for

Fig. 3. Genetic and morphological distances (in parentheses) for *C. mitis* subspecies and for *C. aethiops pygerythrus* populations

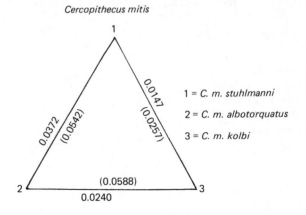

Cercopithecus mitis

1 = *C. m. stuhlmanni*

2 = *C. m. albotorquatus*

3 = *C. m. kolbi*

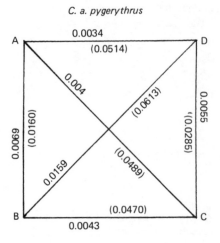

C. a. pygerythrus

assessing differentiation of populations? Conversely, are subpopulations and subspecies distinctions reflected in blood protein differentiation? The morphological distance measures also indicate considerable range and overlap but do not correspond to the genetic distances. A correspondence would not really be expected since morphological differentiation reflects local environmental adaptation and selection, while differentiation in allele frequencies may simply reflect random genetic drift acting on these alleles.

We must ask whether genetic data on structural gene loci can be used to assess population differentiation in a meaningful way or whether the more traditional means of assessing population differentiation such as pelage differences and size differences can give at least as accurate if not more relevant assessments of differentiation since they do reflect local adaptations.

We need to look further at comparisons of subdivided populations, subspecies and species over an array of organisms which would reflect various population parameters, including effective population size and varying reproductive patterns. This comparison of morphological distinctions would allow our two questions to be answered. One of the first steps in this is a refinement of the distance measure we have used, to take into account size and sexual dimorphism. We are currently working on this measure and hope to apply it to other populations in the near future.

References

Atchley, W. R. (1980) M-statistics and morphometric divergence. *Science*, **208**, 1059–60

Ayala, F. J. (1976) *Molecular Evolution*. Sunderland, Mass.: Sinauer Assoc., Inc.

Ayala, F. J., Tracey, M. L., Hedgecock, D. & Richmond, R. C. (1974) Genetic differentiation during the speciation process in *Drosophila*. *Evolution*, **28**, 576–92

Cherry, L. M., Case, S. M. & Wilson, A. C. (1978) Frog perspective on the morphological difference between humans and chimpanzees. *Science*, **200**, 209–11

Dracopoli, N. C., Brett, F. L., Turner, T. R. & Jolly, C. J. (1983) Patterns of genetic variability in the serum proteins of the Kenyan vervet monkey (*Cercopithecus aethiops*). *Am. J. Phys. Anthropol.*, **61**, 39–49

Harris, H. (1966) Enzyme polymorphism in man. *Proc. Soc. Lond., Ser. B*, **1964**, 298–310

Kunkel, J. G., Cherry, L. M., Case, S. M. & Wilson, A. C. (1980) A response to W. R. Atchley. *Science*, **208**, 1060–1

Mott, C. S., Turner, T. R. & Else, J. G. (1984) Genetic differentiation in three populations of Kenyan *Cercopithecus mitis*. *Am. J. Phys. Anthropol.*, **63**, 197

Nei, M. (1975) *Molecular Population Genetics and Evolution*. New York: American Elsevier

Turner, T. R. (1981) Blood protein variation in a population of Ethiopian vervet monkeys (*Cercopithecus aethiops aethiops.*) *Am. J. Phys. Anthropol.* 55, 225–32

Wright, S. (1965) The interpretation of population structure by F-statistics with special regard to systems of mating. *Evolution,* 19, 395–420

IV.3

The genetics of baboons in biomedical research

J. L. VANDEBERG AND M. L. CHENG

Introduction

Of nonhuman primate genera commonly used in biomedical research, *Papio* stands alone as the only one that is not declining in the actual numbers of animals used; according to the National Primate Plan (Interagency Primate Steering Committee, 1978), estimated use of *Papio* remained constant over the 5-year period of 1977 to 1982, whereas estimated use of all other genera declined (*Saguinus* by 9%, *Cercopithecus* by 28%, *Macaca* by 29%, *Saimiri* by 60%, *Aotus* by 66%, and *Pan* by 72%).

The annual number of publications on baboons in biomedical research is also remaining roughly constant. A MEDLINE search (via DIALOGUE) for publications concerning baboons (the search terms were 'baboon' truncated and '*Papio*') revealed 88 publications in 1968, 306 in 1973, 331 in 1978, and 298 in 1983. The percentage of these that dealt with genetic topics (the search terms were 'genet' truncated and the pre-explosion 'genetics') was 0% in 1968, 3% in 1973, 7% in 1978, and 11% in 1983. These figures indicate a substantial and continuing increase in the importance of genetics in research on baboons.

Baboons are used extensively as models for a wide variety of genetically mediated diseases, including alcoholism (Lieber *et al.*, 1975), epilepsy (Ehlers & Killam, 1980), lymphoma (Crawford *et al.*, 1984), hypertension (Smith, De Vitio & Astley, 1982), and atherosclerosis (McGill *et al.*, 1981). The recent discovery of diabetic baboons (W. J. Goodwin, personal communication) and the familial clustering of congenitally blind baboons (T. B. Gage, personal communication) suggest that baboons might also be useful in research on those conditions. Genetics is an important predisposing factor in these diseases, and genetic approaches in research are likely to have considerable impact on our understanding of them.

Because of the increasing importance of baboons in biomedical research, and the increasingly important role of genetics in research involving baboons, we have initiated a long-term effort to characterize biochemical genetic markers in all five subspecies. The importance of genetic markers in this context is fourfold. First, they are required for maintaining accurate pedigree records, even in situations where sire and dam are thought to be known (Curie-Cohen, VandeBerg & Stone, 1983); and accurate pedigree records are a prerequisite for genetic research. Secondly, genetic variation in some proteins is associated directly via physiological processes with particular disease states. For example, it is known that electrophoretic variants of human apolipo-protein E are associated with dysbetalipoproteinemia, either with or without type III hyperbetalipoproteinemia and premature atherosclerosis (Utermann *et al.*, 1984). Thirdly, some polymorphic proteins have advantageous characteristics for investigating particular physiologic processes that are not directly related to the physiologic function of the marker. For example, X-linked markers can be used to investigate phenomena associated with X-chromosome inactivation (reviewed by VandeBerg *et al.*, 1983; VandeBerg, 1983). As another example, markers that distinguish donor from recipient cells in trans-plantation experiments can be used to determine the proportions of the two cell types at various times after the transplant was made. Fourthly, if large pedigreed families in which a genetically mediated disease is present are typed for a large panel of genetic markers, it is sometimes possible to identify the presence and chromosomal location of a specific gene that causes susceptibility to the disease. As examples, this approach, using biochemical genetic markers, has identified genes that control susceptibility in humans to familial hyperchole-sterolemia (Ott *et al.*, 1974) and breast cancer (King *et al.*, 1980); using DNA markers (restriction fragment length polymorphisms), it has located the gene responsible for Huntington's disease to chromosome 4 (Gusela *et al.*, 1983).

This paper summarizes the results to date of our efforts to identify and to characterize biochemical genetic markers in baboons for biomedical research applications. Although the correct taxonomical designations for baboon populations have been disputed for decades, we believe that the evidence for regarding them as subspecies rather than distinct species is overwhelming; it is based on three criteria. First, several subspecies are known to hybridize freely in natural zones of overlap (Jolly & Brett, 1973; Shotake, 1981; Lucotte, 1983). Secondly, no reproductive problems are known in either reciprocal cross between any two subspecies nor are any known in instances when either sex of hybrid progeny is backcrossed to either parental subspecies. Thirdly, as illustrated by data in Table 1, the extent of genetic similarity among baboon subspecies is similar to that among races, subspecies, or geographically isolated populations of other mammals.

Rules for species nomenclature stipulate that the correct name is the one first assigned to any member of that species, so the common long-tailed baboon must be called *Papio hamadryas* Linnaeus 1758. Groves (1972) divides *Papio hamadryas* into five 'subspecies-groups', some of which contain multiple subspecies. We believe that available comparative genetic data are not sufficient to justify the further subdivision of any subspecies-group into multiple subspecies; hence, we consider the species *Papio hamadryas* to comprise five subspecies, namely *anubis* (olive baboons), *cynocephalus* (yellow baboons), *hamadryas* (sacred baboons), *papio* (red baboons), and *ursinus* (chacma baboons). All of these subspecies are maintained at the Southwest Foundation for Biomedical Research (SFBR), and all except *P. h. ursinus* are supported by the National Institutes of Health as a resource that provides baboons for biomedical research.

Materials and methods
The steady-state number of baboons maintained at SFBR includes approximately 1900 *P. h. anubis*, 200 *P. h. cynocephalus*, 200 *P. h. hamadryas*, 30 *P. h. papio*, 15 *P. h. ursinus*, and 400 hybrids, mostly between *P. h. anubis* and *P. h. cynocephalus*. Many of the breeders are maintained in outdoor cages, each of which contains one adult male and approximately 20 adult females, along with infants and juveniles. This caging arrangement enables the maintenance of pedigree records, which can be verified via the use of genetic markers. Another group of several hundred breeders, including only *P. h. anubis*, is maintained in a 6-acre corral for the economic production of baboons for experiments that do not depend on pedigree structure. A second 6-acre corral contains juveniles of the various subspecies.

Blood was withdrawn from the femoral veins of baboons immobilized by intramuscular injection of ketamine hydrochloride (10 mg/kg body weight). Sera were obtained from coagulated blood and stored at $-80\,°C$ in small aliquots that precluded the necessity of repeated freezing and thawing of a serum sample for sequential analyses. Erythrocytes were obtained by collecting blood in acid–citrate–dextrose solution and washing the cells three times in

Table 1. *Estimates of genetic similarity (I = Nei's Identity Coefficient)*

Subspecies of baboons (Lucotte, 1983) (*I* = 0.94–0.97)

	papio	*anubis*	*cynocephalus*
anubis	0.96		
cynocephalus	0.97	0.96	
hamadryas	0.94	0.94	0.94

Mammalian Subspecies or Races of a Single Species (*I* = 0.95–0.98)

Common names	Scientific names	Subspecies or races	*I*	Reference
Baboon	*Papio hamadryas*	4 subspecies	0.95	1
Human	*Homo sapiens*	Caucasians, Blacks and Japanese	0.98	2
Japanese macaque	*Macaca fuscata*	*fuscata* and *yorkui*	0.96	3
House mouse	*Mus musculus*	demes from different farms	0.98	4
Field mouse	*Peromyscus boylii*	5 subspecies	0.95	5
Sheep	*Ovis aries*	7 breeds from western U.S.A.	0.96	6

Mammalian species of a single genus (*I* = 0.85–0.92)

Genus	Species	*I*	Reference
Macaca	rhesus (*mulatta*) and stump-tailed (*speciosa*)	0.91	3
Macaca	rhesus and Japanese	0.89	3
Macaca	rhesus and bonnet (*radiata*)	0.87	3
Macaca	rhesus and pig-tailed (*nemestrina*)	0.85	3
Hylobates	*lar* and *concolor*	0.88	7
Bos	cattle and bison	0.92	8
Odocoileus	mule deer and white-tailed deer	0.86	8

Mammalian genera of a single family (*I* = 0.39–0.80)

Family	Genera	*I*	Reference
Cercopithecidae	*Papio, Macaca,* and *Cercopithecus*	0.52	9
Cercopithecidae	*Papio* and *Theropithecus*	0.55	9
Pongidae	*Pan* and *Gorilla*	0.69	7
Pongidae	*Pan* and *Pongo*	0.80	7
Cervidae	*Odocoileus* (deer) and *Cervus* (elk)	0.39	8
Cervidae	*Odocoileus* and *Alces* (moose)	0.46	8

References: 1. Lucotte (1983); 2. Nei & Roychoudhury (1974); 3. Nozawa *et al.* (1977); 4. Selander *et al.* (1969); 5. Zimmerman *et al.* (1978); 6. Ananthakrishnan (1973); 7. Bruce & Ayala (1979); 8. Baccus *et al.*, 1983; 9. Shotake (1981).

phosphate-buffered saline. Initially, erythrocytes were stored at −25 °C in an ethylene glycol–citrate freezing solution (VandeBerg & Johnston, 1977). However, because baboon erythrocytes are less stable under these conditions than erythrocytes of many other species, we currently store them in a 0.3M glucose/0.45M sucrose/0.05M NaCl solution in droplets in liquid nitrogen (technique modified from Rowe & Allen, 1965).

Protein variation was assessed by standard electrophoretic methods using hydrolyzed starch, polyacrylamide, cellulose acetate, and agarose as gel media.

Results and discussion

Table 2 provides a summary of biochemical genetic markers that have been identified in baboon blood; this summary is a composite of our results and those of other investigators. Although 30 variable markers seems to be a relatively large number, it is deceiving from a practical standpoint because many of the variations are restricted to particular subspecies or even to particular populations of a particular subspecies.

From the standpoint of biomedical research, it is more important to know which markers are variable in those baboons that are readily available as research subjects. Therefore, our efforts have focused on the baboons at SFBR. Table 3 summarizes our results to date on eight markers that are typed routinely in our laboratory. The distribution of alleles among the subspecies is highly variable. This subspecies distribution of alleles probably is due in part to differences in allelic distribution among subspecies in natural populations and in part to the numbers and origins of the animals of each subspecies at SFBR. For example, the *P. h. ursinus* colony and most of the *P. h. papio* colony were each obtained from a single source on a single occasion, and both are small colonies. Therefore, a broader sampling of these subspecies would probably reveal more extensive genetic variation. Nonetheless, the allelic distribution shown for the eight markers in Table 3 reflects that presently available to biomedical researchers in the USA.

GPI is the only one of the eight markers that unambiguously distinguishes one subspecies from all others. All *P. h. papio* are homozygous for the *b* allele whereas individuals of the other subspecies are all homozygous for the *a* allele, which specifies a more anodally migrating isozyme. This allelic distribution is especially useful for monitoring proportions of donor and recipient cells after transplantation. For example, one research protocol involves injecting

Table 2. *Biochemical markers in baboons (all* Papio hamadryas *subspecies combined)*

Protein or polypeptide	Blood component[a]	Putative no. of alleles	Reference
1. Adenosine deaminase	RBC	2	1
2. Adenine phosphoribosyl transferase	RBC	2	1
3. Adenylate kinase 1	RBC	2	1
4. Albumin	Serum	2	3
5. α_1-Antitrypsin (protease inhibitor)	Serum	3	1
6. Carbonic anhydrase I	RBC	3	1
7. Carbonic anhydrase II	RBC	2	4
8. Catalase	RBC	2	2
9. Complement component 3	Serum	10	4
10. Complement component 6	Serum	3	2
11. Complement component 7	Serum	2	2
12. NADH-diaphorase	RBC	2	5
13. α-Fucosidase	WBC	2	2
14. Glucose-6-phosphate dehydrogenase	RBC	2	4
15. Glucose-phosphate isomerase	RBC	2	4
16. Group specific component	Serum	2	3
17. Haptoglobin	Serum	2	6
18. Malate dehydrogenase 1	RBC	2	6
19. Mannose-phosphate isomerase	RBC	3	4
20. Peptidase B	RBC	2	7
21. Peptidase D	RBC	2	2
22. Phosphoglucomutase 1	RBC	2	1
23. Phosphoglucomutase 2	RBC	2	1
24. Phosphogluconate dehydrogenase	RBC	3	1,4
25. Phosphoglycerate kinase A	RBC	2	4
26. Prealbumin esterase	Serum	2	1
27. Prealbumin 2	Serum	2	1
28. Properdin factor B	Serum	3	7
29. Thyroxin-binding prealbumin	Serum	2	1
30. Transferrin	Serum	4	1

[a]RBC = red blood cells; WBC = white blood cells.

References: 1. Shotake *et al.* (1977); 2. R. Fisher, personal communication; 3. Kitchin *et al.* (1967); 4. J. L. VandeBerg and M.-L. Cheng, unpublished; 5. Vergnes *et al.* (1978); 6. McDermid *et al.*, 1973; 7. Dykes *et al.*, 1981.

blood from a *P. h. papio* into *P. h. anubis* fetuses at different stages of development, with the objective of producing fetal chimeras and using the GPI marker to determine the timing of critical events in the development of the hematopoietic system (Roodman, VandeBerg & Kuehl, 1985). Upon sacrifice of the chimeric fetuses, electrophoretic analyses can determine the proportion of donor and recipient cells in various hematopoietic tissues, and inferences can be made regarding the timing and sequence of developmental switches in the sites of hematopoiesis.

G6PD is specified by an X-linked gene in baboons (and other mammals), and this characteristic makes it an especially valuable marker. The *b* allele is fixed in all subspecies except *P. h. papio*, which is polymorphic for the *b* allele and the *a* allele, which specifies a more anodally migrating isozyme. Early in embryonic development, one X chromosome is inactivated in each cell of females (reviewed by Lyon, 1974). Studies on mice have revealed that X chromosome inactivation takes place via a series of events that differ in different embryonic and extraembryonic tissues (reviewed by VandeBerg, 1983), but the events surrounding X chromosome inactivation in primates are not well characterized. The X-linked G6PD marker in baboons will enable the

Table 3. *Polymorphic protein systems in baboons* (Papio hamadryas subspecies) *at the Southwest Foundation for Biomedical Research*

Protein[a]	Alleles[b] present in each subspecies				
	anubis	cynocephalus	hamadryas	papio	ursinus
CA-I	a,b	a,b	a,b	b	b,c
CA-II	b	a,b	b	b	b
C3	a,b,c,d,e, f,g,h,i,j	c,d,f, g,h,i	f,g,h	h	d
G6PD	b	b	b	a,b	b
GPI	a	a	a	b	a
MPI	a,b,c	a,b,c	b,c	b	b
PEP-B	b	b	b	b	a,b
6PGD	a,b	b	b,c	b	b

[a] CA-I = carbonic anhydrase-I; CA-II = carbonic anhydrase II; C3 = third component of complement; G6PD = glucose-6-phosphate dehydrogenase; GPI = glucose–phosphate isomerase; MPI mannose–phosphate isomerase; PEP-B = peptidase B; 6PGD = 6-phosphogluconate dehydrogenase.

[b] Allelic designations were assigned on the basis of decreasing anodal migration of the protein specified; in each case the *a* allele specifies the most anodally migrating allelic form of the protein.

characterization of those events, via the dissection of early heterozygous embryos, into embryonic and extraembryonic tissues and the
determination of the state of X chromosome activity in each by
electrophoresis of G6PD.

G6PD also will be a valuable marker for investigating the development of atherosclerotic plaques. Because one X chromosome is inactive
in somatic cells of post-embryonic females, each cell of heterozygotes
can express only one of its two G6PD alleles. Therefore, if an
atherosclerotic plaque (or a neoplasm) arises via the proliferation of a
single cell, then all the cells in it will express only one X chromosome.
Electrophoresis of fatty streaks, fibrous plaques, and thrombi from
human G6PD heterozygotes at autopsy has revealed an increasing
tendency to express only one allele as the lesion state becomes more
advanced (Pearson *et al.*, 1978, 1979). Because these results are subject
to alternative interpretations (Thomas *et al.*, 1979), the availability of a
suitable nonhuman primate model will be an important factor in
determining the progression of cellular events that lead to the
endpoints observed at autopsy in humans.

The C3 marker is of special interest because of its high level of
polymorphism. Ten allelic forms of C3 have been identified in
baboons, thereby making it the most highly polymorphic marker
known in baboons. This property makes C3 especially valuable for
resolving disputed paternity cases and monitoring pedigree records.
Human C3 variants are thought to be associated with differential
predisposition to atherosclerosis and essential hypertension (Sorensen & Dissing, 1975; Kristensen & Petersen, 1978; Schaadt, Sorensen &
Krogsgaard, 1981), so the highly polymorphic baboon C3 will be useful
for testing this hypothesis in a nonhuman primate in which dietary
and other environmental factors can be carefully controlled.

As new genetic markers are discovered and characterized, we can
expect the baboon to become increasingly popular as an experimental
subject in biomedical research, and we can expect substantially
increased contributions to our understanding of normal physiologic
processes and disease states.

Acknowledgements

We thank Drs W. J. Goodwin, T. J. Kuehl, and H. C. McGill, Jr, for providing
blood samples; we thank M. J. Aivaliotis, L. A. Landry, Jr, M. C. McKown, and
K. A. Quinlan-Walshe for conducting many of the electrophoretic analyses;
and we thank Dr B. Dyke, Dr J. W. MacCluer, L. J. Collins, and J. M. Bridges for
maintaining the data base on the baboons and genetic marker results. The
research was supported by NIH grants RR01104 and HL28972, and by a grant
from R. J. Reynolds Industries, Inc.

References

Ananthakrishnan, R. (1973) A study of gene differences between some breeds of sheep. *Anim. Blood Groups Biochem. Genet*, **4**, 141–6

Baccus, R., Ryman, N., Smith, M. H., Reuterwall, C. & Cameron, D. (1983) Genetic variability and differentiation of large grazing mammals. *J. Mammal.*, **64**, 109–20

Bruce, E. J. & Ayala, F. J. (1979) Phylogenetic relationships between man and the apes: electrophoretic evidence. *Evolution*, **33**, 1040–56

Crawford, M. H., O'Rourke, D. H., Dykes, D. D. Yakovleva, L. A., Voevodin, A. F., Lapin, B. & Polesky, H. F. (1984) Inbreeding heterozygosity, and lymphoma risk among the baboons (*Papio hamadryas*) of Sukhumi, USSR. *Am. J. Primatol.*, **6**, 143–53

Curie-Cohen, M., VandeBerg, J. L. & Stone, W. H. (1983) Opportunities for genetics in research on non-human primates. *J. Hum. Evol.*, **12**, 573–85

Dykes, D. D. Crawford, M. H. & Polesky, H. F. (1981) Genetic variants of properdin factor B (Bf) in *Papio hamadryas* baboons. *Folia Primatol.*, **36**, 226–31

Ehlers, C. L. & Killam, E. K. (1980) Circadian periodicity of brain activity and urinary excretion in the epileptic baboon. *Am. J. Physiol.*, **239**, R35–R41

Groves, C. P. (1972) Phylogeny and classification of primates. In *Pathology of Simian Primates*, Part I, ed. R. N. T-W-Fiennes, pp. 11–57. Basel: S. Karger

Gusela, J. F., Wexler, N. S., Conneally, P. M., Naylor, S. L., Anderson, M. A., Tanzi, R. E., Watkins, P. C., Ottina, K., Wallace, M. R., Sakaguchi, A. Y., Young, A. B., Shoulson, I., Bonilla, E. & Martin, J. B. (1983) A polymorphic DNA marker genetically linked to Huntington's disease. *Nature, Lond.*, **206**, 234–8

Interagency Primate Steering Committee (1978) National Primate Plan. Washington, D.C.: US Department of Health and Human Services, Public Health Service, National Institutes of Health. (DHEW Publication No. (NIH) 80-1520

Jolly, C. J. & Brett, F. L. (1973) Genetic markers and baboon biology. *J. Med. Primatol.*, **2**, 85–99

King, M.-C., Go, R. C. P., Elston, R. C., Lynch, H. T. & Petrakis, N. L. (1980) Allele increasing susceptibility to human breast cancer may be linked to glutamate-pyruvate transaminase locus. *Science*, **208**, 406–8

Kitchen, F. D., Barnicot, N. A. & Jolly, C. J. (1967) Variations in the group-specific (Gc) component and other blood proteins of baboons. In *International Symposium on the Baboon and Its Use as an Experimental Animal, 2nd, San Antonio, Texas, 1965, Proceedings; The Baboon in Medical Research, vol. 2*, ed. H. Vagtborg, pp. 637–57. Austin, Texas: University of Texas Press

Kristensen, B. O. & Petersen, G. B. (1978) Association between coronary heart disease and the C3^F-gene in essential hypertension. *Circulation*, **58**, 622–5

Lieber, C. S., Teschke, R., Hasumura, Y. & DeCarli, L. M. (1975) Differences in hepatic and metabolic changes after acute and chronic alcohol consumption. *Fedn Proc. Fedn Am. Socs Exp. Biol.*, **34**, 2060–74

Lucotte, G. (1983) Bases génétiques de la spéciation et de la taxonomie chez les babouins. *Biochem. Syst. Ecol.*, **11**, 145–58

Lyon, M. F. (1974) Mechanisms and evolutionary origins of variable X-chromosome activity in mammals. *Proc. R. Soc. Lond., Ser. B, Biol. Sci.*, **187**, 243–68

McDermid, E. M., Vos, G. H. & Downing, H. J. (1973) Blood groups, red cell enzymes and serum proteins of baboons and vervets. *Folia Primatol.*, **19**, 312–26

McGill, H. C., Jr, McMahan, C. A., Kruski, A. W. & Mott, G. E. (1981) Relationship of lipoprotein cholesterol concentrations to experimental atherosclerosis in baboons. *Arteriosclerosis*, 1, 3–12

Nei, M. & Roychoudhury, A. K. (1974) Genic variation within and between the three major races of man, Caucasoids, Negroids, and Mongoloids. *Am. J. Hum. Genet.*, 26, 421–43

Nozawa, K., Shotake, T., Ohkura, Y. & Tanabe, Y. (1977) Genetic variations within and between species of Asian macaques. *Jap. J. Genet.*, 52, 15–30

Ott, J., Schrott, H. G., Goldstein, J. L., Hazzard, W. R., Allen, F. H., Jr, Falk, C. T. & Motulsky, A. G. (1974) Linkage studies in a large kindred with familial hypercholesterolemia. *Am. J. Hum. Genet*, 26, 598–603

Pearson, T. A., Dillman, J. M., Solez, K. & Heptinstall, R. H. (1978) Clonal markers in the study of the origin and growth of human atherosclerotic lesions. *Circulation Res.*, 43, 10–18

Pearson, T. A., Dillman, J., Solez, K. & Heptinstall, R. H. (1979) Monoclonal characteristics of organising arterial thrombi: significance in the origin and growth of human atherosclerotic plaques. *Lancet*, i, 7–11

Roodman, G. D., VandeBerg, J. L. & Kuehl, T. J. (1985) Expression of latent hematopoietic progenitor cells in cultures of newborn and adult baboon liver. *Blood*, 65, 1518–25

Rowe, A. W. & Allen, F. H., Jr (1965) Freezing of blood droplets in liquid nitrogen for use in blood group studies. *Transfusion*, 5, 379–80

Schaadt, O., Sorensen, H. & Krogsgaard, A. R. (1981) Association between the $C3^F$-gene and essential hypertension. *J. Clin. Sci.*, 61, 353s–365s

Selander, R. K., Hunt, W. G. & Yang, S. Y. (1969) Protein polymorphism and genic heterozygosity in two European subspecies of the house mouse. *Evolution*, 23, 379–90

Shotake, T. (1981) Population genetical study of natural hybridization between *Papio anubis* and *P. hamadryas*. *Primates*, 22, 285–308

Shotake, T., Nozawa, K. & Tanabe, Y. (1977) Blood protein variations in baboons. I. Gene exchange and genetic distance between *Papio anubis*, *Papio hamadryas* and their hybrid. *Jap. J. Genet*, 52, 223–38

Smith, O. A., de Vitio, J. L. & Astley, C. A. (1982) Cardiovascular control centers in the brain: one more look. In *Working Conference on Circulation, Neurobiology and Behavior, 1981, Dallas, Texas, Proceedings; Circulation, Neurobiology and Behavior*, ed. O. A. Smith, R. A. Galosy & S. A. Weis, pp. 233–48. New York: Elsevier Biomedical

Sorensen, H. & Dissing, J. (1975) Association between the $C3^F$ gene and atherosclerotic vascular diseases. *Hum. Hered.*, 25, 279–83

Thomas, W. A., Reiner, J. M., Janakidevi, Florentin, R. A. & Lee, K. T. (1979) Population dynamics of arterial cells during atherogenesis. X. Study of monotypism in atherosclerotic lesions of black women heterozygous for glucose-6-phosphate dehydrogenase (G-6-PD). *Exp. Molec. Path.*, 31, 367–86

Utermann, G., Weisgraber, K. H., Weber, W. & Mahley, R. W. (1984) Genetic polymorphism of apolipoprotein E: a variant form of apolipoprotein E2 distinguished by sodium dodecyl sulfate-polyacrylamide gel electrophoresis. *J. Lipid Res.*, 25, 378–82

VandeBerg, J. L. (1983) Developmental aspects of X chromosome inactivation in eutherian and metatherian mammals. *J. Exp. Zool.*, 228, 271–86

VandeBerg, J. L. & Johnston, P. G. (1977) A simple technique for long-term storage of erythrocytes for enzyme electrophoresis. *Biochem. Genet.*, 15, 213–15

VandeBerg, J. L., Johnston, P. G., Cooper, D. W. & Robinson, E. S. (1983) X-Chromosome inactivation and evolution in marsupials and other mammals. *Isozymes: Curr. Top. Biol. Med. Res.*, 9, 201–18

Vergnes, H., Cambefort, Y. & Gheradi, M. (1978) Red cell and serum enzymes of Guinea baboon (*Papio papio*). *J. Med. Primatol.*, 7, 8–18

Zimmerman, E. G., Kilpatrick, C. W. & Hart, B. J. (1978) The genetics of speciation in the rodent genus *Peromyscus*. *Evolution*, 32, 565–79

INDEX